Crisis and Prosperity
in
Sung China

John Winthrop Haeger
editor

The University of Arizona Press

Tucson, Arizona

The Sung II Conference was sponsored and supported by the
Committee on Studies of Chinese Civilization of the American
Council of Learned Societies. The publication of this volume
has also been assisted by the Council.

THE UNIVERSITY OF ARIZONA PRESS

I.S.B.N.-0-8165-0494-6
L.C. No. 74-15603

The Contributors
dedicate this volume to

SADAO AOYAMA
and
ICHISADA MIYAZAKI
invaluable contributors to
international Sung studies

and acknowledge with thanks

> HAN-SHENG CH'ÜAN
> HERBERT FRANKE
> PETER J. GOLAS
> JAMES T. C. LIU
> GABRIELLE SATTLER
> JING-SHEN TAO
> *Participants in the Sung II Conference*
>
> *and*
>
> MALINDA MARR COX
> the editor's assistant

About the Authors . . .

JOHN WINTHROP HAEGER was chairman of the 1971 Sung II Conference in Germany which gave rise to the development of this volume. A Princeton graduate with a doctorate from the University of California at Berkeley, he was chairman of the Department of Chinese at the Claremont Colleges from 1968 to 1973, becoming director of the Luce Scholars Program for the Asia Foundation in 1974.

E. A. KRACKE JR. has served on the board of directors of the Association for Asian Studies and as president of the American Oriental Society. Professor Emeritus of Chinese Literature and Institutions at the University of Chicago, he served on that faculty from 1946 to 1973, and was honorary chairman of the Sung II Conference.

BRIAN E. MCKNIGHT became a member of the history faculty at the University of Hawaii following completion of a doctorate at the University of Chicago. Among his published writings is *Village and Bureaucracy in Southern Sung China*.

CHARLES A. PETERSON was coordinator of the first Sung project in 1965-66. His writings have focused on problems of China's foreign relations in the medieval period and the dynamics of central government-provincial relations in middle and late T'ang. Following post-doctoral studies in Paris and Kyoto, he joined the Chinese history faculty at Cornell University.

CONRAD SCHIROKAUER has written widely on the personalities and problems of neo-Confucianism, especially Chu Hsi, and his articles have appeared in the *Journal of the History of Ideas* and the *Encyclopedia Britannica* as well as in several symposium volumes. Holder of a Ph.D. from Stanford, he later joined the history faculty at the City College of the City University of New York.

YOSHINOBU SHIBA studied Chinese economic history at Tokyo University, in 1962 joining the faculty at Kumamoto University and later becoming associate professor at Osaka. His *Studies in the Commerce and Society of Sung China*

[vii]

(1968) was issued in abstracted English translation as *Commerce and Society in Sung China* by the University of Michigan.

ROLF TRAUZETTEL's chief interest has been in Chinese political and intellectual history, his publications including *Ts'ai Ching als Typus des illegitimen Ministers* and, with Herbert Franke, *Das chinesische Kaiserreich*. After receiving his doctorate from Munich in 1964, he taught there until 1971 when he became professor of Far Eastern Studies at the University of Göttingen.

EDMUND H. WORTHY was founding editor of the *Sung Studies Newsletter* and has contributed numerous articles on various aspects of Sung and modern Chinese history. Following graduation from Yale and graduate studies at Princeton, he became Visiting Lecturer in the Department of History at New Asia College in the Chinese University of Hong Kong and also represented the Yale-in-China Association.

Contents

ILLUSTRATIONS

TABLES

Crisis and Prosperity in
Sung China

Abbreviations Used in the Text

APT   Ch'en Ch'un, *Ao-po t'u* 熬波圖。

CKCHL   Li kang, *Ching-k'ang ch'uan-hsin lu* 靖康傳信錄。 Ssu-pu pei-yao ed.

CKFC   Sun Feng-chi, *Chih-kuan fen-chi* 職官分紀。 Ssu-k'u chen-pen ed., Shanghai 1934–5.

CS   T'o T'o et al, *Chin-shih* 金史。 Po-na pen ed.

CSPM   Feng Chi, comp., *Sung-shih chi-shih pen-mo* 宋史紀事本末。 KHCPTS ed., Taipei 1956.

CTYL   Li Ching-te, comp., *Chu-tzu yu-lei* 朱子語類。

CWTS   Chiu wu-tai shih 舊五代史。 Po-na pen ed.

CYTC   Li Hsin-ch'uan, *Chien-yen i-lai ch'ao-yeh tsa-chi* 建炎以來朝野雜紀。 Reprint of Shih-yuan ts'ung-shu ed., Taipei 1967.

HCP   Li Tao, *Hsü tzu-chih t'ung-chien ch'ang-pian* 續資治通鑑長編。 Chekiang shu-chü ed., 1881.

HFHC   Shen Fu-yi, *Hsiang-fu hsien chih* 祥符縣志。 1898 ed.

HNYL   Li Hsin-ch'uan, *Chien-yen i-lai hsi-nien yao-lu* 建炎以來繫年要錄。 KHCPTS ed.

HSJC   Huang Chen, *Huang-shih jih-ch'ao fen-lei* 黃氏日抄分類。 1767 woodblock ed.

HTCTC   Pi Yüan, comp., *Hsü tzu-chih t'ung-chien* 續資治通鑑。Ku-chi ch'u-pan-she ed., Peking 1957.

HWHTK   Wang Ch'i, *Hsü wen-hsien t'ung-k'ao* 續文獻通考。KHCPTS ed.

KFFC   Kuan Chieh-chung, *K'ai-feng fu chih* 開封府志。1863 ed.

LS   T'o T'o et al, *Liao-shih* 遼史。Po-na pen ed.

MHL   Meng Yüan-lao, *Tung-ching meng-hua lu* 東京夢華錄。Ssu-k'u ch'üan-shu ed.

MHLC   *Tung-ching meng-hua lu chu* 東京夢華錄注。With notes by Tang Chih-ch'eng, Peking 1959.

PCSMC   Lo Chün, comp., *Pao-ch'ing ssu-ming chin* 寶慶四明志。Sung-Yüan ssu-ming liu-chih, 1854–79.

PMHP   Hsü Meng-hsin, *San-ch'ao pei-meng hui-pien* 三朝北盟會編。Yüeh t'ung chi ed.

SHY   *Sung hui-yao chi-pen* 宋會要輯本。Shih-chieh shu-chu ed., Taipei 1963.

SL   Wang Fu-chih, *Sung lun* 宋論。KHCPTS ed.

SS   T'o T'o et al, *Sung-shih* 宋史。Po-na pen ed.

SYHA   Huang Tsung-hsi, comp., *Sung-Yüan hsüeh-an* 宋元學案。Wan yu wen-k'u ed.

TCKC   Yü-wen Shu-chao, *Ta-Chin kuo-chih* 大金國誌。KHCPTS ed., 1936.

TFSL   Hsieh Shen-fu, *Ch'ing-yüan t'iao-fa shih-lei* 慶元條法事類。Yen-ching ta-hsüeh t'u-shu-kuan, Peking 1948.

THY   Wang P'u, *T'ang hui-yao* 唐會要。Wan yu wen-k'u ed.

TLT   *Ta T'ang liu tien* 大唐六典。Wen-hai Publishing Company, Taipei 1962.

TML   Li Hsin-ch'uan, *Tao-ming lu* 道命錄。TSCC ed.

TPHY   *T'ai-p'ing huan-yü chi* 太平寰宇記。Chin-ling shu-chü ed., 1882.

TTSL   Wang Ch'eng, comp., *Tung-tu shih-lüeh* 東都事略。Sung-shih tzu-liao hui-pen ed., Taipei 1967.

WHTK   Ma Tuan-lin, *Wen-hsien t'ung-k'ao* 文獻通考。KHCPTS ed.

YFCY   Wang Ts'un, *Yüan-feng chiu-yü chih* 元豐九域志。TSCC ed.

YH   Wang Ying-lin, *Yü hai* 玉海。Kua-lien ch'u-pan-she ed., Taipei 1964 (photo offprint of 1337 woodblock edition).

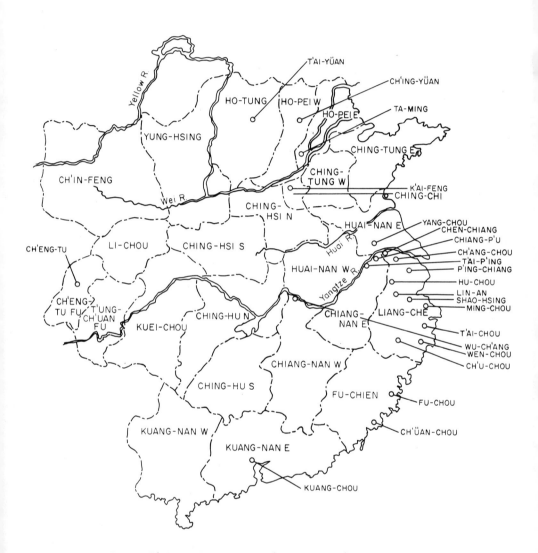

Sung China: Circuits and Major Urban Centers

Introduction:
Crisis and Prosperity
in Sung China

JOHN WINTHROP HAEGER

THE DYNASTS OF THE CHAO FAMILY ruled most of China from the fall of Later Chou by coup d'état in February of 960 until Ping-ti was drowned on the South China Sea following the Mongol invasion in the spring of 1279. They called themselves Sung, to honor their ancestral home in Ho-nan, the historic fiefdom granted by the ancient Chou to the hapless descendants of the last king of the Shang, and with this name they struck a distinctive timbre in three centuries of time. They were no match for the Han in longevity, for the T'ang in power, for the Ming in imperial grandeur, nor for the Yüan in cosmopolitan achievement. They presided simultaneously over political disaster and cultural efflorescence, over the shrinking of their borders and the rigorous development of their land, over humiliating treaties and an intense quickening of domestic political economy. Their historical significance is tied on the one hand to the internal dynamics of dynasties as a political institution and on the other to the independent movements of economic, social and intellectual change which they neither began nor ended but upon which they were superimposed.

Chinese dynasties were very different from the ruling families of European history. The latter were mostly the linkage in a pageant of individual princes and kings, who in their turn held court and made laws, convened their barons and settled disputes, erected palaces and patronized art. The familial linkage governed their marriages, because dowry often paid for land and blood determined who were their friends, allies and enemies. Families were the authority for succession, but not the legitimation for rule, which had to be sought either from the feudal compact and its proto-parliamentary descendants, or from transcendent ecclesiastical authority, and which had a limited ability to support the reign of grossly weak individual kings. In China both the individual

[1]

rulers and the authentic blood links between them were of smaller significance, and the dynasty was an institution far greater than its familial aspect.

In the first place Chinese dynasties were an essential compromise between a basic principle of political philosophy and a realistic approach to the transfer of political power. Yao's transmission of the throne to Shun rather than his own son is of only minor and dubious interest as a historical fact, but enormously important as the metaphorical expression of a central tenet of classical Confucian thought: that the ablest and justest should always rule the land. Yet with practice as the only guide to the recognition of ability and justness, and with royal birth the best guarantee of appropriate apprenticeship in statecraft, the ideal was tempered by the realities of life. The dynasty became accepted as the best compromise between the affinities of blood and the determination to seek rulers by ability — a king and his descendants might rule until they demonstrated incompetence and fell from harmony with the natural order.

It follows that the succession of individual rulers within a dynastic line was much less important than the succession of dynasties themselves, for only the transfer of the mandate, as it was called, could appropriately celebrate the Confucian ideal. Moreover, the succession of dynasties was the primary expression of the continuity of political time. As the relationship between history and mythology was worked out in the last five centuries B. C., and particularly as the lessons of dynastic rise and fall were imprinted on the minds of a single generation at the beginning of the Han, the centuries before the beginning of recorded time were invested with the same dynastic pattern which had maintained the Chou and which destroyed the Ch'in after scarcely twenty years. History without dynasties became unthinkable, for dynasties reflected in the world of men and institutions what the pattern of the seasons and the stars represented about the world of nature: a transcendent pattern of change in which rise and fall did not challenge but affirmed the essential changelessness of life.

The dynastic institution also absorbed some of the attributes of personality which might otherwise have inhered in the record of individual sovereigns, largely by maintaining the style and to some extent the situation of each founder. Because of the historical and moral significance attached to the end of one dynasty and the commencement of another, the personality of first and last emperors acquired unusual importance. Part of this importance is expressed in the stereotypes of hapless degeneration and enlightened vigor which characterize the last and first respectively, but part also lies in the fact that each founding emperor was possessed of a private career and a non-imperial approach to life and history before he ascended the throne. This amounted to a link between human personality and political institutions which to some degree anthropomorphized each dynasty in the image of its founder. Because Kao-tsu of the Han was a provincial leader of peasant extraction, the dynasty itself was never entirely rid of its peasant origins, and its institutional history is suffused with the efforts of statesmen to hedge their sovereigns with dignity, to invent ceremony worthy of imperial aspirations, and to build institutions more durable than the peasant descendants who governed them. In the same way Chao K'uang-yin's experience as a general for the later Chou conditioned the later history of the Sung. Partially as a consequence of deliberate institutional innovations, partially by his supervision of the succession, and partially by the balance he established between family and bureaucracy, Chao stamped the whole dynasty with his interpretation of tradition, his hierarchy of values and his style of government.

Chao was a military man who distrusted military solutions. As a student of history he drew little solace from the story of the T'ang, which seemed to have perished as it had lived — by the sword. The very institutions which had produced its glory — the huge standing army, the hereditary military commands, the independence of the frontier, and imperialist use of non-Chinese in the army — had torn the dynasty apart in the eighth and ninth centuries. As a Chinese, Chao was no more consoled by the depressing history of divisions in the early part of the tenth century, which seemed prima facie evidence of a misorganized world in which the institutions of civilization were endangered. But when the young Kung-ti had been deposed and the Sung set up in place of the Later Chou, Chao K'ung-yin contemplated this example nervously and set about to ensure that his own coup d'etat would terminate a period of dynastic evanescence and inaugurate an era of relative stability. He delegated great authority to no one, recalled his generals to K'ai-feng, rewarded military prowess with civilian rank, cut the standing army to half the size of T'ang and ensured that his mature and lettered brother would succeed him on the throne. His testament to twelve generations of Chao rulers was symbolized in an almost legendary banquet where he traded his generals' appointments to civil office for their swords, and sealed the new agreement with a famous "cup of wine." However the Sung may have resembled the other major dynasties in Chinese history, it was unique and consistent in its adherence to this testament of distrust for military solutions. These sentiments were part of a larger orientation toward moderation and introspection in all aspects of life. Not only were T'ang institutions regarded with discomfort and suspicion, but also the colors of T'ang art and the thrust of T'ang painting were subdued and redirected. Emerald green and ochre were slowly displaced by subtle shades of sage and grey and brown. Landscapes full of men and horses and the first serious forays into portraiture virtually disappeared, replaced by a more modest vision of men in the natural scene and by the nearly photographic study of birds and flowers, small and delicate representatives of nature's craftsmanship. The color and bustle of urban life actually intensified from T'ang to Sung, but the Sung eradicated most of the T'ang exotica in men and goods and taste, and overlaid their public lives with greater domestic sophistication and refinement. All this was part of Sung's modest, civilistic personality, a socio-psychological phenomenon of vast complexity, fed by a score of stimuli and to some extent self-reinforcing, but partially related to the known, human personality of its illustrious founder.

In spite of its personality and internal dynamics, however, the Sung was, like most political institutions more significant as a respondent to historical events than as a creative force in its own right. Since the writings of Naito Torajiro nearly seventy years ago, it has been clear that Chinese history cannot be satisfactorily unravelled from the perspective of dynastic pattern alone. At first through a rather clumsy analogy with the aging process of the human body and then through more sophisticated scholarship, secular patterns have been discerned in the fabric of Chinese history, reaching beyond the chronological limits of any single dynasty and describing historical tendencies more significant than the rhythm of political rise and fall. It is by now almost in the nature of truism that the beginnings of "modern" Chinese history can be traced to the so-called T'ang-Sung transition in the eighth, ninth and tenth centuries. In the wake of a general migration of northern families from the North China Plain and Kuan-chung into the Yangtze delta, which in its turn had begun around the middle of the Han, the T'ang-Sung transition represents the nexus of ensuing economic and social developments. The concentration of population and economic strength away from the political center of gravity stimulated the first significant long-distance trade in Chinese history, and the first cities of nonpolitical character. The relative surplus of fertile, arable land in and near the new economic centers tended to modify the pattern of landholding, to stimulate tenancy and absentee ownership and to encourage some kinds of social mobility. The growth of commerce affected the social distribution of wealth, which in turn changed the avenues of access to power and influence.

The Sung reaction to these developments was infinitely complex. Contemporary men, of course, were not consciously aware that any transition had occurred, nor for the most part that their own times were faced with problems of any greater scope than the Han or T'ang before them. A general pattern of response can still be discerned, however, which was both rationalist and classicist. The separation of the economic and political centers of gravity in the T'ang-Sung transition not only created the obvious necessity of feeding the capital from a significant distance, but also stimulated recognition for the basic idea of specialized economic function. When this was translated into the organization of the national market, it had a dramatic impact on regional trade. Self-sufficiency in given townships or cities not only disappeared in fact but was also eradicated in theory. As increasingly specialized commercial and craft guilds appeared in all the major cities of the south, they had no difficulty gaining official recognition, and as they proliferated, the national use of labor was increasingly rationalized. The circulation of money and the consequent determination of a money value for goods and services alike gave great impetus to the rationalization of the entire social order. By the middle of the dynasty, compulsory labor and administrative services had been almost entirely transformed into simple taxation, eliminating cumbersome status gradations between households, permitting labor to be weighed against profit in the determination of value, and allowing the government to find and buy exactly the goods and services it required, instead of having to make do with whatever was available in a given year in a given locality. Finally, the Sung stripped the civil service recruitment system of its least rational accretions in order to tap the human resources of the whole society for the duty of governance. Commercially generated wealth became a means of access to education, and education, in effect, the only significant means of access to official position. The mobility which this engendered served to reinforce the linkage between government and society and between society and its civilized heritage. Simultaneously it rationalized the access to talent, and the development of individual talent for the common welfare. In the end the Sung became so immersed in the rationalization of affairs and so enamored of the universal convertibility of goods, services and intangible benefits that they even became willing to set a price on war and peace. When they negotiated treaties with the Liao and Chin whose terms called for subsidies to guarantee freedom from attack, however pragmatic their approach to the problems at hand, the Sung in effect committed the ultimate rationalization: prosperity in the towns and the countryside was used to buy the peace their armies could not win.

The second aspect of the Sung reaction was classicist. As the process of rationalization proceeded, Sung Chinese became increasingly aware that their historical position was unique. In the 1060s Wang

An-shih's reforms seemed all too clearly directed toward accelerating the pace of change. The various avoidance taxes were a bald admission that economic factors had become universally convertible on the basis of cash value; the reforms he suggested in the civil service examinations favored the specialization of talent in government as labor had already become specialized in the countryside; and Wang's own influential position testified to the dramatic effect of social and economic mobility on the recruitment of talent and the role of prestige in the bureaucracy. The conservative reaction which followed Wang's demise in the 1080s temporarily undid most of his specific reforms, but it also raised to consciousness deep-seated uncertainties about the nature of the Sung task and the meaning of its responsibilities. Chao K'uang-yin had been anxious to avoid certain specific mistakes of T'ang practice; his eleventh-century successors found themselves confronted with wholesale distaste for the entire T'ang period, and with a determination among some reflective contemporaries at least to link Sung policies and Sung trends of thought directly with classical antiquity, rejecting completely the intervening experience of the Han and T'ang. On the one hand this argument inescapably implied that the Sung had recognized the historical distance between the northern, aristocratic, megalomaniacal T'ang and themselves, on the other it suggested that the most efficacious way of dealing with economic and social change was to confront contemporary problems with the wisdom of pure, classical texts. It is for this reason that the political debates of the eleventh century were phrased in terms of conflict between the *Rites of Chou* and the *Book of Ceremony,* and also for this reason that the early Neo-Confucians dismissed Han and T'ang commentaries in favor of undivided attention to the ancient texts themselves. In a sense the Sung policy on war and peace was also a classical reversion, for it exalted the Mencian conviction that the victory of life and culture was won, not by force of arms, but by civilized example.

The essays in this volume are all concerned with the central irony of Sung history: that a period of towering achievement in material culture and intellectual subtlety should also have been shaken by a crippling succession of political and military crises. Mr. Shiba's essay traces the consequences of the T'ang-Sung transition in the lower Yangtze valley, showing that the quickening pulse of trade and urbanization were not spontaneous, haphazard developments spattering the countryside with a confetti of cash crops, wealth and towns, but were, on the contrary, an orderly process resulting in a hierarchy of differentiated urban centers of graded size with specific marketing functions. This hierarchy, combined with an overriding specialization of function between the hilly areas and the plains, gradually linked the entire Yangtze region in an integral market maintained through local, interregional, and interurban communications networks. Mr. Kracke turns the discussion of urbanization to the capital city of the Northern Sung at K'ai-feng. He finds the same tendencies toward rapid urban growth, urban concentration of population, increasing wealth and dynamic commercial enterprise which were characteristic features of the T'ang-Sung progress in the lower Yangtze, combined with a remarkable magnetism for intellectual talent that only the capital of a very literate dynasty—which tapped its finest minds for government service—could manage. The development of K'ai-feng during the first century of Northern Sung seems to have been marked by a general prevalence of practical convenience and permissiveness over traditional scholarly partiality to formal order so that the imperial palace did not bear its proper relation to the rest of the city, population growth and construction were unbalanced among quarters, and finally the whole city became skewed on its north-south axis, looking more rhomboidal than rectangular. In this respect tenth-century K'ai-feng prefigured the great cities of the south, which in their time wholly abandoned any pretense of rectangularity. Mr. McKnight's essay is concerned with the consequences of economic prosperity in the countryside. By analyzing the way in which government regulations treated various categories of rural households in respect to their liability for or exemption from certain village service obligations, he is able to see a gradual but unmistakable decline in the special privileges associated with ascribed status during the Sung. The association among money, trade and urbanization is obvious and universal, but the spread of a money economy and the distribution of wealth into rural areas to pay for the agricultural surplus which sustained urban life had important consequences in the countryside as well: it slowly eliminated the last traces of an aristocratic system of social leadership inherited from the T'ang and made wealth practically the sole determinant of rural prestige and status. Finally, Mr. Worthy's essay discusses the problems of monopoly management in an age when all goods and services were theoretically convertible at cash value. The extensive development of commercial enterprise, by its reliance on market mechanisms to determine value and by its inevitable introduction of competition into economic life, was ill-suited to cooperate with government monopolies, and only precarious balance was achieved.

Because our own times are acutely conscious of the dangers to life which inhere in the limitless extension of economic progress and social development we can perhaps appreciate that some seeds of crisis were contained within Sung prosperity. There is some evidence that

Sung K'ai-feng may have prospered too much and begun to suffer from a twelfth-century strain of urban blight. Calculations of population density are difficult to make with precision, but the crowding in some quarters of the old city must have been excruciating, expecially if we envision (as we must) that traditional north Chinese one-story houses had not given very much way to the two- and three-story dwelling places of later Hang-chou. Mr. Kracke finds some interesting evidence that the oldest and wealthiest official families of the Northern Sung may have moved their primary places of residence from the traditional residential quarters to the hilly suburbs of K'ai-feng before the end of the eleventh century leaving the "center city" to the increasing profusion of merchants, craftsmen and nouveaux riches. There were repeated efforts to clean and beautify the bustling but esthetically unedifying capital, and Emperor Hui-tsung even encouraged a mild mania for rock gardens which imitated in miniature the majestic drama of wilderness landscape. While the great cities of the south apparently escaped the worst aspects of K'ai-feng's distress, at least for the duration of Southern Sung, the countryside suffered in another way from excess growth. Mr. Shiba points out that the widening differentiation between urban and rural areas not only contributed to the gradual creation of an identifiable "urban" class, possessed of distinctive interests and a distinctive mode of life, but also worked to the disadvantage of the countryside, which tended to bear more and more of the total tax burden levied by the government. Partially because Chinese government never really adjusted to the idea that wealth was separable from the land, partially because the complexity of commercial organization defied the full comprehension of nonspecialist officials, and partially because the nouveaux riches and their families became rapidly influential in government circles, the state was never able to derive proportionate revenue from the cities and from commerce, relying instead on the land, which they had taxed from the beginning of time. By the end of Southern Sung much of the countryside had been impoverished by the selfsame forces which had sparked the agricultural and commercial revolutions in the first place.

The sour fruit of prosperity itself was by no means the only source of problems for the Sung. From the very beginning of the dynasty, Chao K'uang-yin's decision to limit the court's military strength, set against the increasing restlessness of the Jürchen and Khitan, made for a season of traumatic encounters between the Sung and its northern neighbors. My own essay and Mr. Peterson's are devoted to the formulation of Sung policy in the face of major threats to their national security; mine in respect to the Chin attack on K'ai-feng in the winter of 1125-26, Mr.

Peterson's in respect to the Mongol attack on the Chin in 1211 and their subsequent conquest of north China. In both cases the external crisis precipitated a major policy debate between high officials of moderate persuasion and a group of hard-line irredentists, who favored the adoption of a more aggressive posture and held out the promise that parts of north China could and should be recovered from barbarian rule. In 1126 the moderates showed an unmistakable reluctance to admit that a crisis had actually occurred and a preference for believing that a right-ordered world was still intact. They comforted themselves at every indication of normalcy and steadfastly refused to commit themselves to any major military action, which might have catapulted generals into significant positions of leadership. The apparent determination to frame policy according to conditions rather than principles which characterized the moderate position in both crises may be deceptive, however: while the irredentist voice is shriller, the comparative silence of the moderates is more Chinese, and probably denotes an almost unutterable faith in the verity of Confucian principles even under fire. Mr. Trauzettel's essay provides another perspective on the world views which lay behind the moderate and irredentist positions. In the context of a general decline of emphasis on the concentric, radiant world order of Han and T'ang described in the concept of *t'ien-hsia,* and the concurrent development of a more circumscribed, less grandiose vision of China's place in the world the moderates (or pacifists, in Mr. Trauzettel's phrase) were the dying universalists, while the irredentists renounced universalism, and considered the barbarians as enemies of the fatherland, the fatherland *qua kuo,* not as potential members of the cultural *oikumene.* The transformation of empire into country was probably rooted too firmly in the Sung approach to history and value to have been a wholly partisan issue, however, and the moderates apparently abandoned their share of universalism too. On the one hand they maintained that the end of the Confucian state was the whole end, on the other they were prepared to recognize that the limits of their effective power no longer coincided with the farthest edges of Chinese cultural influence, and they took occasional perverse pleasure at the mimicry of Chinese social and political institutions by the Jürchen and Khitan.

Ideas were more than a backdrop for political debate, however, and at the end of the twelfth century, intellectual and political crises became interwoven. Mr. Schirokauer's essay describes the bitter debate over "spurious learning," which had its origins in the genuine Neo-Confucian effort to sort through the parentage of ideas, was fueled by factional politics and personal grudges, and finally led to a temporary ban on the most influential thinkers of the day. While the direction of

Neo-Confucian thought after the end of Northern Sung was certainly toward the establishment of intellectual lines of descent from classical masters, free from the elaborations of Han and T'ang scholars, and while this was probably related to the socio-intellectual effect of the loss of north China and the recognition of Sung's unique character, the spurious learning crisis is remarkable for its rather poor reflection of social, economic or regional divisions in society. In purely intellectual terms too, it was filled with sound and fury signifying little, except a manifest desire for ideological normalcy to end a long period of rapid change which had involved more people in the world of ideas than any age before or since.

One of the unifying themes in Sung response to crisis is formalism. In describing the evolution of K'ai-feng, Mr. Kracke identifies formalism as the obverse of pragmatism. To counter the relative permissiveness and spontaneity of the tenth century and the consequent disorder of the city's growth, efforts were made in the second half of the eleventh century to broaden some of the major avenues, to relocate gates symmetrically in the walls and above all to change the names of streets, gates and landmarks to eradicate localisms and evidences of spontaneity and to replace these with classical allusions symbolizing the proper configuration of an imperial capital. Mr. Kracke also notes the analogy between this structural formalism in the renovation of K'ai-feng and the tendency of major reform programs in Northern Sung to grow more sweeping, more utopian and more decorated with classical precedents, and less responsive to specific problems or abuses. Although reform began as a genuine response to the problems and possibilities of social change in the post-T'ang period, it ended as a method of governance in its own right. At court, legislation began to overpower adjudication as the central posture of government, and even crises were met not with individual decisions toward a single specified course of action, but with barrages of planning and new law. Crises were also met by a second variation on formalism: renewed emphasis on symbolic order. Nothing was more important in the wake of the Chin attack in 1126 than proper arrangements for Hui-tsung's orderly abdication and Ch'in-tsung's accession to the throne. Contemporaries perceived that when the real world was disarrayed, artificial order in matters of ceremony partially compensated. The world of titles, rank and symbols was not an illusion, but the mirror of reality, and therefore also an instrument for the adjustment of reality. Finally, Mr. Schirokauer's paper suggests that a third variation on formalism is orthodoxy. The tendency to claim exclusive access to the truth and to cast disagreements in the vocabulary of error and perversion was very strong in *tao-hsüeh* from its beginning in the first years of Southern Sung. Decades of bitter debate, including some unseemly character assassination, did nothing to instill a sense of intellectual humility or relativity among Sung thinkers; on the contrary it seemed to intensify the desire for one, dependable, orthodox truth. But in this respect, it was left to the Yüan to complete Sung work — there was no certified orthodoxy until Chu Hsi's commentaries on the classics were made standard for the purpose of state examination in 1313.

While the effort to achieve clear, decisive historical periodization is obviously mocked by the certainty that each moment holds within itself some vestige of the past and some seed of the future, it may still be useful to distinguish broadly between Northern and Southern Sung. Mr. McKnight's essay calls attention to the transitional character of Northern Sung. With its roots in Ho-nan, it was in a sense the last successor state of the T'ang and the natural heir to many aspects of T'ang culture and institutions. Much of this it resented, however, and found burdensome to the development of its own personality. By contrast, the geography of Southern Sung did not even include the old heartland of Chinese culture, and its history risked comparison only with Northern Sung, never with the T'ang. Unlike Northern Sung, which had to sort out a complicated heritage full of alien influence and exotic overlay and had to build unity from the piecemeal conquest of a dozen splinter states, the southern dynasty started from a relatively clean slate. The ninth son of Hui-tsung, who had never been Grand Heir or prepared in any way to rule, was arrested fleeing in the countryside and enthroned; a new capital was virtually built from scratch beginning in 1129; and the political and economic centers of gravity were finally made to coincide. The Southern Sung was a "financial" state in a way the northern dynasty could never have been; wealthy city-dwellers came powerfully close to establishing a distinctive urban class, and social leadership in the countryside was lodged firmly in the hands of men whose only common characteristic was their wealth. In the end, the loss of the north was less a liberation than a new constraint. The practical problems of providing for a considerable influx of northern refugees, most of them unreconciled to separation from their ancestral homes, was added to the immense psychological burden of being cut off from the roots of Chinese civilization. The material comforts of life in the southeast never entirely offset an atmosphere of impermanence. The elegant and charming new capital at Hang-chou, the largest city in the medieval world, they called *hsing-tsai,* the "halting place." Their houses and even their public buildings were built of wood, which in spite of advanced urban services, frequently were consumed in flame. Their poetry is pervaded with introspective melancholia expressed in the juxtaposition of southern pleasure and beauty with emotional commitment to the north.

Perhaps the men of Southern Sung sensed some larger historical impermanence in their experience. The final approach to the significance of Sung is to see what did not happen, to estimate what in the end was not achieved. The T'ang-Sung transition is real enough, but the Sung-Yüan (or even Sung-Ming) transition seems rougher by comparison. The roads which led to Southern Sung, in both a literal and figurative sense, led nowhere, and the process of historical evolution was in one sense interrupted. The agricultural revolution on which markets, commerce and cities had been based was eventually reversed, and the countryside slowly reduced, first to subsistence and then to poverty. As Mr. McKnight points out, the Yüan reinfused south China with T'ang values, essentially northern ideas about the organization of society and the management of economy, which had passed from T'ang to Yüan through Liao and Chin. The leveling of social distinctions based on ascribed characteristics and the beginnings of capitalist enterprise were essentially ended. Introspection and subtlety gave way to eremitism on the one hand and to a brutal cosmopolitanism on the other. With the drowning of Ping-ti in 1279 and the fall of Hang-chou to a Mongol army, the great Sung experiment was over. The effort to confront the pressure of social and economic quickening and the aggression of settling nomads with modesty, rationalism and formalism had produced a generous and brilliant age, but no more permanence than the crudest forms of power.

Urbanization and the Development of Markets in the Lower Yangtze Valley

YOSHINOBU SHIBA

DURING THE PERIOD from the eighth to the thirteenth centuries Chinese society underwent a great transformation. Among the most striking features of this change were the rapid growth and diversification of trade, the development toward a money economy with adequate facilities for the transfer of funds and the provision of credit, the progressive urbanization of society, and the growth to prosperity of an urban class with its own distinctive culture.

Kato Shigeshi, a pioneer in Chinese economic history, pointed out the enormous progress in urbanization during the T'ang-Sung transition. He emphasized the following developments: (1) the rapid decline of the old "ward system" and "official market system" along with the collapse of restrictions which theoretically confined activities of merchants and artisans to specific "wards" of cities serving as administrative centers and (2) the proliferation of interconnected small and medium-sized marketplaces throughout the country, indicative of the progressive commercialization of the peasant economy.[1] Kato also suggested that through the analysis of statistical data on the commercial tax which has survived in the *Sung hui-yao*,[2] the nationwide pattern of the distribution of urban centers could be estimated. This line of inquiry has been developed in studies by Etienne Balazs[3] and Laurence J. C. Ma.[4]

Other economic historians have contributed much toward elucidation of the economic background of urbanization and toward study of the relationship between urbanization and the overall character of the social division of labor. Ch'üan Han-sheng did much to explain the extension of interlocal trade centered at state capitals, large regional cities, and temple fairs, and the function of these markets as collection and distribution centers for various kinds of staple goods.[5] Miyazaki

Ichisada has discussed the general tendency for rural populations to concentrate in urban centers, the relative wealth of the new urban populations and the sharp disparity in the distribution of wealth between a few rich investors on the one hand and the majority of petty entrepreneurs on the other. According to Miyazaki, the State Trade System (3rd/1072) was a measure which extended government loan facilities to small merchants whose businesses would otherwise have suffered from the stringency of capital.[6] Studies of the development of Sung cities in terms of the state's financial control have only recently begun. These have already demonstrated, however, the considerable growth of citizens' private rights, the increased importance of urban ownership as a lucrative source of income, and the concomitant introduction of taxes on city houses and lands.[7]

Sudo Yoshiyuki and others have collected a great deal of data regarding small market towns and rural market-gatherings in Sung times, and have pursued various lines of inquiry concerning their origin, etymology and function.[8] Fujii Hiroshi, in a study concerning the relationship between the development of rural markets and long-distance trade under the Sung, maintained that a qualitative change in the nature of internal trade took place during the T'ang-Sung transition. He proposed three essential elements of this change: (1) commodities collected and distributed by itinerant merchants were, from Sung times on, no longer limited to luxury goods for the rich, but grew to include daily necessities for a broader base of the population, including petty rural landowners and the poor; (2) farmers in various regions of China were no longer economically self-sufficient, but were involved in a network of internal trade; and (3) internal trade was no longer confined to urban and quasi-urban areas, but extended to include border villages located far from major cities.[9] This qualitative change in agrarian economy and in rural society has also been emphasized by many other scholars.[10] Denis Twitchett, whose studies have stressed the overall pattern of rural development during the T'ang-Sung transition, has postulated that

the hierarchy of settlements in the provinces seems to have changed from the comparatively simple pattern of

village —— administrative town (*hsien*)

in the early T'ang, when the intermediate category of small country town without administrative status was still rare, to a more complex model

village —— subordinate (market) town —— administrative town

by Sung times. This hierarchy of settlements was essentially an economic and social one, and was both formally and functionally completely independent of the purely fiscal-administrative hierarchy of

li —— hsiang —— hsien

which provided the local government with its chain of command in the countryside. Only at the level of the county town did the two systems come together.[11]

Twitchett also argued that in T'ang times every county capital was ipso facto an administrative center, and was normally a market center as well.[12]

In spite of the accumulation of such research, the full dimensions of the process of urbanization and the operation of markets in Sung times are not yet clear. For example, in previous studies villages and cities have not been considered together as parts of a single system. Further, relatively little research has been done on small urban centers, in contrast with the detailed information available regarding large urban centers. Nor have the demographic and social aspects of Sung urbanization been adequately studied.

To go a step further in researching the cities and markets of Sung times, we need to concentrate our efforts on a few particular regions. The lower Yangtze valley,* which was the most developed region economically and which had the largest concentration of major cities in the country, will be the focus of attention in this paper. What follows is therefore an inquiry which first explores the general features of urbanization in the lower Yangtze, and then proceeds to focus on particular prefectures (Hu-chou and Hui-chou) to demonstrate the difference between level and hilly districts in commercial development. Finally, the impact of urbanization on Sung culture and the response of the state to this social change will be discussed.

The general features of urbanization in the lower Yangtze valley include population concentration and its relationship to the process of urbanization, density of urban compared with rural population, the rearrangement of administrative divisions in prefectures and counties, and the economic background of urbanization.

Population Concentration and Urbanization

Prior to considering the rapid rise of urban centers, towns, and market-assemblies throughout the lower Yangtze valley during the period from late T'ang to Sung, it should be kept in mind that this change was paralleled by another important development: the tremendous movement in the mass of China's population from the northern plains to the mountainous south and to the southeast coast. To be sure, this southward migration had a long history even before the T'ang, but its magnitude in spatial extent, in number of migrants, and in degree of resultant sinification of the south exceeded previous population movements by a great deal. Even later counterparts, such as the movement to Manchuria and Mongkiang under the Manchu conquest, could not

---

* "The lower Yangtze valley" refers to the area including the south of the Yangtze River in present-day Kiangsu and Anhwei, together with the whole territory of Chekiang.

match the enormous scope of the T'ang-Sung migration. The increase in southern population did not, of course, occur solely as a result of immigration from the north. Higher population figures can also be accounted for by the natural increase in indigenous population as well as by intensified efforts on the part of the government to register previously uncounted population. Nonetheless, migration was the primary reason for sudden population growth. In this regard, a brief review of the demographic change between the Sui and the Sung will be instructive.

According to the census of 606, only 23 percent of registered households lived in the south, and 77 percent lived in the north. By 742, however, the southern population had grown to 43 percent of the whole empire. Table 2.1 shows prefectural population by households in the years 606 and 742, during which time the population more than doubled in each prefecture.

The following propositions could be advanced on the basis of this table: (1) in regions where both the ratio and the amount of increase were high (northern Chekiang, southern Kiangsu, and Fukien), the population had increased at a normal rate before the Sui, but began to increase at a swifter pace thereafter because a great deal of land was still open for settlement. (2) In regions where the ratio of increase was relatively low but the amount of increase was high (the Chengtu basin, the lower reaches of the Yangtze valley, and the mouth of the Pearl River valley), the same pace of increase was maintained from the earliest periods until mid-T'ang times. (3) In hitherto underdeveloped areas where the ratio of increase was high while the amount was low (Lu-chou on the upper course of the Yangtze, and northern Kiangsi), the rapid increase following the Sui was due to migration. (4) The population in the southernmost provinces of Kwang-nan, northern Hunan, southwestern Szechwan, and southern Kiangsi remained almost unchanged. (5) The relative balance of population between the north and the south was completely altered.[13]

During the mid-T'ang and Sung the southward migration was accelerated by social disorder in the north and by the transfer of the Sung capital to Hang-chou. The predominance of the southern population over the northern was decisive: 65 percent in the south, 35 percent in the north. Moreover, the pattern of population distribution was somewhat different from that of the T'ang, as shown in Table 2.2.

Generally, the front line of migration moved from middle and southern Chekiang, southern Anhwei, northern Kiangsi, and middle and southern Hunan to the hitherto sparsely settled areas of Fukien, central Anhwei, eastern Hupei, southern Kiangsi, eastern Kwangtung, and the upper reaches of the Pearl River valley in Kwangsi. Although

TABLE 2.1.
Population by Household in 606 and 742.

Modern Province	Prefecture in T'ang	Number of Commanderies in Sui	Number of Households in 606	Number of Households in 742	Ratio of Increase
Chekiang	Ch'ü, Wu, Wen, T'ai, Ch'u	2	30,347,000	382,176,000	13.9
Szechwan	Lu	1	1,802,000	16,594,000	9.1
Chekiang	Mu	1	7,343,000	54,961,000	7.4
Fukien	Fu, Ch'üan, Chien, T'ing, Chang	1	12,420,000	90,686,000	7.3
Kiangsu and Chekian	Ssŭ, Hu, Hang	2	33,757,000	235,985,000	7.2
Chekiang	Ming, Yüeh	1	20,271,000	132,406,000	6.5
Anhwei	She	1	6,164,000	38,330,000	6.1
Szechwan	Ho	1	6,921,000	66,810,000	6.0
Kiangsu	Ch'ang	1	17,599,000	102,631,000	5.8
Hunan and Kwangtung	Heng, Liu, Yung, Tao, Lien	4	26,844,000	147,246,000	5.5
Kiangsi	Hung, Chiang, Jao	3	29,740,000	120,454,000	4.0
Szechwan	Ch'ien, Fei	1	1,460,000	4,699,000	3.2
Szechwan	T'ung	1	12,624,000	40,743,000	3.2
Anhwei	Ho	1	8,254,000	24,794,000	3.0
Hunan	Yüeh, T'an, Shao	2	21,209,000	61,085,000	2.9
Kwangsi	Wu, Ho, Feng	1	4,578,000	13,400,000	2.9
Szechwan	Ya, K'ou, Li, Mei, Chia, Ling, Jung, Hsieh	4	63,048,000	171,964,000	2.8
Szechwan	Ch'eng-tu, Han, P'eng, Chien, Shu, Lang, Kuo	2	147,190,000	500,197,000	2.8
Szechwan	Sui	1	12,622,000	35,632,000	2.8
Szechwan	Tzu, P'u, Jung	1	25,722,000	60,967,000	2.4
Hunan	Ch'en, Wu, Chin, Ch'i, Lang	4	19,120,000	46,463,000	2.4
Kiangsu and Anhwei	Yang, Jun, Ch'u, Hsüan, Ch'u	3	159,628,000	353,890,000	2.3
Kiangsi	Wu, Chi, Ch'ien	3	45,782,000	106,004,000	2.3
Kwangtung	Kuang, Shao, Kang	1	37,482,000	78,885,000	2.1

Source: Aoyama Sadao, "Zui, Tō, Sō sandai ni okeru kosū no chiiki teki kōsatsu [An Areal Study on the Change in Population during Sui, T'ang, and Sung]," *Rekishigaku Kenkyū*, 6, No. 4 (1936), pp. 441–446.

TABLE 2.2.
Prefectures in which Population by Household
Increased More than 200 percent from 742 to ca. 1078.

Modern Province	Prefectures	Ratio of Increase	Modern Province	Prefectures	Ratio of Increase
Kwangtung	Ch'ao	16.8	Kwangsi	Liu	3.9
Fukien	Ch'üan, T'ing, Chang	16.3	Kwangsi	Kuei, Jung	3.8
			Szechwan	Ch'in	3.7
Fukien	Chien	13.4	Kiangsi	Ch'ien	3.5
Kwangtung	Hsün	11.3	Anhwei	Shou	3.5
Shensi	Shang	9.0	Hunan	Yung, Ch'en	3.4
Kwangsi	Ho	8.9	Anhwei	Lu, Wu-wei	3.2
Szechwan	Min	8.6	Kwangtung	Lei	3.1
Hunan	Yüeh, T'an, Heng	8.2	Anhwei and Kiangsu	Ch'u, Hao, Ssu, Ch'u, Su	3.1
Kiangsi	Chi, Yüan	7.3	Szechwan	Ch'eng	3.1
Shensi	Feng	6.4	Hunan	Li	2.9
Szechwan	Yü	6.3	Anhwei	Ying	2.9
Hupei	Ching	6.3	Anhwei	She	2.9
Fukien	Fu	6.2	Szechwan	Jung	2.9
Shensi	Wei	5.8	Chekiang	Wen	2.8
Hunan	Shao	5.7	Szechwan	Lu	2.8
Szechwan	Wan, Liang-shan, Chung	5.7	Chekiang	Ch'u	2.7
			Hupei	Chün	2.7
Hupei	Hsia	5.6	Kwangsi	Chao, Meng, Fu	2.7
Shantung	Mi	5.3			
Kiangsi	Hung, Chiang, Nan-k'ang	4.9	Kansu	Ch'in	2.7
			Kansu	Pin	2.6
Chekiang and Kiangsi	Ch'ü, Hsin, Jao, Wu	4.8	Kwangsi	Hsün	2.4
Hupei	Huang	4.6	Kwangtung	Kwang, Shao, Kang, Tuan, Hsin, K'ang	2.3
Shantung	Lai	4.5			
Hupei	An, E	4.5	Szechwan	P'eng	2.3
Hunan	Lang	4.4	Shantung	Ti, Pin	2.1
Szechwan	K'ai	4.4	Szechwan	Ya	2.1
Hupei	Ch'i	4.3	Hunan	Ch'en	2.1
Kiangsu	Ssu	4.0	Hunan	Kuang	2.0
Shantung	Teng	3.9	Chekiang	Ming, T'ai	2.0
			Kwangsi	Pin, Ch'eng	2.0

Source: Aoyoma Sadao, "Zui, Tō, Sō sandai ni okeru kosū no chiiki teki kōsatsu [An Areal Study on the Change in population during Sui, T'ang, and Sung]," *Rekishigaku Kenkyū*, 6, No. 5 (1936), pp. 529–554.

the northern population was generally characterized by stagnation or decline, in certain areas the population rose locally – in the lower reaches of the Yellow River valley, in the national capital and its adjacent areas, in Shantung, and in regions along the northern border. On the other hand, in the most advanced areas of the lower Yangtze valley the ratio of increase was rather modest, except for Ssu-chou and Ch'ü-chou in the upper reaches of the Tsientang River. This indicates that the population of the Yangtze River delta had reached its saturation point by the time of the Northern Sung.[14]

After the Jürchen capture of the old capital at K'ai-feng and two years' hesitation in selecting the site for a new capital, the "temporary residence" of the Sung was established at Hang-chou. Coincidentally, hundreds of thousands of people of northwestern origin – approximately 20,000 salaried high officials, tens of thousands of clerks, and the greater part of 400,000 regular soldiers and their families – moved to Hang-chou and adjacent areas, including Ssu-chou, Chien-k'ang, and Chen-chiang. Poor families occupied lands unsuited to rice cultivation, such as sandy land along the seashore, low land vulnerable to sea water, and narrow valley floors in the mountainous districts. On the other hand, the rich but landless immigrants from northwestern China generally settled in the cities. In Hang-chou, for example, they occupied the traditional residential areas of the city, forcing the former inhabitants out into the suburbs. These wealthy immigrants eagerly sought land for permanent residences and for safe investment. The growing surplus of population relative to land and the rapid rise in the price of land, though partly due to inflation and in some measure to excessive investment in land,[15] were a widespread phenomenon in the lower Yangtze during the Southern Sung. *"Fan Huai-nan,"*[16] meaning a mass influx of migrants from the Huai River valley into the Yangtze delta and farther to Fukien, became a common expression. Rampant infanticide in hilly districts south of the Yangtze delta, particularly in southern Anhwei and Fukien, indicates that there was little land available to new settlers.[17] The excess population from Hui-chou and Ssu-chou settled in central Anhwei, living mainly as migrant laborers.[18] Similarly, Fukienese farmers emigrated to Kwangtung.[19] Many landless farmers emigrated to cities to take up other occupations or to become simple vagrants.[20] Interestingly, there was a kind of popular preference poll among cities in the lower Yangtze basin.[21] Chien-k'ang (Nanking) was most preferred, followed by Chen-chiang, Ch'ang-chou, and Hu-chou. Hang-chou came next, followed by Ssu-chou, but these cities were not so favored because of their hurried pace of life. Then, in descending order, were frivolous

Shao-hsing, shameless Ming-chou (Ningpo), obscene Wen-chou, cunning T'ai-chou, and at last noxious Ch'ü-chou and Wu-chou. But apart from this ranking, Ssu-chou, Hang-chou, and Hu-chou were generally regarded as very attractive places to settle because of their beautiful environments and their prosperity, the latter derived from well-developed, stable farm productivity. As early as late T'ang and throughout the Five Dynasties period, it was proverbially said that "being able to live in Hu-chou as a landholder would offset risking one's life."[22] A similar proverb gained currency regarding Ssu-chou and Hang-chou, calling each of them "a heavenly palace on earth."[23] Thus, the population migration speeded the process of urbanization in the lower Yangtze and the south in general by concentrating into these areas a population far greater than they had previously supported.

Urban Population

Estimating the density of urban populations in Sung times is problematical. As a rule, Sung statistics on population were compiled by county, not by individual city or rural area. The situation is further complicated by the fact that women, children, soldiers, travelling merchants, vagrants, and slaves were not ordinarily recorded; nor were those who lived in small towns recorded as a component of the urban population. Sometimes the population figures themselves are suspicious because of under-reporting. Nonetheless, some information can be gleaned from the available materials, such as the figures provided by local gazetteers, in which urban and rural population statistics are broken down.

According to the gazetteer for Ssu-ming in the Pao-ch'ing reign period (1225-27) the population of Yin county (modern Ningpo) was as given in Table 2.3. Since the total population by households of Ming-chou (excluding the Chusan Archipelago) was around 200,000, this means that about 20 percent of the prefectural population lived in the prefectural seat, and that 13 percent of this population were city-dwellers. Similarly, according to the gazetter for Hsin-an (Hui-chou) in the Shun-hsi reign period (1174-89), the population of She county (the prefectural seat) was classified as given in Table 2.4. As there were 122,014 households in the entire territory of She prefecture, about 23 percent of the population were in She county and of the latter 7 percent were urban.

The statistics from the gazetteer for Chen-chiang in the Chih-shun reign period (1330-32) tell us the distribution of population in Tan-t'u county (the prefectural seat) (Table 2.5). Since the population of the whole prefecture was 108,500 households in 1208-24 and 72,427

TABLE 2.3.
Population of Yin County, 1225 – 27.

Population	Number of households	Percentage of total population
two urban localities	5,321	13
eleven rural localities	36,296	87
Total	41,617	100

Source: *Ssu-ming chih* (for Pao-ch'ing period), chüan 13.

TABLE 2.4.
Population of She County, 1172.

Population (1172)	Number of households	Percentage of total population
inside the city wall	1,281	7
outside the city wall	650	
in rural areas	25,943	93
Total	27,874	100

Source: *Hsin-an chih* (for Shun-hsi period), chüan 3.

TABLE 2.5.
Population of Tan-t'u County.

Population	Number of households	Percentage of total population
1208 – 24		
in the city	14,300	37
in Chiang-k'ou port	1,600	
in rural areas	27,000	63
Total	42,900	100
1265 – 74		
in the city	8,698	38
in rural areas	14,081	62
Total	22,779	100

Source: *Chen-chiang chih* (for Chih-shun period), chüan 3.

households in 1265-74, about 31 to 40 percent of the entire population lived in the county in which the prefectural capital was located, and the ratio of urban concentration to total population in the county was 37 to 38 percent.

These percentages of urban population concentrations are not

exceptionally high. In T'ing-chou, a prefecture located at the southern
edge of Fukien, 33 percent of the people were urban during the middle
period of Southern Sung.[24] Two prefectures in the middle reaches of
the Yangtze River also show relatively high concentrations: 13 percent
at Hanyang[25] and 17 percent at Ching-men.[26] These figures are also
roughly consistent with those for the Ch'ing period: 39 percent at
T'ien-chin in 1846, 21 percent at Li-ch'eng (the provincial capital of
Shantung) in 1772, 24 percent at Chi-ning (a prefectural capital in
Shantung) in 1840, 24 percent at Ta-t'ung (a prefectural capital in
Shansi) in 1830, 10 percent at Chieh-chou (another prefectural capital
in Shansi) in 1764.[27]

With regard to most other cities in the lower Yangtze the relevant
data are lacking. For Chien-k'ang, however, there is ample evidence to
estimate that from 300,000 to 400,000 people lived in and just outside
of the city, among which 170,000 were permanent residents.[28] As for
Ssu-chou, as early as mid-T'ang times about 45 percent of the prefecture's population lived in two counties that formed the prefectural
seat,[29] but there is no clue to determine what proportion of the prefecture's population lived in the city itself. For the city of Hang-chou in
the Southern Sung, the best estimates range from 1.5 to 5 million.
Kato's conservative estimate, supported by Etienne Balazs, suggested
a total of 1,500,000 persons made up as shown in Table 2.6.

TABLE 2.6.
Population of Hang-chou, according to Kato.

Section of city	Number of Households	Number of Persons
inside the walled city	180,000	900,000
southern suburbs	80,000	400,000
northern suburbs	40,000	200,000
Total	300,000	1,500,000

Source: Kato Shigeshi, *Shina Keizaishi Kosho,* II: 417—
18. E. Balazs, *Chinese Civilization and Bureaucracy*
(New Haven: Yale University Press, 1964), p. 84.

Calculating maximum total figures from the same data for the same date,
Ikeda Shizuo suggested figures consistent with Kuwabara Jitsuzo's
estimate of about 5 million total population in Hang-chou, as shown
in Table 2.7. This estimate has been supported recently by Hino
Kaizaburo and T. H. Hollingsworth,[30] but it seems to me unrealistic

TABLE 2.7.
Population of Hang-chou, according to Ikeda.

Section of city	Number of Households	Number of Persons
inside the walled city	300,000	1,500,000
southern suburbs	400,000	2,000,000
northern suburbs	200,000	1,000,000
Total	900,000	4,500,000

Source: Ikeda Shizuo, *Shina Suiri-chirishi Kenkyu,* pp. 111 – 29.

to assume five million people in the city of Hang-chou during the Sung solely on the basis of grain supply data.*

Rearrangement of Administrative Divisions

Faced with a massive influx of migrants and rapid growth of wealth in the lower Yangtze, the state learned to apply the fiscal-administrative system more flexibly. The 44 counties into which the region had been divided in Sui times grew to 106 by the middle of Sung. This process of administrative division may be considered in three stages. In the first stage, from Sui through mid-T'ang, the two commanderies of Yung-chia and Tung-yang in southern Chekiang were divided into five prefectures and 25 counties. Meanwhile, in the heart of the Yangtze delta, Hu-chou was established out of territory previously assigned to the western parts of Ssu-chou and the northern parts of Hang-chou. In the second stage, from Hsüan-tsung's reign to the end of the Five Dynasties period, Ming-chou was established in the northeastern corner of Chekiang, and the area south of the Yangtze River (in modern Anhwei province) was more finely divided. At the prefectural level, all the territorial divisions up to this point coincided roughly with natural boundaries. In the third stage, after the beginning

---

* Assuming there were five million people, the total annual consumption of rice would amount to somewhere between 18,000,000 piculs and 36,000,000 piculs (provided we count .01 or .02 piculs of rice as a man's daily consumption); if there were 1.5 million people, the total annual consumption of rice would amount to somewhere between 5,400,000 piculs and 10,800,000 piculs. But in reality, about 1,500,000 to 1,700,000 piculs of official rice were consumed in Hang-chou each year at the beginning of the Southern Sung (see Shiba Yoshinobu, *Sodai Shogyoshi Kenkyu* [Tokyo: Kazama-shobo, 1968], pp. 157 – 158). About 800,000 of these were tax rice from Liang-che circuit and the remainder was bought from merchants by the government. By the end of the dynasty the latter purchases had increased to 1 to 3 million piculs. Besides these, at least 3,000 to 4,000 piculs per day, or 1,100,000 to 1,400,000 piculs annually, were consumed by commoners. If we count up some 2 to 3 million piculs of rice as the consumption of rich people and landlords in the city, the figure of 1.5 million people is understandable.

of the Sung, an intensified effort was begun to divide prefectures and counties into even smaller units, particularly in the so-called Sung-chiang delta. These Sung divisions were of a rather artificial nature, deviating from natural boundaries even at the prefectural level.

The criteria by which the state regulated the size of a given county were rather complex. Initially, the state intended to draw boundary lines so that they might contain the minimum number of people needed to qualify as a county. This was particularly true of administrative divisions in T'ang times: on the average a county was constituted of ten *hsiang* or 5,000 households.[31] But as the economic system of a given region developed and as the population became more dense, the division of county boundaries tended to become increasingly artificial. Moreover, with the growth of rural-urban diversification as reflected in the rise of large cities, and with the advent of an intermediate category of small towns, the division of county boundaries by population became meaningless. Thus in Sung times, the state gave up the endless proliferation of counties in favor of intensified control through a tight network of administrative subdivisions. Logically, this network of administrative subdivisions was the means by which the state established uniform control over the country, irrespective of the differences between cities and rural areas, but in reality the state had to deal with the growth of differentiation, particularly with respect to fiscal matters. Thus in the cities the system of urban localities called *hsiang, yü,* or *chieh* was introduced, partially to maintain security but mostly to facilitate the distribution of urban taxes. In addition, a chain of supervisory stations was established at economically important towns in the countryside to collect commercial taxes and to control the state monopolies.

The Economic Background of Urbanization

It is apparent from the previous discussion that the two hierarchies of cities and towns — the "natural" economic one and the "artificial" administrative one, which came together for the most part at the level of prefectural capitals — tended to become divorced from one another toward the bottom of the scales. To inquire more critically into the problem of the nature and operation of this economic hierarchy, Table 2.8 provides an overview of the national distribution of commercial tax-collecting stations, classified according to their quotas and to the kinds of cities and towns in which they were located in 1077. On the basis of similar data, Etienne Balazs estimated that revenue from the two principal forms of commercial tax (i.e., *kuo-shui* or tax levied on the goods carried by travelling merchants when they passed a custom-house in transit and *chu-shui* or tax levied when travelling merchants sold their goods at market, or when a producer sold goods to a travelling

TABLE 2.8.
Frequency Distribution of Stations for Commercial Tax in 1077.

Amount of tax quota in strings of cash	chou capital	hsien capital	chen	ch'ang	wu	chai	pao	p'u	kuan	tu	chin	tien	hsü	k'eng	others
1 – 999	7	199	283	98	22	57	6	10	7	15	13	7	21	14	26
	*5**	*116*	*98*	*96*	*19*	*4*		*10*					*21*	*13*	*12*
1000 – 1999	15	148	136	12	6	9	1			13	1	1			3
	10	*69*	*43*	*11*	*5*	*2*					*1*				*1*
2000 – 3999	35	202	61	9	3	2				10	2		1	1	4
	14	*90*	*28*	*8*	*2*	*1*				*1*			*1*	*1*	*1*
4000 – 5999	34	98	17	3		1				1					2
	18	*50*	*10*	*3*											
6000 – 7999	24	43	6	1	1					1					2
	11	*26*	*4*	*1*	*1*					*1*					*2*
8000 – 9999	21	23	3	1	1	1									1
	10	*19*	*2*	*1*											*1*
10000 – 11999	17	11	3	1											
	8	*8*	*2*	*1*											
12000 – 13999	14	9	4												1
	7	*7*	*2*												*1*
14000 – 15999	15	7	1												1
	12	*6*	*1*												
16000 – 17999	15	4	1	1											1
	11	*3*	*1*	*1*											
18000 – 19999	12	3	1	2											
	6	*3*		*1*											
20000 – 21999	11	1													
	9	*1*													
22000 – 23999	4	1	1												
	2	*1*													
24000 – 25999	5		1												
	5														
26000 – 27999	5	1	2												
	3		*1*												
28000 – 29999	3	2													
	3	*1*													
30000 – 39999	26	1													
	15														
40000 – 49999	5														
	5														
50000 – 59999	7														
	6														
60000 – over	5														
	3														
Total	280	753	520	128	33	70	7	10	8	38	17	8	22	15	41
	163	*400*	*192*	*123*	*27*	*7*		*10*	*1*	*1*	*1*		*22*	*14*	*18*

* Figures in italics represent tax stations in south China.

merchant) amounted to 6,918,159 strings of cash, or 5 to 10 percent of the value of merchandise traded. Thus the total taxed trade ranged in value between 70 and 140 million strings.[32] Dwight H. Perkins has postulated that this trade represented about 20 to 30 percent of total farm output in 1077 — assuming that per capita farm output in real terms was not much different in 1077 from 1933.[33]

Of the cities at the prefectural level, 95 percent had commercial tax stations which also functioned as prefectural "central supervisory offices." Furthermore, the tax quotas, or the amount of trade recorded at these prefectural stations, surpassed by far most other stations of lower levels in the territory as a whole. Those tax stations whose quota was more than about 30,000 strings of cash were predominantly located at the prefectural capitals.

County capitals, on the other hand, were significantly lower in the hierarchy of economic importance. Of the 1,135 county capitals extant during the same period, only 743 (or 65 percent) had stations for collecting the commercial tax. In other words, about 35 percent of the county capitals were economically negligible. Moreover, the tax quota in more than half of the county tax stations was considerably lower than in the prefectural stations. This may, in part, be due to the fact that the county capitals' predominance in local trade was often challenged by other urban and quasi-urban centers. Among these, the importance of *chen,* towns in the local trading system, was remarkable. Sometimes the tax quotas at *chen* matched those of county stations, particularly in the north. More important, though, is the fact that the 520 *chen* stations in Table 2.9 represent only one quarter of a total 1,815 extant towns, which suggests that the tax stations in these towns should be counted among the intermediate category of rural market towns. Other centers of local communications, such as *kuan* (check stations), *tu* (ferries), *chin* (wharves), and *tien* (hostels or inns acting as general stores) were predominant in the north, while urban centers connected with mining, or with salt or tea manufacturing were distributed mainly in the south.

In the lower Yangtze the supremacy of strongly commercial prefectural cities in the urban economic hierarchy was much more evident, as is demonstrated in Table 2.9. If the tax quotas of all the prefectural stations in the country are arranged in descending order, 15 out of 19 prefectural stations in the lower Yangtze ranked somewhere between second and seventy-eighth in the country as a whole; Hang-chou was second, Ssu-chou tenth, Chien-k'ang fourteenth, Ch'ü-chou nineteenth, Hu-chou twentieth, Ming-chou twenty-sixth, and Hui-chou seventy-eighth. A typology ranking prefectural capitals in the lower Yangtze according to the commercial tax quota of each — 3,000 strings

TABLE 2.9.
Frequency Distribution of Stations
for Commercial Tax in the Lower Yangtze in 1077.

Amount of tax quota (strings of cash)	*Chou* capital	*Hsien* capital	Town	Others (Ch'ang, Wu, etc.)
1 — 999		8	22	5
1,000 — 1,999		9	13	2
2,000 — 3,999	1	24	12	2
4,000 — 5,999	1	15	2	
6,000 — 7,999	1	10		
8,000 — 9,999	1	5		
10,000 — 11,999		4		
12,000 — 13,999	1	3	1	
14,000 — 15,999			1	
16,000 — 17,999	1	1	1	1
18,000 — 19,999				
20,000 — 21,999	1			
22,000 — 23,999	1			
24,000 — 25,999	2			
26,000 — 27,999	3			
28,000 — 29,999	1			
30,000 — 39,999	2			
40,000 — 49,999	1			
50,000 — 59,999	1			
60,000 — and over	1			
Total	19	79	52	10

of cash as the minimum requisite amount to be classed in the category "central market town," 10,000 for "local city," and 30,000 for "regional city," for example — would arrange the cities as follows:*

> Regional cities: Hang-chou, Ssu-chou, Chien-k'ang, Ch'u-chou, and Hu-chou.
> Local cities: Shao-hsing, Hsiu-chou, Wu-chou, Chang-chou, Wen-chou, Chen-chiang, T'ai-chou, Ming-chou, Hsüan-chou, and Hui-chou.
> Central market towns: Chu-chou, Mu-chou, Ch'i-chou, and T'ai-p'ing-chou.

---

* The typology and terminology used here are applied in the sense given to these by G. William Skinner in his article "Marketing and Social Structure in Rural China," *The Journal of Asian Studies,* 24, Nos. 1, 2, 3 (1964, 1965).

If the county capitals in this region are classified according to the
same typology (with the addition of the category "intermediate market
towns" in which the quota was less than 3,000 strings of cash), the
county capitals would be arranged as follows:

> Local cities: Fu-yang (Hang-chou), Lin-an (Hang-chou), Wu-hu
> (T'ai-p'ing), An-chi (Hu-chou), T'ung-lu (Mu-chou), Hua-
> ting (Hsiu-chou), Chiang-yin (Chang-chou), and Wu-shih
> (Chang-chou).
>
> Central market towns: I-wu (Wu-chou), Chu-chi (Shao-hsing),
> Lan-ch'i (Wu-chou), Chang-shu (Ssu-chou), I-hsing
> (Chang-chou), and thirty-five other capitals.
>
> Intermediate market towns: Ch'i-men (Hui-chou), Chi-hsi (Hui-
> chou), Lung-ch'üan (Ch'u-chou), Feng-hua (Ming-chou),
> Chin-t'an (Chen-chiang), and twenty-six other capitals.

It must be remembered that these classifications are based solely on
the amount of tax, and not on marketing function.

Most of the other towns (*chen, kuan, tu*, etc.) were "intermediate
market towns" economically, but some of them were so important in
internal trade that they had tax quotas high enough to be classed as "local
cities" or "central market towns." These are Chekiang ferry (16,446
strings) near Hang-chou, Ch'ing-lung port (15,879 strings) in Hsiu-chou,
Ch'i-kou port (13,386 strings) in Ch'i-chou, Tsao-o junction (4,936
strings) in Shao-hsing, Yung-an (4,703 strings) in Wen-chou, Ta-tung
port (3,616 strings) in Ch'i-chou, and Yu-p'u ferry (3,240 strings in
Shao-hsing.

At the bottom of the economic hierarchy were numerous rural
assemblies or marketplaces, classified as "standard markets." With the
development of these rural markets, the mesh of the urban network
became more closely drawn than it had been previously. Illustrative of
the new situation is a passage from the Chen-chiang gazetteer for the
Chih-hsün reign period (1330-32) describing the town of T'ing-ch'iao:

These days, wherever there is a settlement of ten households, there is always a
market for rice and salt. The use of the term 'market' indicates that business is
going on there. At the appropriate season people exchange what they have for
what they have not, raising or lowering their prices in accordance with their
estimate of the eagerness or diffidence shown by others, so as to obtain the last
small measure of profit. This is of course the usual way of the world. Although
Ting-ch'iao is no great city, its river will still accommodate boats and its land
routes carts. Thus it too serves as a town for peasants who trade and artisans
who engage in commerce.[34]

This market site clearly served a standard marketing area in which the typical transactions were the exchange of surplus products from local farms and workshops for commodities brought in by long-distance trade. The operation of these local markets was not dominated solely by landlords and great merchants; individual peasant farmers engaged in trade at this level as well, although the scale of their operations was much smaller.

Market towns were established either on the borders of two counties or on important lines of communication well away from the county capitals. Something of their density of distribution in Ch'ang-shu county in Ssu-chou prefecture is known from the Ch'in-ch'uan gazetteer for the Shun-yu reign period (1241 – 52).[35] The county consisted of nine rural areas (*hsiang*), fifty boroughs (*tu*), and 386 villages (*li*). Of the last, about forty appear from their names to have supported markets of some sort and six to nine of these were actually classified at the next higher level in the system, although they partially overlapped in function with those of the lower category. The Ch'ang-shu county gazetteer for the Hung-chih reign period (1488 – 1505) also quotes an old gazetteer: "The fields are arrayed like fishes' scales. On a level plain of a hundred *li* villages and markets will be linked together continuously in all directions."[36] Other data from the Chiang-yang gazetteer and Lu-chou prefecture gazetteer (recorded in *Yung-lo ta-tien*) written in Southern Sung indicate that the dense distribution of rural markets was not peculiar to the Yangtze delta.[37]

The economic hierarchy of cities and towns described above developed real significance only as long-distance trade, farm productivity, and division of labor progressed after the middle of the T'ang. The great amount of surplus rice produced in Ssu-chou and adjacent areas (Chang-chou, Hsiu-chou, and Hu-chou) was a crucial determinant of urban development throughout the lower Yangtze valley. Ssu-chou alone had 3,400,000 *mou* of taxable paddy-fields. But even this huge figure probably represents only a part of the total arable land: miscellaneous evidence shows that some estate owners had hundreds of thousands or even a million piculs in their storehouses, and there was unregistered land and production besides. The high productivity in Ssu-chou is partly due to the natural fertility of the land, and partly to intensified utilization of land through a well-developed water control system. Farther south, however, the land grows poorer. Table 2.10 shows the amount by prefecture of the Autumn Tax rice in Liang-che circuit. In sharp contrast with the highly productive paddies of Ssu-chou, land in the mountainous districts of the lower Yangtze valley was limited

TABLE 2.10.
The Amount of Autumn Tax
Rice by Prefecture in Liang-che.

Prefecture	Amount of Rice (piculs)
Ssu-chou	ca. 340,000
Chang-chou	ca. 220,000
Hu-chou	ca. 50,000
Hang-chou	ca. 120,000
Chen-chiang	ca. 100,000
Ming-chou	ca. 110,000
Shao-hsing	ca. 250,000
Wen-chou	ca. 50,000
Yen-chou	8,751
Wu-chou	ca. 133,000
T'ai-chou	ca. 140,000
Total	ca. 1,500,000

These figures are from various sources of
wen-chi and local gazetteers.

in extent and not very fertile. Thanks to growing long-distance trade, production in these districts was intended from the beginning for the market, and in turn, the farmers had to supply their own food by buying rice from Ssu-chou and other flatland areas.

The development of communication networks, particularly the waterways system, and much decreased transport costs were other significant features of commercial growth in the lower Yangtze. As Owen Lattimore has suggested, [38] the impossibility of extending the Grand Canal to the south forced the development of coastal shipping in the southern provinces. This organization was subsequently extended to trade with Nan-yang in the south, and with Shantung, Kaoli, and Japan in the north and northeast. Seaports, such as Chen-chiang, Ch'ing-lung, Hua-ting, Kan-p'u, Hang-chou, Ming-chou, T'ai-chou, and Wen-chou, thrived on the coastal trade. Among them, Ming-chou (Ningpo) monopolized the role of transshipment center in the Yangtze delta region from the Sung until the end of the nineteenth century. Here products from distant regions were transferred to small boats to negotiate the canals and other inland waterways which led to cities throughout the country.

Hang-chou was located at the nexus of the whole system. Three routes ran to the north. To the northeast was the sea route which reached Hang-chou through the Yangtze River ports. Silk was the main item shipped from the north via this route; the return cargo was comprised of incense, ivory, rhinoceros horn, and rice. The central route, the Grand Canal, was the main artery through which the bulk of official and private goods including rice, silk, metals, and other specialties from semi-tropical southern provinces were exported to the north in exchange for salt from the northeast coast of Kiangsu. The route to the northwest was an overland route which functioned as the by-road of the Grand Canal. Through this route metals, incense, and other hill-area products from Kiangsi and Kuang-nan were carried via Hui-chou to the port of Wu-hu on the Yangtze. Then, after crossing northern Anhwei, the route joined with the Pien Canal. Parallel to this highway was another shortcut which started from Hui-chou, continued to Ta-tung port on the Yangtze and led finally to K'ai-feng, crossing Anhwei northward. Products from the west (i.e., silk, lumber, hemp, etc.) made their way downstream on the Yangtze. The Yin-lin Canal, which branched from Wu-hu port and led to T'ai-hu Lake, was also opened to shorten the journey. Lumber, porcelain, paper, silk, hemp, lacquer, oil, and fruits from the southern hinterland of Fukien, western Chekiang and the Tsientang River valley including Hui-chou and Hsin-chou, were shipped through the Tsientang River to its terminus, Lung-shan ferry near Hang-chou. Products from Nan-yang and the southeastern coasts of China (ivory, rhinoceros horn, medicines, pearls, iron, copper, lumber, dried fish, fish glue, sugar, hemp, paper, and so forth) arrived at Chekiang ferry near Hang-chou through Ming-chou. The return cargo on these two routes was mainly rice from the Yangtze delta.[39]

Linked with the growing communication system and the efficient circulation of goods was the development of wholesaling in large cities located at strategic points in the transportation network. In Hang-chou there were a great variety of trades, guilds organized by business type, and highly specialized wholesaling markets. According to Balazs' description, Hang-chou's organization of wholesalers and retailers approached that of a modern town in terms of the technique for credit arrangements. There were similar developments in other commercial cities in the lower Yangtze, although on a lesser scale. The following list of markets and shopping areas found within a variety of cities indicates the extent of specialization in Sung times:

> Ssu-chou: *Markets:* The large market, the small market, the eastern market, the western market, the market for grain, the market for vegetables.
>
> > *Shopping areas:* For fruits, rice, fish, silk thread, matting, gold and silver, brocade and embroidery, and iron cooking ware.[40]

Chien-k'ang: *Markets:* The eastern market, the western market, the fish market, the thin silk market, the salt market, the fodder market, the livestock market, the grain and shellfish market, the small market, Chen-huai-ch'iao market, Hsin-ch'iao market, Ch'ieh-ch'iao market, Ch'ing-hua market.

Shopping areas: For silver, flowers, and poultry.[41]

Chen-chiang: *Markets:* The large market, the small market, the horse market, the rice and vegetables market.

Shopping areas: For bamboo, small-sized bamboo, lumber, matting, lime, glutinous rice, fruit, fodder, horses, poultry, pigs, rice cakes, boiled water, wooden spoons, hemp sacks, hats, waistbands, grinders, and needles.[42]

Ming-chou: *Markets:* The large market, the rear market, Yung-tung market.

Shopping areas: For dried fish, rice, bamboo, lumber, flowers, incense, matting, salted fish, coffin-boards, slates, oil-pressing, and foodstuffs.[43]

Hu-chou: *Markets:* The southern market, the western market, the small market.

Shopping areas: For bamboo and lumber, straw, firewood, fodder, straw-rope making, lime, fish, dried fish, poultry, flowers, lacquerware, silver, bamboo baskets, carpenter's squares, carriage horses, and oil-pressing.[44]

Shao-hsing: *Markets:* Chao-shui-fang market, Ta-yung-ch'iao market, Yüeh-ta market, Ch'ing-tao-ch'iao market, Lung-hsing-ssu market, I-pei market, Chiang-ch'iao market.[45]

Furthermore, there is considerable evidence of progressive diversification of the commercial system in county capitals. For example, in the town of Ch'ang-chou there were at least two markets in addition to the shopping areas specializing in fish, nutmeg, nails, vegetables, firewood, and sheep.[46] Again, in the county town of Ch'ang-hsing in Hu-chou there were a variety of commercial and other kinds of guilds grouped according to occupational specialities, such as dealers in the five condiments, in incense and candles, in silver, in priests' fly-whisks, in symbolic paper money for sacrifice to the gods, in fruits, wine, foodstuffs, silk cloth, sweet rice cakes, and fish; and guilds of boatmen, cooks, clerks, tanners, barbers, and tailors.[47]

Lodges to accommodate merchants, inns-cum-stores, establishments for stockpiling and storage as commission agents, and wholesaling firms were the indispensable facilities of commercial centers, but they ranged widely in size and role. The degree of their specialization varied according to the level of their particular market in the whole marketing structure. In general, the smaller the market the more likely a broker was to be engaged in activities other than simple brokerage. In rural towns he might be a broker who ran a merchant hostel, or a retailer, a weights and measures expert, or a tax payment agent for wealthy families. In addition, rich farmers and landlords who dwelt in such towns were not infrequently the proprietors of *t'ing-t'a* (warehouses) in which capacity they made speculative purchases of goods in bulk.

On the other hand, in prefectural or county capitals there were *ti-tien* (warehousemen-cum-innkeepers who served as commission agents and wholesalers), *fang-lang* (ateliers and marketing arcades), and, particularly in large commercial cities, *t'a-fang* (storehouses). In county capitals incomes from these businesses were far smaller than in prefectural cities. In Ch'u-jung county of Chien-k'ang the owners of ateliers and marketing arcades drew an income of five to seven thousand strings of cash per day as rent, while in the city of Chien-k'ang such people enjoyed a daily income of twenty to thirty strings of cash at least, and the owners of pawnshops and other stores earned an income of several tens of thousands of strings of cash per day.[48]

Since the geography of an area played an important part in determining its economic development, Hu-chou and Hui-chou illustrate differences in the process of commercialization between level plains and mountainous regions.

Commercial Development of Hu-chou

The physical environment of Hu-chou was complex. Its territory consisted of two different types of land: a vast stretch of rich plain to the east, and mountainous, unproductive districts to the west. In terms of topography, Hu-chou was a microcosm of the whole lower Yangtze valley. The capital of Hu-chou prefecture, functionally a central market of its dependent areas, was located at the nexus of the communication system of the Tiao River valley, at the junction of two tributaries of that river and a branch line of the Grand Canal. In Ch'in and Han times, before the territory had been consolidated into one regional unit, the eastern plain was assigned to Wu-ch'eng county, while the hilly western district was a part of Ku-chang county, later renamed An-chi in 266. It was not until the end of the Wu Dynasty of the Three Kingdoms and the early years of the Chin Dynasty that the whole territory was unified into Wu-hsing commandery, subdivided into nine counties: Wu-ch'eng, Ch'ang-ch'eng (renamed Ch'ang-hsing in 908), Wu-k'ang, An-chi and others. During the Sui-T'ang transition the provincial territory was unified as Hu-chou prefecture (as stated above). Later, Te-ch'ing

county was established to the south of the prefectural capital, drawing
from the eastern part of Wu-k'ang, and in 979 Kuei-an county was established, dividing Wu-ch'eng in two. The establishment of the latter
two counties was due to the urban concentration of population. Indeed,
the population of Hu-chou doubled between Sung and early Ming,
excluding An-chi and Te-ch'ing. Table 2.11 shows that in sharp contrast
to the stagnation in the hilly districts, about 40 percent of the whole
population became concentrated in Wu-ch'eng, the prefectural capital,
and in the Kuei-an counties, its suburbs on the eastern plain. Growing
urban markets for food and handicrafts and urban sources of exotic
goods had a great impact upon the economy of the rural households in
surrounding areas. Inside the city wall, built in 621 and measuring
11,384 meters in circumference, there were at least three markets in
addition to shopping areas which specialized in lumber, bamboo,

TABLE 2.11.
Change in Population in Hu-chou.

County	Dynasty	Date	Number of Households	Population
Change in whole prefecture				
	T'ang	618 – 626	14,135	76,400
	T'ang	742	73,306	470,000
	Sung	1008 – 1016	129,540	436,372
	Sung	ca. 1078	145,121	–
	Sung	1182	204,588	571,812
	Yuan	1290	236,570	–
	Ming	1391	200,048	810,244
Change by county				
Wu-ch'eng	Sung	1008 – 1016	26,357	90,373
	Sung	1290	68,437	–
	Ming	1391	58,617	226,008
Kuei-an	Sung	1008 – 1016	26,913	12,119
	Sung	1290	49,894	–
	Ming	1391	61,950	–
Ch'ang-hsing	Sung	1182	49,811	54,838
	Sung	1290	54,151	–
	Ming	1391	40,124	167,707
An-chi	Sung	1008 – 1016	22,185	71,062
	Sung	1290	25,298	–
	Ming	1391	18,044	77,216
Te-ch'ing	Sung	1008 – 1016	10,434	33,002
	Ming	1391	11,057	53,781
Wu-k'ang	Sung	1007	4,619	–
	Sung	1290	17,261	–
	Ming	1391	10,256	44,991

Source: *Yung-lo ta'tien*, chüan 2276 (pp. 2 – 3).

straw, firewood, fuel, lime, flowers, fish, dried fish, lacquer manufacture, bamboo basket manufacture, and oil pressing. In addition there were moorages for sampans, carriage horses, and amusement centers.

To provide food for urban consumption, hydraulic enterprise was expanded. In the eastern lowlands the water-control system was extensively developed, providing drainage for areas which were formerly nonarable. As is illustrated in Table 2.12, the reclamation of land by constructing dams and sluices centered mainly in the lowlands of the eastern plain. According to Wang Yen, who flourished in the middle of Southern Sung, about 100,000 *mou* of land were reclaimed in Hu-

TABLE 2.12.
Diked Lands in Hu-chou in 1377.

County	Cultivated Acreage (*mou*) of Diked Lands
Wu-cheng	3,114
Kuei-an	1,715
Chang-hsing	867
Te-ch'ing	980
Wu-k'ang	201
An-chi	18

Source: *Yung-lo ta-tien,* chüan 2277 (p. 4).

chou around 1209.[49] Due to the success of water control, rice production developed extensively on the eastern plain. Wang observed: "Boats and carts will usually set out in all directions to sell the surplus in a year when the harvest has been good." It was for the most part high quality, moderately glutinous rice which was produced in this area. Peasants who dwelt in the vicinity of cities and towns, however, did not eat such high quality rice, but usually bought brewer's grains or rice brans instead.[50] Early-ripening Champa rice was also produced in this area in small amounts to feed army horses and to be eaten by all households, from those owning a modest amount of property on down.[51]

A much more important crop produced in this area was the highly glutinous rice used by city-dwellers for wine brewing and other luxuries. Indeed, wine brewing had been one of the most famous specialties in Hu-chou since Han times. Wine brewing was encouraged by the Wu-yüeh Kingdom during the Five Dynasties period and by the warlords in the early Southern Sung as a source of revenue. Thus in the

Southern Sung the production of highly glutinous rice spread so much on the eastern plain that a proposal was submitted to the government to monopolize its production and sale. The wine breweries were located not only in prefectural and county capitals, but also in thirty-five towns scattered on the eastern plain.[52] It is reasonable to conclude, therefore, that the commercialization of rice in Hu-chou did not result from marketing incidental surplus production, but rather from a deliberate effort to produce a cash crop.

Similarly, along the shore of T'ai-hu Lake people specialized in gardening, fishing, fish hatching, and pomiculture for the market. Their ginger, radishes, and oranges achieved a national reputation. A cloth made from yellow grass and a fabric made from hemp were also produced on the eastern plain, with production centered in such towns as Ssu-ch'i and Tao-ch'ang-shan.

In the western district the flat land was limited by a chain of mountains and was not very fertile. Early-ripening Champa rice was the main crop of the district, but its yield could not satisfy demand. Instead, sericulture, tea, pottery manufacture, lacquer, and other hill industries were emphasized. Towns like P'ing-yao and Hsia-chu in Wu-k'ang and Shih-ting-shan in Te-ch'ing were famous for their pottery, which was sold as far away as southern Kiangsu.[53] Silk was another local specialty of particular importance. By the middle of the Ming this industry had become concentrated in the prefectural capital and the surrounding towns,[54] but in Sung times it remained peculiar to the hilly districts of An-chi and Wu-k'ang. The thin silk and silk thread made in the county of An-chi as well as thin silk made in Mei-ch'i, a town in An-chi, were famous nationally for their excellent quality. A passage from Ch'en Fu's *Treatise on Agriculture,* printed in 1154, illustrates the extent of specialization:

All the men of An-chi county can [graft mulberry trees]. Some of them make their living solely by sericulture. [For subsistence, it is necessary that] a family of ten persons rear ten frames of silkworms, obtaining twelve catties of cocoons from each frame. Each catty yields 1.3 ounces of thread, and from every five ounces of thread one length of small silk may be woven, and this exchanges for 1.4 piculs of rice. Supplying one's food and clothing by these means insures a high degree of stability. One month's toil is better than a whole year's exertions [at farming], and one is afflicted neither by parching drought nor by overflowing floods.[55]

Thus, some well-to-do families in An-chi had several tens of *mou* of mulberry trees, and the richest of the specialized weaving households reared several hundreds of frames of silkworms. Each *mou* of mulberry land produced 160 catties of mulberry leaves.[56]

On the basis of such rural specialization, a fairly dense distribution of markets emerged. But the pattern in the mountainous areas was quite different from that of the level plains. In the latter case the mesh of the net of distribution was close. The trade in some towns like Wu-tun, Hsin-shih, Nan-lin (Nan-hsün), and Shang-po usually equalled but sometimes exceeded the county capitals.[57] Furthermore, there were towns like Ssu-ch'i, Tao-ch'ang-shan, Shih-ting-shan, and Hsia-chu which prospered on specialized industries. In the hilly districts, however, the market towns were dotted sparsely in the narrow valleys along the water routes. It appears that the location of towns depended primarily on the ease of access to the transportation system.

Commercial Development of Hui-chou[58]

In contrast to Hu-chou, Hui-chou provides a model for examining the impact of commercialization on mountainous areas. The territory of Hui-chou, first designated during the transitional period from Sui to T'ang and unchanged thereafter until the end of the Ch'ing, was located on the watershed which divided the three provincial regions of Anhwei, Chekiang, and Kiangsi. Before the formation of Hui-chou itself, a loose, natural administrative-territorial unit which included the Hsin-an River valley (the future territory of Mu-chou) was recognized as early as the Wu Dynasty of the Three Kingdoms, when Sun Ch'üan established the Hsin-tu commandery (later renamed Hsin-an) in 208. Throughout the succeeding centuries, the high mountains surrounding the commandery afforded good shelter for immigrants from the north. Farm productivity was improved by powerful landlords such as Pao An-kuo, Hu Ming-hsing, and Ch'eng Ling-hsi, but the effect of their efforts was limited. In the Sui-T'ang transition, Wang Hua (586-649), a powerful, militant native landlord, assumed command of about 100,000 militia, protected his homeland against attack from other warlords, and consequently attained hegemony over six prefectures including Hui-chou. Wang's control is an indication of Hui-chou's increasing internal homogeneity in the overall territorial differentiation of the Yangtze valley. The eastern fringes of Hui-chou were ceded to neighboring Mu-chou in the Sui, and the remaining territory was slowly subdivided into six counties during the course of the T'ang and Five Dynasties, primarily in consequence of immigration and the accumulation of wealth in the area. Indeed, the population almost sextupled between 606 and 742, then nearly trebled again between 742 and 1078. Under the Sung the population quadrupled in the county of She (the prefectural seat), trebled in Wu-yüan county, and approximately doubled in Ch'i-men and Hsiu-ning counties (Table 2.13). This indi-

TABLE 2.13.
Change in Population in Hui-chou.

County	Dynasty	Date	Number of Households	Population
Change in whole prefecture				
	Sui	606	6,154	—
	T'ang	742	38,320	269,109
	Sung	976–83	11,763	—
	Sung	1017–21	127,203	192,292
	Sung	ca. 1078	105,984	—
	Sung	1165–73	120,083	—
	Ming	1391	131,662	581,082
Change by county				
She	Sung	1017–21	6,474	28,491
	Sung	1165–73	25,534	—
	Sung	1208–24	22,613	39,783
	Ming	1391	40,064	177,304
Hsiu-ning	Sung	1017–21	13,871	25,105
	Sung	1165–73	19,599	—
	Sung	1225–27	19,626	46,038
	Ming	1391	36,863	174,114
Wu-yuan	Sung	1017–21	14,614	31,341
	Sung	1165–73	41,864	—
	Sung	1234–36	44,432	55,932
	Ming	1391	28,027	137,701
I	Sung	1017–21	6,649	18,511
	Sung	1165–73	7,769	—
	Sung	1234–36	8,336	19,347
	Ming	1391	6,380	22,001
Chi-ch'i	Sung	1017–21	8,235	16,004
	Sung	1165–73	8,391	—
	Sung	1225–27	9,684	26,297
	Ming	1391	13,385	39,213
Ch'i-men	Sung	1017–21	5,921	8,289
	Sung	1165–73	15,536	—
	Sung	1234–36	16,683	—
	Ming	1391	6,943	30,749

Source: Shiba Yoshinobu, "Sōdai Kishū no Chiiki Kaihatsu," p. 220.

cates the concentration of population in the prefectural capital itself and in the basin surrounding it, and new colonization of the peripheral areas to the south and west which were connected with Kiangsi through waterways.

In response to growing urban consumption the land was seriously exploited. According to the official tally of irrigation ponds in Hui-chou prefecture (shown in Table 2.14), about half of the total number were concentrated in the central basin or outlying areas of She and Hsiu-ning counties. Furthermore, in the central basin and in Ch'i-men county offi-

TABLE 2.14.
Irrigation Ponds in Six
Counties in Hui-chou in the
Southern Sung.

| County | Kind of irrigation pond | | |
	Pei	Chieh	T'ang
She	—	226	1,207
Hsiu-ning	—	210	510
Ch'i-men	—	975	237
Wu-yuan	157	17	—
Chi-ch'i	—	117	95
I	—	190	—
Total	157	1,735	2,049

Source: *Hsin-an chih* (for the Shun-hsi
period), chüan 3, 4, and 5.

cially registered cultivated fields doubled during the Sung and early
Ming. A variety of improved early-ripening Champa rice was produced
in Hui-chou to compensate for the land's relative unsuitability to rice
culture. As in Hu-chou, high quality rice of moderate glutin content
was produced as tax rice and as food for relatively well-to-do families,
while Champa rice was the most common food for households of middle
to low status. In addition, farmers began to terrace the hillsides for
cultivation, so that new fields rose level upon level like steps in a stair-
case. Since rivers and irrigation ponds were shallow and remote, the
farmers worked extremely hard, but were limited by what could be
achieved by labor-intensive cultivation. The population remained nearly
the same — 127,083 in 1173, and 131,662 in 1391 — from the Southern
Sung to early Ming. Gradually, people were induced to turn to commercially oriented farming or to take up nonagricultural pursuits. In
this regard, the improvement of the communication system was vitally
important to Hui-chou's economic development. Ch'i-men county in
late T'ang times exemplifies this development. The land in Ch'i-men
was so limited by its hilly setting that almost seven-tenths of the 5,400
households in the county drew their livelihood from tea manufacture
and businesses connected with it. Government income too was obtained
from the taxes on tea manufacture. Among tea merchants from other
cities, the teas produced in Ch'i-men were much reputed for their excellent flavor and color, but in spite of the increasing demand, natural
barriers — especially the Ch'ang-men rapids at Ch'i-men River, thirteen
li southwest of the county capital — prevented the tea cargoes from being efficiently shipped in bulk. Between 860 and 862 a prefect named
Ch'en Kan-chih resumed river improvements which had been com-

menced by his predecessors, financing these partly by diverting official
money (such as profits from tea monopoly), partly by raising money
from beneficiaries, such as tea merchants and shipping agents, and partly
from his own salary. A dam and a drainage canal were thus constructed
at the rapids, greatly facilitating the shipment of tea.[59]

In the Southern Sung, tea, lacquer, lumber, and paper were common exports from Ch'i-men to Kiangsi via the Ch'i-men River, and
they were exchanged for rice, cattle, and fish. The hills in Hsiu-ning
and Wu-yüan were so well suited for growing cryptomeria that few of
the local people cultivated fields, preferring to make their living from
cryptomeria wood cultivation. The lumber was usually collected at a
logging yard, bound there into rafts and floated downstream to Hang-
chou, a central market, where other hill region products from Hui-chou,
such as paper, wax, lacquer, and dyes, were also brought together.
Returned from the Yangtze delta were rice and salt. Paper made from
the bark of the paper-mulberry in Chi-ch'i county surpassed by far
that from other regions in the Yangtze valley both in quality and quantity, and almost monopolized the market.

The pursuit of knowledge might also be included among the
nonagricultural activities in this prefecture. Table 2.15 shows the
increase in number of *chin-shih* degree holders in Hui-chou, with the
greatest increases in Wu-yüan and Hsiu-ning counties.

Hui-chou not only was an important commercial center regionally,
but also served as a focal point for competitive trade with the rest of
the empire. Indeed, Hui-chou was the base of a unified economic
organization in which division of labor, specialization of local products,
and differentiation of demand and consumption were combined. On
the occasion of an annual Buddhist festival (eighth day of the fourth
month) worshippers from all over the empire, particularly merchants,
converged in the capital of Wu-yüan county to give thanks to Hui-chou's
special deities, the Five Shining Spirits, or Five Lumber Trading Spirits.
The extent of Hui-chou's marketing area is reflected by the diffusion
of its deities to southern Anhwei, Kiangsi, Kiangsu, and notably to the
city of Ssu-chou.

In summary, Hui-chou's interregional trade developed not as a
result of purely local commercial demands, but primarily as a response
to the demand for its special products in other regions. The progress
of commercialization in hilly areas such as Hui-chou, then, is as follows:
the wealth and population of the agrarian society increases slowly,
trade routes are extended into the area from other regions, fairs are
established along the routes, the inhabitants of the locality turn to
commercially oriented farming or nonagricultural pursuits in response

TABLE 2.15.
**The Number of *Chin-shih* Holders in
Hui-chou during the Sung.**

Counties	Dynasty		
	Northern Sung	Southern Sung	Total
Wu-yuan	61	124	185
Hsiu-ning	15	138	153
She	34	65	99
I	37	38	75
Ch'i-men	16	38	54
Chi-ch'i	18	13	31
Unknown	16	11	27
Total	197	427	624

Source: Shiba Yoshinobu, "Sōdai Kishū no Chiiki Kaihatsu," p. 224.

to the new demand from distant areas, and finally the region manufactures special products using its particular resources.

Largely as a result of such a pattern of commercialization, few large urban centers with a differentiated hierarchy of marketing functions developed. Only six towns are recorded. With the exception of Yüeh-ssu in She county, which was known for its lacquerwork, the towns were only small trading posts or break-points on transportation routes.

Conclusion

China's predominantly rural society in pre-T'ang times was essentially self-sufficient. Neither periodic markets in systems of local trade nor the development of long-distance trade disturbed the subsistence basis of the peasant society. The cities which were seats of prefectural or county government performed primarily political, military, religious, or administrative functions, and only secondarily served as market centers for their hinterland. These cities obtained foodstuffs from the surrounding countryside mainly by a pattern of redistribution — collecting local surplus as taxes in kind and distributing them through official expenditure. Villages were linked to cities through *hsiang,* sub-urban administrative jurisdictions. The rural-urban relationship was therefore less economic than political.

With the series of revolutions — agricultural, commercial, industrial, and political — which took place during the great transitional period from mid-T'ang to Sung, the traditional subsistence basis of society was greatly changed by increasing specialization of the economy and the consequent breakdown of local self-sufficiency. However, since the upsurge in rural productivity, especially in the lower Yangtze valley, varied locality by locality, the inequality of demand and supply had to be adjusted by the intermediary services of trade. Thus a hierarchy of urban centers with marketing functions developed to mediate local, interregional, and interurban trade. According to Chi Ch'ao-ting (b. 1903), "The Yangtze Valley, though economically greatly developed during the T'ang dynasty by water-control undertakings, had not yet advanced far enough to overcome natural and historical barriers between the various independent and self-sufficient constituent units." But after the Sung dynasty, "the whole valley, except Szechwan, was sufficiently developed in regard to communications as well as cultural homogeneity to allow the major part of the territory to be woven into one regional unit."[60] In other words, the Yangtze valley became an integral market.

The massive influx of migrants from the north to the fertile Yangtze valley was another characteristic feature of urbanization and commercialization during this period. Wealthy immigrants preferred to live in the cities, while the poor settled in sparsely settled borderlands as migrant laborers or emigrated to cities to take up occupations other than farming. The high population density in the lower Yangtze valley brought about urbanization and reorganization of the administrative hierarchy linking towns and cities. Increasing population density, especially in the cities, also stimulated further progress in specialization. Because a large amount of city residents' grain demand had to be supplied from its direct hinterland, the rich delta lands of the lower Yangtze became the chief supplier of China's granaries, and showed the greatest advances in agricultural productivity. The grain not only fed those living in the cities but also supplied those farmers who devoted their land to the production of raw materials for urban industries and for luxury consumption.

Major cities selected as the sites of administrative centers were located at the natural centers of local trade and communications. Hang-chou, for example, was a terminal of the Grand Canal and a node of exchange between the level plains and hilly districts, and remained so even after the end of its political role as state capital. Among the distinct changes in these cities were the collapse of the system of officially controlled markets, the rise of prototype merchant and craft guilds, and the advent of "city bourgeoisie" that created their own new culture.[61]

With the increase in population density and the proliferation of trading posts and periodic markets, the number of rural households participating in the local marketing process increased. As long as these local markets were held only periodically through the medium of mobile firms, the commercialization of rural households was limited. But in ever widening areas, these market sites developed into *chen* (towns), the intermediate category of urban centers with a certain minimum density of population and the facilities of permanent firms. The trade of these towns was intermediate because their function as collection, distribution, and financial centers for their marketing areas linked interregional or interurban trade at the county capital (or central market) to the intra-local trade at rural market sites. As a consequence the pattern of rural-urban relationships changed greatly. The old system of sub-urban administrative jurisdictions (*hsiang*), which politically linked self-sufficient villages (*li*) to county capitals, collapsed. Instead a new economic linkage of cities and villages through *chen* emerged. In spite of its effort to control both rural and urban areas under a uniform administrative system, the government had to take into account the growing economic differentiation between rural and urban areas. The traditional administrative subdivision *li,* which had been applied indiscriminately to rural and urban areas alike was replaced by a more differentiated system: *yü* and *hsiang* for subdivisions in cities and their direct suburbs, and *ts'un* and *li* for those in the countryside.

Taxation also tended to differentiate urban from rural areas. Not only did the tax systems differ, but also the tax burden, with rural areas bearing the heavier load. Hsia Sung (985-1051), a high official in the middle of the Northern Sung, observed that

...since the unification of the empire, control over the merchants has not yet been well established. They enjoy a luxurious way of life, living on dainty foods of delicious rice and meat, owning handsome houses and many carts, adorning their wives and children with pearls and jades, and dressing their slaves in white silk. In the morning they think about how to make a fortune, and in the evening they devise means of fleecing the poor. Sometimes they ride through the countryside behaving haughtily, and sometimes they inveigle rich profits from the poor. In the assignment of corvee duties they are treated much better by the government than average rural households, and in the taxation of commercial duties they are less rigidly controlled than commoners. Since this relaxed control over merchants is regarded by the people as a common rule, they despise agricultural pursuits and place high value on an idle living by trade. They also want to sell farm tools in exchange for carts and vessels, letting the land lie waste and meeting at markets....[62]

The gradual, consequent impoverishment of rural communities was decisive, and this in turn fettered further urbanization. It is worth noting that the efforts made by some officials to reduce such inequalities between the urban and rural areas almost always ended in failure.

Booming trade and urban prosperity had a marked influence on the general cultural environment. E. A. Kracke, Jr. observed that a certain minimum literacy was a prerequisite to the operation of all but the simplest businesses.[63] This is illustrated in a passage of Fang Ta-tsung, who flourished in the Southern Sung:

In my own county [Yung-fu in Fu-chou] every family is adept at music and the chanting of texts. People know the laws; and this is true not only of the scholars — every peasant, artisan, and merchant teaches his sons how to read books. Even herdsmen and wives who bring food to their husbands at work in the fields can recite the poems of the men of ancient times.[64]

Moreover, there is good reason to assume the diffusion of various kinds of entertainment connected with religious-cum-commercial assemblies whose audiences were mostly farmers. According to Tanaka Kazushige's recent work on local theatrical performances in Fukien under the Sung, there were several hundred temples to local spirits in Chang-chou (Fukien) where gatherings were held periodically. Prior to the gathering a group of the devout was usually organized to raise funds for preparation of the festival. On festival days the group paraded through villages carrying the statues of the spirits and enjoyed open-air theatrical performances, such as puppet shows, shadow plays, and dramas. Theatrical companies were called to these ritual assemblies from Hang-chou and other cities.[65]

Through these itinerant troupes and travelling merchants who gathered at such ritual assemblies, farmers must have learned a good deal about the urban way of life, its extravagance and exchange economy. Ts'ai Hsiang, who flourished in the middle of the Northern Sung, felt obliged to issue a warning against the exorbitant expenditures and excessive debts incurred in rural villages on the occasion of coming-of-age ceremonies, marriages, funerals, and festivals.[66] On the other hand he observed that "it is human nature for everyone to desire riches. Even peasants, artisans, and merchants all scheme away night and day in search of profit"[67] — and it was increasingly agreed that a desire for wealth was both natural and acceptable.[68] The custom of extravagance spread downwards from officialdom into the lower classes and outwards from the capital into the provinces. Wang Mai, a thirteenth-century official, observed that "adornments which make their appearance in the Rear Palace in the morning will have become the fashion among the commoners by evening."[69] Shops that dealt in gold and silver, and silversmiths, were to be found in many prefectural and county capitals, and even in some market towns. And Fang Ta-tsung, writing about his travels in thirteenth-century Fukien, noted: "Trade in the markets is customarily carried on by means of strings of a thousand copper cash. The people from the country villages take what they have produced to the markets and exchange it there for these strings."[70] Many peasants went into other occupations. For example, Tai Hsü, a thirteenth-century scholar-official, wrote about the class of peasant-artisans which grew up around Ting-hai county in Ming-chou: "Even if they do own only a few *mou* of land, one has to regard them as practicing agriculture; and yet, since they work as artisans, craftsmen, knife smiths, or peddlers, one must speak of them as pursuing skilled trades."[71] Tseng Feng, an official of the mid-twelfth century, also noted that "Everywhere these days there are persons leaving agriculture to become scholars, Taoists, Buddhists, or professional entertainers, but those from Fukien are the most numerous. The land of Fukien is cramped and inadequate to feed and clothe them, so they scatter to all the four quarters."[72]

Finally, the general impact of urbanization on social mobility has been discussed by E. A. Kracke, Jr.

Data from two lists of graduates that have come down to us from the twelfth and thirteenth centuries show that the regions with more and larger urban concentrations tended to supply not only more graduates in proportion to their area, but also more graduates per family, so that they clearly dominated the field. Moreover, the largest proportion of apparently new blood tended to appear in the circuits of most rapid population growth, if we may judge from the numbers of graduates counting no officials among their direct paternal forebears. Conspicuous among these regions of growing population were again those containing the great coastal cities and those on the main inland trade routes.[73]

Kracke's data are confirmed by the study of Hui-chou. For those who were not gifted with outstanding intellectual ability, several occupations were available besides official careers. Yüan Ts'ai, a county magistrate in Wen-chou, Chekiang, who flourished in the middle of the Southern Sung, wrote:

If the sons and younger brothers of an official have no hereditary stipends by which they may be maintained, and no landed property on which they may depend, and they want some way of serving their parents and caring for their dependents, the best thing for them to do is to become Confucian scholars. Those of them who are endowed with outstanding talents and able to pursue the calling of a scholar fitting himself for appointment to office will, if of the first quality, gain riches and honors through success in the examinations, and if of the second quality, give instruction to disciples and receive the offering due to a master; while those who are not able to pursue the calling of a scholar fitting himself for appointment to office will, if of the first quality, be able to fulfill the tasks of writing letters and drawing up documents for others, and if of the second quality, be able to give primary instruction to boys in the arts of punctuating and reading. Those who are not capable of being Confucian scholars may make their living without disgracing their ancestors by working as spirit-mediums, doctors, Buddhists, Taoists, farmers, merchants or experts of some sort. It is the greatest disgrace to the ancestors if sons or younger brothers degenerate into beggars or thieves....[74]

Indeed such relaxation of rigid social stratification which originated in the Sung and increasingly permeated society under the Ming and Ch'ing dynasties, distinguished China from other medieval societies.

Notes to Chapter 2

1. Kato Shigeshi, *Shina Keizaishi Kosho* [Studies in Chinese Economic History] (Tokyo: The Toyo Bunko, 1952), I: 199–421.
2. Kato Shigeshi, *Shina Keizaishi Kōshō* (Tokyo: The Toyo Bunko, 1953). II: 176–221.
3. Etiènne Balazs, "Une Carte des Centres Commerciaux de la Chine à la Fin du XIᵉ Siecle," *Annales: Economies Societes Civilisations,* 12, No. 4 (Oct.–Dec. 1957), 587–93.
4. Laurence J. C. Ma, *Commercial Development and Urban Change in Sung China (960–1279),* Michigan Geographical Publication, No. 6. (Ann Arbor: Michigan University Press, 1971).
5. Ch'üan Han-sheng, "Pei-Sung pien-liao ti shu-ch'u-ju mao-i" [The Problem of Export and Import Trade in K'ai-feng under the Northern Sung], *Academia Sinica Bulletin,* 8, No. 1 (1939), 189–301. Ch'üan Han-sheng, "Nan-Sung Hang-chou ti hsiao-fei yü wai-ti shang-p'in ti shu-ju" [Consumption and Supply of External Goods in Hang-chou under the Southern Sung], *Academia Sinica Bulletin,* 7, No. 1 (1936), 91–119. These have recently been reprinted in the collected essays of Ch'üan Han-sheng, *Chung-kuo ching-chi-shih lun-ts'ung* [Studies in Chinese Economic History] (Hong Kong: The New Asia Research Institute, 1972), I: 87–199 and 295–323, respectively.
6. Miyazaki Ichisada, "Chugoku Kinsei ni okeru Seigyō-shihon no Taishaku ni tsuite" [On the Loan of Working Capital in the Cities of Modern China]. First published in *Toyoshi Kenkyu,* 11, No. 1 (1950) and reprinted in Miyazaki Ichisada, *Ajia-shi Kenkyū* [Studies in Asian History] (Kyoto: Toyoshi-kenkyu-kai, 1963), 3: 176–97.
7. Kusano Yasushi, "Sōdai no Okuzei, Chizei ni tsuite" [On Urban Taxes in the Sung], *Shigaku-Zasshi,* 68, No. 4 (1959), 71–88. See also Umehara Kaoru, "Sōdai Toshi no Zeifu" [On Urban Taxation in the Sung], *Toyoshi-Kenkyu,* 28, No. 4 (1970), 42–74. Shiba Yoshinobu, *Sōdai Shōgyoshi Kenkyū* [Commercial Activities in the Sung] (Tokyo: Kazama-shobo, 1968), pp. 318–28.
8. Sudo Yoshiyuki, "Sōdai no Kyō-son ni okeru ten, shi, ho no hatten" [The Rise of Rural Markets in the Sung]. First published in *Shigaku-Zasshi,* 59, Nos. 9 and 10 (1950), and reprinted with minor revisions in Sudo Yoshiyuki, *Tō-Sō Shakai-Keizaishi Kenkyū* [Studies in the Socio-economic History of T'ang and Sung China] (Tokyo: Tokyo University Press, 1965), pp. 783–866. Ch'üan Han-sheng, "Sung-tai nan-fang ti hsü-shih" [Periodic Markets in Kiangnan under the Sung], *Academia Sinica Bulletin,* 9 (1947), 265–74; now reprinted in Ch'üan Han-sheng. *Chung-kuo ching-chi-shih lun-ts'ung,* I: 201–210. See also Chü Ch'ing-yüan, T'ang-Sung shih-tai Ssu-ch'uan ti ts'an-shih" [On Fairs Trading in Sericultural Tools in Szechwan during the T'ang and Sung], *Shih Huo,* 3, No. 6 (1936), 28–34. Hino Kaizaburo, *Zoku Tōdai Teiten no Kenkyū* [The Continuation of the Study of Inns-cum-stores in T'ang times] (Fukuoka: the author's publication, 1970), pp. 1–548. Umehara Kaoru, "Sōdai Chihō-shōtoshi no Ichimen" [An Aspect of Towns in the Countryside in the Sung], *Shirin,* 41, No. 6 (1958). Umehara Kaoru, "Sodai no Chiho-toshi" [Local Urban Centers in the Sung], *Rekishi Kyoiku,* 14, No. 12 (1966), 52–58. Shiba Yoshinobu, *Sōdai Shōgyōshi Kenkyū.*

9. Fujii Hiroshi, "Shin-an shōnin no Kenkyū" [A Study of Hsin-an Merchants], *Toyo Gakuho*, 36, No. 1 (1953), 2−7.
10. Nishijima Sadao, *Chū-goku Keizaishi Kenkyū* [Studies in Chinese Economic History] (Tokyo: Tokyo University Press, 1966), pp. 729−52.
11. Denis Twitchett, "The T'ang Market System," *Asia Major*, 12, No. 2 (1966): p. 204.
12. *Ibid.*, pp. 225−6.
13. Aoyama Sadao, "Zui, Tō, Sō sandai ni okeru kosū no chiiki teki kōsatsu" [An Areal Study on the Change in Population during Sui, T'ang, and Sung], *Rekishigaku Kenkyu*, 6, No. 4 (1936), 411−46. See also E. G. Pulleyblank, *The Background of the Rebellion of An Lu-shan* (Oxford: Oxford University Press, 1955), pp. 172−177. Denis Twitchett, *Financial Administration under the T'ang Dynasty* (Cambridge: Cambridge University Press, 1963), pp. 12−14, and 22.
14. Aoyama Sadao, "Zui, Tō, Sō sandai ni okeru kosū no chiiki teki kōsatsu" [An Areal Study on the Change in Population during Sui, T'ang, and Sung], *Rekishigaku Kenkyū*, 6, No. 5, pp. 529−554.
15. Shiba Yoshinobu, *Sōdai Shōgyōshi Kenkyū*, pp. 461−65.
16. Yeh Shao-weng, "Huai-nan chiang-tsao" [On Juicy Jujube in Huai-nan], *Ssu-ch'ao wen-chien-lu* [A Record of Personal Experiences during the Four Reigns], chüan 5.
17. *Sung hui-yao chi-kao* (Shanghai: Chung-hua shu-chü, 1957), ts'e 165, Hsing-fa, 2, pp. 49b, 50a, 56b, 57a. See also Shiba Yoshinobu, *Sōdai Shōgyōshi Kenkyū*, pp. 429−30.
18. Shiba Yoshinobu, "Sōdai Kishu no Chiiki Kaihatsu" [Development of Hui-chou and its Hinterland in the Sung], *Yamamoto-hakushi Kanreki-kinen Toyoshi Ronso* (Tokyo: Yamakawa Shuppansha, 1972), p. 227. See also Chu Mu, *Fang-yu sheng-lan* [A Triumphant Vision of the World], chüan 48.
19. Shiba Yoshinobu, *Sōdai Shōgyōshi Kenkyū*, pp. 429−30.
20. Miyazaki Ichisada, *Ajia-shi Kenkyu*, pp. 176−179.
21. K'ung Ch'i, "Chih-cheng chih-chi" [Straightforward Notes of the Chih-cheng Period (1341−1367)] *Yüeh-ya-t'ang ts'ung-shu*, (in *Pai-pu ts'ung-shu chi-ch'eng* ed.). See also Ikeda Shizuo, *Shina Suiri-chirishi Kenkyū* [A Study of the History of Water-control Undertakings and Historical Geography in China] (Tokyo: Seikatsusha, 1940), pp. 141−142.
22. Hsü Hsien-chung, "Wu-hsing-chang-ku-chi" [Historical Precedents in Wu-hsing], *Wu-hsing hsien-chei-shu* 14.
23. A. C. Moule, *Quinsai, with Other Notes on Marco Polo* (Cambridge: Cambridge University Press, 1957), p. 11.
24. See "Lin-t'ing chih" in *Yung-lo ta-tien*, chüan 7890.
25. Huang Kan, "Mien-chai chi" [Literary Works of Huang Kan], in *Ssu-k'u ch'üan-shu chen-pen*, 2nd Series, chüan 30.
26. Hung Kua, "P'an-chou wen-chi" [Literary Works of Hung Kkua] in *Ssu-pu ts'ung-kan*, chüan 49.
27. Nakamura Jihei, "Shin-dai Kahoku no Toshi no Kokō ni kansuru ichi-kōsatsu" [A Study of Urban Population in North China in the Ch'ing period], *Shien*, (March, 1968). See also Momose Hiroshi, "Shin-mon Ho-kō Zusatsu ni tsuite" [A Study on *Chin-men pao-chia t'u-ts'e*, or Statistics on Households of Merchants, Artisans, and Farmers in Tientsin in the Ch'ing period], *Ono-Takeo Hakushi Kanreki-kinen Tōyō-Nōgyō-keizaishi Kenkyū* (Tokyo: Nihon-Hyoronsha, 1948), pp. 125−34.
28. Shiba Yoshinobu, *Sōdai Shōgyōshi Kenkyū*, pp. 157−58. See also Yeh Meng-te, "Chien-k'ang yen-ko chi" [A Description of Burials of War Victims in Chien-k'ang], *Chien-k'ang chi*, chüan 4. Li Ts'eng-po, *K'o-dhai hsü-kao*, chüan 19. Chen Te-hsiu, *Hsi-shan hsien-sheng Chen Wen-chung kung wen-chi*, chüan 6.
29. Hino Kaizaburo, *Tō-dai Teiten no Kenkyū* [A Study on Inns-cum-stores in the T'ang period] (Fukuoka, author's own publication, 1968), p. 331.
30. T. H. Hollingsworth, *Historical Demography* (London: Hodder and Stoughton, Ltd., 1969), pp. 244−47.
31. Nakamura Jihei, "Tōdai no Kyō" [On administrative subdivisions in T'ang times]. *Suzuki Shun Kyōju Kanreki-kinen Toyoshi Ronsō* (Tokyo: Sanyosha, 1964), pp. 419−46.
32. E. Balazs, "Une Carte des Centres Commerciaux," *Annales: Economies Societes Civilisations*, 12, No. 4 (1957), 587−93.
33. D. H. Perkins, *Agricultural Development in China, 1368−1968* (Edinburgh: Edinburgh University Press, 1969), p. 117.

34. See *Chen-chiang chih* (for Chih-shun period), chüan 10.
35. See *Ch'in-ch'üan chih* (For Shun-yu period), chüan 1.
36. See *Ch'ang-shu-hsien chih* (for Chia-chin period), chüan 1.
37. See "Chiang-yang p'u" in *Yung-lo ta-tien*, chüan 2217.
38. Owen Lattimore, "The Mainsprings of Asiatic Migration," in *Limits of Land Settlement*. ed. Isaiah Bowman (New York: Council of Foreign Relations, 1937), pp. 119–135.
39. Shiba Yoshinobu, *Sōdai Shōgyōshi Kenkyū*, pp. 133–140. Aoyama Sadao, *Tō-Sō Jidai no Kōtsū to Chishi Chizu no Kenkyū* [Studies on the Transportation System and Geographical Documents in T'ang and Sung times] (Tokyo: Yoshikawa Kobunkan, 1963), pp. 29–49.
40. Wang Chien, *Sung p'ing-chiang ch'eng-fang k'ao* [A Study of Ssu-chou in the Sung]. (1928 edition). Chüan 1 and 2.
41. See *Chien-k'ang chih* (for the Ching-ting period), chüan 16.
42. See *Chen-chiang chih* (for the Chih-hsun period), chüan 13.
43. See *Ssu-ming chih* (for the Pao-ch'ing period), chüan 13.
44. See *Wu-hsing chih* (for the Chia-t'ai period), chüan 2.
45. See *Hui-chi chih* (for the Chia-t'ai period), chüan 3.
46. See *P'i-ling chih* (for the Hsien-shun period), chüan 3.
47. Kato Shigeshi, *Shina Keizaishi Kōshō*, I: 448–49.
48. Shiba Yoshinobu, *Sōdai Shōgyōshi Kenkyū*, pp. 391–424.
49. *Sung hui-yao chi-kao*, ts'e 123, Shih-huo 6, pp. 31a–31b.
50. Wang Yen, *Shuang-ch'i wen-chi* [Literary Works from Shuang-ch'i], chüan 16.
51. Wang Yen, *Shuang-ch'i wen-chi*, chüan 26.
52. See *Hu-chou-fu chih* (for the Ch'eng-hua period), chüan 13.
53. See *Wu-hsing chih* (for the Chia-t'ai period), chüan 4.
54. Fu I-ling, *Ming-Ch'ing shih-tai shang-jen chi shang-ye tzu-pen* [Merchants and Commercial Capitals in Ming and Ch'ing times] (Peking: Jen-min ch'u-pan she, 1956), p. 46.
55. Ch'en Fu, *Nung-shu* [Treatise on Agriculture], chüan 2.
56. See *Wu-hsing chih* (for the Chia-t'ai period), chüan 4.
57. *Sung hui-yao chi-kao*, ts'e 123, Shih-huo 16, p. 8a.
58. Shiba Yoshinobu, "Sōdai Kishū no Chiiki Kaihatsu."
59. Ibid., pp. 224–27.
60. Chi Ch'ao-ting, *Key Economic Areas in Chinese History* (London: Allen and Unwin, 1936), p. 132.
61. E. Balazs, *Chinese Civilization and Bureaucracy*, pp. 66–100. See also Denis Twitchett, "The T'ang Market System," *Asia Major*, 12, No. 2, 205–7. Denis Twitchett, "Merchants, Trade and Government in Late T'ang," *Asia Major*, 14, No. 1 (1968), especially pages 94–5.
62. Hsia Sung, "Wen-chuang chi" [Literary Works of Hsia Sung], *Ssu-ku ch'uan-shu chen-pen, ch'u-chi*, chüan 13.
63. E. A. Kracke, Jr., "Sung Society; Change Within Tradition," *Far Eastern Quarterly*, 14 (1954–1955), 479–88.
64. Fang Ta-tsung, *T'ieh-an Fang-kung wen-chi* [Literary Works of Fang Ta-tsung], chüan 33.
65. Tanaka Kazushige, "Nan-sō jidai no Fukken chihō-geki ni tsuite" [On Local Theatrical Performances in Fukien in the Southern Sung], *Nihon Chūgoku Gakkaihō*, 22 (1970).
66. Ts'ai Hsiang. *Ts'ai chung-hui-kung wen-chi* [Literary Works of Ts'ai Hsiang], chüan 29.
67. Ibid.
68. Shiba Yoshinobu, *Sōdai Shōgyōshi Kenkyū*, pp. 493–94.
69. Wang Mai, "Ch'u-hsüan chi" [Literary Works of Wang Mai]. *Ssu-k'u ch'uan-shu chen-pen, ch'u-chi*, chüan 10.
70. Fang Ta-tsung, *T'ieh-an Fang-kung wen-chi*, [Literary Works of Fang Ta-tsung], chüan 14.
71. Tai Hsü, *Huan-ch'uan chi* [Literary Works of Tai Hsü], chüan 4.
72. Tseng Feng, *Yüan-tu chi* [Literary Works of Tseng Feng], chüan 17.
73. E. A. Kracke, Jr., "Sung Society; Change Within Tradition," pp. 479–88.
74. Yüan Ts'ai, "Yüan-shih shih-fan" [Family Precepts by Yüan Ts'ai], chüan 2, in *Chi-pu tsu-chai ts'ung-shu*, chi 14. See also Ho Ping-ti, *The Ladder of Success in Imperial China* (New York: Columbia University Press, 1967), p. 74. Denis Twitchett, "Merchant, Trade and Government in Late T'ang," pp. 94–5.

Sung K'ai-feng:
Pragmatic Metropolis and
Formalistic Capital

E. A. KRACKE, JR.

DURING THE PAST THREE THOUSAND YEARS ONLY FOUR CITIES, each varying in name and exact site, have served as the principal capital of a united China for a period of a century or more. During the two millennia before the Sung, such capitals were either at Ch'ang-an or at Lo-yang. During the six centuries after the Sung, they were always at Peking. K'ai-feng, the Northern Sung capital, had much in common with these, but it differed from them in one important respect. Capitals were usually located at the three places first named in order to further long-term political and military strategy; they were, especially after the sixth century A.D., generally planned or rebuilt to be capitals; economic considerations were only minor factors in their original growth as cities and their selection as seats of government. K'ai-feng, however, came in a different way to the role of capital, and the circumstances of its rise and continued existence gave it a distinctive character of its own.

Dynasties ruled at K'ai-feng only a little over two centuries, from 907 to 1127, and it served a united China for only a little over a century and a half.* During these years it passed, like China as a whole, from times of hardship and precarious survival to stability, confidence, and prosperity, and then to new difficulties heralding the crisis that ended its active function in Sung government.

During most of the tenth century its rulers lived in constant apprehension of rebellion, coup d'état, or rival warlords, and, until 1004,

---

* It lost the function of capital and the name K'ai-feng under the Latter T'ang (923-936) but these were restored in 938 (see *CWTS* 3.4a-b; 7a; 76.8b-11b; 77.7b-8b; 150.1b). In the Sung it was called also the Eastern Capital (Tung-ching or Tung-tu); however, the other three (the Western, Ho-nan; the Northern, Ta-ming; and the Southern, Ying-t'ien) had no capital functions apart from the titles of their officials and a few other ceremonial attributes. In familiar but nonofficial usage K'ai-feng was called also Pien-ching, Pien-liang, etc.

of imminent Khitan occupation. A period of rapid growth and flowering followed. A military threat from the Tangut people, which grew serious about 1040, brought fiscal and economic stringencies for the empire, but for long the material prosperity of the capital itself did not seem to suffer. The city's dynamic life was more fundamentally shaken with the eruption after 1120 of the Jürchen invasions, which led to its sacking and its permanent loss by the Sung. It remained a great city for another century, however. At times it would serve as a secondary capital, and even briefly as seat of government, under Jürchen and Ming rulers, but after the thirteenth century it showed only the face of a modest provincial city.

Yet K'ai-feng did not end its political service to the Sung in 1127. Even when Hang-chou became the dynasty's temporary political seat, and then, as hope of reconquering the North faded, acquired all features of an established administrative center, K'ai-feng still kept the formal and symbolic role of capital. The memories of its life were preserved in the nostalgic guide to its famous spots written in 1147 by Meng Yüan-lao, a former citizen.[1] The emotions it invoked remind us of those inspired by Rome in the European Middle Ages or in nineteenth-century Italy. Could it have been so much more attractive than the idyllically situated Hang-chou? Or was it simply a token of the lost but never renounced northern third of China's territories? Or did it represent something more?

In this essay I shall endeavor to find hints to the answers to these questions through considering a few selected aspects of the city's national role and of its changes in character before 1127 in response to its varying fortunes.

K'ai-feng's character reflected from the first its peculiar place in China's life. Like the other great capitals, it became the central stage for a political and military power which owed its success and brilliance to the talents and resources of the nation it controlled. But K'ai-feng did more than this. It made a contribution beyond the passive provision of a strategic location for rulers, their governments, and their armies.

Military and political strategy was not entirely absent from the reasons that dictated the original choice of K'ai-feng as capital. When Chu Wen seated his new Latter Liang dynasty there in 907, it was already his base of power, partly because its proximity to northeastern China helped him control the unruly warlords there. But the city had already gained economic importance in the T'ang dynasty as a center of communications, near the junction of the Yellow River and the Pien

Canal, chief artery for the vital traffic to and from China's southeast coast.*

The gradual restoration of national unity after 960 freed China's long developing but inhibited commercial energies. K'ai-feng's importance as a trade entrepôt grew rapidly. Its commerce was complemented by the growing production of its workshops. A century after the founding of the Sung, if not earlier, the city had evidently far outdistanced all its rivals among China's economic centers. Its role as capital certainly affected this development, and it is scarcely possible to separate clearly the interacting forces of political and economic factors, governmental and private initiative that brought the final result. With the expansion and centralization of government the city took on new political, military, and economic functions. Its arsenals served the country as a whole by supplying the national armies at a time when military technology was developing rapidly. An increasing flow of goods was demanded by the city's residents, including large military contingents stationed near it, an expanding bureaucracy, merchants, and craftsmen, people employed in services for all these, and seekers for opportunities to invest in business enterprises, or for office, or for humbler governmental or private employment.[2]

K'ai-feng was the marketplace for its immediate population, for places in the market area of which it was the center, and for more distant places in North or South China or foreign countries. Beyond the things produced or made in K'ai-feng or its satellite cities, it consumed or exported (sometimes after processing) many products or commodities from elsewhere. The first Sung emperors had fostered the textile industries, resettling textile workers from Szechwan and the Yangtze delta. The iron and steel industries of the K'ai-feng market area for the first time replaced small-scale and more or less seasonal operations with highly organized enterprises dependent on more sophisticated

---

* Wang Gungwu, *The Structure of Power in North China During the Five Dynasties* (Kuala Lumpur: Univ. of Malaya Press, 1963), pp. 47–8; Miyazaki Ichisada, "Tokushi sakki [historical notes]," *Shirin* 21, No. 1, 124–58; Ch'üan Han-sheng, "Pei-Sung Pien-liang ti shu ch'u ju mao-i [Export-import trade of Pien-liang in the Northern Sung]," *Chung-yang Yen-chiu Yüan Li-shih Yü-yen Yen-chiu So shi-k'an* 8, No. 2, 189–301, esp. 189–194. This and other cited articles by Ch'üan are also reprinted in his *Chung-kuo ching-chi shih lun-ts'ung* [Studies in Chinese economic history] (Hong Kong: Hsin-ya Yen-chiu So, 1972); Aoyama Sadao, *Tō-Sō jidai no kōtsū to chishi chizu no kenkyū* [Study of communications and gazetteer maps of the T'ang-Sung period] (Tokyo: Yoshikawa Kobunkan, 1969), 213–56; *HCP* 118.9a-b; Aoyama Sadao, "Tō-Sō Ben-ka kō [An investigation of the T'ang-Sung Pien River]," *Tōhōgakuhō*, Tokyo 2:49; Ch'üan Han-sheng, *T'ang Sung ti-kuo yü yün-ho* [The T'ang and Sung empires and the Grand Canal] (Taipei: Academia Sinica Historical-Linguistic Section, 1956), especially pp. 93–113. K'ai-feng's location also opened it to attack over the northern delta plain, a serious long-term military weakness.

techniques, great investments in equipment, and large numbers of workers. The industries were developed both by the government and by private iron masters with extensive capital resources. K'ai-feng workshops of many kinds, of course, produced articles of luxury for the imperial family, high officials, and wealthy businessmen or other residents, and such special products naturally figured in the export trade. Tea from the south was an important item for re-export. But such a city could scarcely thrive by catering to wealthy patrons alone, and it is interesting to note also among exported items some of a rather more practical appeal, such as measures, building materials, chemicals, books, and clothing.*

No simple explanation seems adequate to account for K'ai-feng's economic development. Its site at the hub of national communications surely remained the essential condition, but the above-noted factors all contributed, and perhaps its expansion to some extent also fed on its own momentum in this period. While the state in many ways promoted K'ai-feng's economic development, merchants and other inhabitants paid heavily into the state treasuries through business taxes and other primarily urban taxes which formed an ever-growing source of governmental income.† Thus the capital and its market area contributed in varied and significant ways to the national economy on which it depended.

The reasons for K'ai-feng's economic decline after 1127, which might illumine those for its rise, are also not simple. Its strategic position as a center of communications was eroded after 1127 by a century and a half of separation from South China's markets, by disruptions of

---

* See Ch'üan Han-sheng, "Pei-Sung Pien-liang ti shu ch'u ju mao-i [Export-import trade of Pien-liang in the Northern Sung]," *Chung-yang Yen-chiu Yüan Li-shih Yü-yen Yen-chiu So chi-k'an* 8, No. 2, pp. 196−223 and 275−301; Robert Hartwell, "Markets, Technology, and the Structure of Enterprise in the…11th century Chinese Iron and Steel Industry," *Journal of Economic History,* 26 (1966), pp. 37−8 and 45−8; R. Hartwell, "A Cycle of Economic Change in Imperial China: Coal and Iron in Northeast China, 750−1350," *Journal of the Economic and Social History of the Orient,* 10 (1967), pp. 129−30 and 142−43. I suspect that statistics based on *MHL* (Ma, *Commercial Development,* pp. 139−140) and suggesting a city economy dominated by luxury trades and amusements call for caution in view of *MHL's* purpose of entertainment and lack of concern with practical matters as such.

† In accounting for K'ai-feng's growth, Ma's view tends to weigh strategic economic location more lightly than political factors, and stresses an apparent statistical excess of imports over exports. But this evidence may not reflect certain factors, such as the considerable volume of untaxed governmental shipments from the capital, or the fact that K'ai-feng as an economic entity included important places outside its political borders. K'ai-feng's economic contribution included also, or course, the heavy payments of its citizens through taxes and state monopoly revenues. See Ch'üan Han-sheng, "T'ang Sung cheng-fu sui-ju yü huo-pi ching-chi ti kuan-hsi [T'ang and Sung annual governmental income in connection with monetary economy]," *Chung-yang Yen-chiu Yüan,* 20 (1948), 189−221. The complex effects of urbanization on the urban-rural balance of tax burdens need further study.

its local canal systems through floods, and by the rerouting of the Grand Canal in the Mongol period. The last of these was prompted chiefly by the shifting of the capital to Peking for military and political reasons, but it may also have been influenced by the economic decline of K'ai-feng in the meantime through a combination of causes. The city had twice been destroyed in war, it had lost markets and entrepôt functions in a divided China, it had suffered from early Mongol economic policies, and no doubt forgot old habits and skills during the centuries unfavorable to its economic activities.[3]

Politically, K'ai-feng was not merely a complacent host to the government that functioned there. Its role was enhanced by the administrative centralization that reached a peak in the Northern Sung. The officials who went out to all parts of the empire for short tours of duty tended to make it their home. Energetic rivalry was typical of its political life as of its trade and industries. At court the parties fought for dominance. In the prestigious examinations for the doctorate in letters which produced the leading government officials, candidates from families of the prefecture of K'ai-feng won the lion's share of degrees. In the years 1059 – 1063, they took 179 of the 541 such degrees awarded in the empire — nearly a third — although the prefecture's population was only about 1.6 percent of Sung China's. Thus, even though K'ai-feng citizens (like those of other places) had no independent city government as their organ of expression, and their guilds were subject to government supervision, men bred in the city or its surroundings exercised much influence in the bureaucracy.*

In the realms of thought, literature and scholarship the natives of K'ai-feng did not seem outstanding among Sung Chinese. But the Northern Sung capital seems to have drawn outstanding minds to itself rather more than its Southern Sung counterpart would do, perhaps because in the earlier Sung a larger proportion of the most creative intellectuals were active and prominent in government. The nation's ablest students were also attracted to its governmental schools, which were several times expanded after 960. The National University (the T'ai-hsüeh) came to stand as the apex of the empire's pyramid of public education, to which the best graduates of the more advanced local schools were promoted.[4] The books and writing materials produced there were known for their quality, and beyond the collections of the Imperial Library, the greatest in China, outstanding private collections

---

* Ssu-ma Kuang, *Wen-kuo...wen-chi* [Collected papers], Ssu-pu ts'ung-k'an ed., 30, 1a – 5b. There is also some evidence that merchant families contributed their share of urban graduates. Apart from men with K'ai-feng homes, National University students from elsewhere also played a political role, especially after 1200.

also existed. A number of scholars bought houses in the convenient neighborhood of one of the latter.[5]

If apart from its service as host to immigrant scholars and seat of the state schools, K'ai-feng seemed to be on the whole more of a beneficiary than a major force in Sung China's intellectual life, it is possible that intangible factors redressed the balance somewhat. It is hard to say how far the tempo of the city's life and its varied activities helped to stimulate the originality that marked both political thought and speculation of other kinds in the years of its flourishing.

The gradual transition in the outlook of K'ai-feng officialdom, from early apprehensiveness to confidence (and perhaps overconfidence), saw many subtle changes in the character of the city and in men's attitudes toward it. Little by little, the regulation of the life carried on in the city and the planning of the edifices and public spaces that formed its arena came to be rather less the results of practical considerations and rather more those of ideal and metaphysical concepts. But the alterations were not sudden or obvious; they came about gradually, and at differing pace in different aspects. Even the first Sung rulers and their ministers sought to mitigate the prosaic atmosphere of their capital, and the effort continued. But the contrasting concepts and their reflection in K'ai-feng can be seen more clearly if we consider first the pragmatic and utilitarian aspects of the city and thereafter seek the evidences of a shift in attitudes favoring a more ideal, formalistic and symbolic capital.

During the tenth century, when both rulers and subjects were fully preoccupied with emergencies of the moment, K'ai-feng can have had only a very minimal beauty and charm. It lacked romantic or historical associations, unless one thought twelve centuries back to feudal Liang of Mencius' day. The Sung founder was tempted to move his new regime to his birthplace, Lo-yang, capital of the T'ang in its later years.[6] For many years, we may imagine, the life and atmosphere of K'ai-feng reflected strongly the less attractive consequences of the pragmatism that seemed basic to its growth as it was to Sung government. In payment for the relative freedom allowed the commercial imagination there, for the individual vitality and prolific diversity in its enterprises, for its innovations and achievements (and their direct or indirect social, political, and intellectual benefits), those who lived at K'ai-feng were obliged to suffer a pervasive atmosphere of competition, conflicting aims, utilitarian plainness, if not ugliness, neglect of cherished social patterns and norms, and inequities arising from new untried ways. To a tradition-minded Sung man, the city would seem organic or efficient only insofar as its tensions and disorder were necessary conditions to its creativity (to which a contemporary was often blind). It was surely a far cry from the ideal capital. At most, he might find it a reasonably appropriate setting for a government which itself showed the same ad hoc and disorderly character in its organizational patterns and its practices. City and government functioned, but they lacked both intellectual neatness and the aura of tradition.

Pragmatism was reflected in the very arrangement of the city. It seems to have contrasted especially strikingly with Ch'ang-an of the T'ang, and almost as greatly with Peking of the Mongol and Ming periods. It was built on a relatively even terrain, as were those cities, but it clearly lacked their sense of orderly distribution, ample space, symmetry, and dramatic alignments of avenues, gates, and palaces, building to a climactic confrontation with the majestic throne-hall and its surrounding edifices.*

Like several Sung cities, it had more than one walled area. The inner city was essentially the T'ang city of Pien-chou, in which changes of detail were introduced from time to time. It had been supplied in 781 with walls that remained through 1127. The headquarters of the former regional commanders in the northwest corner of that city, had been converted in 907 by Chu Wen to serve as an imperial palace. By 956, in the Latter Chou dynasty, this city had grown overcrowded and settlements, perhaps more or less spontaneous and unplanned, occupied lands outside its gates. An outer wall was erected to protect the new settlements. A tradition tells that in 968 it was proposed to straighten the wriggly line of this wall and impose some order on its plan, but the Sung founder sternly rejected the project as unfunctional, and the old design remained.[7] Soon the crowding population created outside its gates new bustling faubourgs.

No accurate maps survive to show the city's proportions, though the certainly schematic and idealized maps shown in a Yüan encyclo-

---

* For Ch'ang-an see A. F. Wright, "Viewpoints on a City: Ch'ang-an," *Ventures,* Winter 1965, 15 – 23; Wright, "Symbolism and Function," *Journal of Asian Studies,* 24, 667 – 73; Robert des Rotours, *Journal Asiatique,* 244, 240 – 43. For Peking see Oswald Sirén, *The Walls and Gates of Peking* (London, 1924); L. C. Arlington and William Lewisohn, *In Search of Old Peking* (Peking, Vetch, 1935). Nanking and Lo-yang were less symmetrical, though even Lo-yang of the Northern Wei had much regularity: see Ping-ti Ho, "Lo-yang," *Harvard Journal of Asiatic Studies,* 26, 52 – 101 and Ho, "Pei-Wei Lo-yang," in *Symposium in Honor of Dr. Li Chi* (Taipei, 1965). Apart from some Roman and Greek cities, medieval exceptions like Aigues Mortes, or new model plans of the eighteenth century, European cities, of course, showed little of the Ch'ang-an or Peking symmetry or rectangularity.

pedia, the *Shih-lin kuang-chi,* may supplement in some respects the testimony of other materials.* Our chief reliance must be on literary sources aided by a very limited number of surviving Sung edifices. No evidence has yet been made available through archeological investigation.

The schematic plan in Figure 3.1 shows the probable general arrangement of the K'ai-feng boroughs after 1021, and indicates the recorded numbers of wards (*fang*) and households for each.

The literary evidence for the early Sung city is summarily indicated on the schematic plan. I should emphasize that the only accurate dimensions on this plan are the relative perimeters of the outer city wall, the inner wall, and the Imperial Palace. The actual shapes and locations of these evidently made a pattern far indeed from the neat and symmetrical one this plan might suggest.

The circumference of the old inner city rampart, about 11.4 kilometers, was apparently unchanged from that of the T'ang Pien-chou, and remained so until alterations after 1127.† There were apparently twelve gates, including three water gates; three of the gates (including one water gate) were added in the Sung. The Imperial Palace was enlarged by T'ai-tsu of the Sung in 962, in emulation of the Lo-yang palace, and it attained a circuit of 2.76 kilometers (still modest compared with that of Ch'ang-an).‡ After the Sung court fled southward in 1127, and the city was sacked, the metropolis slowly shrank. The outer walls were abandoned, and those of the old inner city became the main defenses. These were repaired at various times by Mongol rulers, and when the Ming founder made K'ai-feng a capital he rebuilt them more ambitiously.[8] In 1642 the forces of Li Tzu-ch'eng diverted the Yellow River, filling the city with water and mud, and causing its temporary abandonment until a new restoration was undertaken in 1662.[9]

What remains today of the Sung inner city? The walls of 1368 were described as approximating the circuit of the Sung inner walls, and they are believed to be on roughly the same site.§ But few Sung

---

* These maps are often reproduced in Chinese and Japanese histories treating the Sung, as in Fang Hao, *Sung shih* [Sung history] (Taipei: Chung-hua Wen-hua Wei-yüan-hui, 1954), vol. 2, plate 3. Note that the *Shih-lin kuang-chi* map reverses the order of the New Ts'ao and New Sung gates agreed upon by earlier sources, and departs from them in other gate arrangements also.

† *MHL* (ch. 1) p. 19; *SHY* (vol. 15), *fang-yü* 1. 1a; *SS* 85.8b; the two latter give wall circuit as 20 *li* 155 *pu.* Following Wu Ch'eng-lo, the Sung *li* is taken as 552.96 meters.

‡ Sung palace 5 *li* (*SHY* [vol. 15], *fang-yü* 1.2b; *SS* 85.4b; *CWTS* 3.7a); T'ang palace city 13.5 *li* (*Hsin T'ang shu,* Po-na ed., 37.2a).

§ *HFHC* 9.5a; 14.5a; *KFFC* 9.11a. The 1368 wall circuit is given as 20 *li* 290 *pu.*

landmarks survive to demonstrate this. The famous artificial mountain created by Sung Hui-tsung in the northeastern part of the old city and turned into a fantastic garden — the Ken-yüeh — is popularly believed to survive, but actually its earth seems to have been used by the Jürchen Emperor Hsüan-tsung in extending the northern wall.* There may be little more substantiation for a popular identification of the hillock bearing the "Dragon Kiosk" with a hill set up by the Sung founder behind his palace.[10] The rivers of the old city have turned into streams and ponds quite differently distributed, though a stream still runs as of old across the southern part of the city. The most reliable landmark may be the Buddhist shrine of Hsiang-kuo Ssu, in Sung days a magnificent center of both religious and secular activity. It appears today to preserve no actual trace of Sung architecture; but repaired and restored from time to time, it may easily occupy its former site still.[11] It is in the southern part of the city, somewhat east of the center; it is, in fact, situated in modern Kaifeng much as Meng Yüan-lao's descriptions would lead us to picture it in the Sung inner city, somewhere within the east gate of the south wall.†

The first surely authentic architectural relic from the Sung, on the other hand, gives us less help. The tall and slender glazed brick pagoda called from its color the "Iron Pagoda" is not identifiable beyond all question in Sung accounts. An edifice that was certainly very similar was erected soon after 1044 in a part of the temple complex of the K'ai-pao Ssu, which was then outside the Old Feng-ch'iu Gate (c in the plan) in the eastern part of the northern inner city wall.‡ The "Iron Pagoda" today stands *within* the northeast corner of the city, however. How can we explain this discrepancy if the K'ai-pao Ssu identification is correct? Perhaps in one of the post-Sung rebuildings of the wall, the northern part was moved outward some distance, taking in the K'ai-pao temple?[12]

---

* *Honan Sheng ku-wu tiao-ch'a piao* [Inventory of Honan Prov. antiquities] (1918), la, reports hill as still standing, but see Li Lien, 4.13a, contradicting such a popular identification as early as 1546.

† Note location of its bridge over the Pien (*MHL* [ch. 1] p. 22 and *MHLC*, p. 27) and in modern Kaifeng (Fu Shou-t'ung, *Pien-ch'eng ch'ou-fang pei-lan*, [Investigatory tour of Pien city, Kaifeng, 1860] 3.9a etc.).

‡ Yang T'ing-pao, "Pien Cheng ku chien-chu yu-lan chi-lu [Notes on a tour of architectural antiquities in Pien and Cheng]", *Chung-kuo Ying-tsao Hsüeh-she hui-k'an*, 6, No. 3, 1 – 16, pp. 1 – 2. The early source may err on the height of the second pagoda, but the description otherwise fits the present edifice. For location, see *MHL* (ch. 3), p. 63; Chou Ch'eng, *Sung Tung-ching k'ao* [An enquiry into Tung-ching of the Sung] (Liu-yu T'ang, 1731), 14. 10b – 11a.

Fig. 3.1. K'ai-feng About 1021: Schematic Arrangement

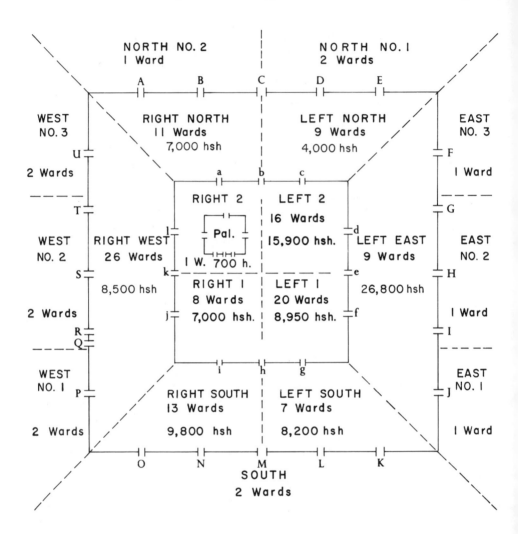

Figure 3.1

The gates admitted the waterways mentioned in parentheses. The names first given for each gate are those seemingly in popular use. In some cases they may have been unofficial from the first (at least in the Sung); in other cases they are the oldest official Sung names. Other names are given in chronological order of official designation. Some names were officially restored after temporary change. In several cases the equivalences of popular and official names are uncertain. While in the old city most gates originated in the T'ang, its two flanking southern gates and its northern water gate were Sung additions. *MHL* (ch. 1), p. 17; *SHY* (vol. 15) Fang-yü 1.1a; 3.44a; *SS* 85.6a; *CWTS* 77.8b; also Chou, *KFFC,* and *HFHC.*

Key to Figure 3.1

— — — —Boundary within or without the walls. Note that exact placing, contours, and relation to gates are in all cases undetermined.

City Gates

A ?Water Gate, Hsien-feng? (Kuang-chi River, North Branch?)
B Wei-chou, An-su
C New Suan-tsao, Hsüan-te, T'ung-t'ien, Ning-te
D (New) Feng-ch'iu, Ch'ang-ching, Ching-yang
E Ch'en-ch'iao, Ai-ching, Yung-t'ai
F Northeast water gate, Hsien-t'ung, Shan-li (Wu-chang River)
G New Ts'ao, Han-hui, Yin-pin
H New Sung, Yen-ch'un, Ch'ao-yang
I East water (1), T'ung-chin, Kuang-chin (Pien River)
J East water (2), Shang-shan, T'ung-chin (Pien River)
K Ch'en-chou, Chu-ming, Hsüan-hua
L Ch'en-chou water, P'u-chi (Hui-min River)
M Nan-hsün (official and popular)
N Tai-lou water, Kuang-li (Hui-min or Ts'ai River)
O Tai-lou, Wei-ching, An-shang
P New Cheng, Ying-ch'iu, Shun-t'ien
Q West water (1), Ta-t'ung, Shun-chi, Li-tse? (Pien River)
R West water (2), Hsüan-tse, Ta-t'ung? (Pien River)
S Wan-sheng, T'ung-yüan, K'ai-yüan
T Ku-tzu, Su-cheng, Chin-yao
U Northwest water?, Yung-shun? (Kuang-chi River, South branch? or Chin-shui River?)
a Chin-shui, Ta-an (?), T'ien-po (water gate)
b (Old) Suan-tsao, Hsüan-hua, Ching-lung
c (Old) Feng-ch'iu, Hsüan-yang, An-yüan
d (Old) Ts'ao, Ho-cheng, Wang-ch'un
e (Old) Sung, Jen-ho, Li-ching (water gate?)
f Chüeh-men-tzu (water)
g Pao-k'ang
h Wei-shih, Hsün-feng, Chu-ch'iao
i New Gate, Hsing-li, Ch'ung-ming
j (Old) Cheng, Chin-i, I-ch'iu
k Chüeh-men-tzu (water gate)
l Liang, Ch'ien-ch'iu, Ch'ien-ming (?), Ch'ang-ho

The plan of the old inner city presents another puzzle, which may
be more easily solved if the configurations of the present city do in
fact largely conform to those of its Sung ancestor. If the Sung city was,
like that of today, slightly rhomboidal, tipping toward the northeast,
then the position of the Imperial Palace in the northwestern quarter
mentioned by Sung writers would not prevent the Imperial Avenue
from running, as Sung writers seem to imply, directly north from the
central gate of the old city to the middle southern palace gateway. We
need not be troubled by the conflict of this supposition with the exact
centrality of the palace in the often-reproduced Yüan maps from the
Shih-lin kuang-chi which, as noted earlier, are schematic and
idealized.* But until more evidence appears, the basic identity of the
present walled city with the inner Sung city (apart from certain specific
changes) must remain merely an attractive hypothesis.

When we look for indications of the layout of the outer walled
area, the "New City," the evidence is still more difficult to find. There
are many reports on its total circuit, from its original construction in
956 through successive slight enlargements until the twelfth century.†
It grew from a little under 27 kilometers to a little under 28. Reports
on the number and exact order of its gates conflict. Most probably
there were twenty-one, distributed by wall as in the schematic plan.
Some of them were seemingly partly or wholly water-gates. We are in
no better position to place accurately the streets and canals within the
city, or the highways and waterways that approached the city
from other places.[13]

The story of the city's gradual destruction thereafter, through
neglect and military operations, remains vague; it may have survived
reasonably well until some time in the thirteenth century.[14] In the fif-
teenth century, its remains were still so recognizable that the sites of a
few old gates were still known by the Sung gate-names. It was called
the "earth wall," and we are told that it was some seven or eight *li*
from the inner wall (then the only functional one).[15]

One piece of architectural evidence also exists: the huge but
truncated pagoda known as the "Fan-t'a." It lies perhaps a little less
than two *li* south of the modern city wall. While it seems clearly to date
from some time in the tenth century, the documentation associating it

---

*See note p. 56.

† *CWTS* 116.1a: over 100,000 corvee workers were employed. The original circuit
of 48 *li* 233 *pu* was repeatedly enlarged, attaining 50 *li* 165 *pu: SHY* (vol. 15) *fang-yü*
1.1b, 13b, 16a, 17a; *SS* 85. 8b; *MHL* (ch. 1), p. 17; *KFFC* 9.1b. The straightening of the
walls in 1075 possibly expanded the area significantly: see note, p. 72.

with the southern part of the Sung outer city is less than conclusive.*

The *Shih-lin kuang-chi* map does suggest that the new city extended farther to the south than to the north of the old, but this may have no significance. The fifteenth-century observer is vague. At what points was the "new city" wall (then abandoned) seven or eight *li* from the old city? What was its shape?

The urban areas outside the wall — the faubourgs, as distinct from suburbs — are still harder to visualize. We know the faubourgs existed and lay on all sides of the walled city. But we have no descriptions of them.

Beyond this point, we must turn to less direct evidence on the city plan. Rich data are of course provided in Meng Yüan-lao's itineraries. We can picture the different quarters, and many important buildings, in a general relationship to each other. But distances are rather vague, relationships are not always clear, and large parts of the city area are insufficiently interesting from Meng's point of view to merit mention.

Further help is provided by data on the administrative structure of the city preserved for certain periods. K'ai-feng was under the general control of a *yin* or metropolitan prefect, who with his staff governed the city and a considerable surrounding area. It was often associated with a changing group of neighboring prefectures, usually four, in a capital regional administration which from 1053 to 1110 and 1114 to 1120 was administered as a circuit (*lu*).[16]

Under this government the territories were divided into a number of *hsien* or subprefectures, each with a subprefect and his staff. The number of *hsien* subject to the prefecture (and thus its area) varied greatly in the course of time. Under its T'ang predecessor, Pien-chou, there had been only 6 *hsien* in all. These multiplied under the Sung both through subdivision of existing *hsien* (adding two) and through transfer of certain *hsien* from six adjacent prefectures, not always permanently. The total of *hsien* under K'ai-feng rose as high as 17 around 1080. The

---

* The Hsiang-kuo Ssu (replaced by a market), the "Iron Pagoda," and the Fan-t'a are located more precisely in early twentieth century maps of Kaifeng, the first two shown much as in maps in *HFHC* and Fu Shou-t'ung. (I am indebted to Arthur F. Wright for copies of the twentieth century maps, in the Yale University collection.) See also Yang T'ing-pao, "Pien Cheng ku chien-chu yu-lan chi-lu [Notes on a tour of architectural antiquities in Pien and Cheng]," *Chung-kuo Ying-tsao Hsüeh-she hui-k'an,* 6, No. 3, 1–16, pp. 6–7; and Chou Ch'eng, *Sung Tung-ching k'ao* [An enquiry into Tung-ching of the Sung] (Liu-yu T'ang, 1731), 15.1a. Early inscriptions date the Fan-t'a in the later tenth century and associate it with the T'ien-ch'ing Ssu (Heavenly Purity Temple). This temple is placed by *MHL* (ch. 3), p. 63, in the northern section of the new city; Li Lien, (10.8b,) writing about 1500, puts the same temple in the southern quarter inside the Ch'en-chou gate (K on schematic plan herewith). Li's placing fits the existing pagoda, but the seeming conflict with *MHL* is disconcerting.

eastern part of the city of K'ai-feng and its adjacent rural area was under the *hsien* of K'ai-feng; the western part and its adjacent rural area under that of Hsiang-fu (at first called Chün-i). The urban parts of the city were divided into wards (*fang*) for purposes of public order and fire protection.

As the city grew, however, this arrangement proved inadequate to deal with the more complex administrative problems, and a structure of urban boroughs (*hsiang*) was superimposed on the wards. The great multiplication of the ward units in the city between 975 and 995 suggests an altered administrative significance for the word *fang,* which might have come to imply a street or street-centered neighborhood. About 975 the two capital metropolitan *hsien* had 8 wards each. In 995 the old city had 4 boroughs (termed "army boroughs" *chün-hsiang*) with 46 wards, and the new city, 4 boroughs and 75 wards. All were then renamed in 1009, the faubourgs were accorded 9 boroughs with 14 wards. In 1021 the units were the same except for elimination of one ward from Borough Right 2. Our sources are inadequate and confusing for the periods thereafter.[17]

Each borough had its contingent of officials of several kinds. A list of 1021 provides quotas for each of six kinds of borough officials, which were at this time reduced from a grand total of 260 to about 180. (In the cases of three boroughs, numbers of officials by kind and in total disagree.) The reduced total quotas were, by borough:

Left 1	24	Right 1	13 [12?]
Left 2	26	Right 2	9 [6?]
Left South	16	Right South	20 [15?]
Left East	19	Right West	25
Left North	16	Right North	13

The boroughs that existed from 995 to 1021 have special interest also because their names give some clue to their relative locations, as shown on the schematic plan, and other valuable data are also supplied for them. Those within the old and new cities or outside of both are specifically so described. In the case of those merely numbered within a certain area, a reading from south to north and from east to west seems in harmony with the general scheme of listing, and with other information. The conjectural boundaries between the boroughs are no doubt too regular and symmetrical.

The resulting arrangement is not without logic. In borough "Right 2," the single ward, named the "South Ward," has few households: understandably in a borough chiefly occupied by the Imperial Palace.

Other supporting evidence will be noted below. But one striking discrepancy quickly meets the eye. Why has the Left East borough so few wards and so many households, while the Right West borough has just the reverse? Other boroughs also show similar, though less extreme, eccentricities in their household/ward ratios. In fact, populations and numbers of wards seem to bear no consistent relationship at all. Numbers of wards evidently do not depend on population. On what basis, then, are the wards determined? Having multiplied greatly in a short time, the wards do not represent merely an outmoded population pattern.* In a few cases, like that of Borough Right 2 which was probably occupied chiefly by the Imperial Palace, security or other special considerations may have determined the ward distribution and staff. In most cases, however, we are led to conclude that the ward distribution relates substantially to the extent of *space* that could be administered effectively by a given number of police and other borough officials. This conclusion is consistent with the numerical quotas of borough officials in different boroughs; the ratio of officials to numbers of wards generally varies little, customarily providing slightly more officials than wards in a borough. Staff sizes are less consistent with population: there are commonly fewer than two officials per thousand households, but in the boroughs with most wards there are nearly three, though still only about one per ward. More wards seem to imply more *area* to administer. From this one is led to infer that the Right West borough was considerably larger than the Left East, so that the old city was not symmetrically placed on the axis of the new, but distinctly nearer to the eastern side. The comparative ward numbers of Right and Left North, and Right and Left South, tend to support this inference. As we shall see later, there is some reason to think that the wards in the western boroughs were still larger in area, placing the old city still more to the east and adding to the asymmetry. On the same principles, the distribution of wards within the old city would be accounted for by an asymmetrical arrangement of the boroughs there also.

These hypotheses obviously need further factual support. Since we have a list of the wards as they were renamed in 995, the task of relating these wards to buildings and districts in Sung writings should not be impossible. But identifications face several handicaps. It is clear that ward names were changed to some extent after this time, and that new wards were added. Moreover, places mentioned in Meng Yüan-

---

* Exact household figures to confirm this are found only for 1021. See also below on population density as it affected quotas by area.

lao's itineraries and other sources are not often identified by ward.*

For the nine faubourg boroughs outside the new city, the 1021 list offers little more than a suggestion that the more or less urbanized areas there were already substantial. Containing altogether 14 wards, in cumulative importance they perhaps resembled an average borough within the walls. The ward distribution hints interestingly that the faubourgs adjacent to the western and northeastern walls were then rather more settled than others, but we may surmise that in the century after 1021 the growing population settled to some extent in all wards. The "Peking version" of the Ch'ing-ming Festival landscape hand-scroll by Chang Tse-tuan, possibly reflecting the city in the early twelfth century, may help to support such an assumption: while three-fourths of it shows scenes of busy commercial life, on land and river, more than two-thirds of these urban activities are indeed outside of the city wall.†

The pattern of settlement had evidently grown unplanned, following especially the convenience of commerce. Commercial activities, confined in Ch'ang-an and Lo-yang of the T'ang to the symmetrically located great city marketplaces, now spread to many parts of the city and were found in streets, along river banks near bridges, or in open spaces outside the walls. The banks of the Pien canal, coming from the commercial and food-producing southeast, and those of the Wu-chang River, coming from the industrially developed near northeast and skirting the Ts'ao Gate quarter, were especially busy. The Pien was bridged by great single high wooden spans, to allow for the large vessels that were constantly moving up or down and were moored by the banks. Only the carved stone bridge carrying the Imperial Avenue stopped their way upstream. No space in the city could be wasted. Even the fine and ample precincts of K'ai-feng's great Buddhist temple, the Hsiangkuo Ssu, were turned to practical purpose as the site of monthly fairs where everything could be found. Even the Imperial Avenue, the cere-

---

* For several boroughs in the 995 ward list, seeming lacunae have eliminated some names and rendered others uncertain. Change of two ward names is directed in an order of 1013 (*SHY* [vol. 15], *fang-yü* 1.13b). But the home ward names of four urban K'ai-feng *chin-shih* of 1148 all dated back to 995. (See note p. 75.)

† Chang supposedly flourished before 1120; his scroll was mentioned as in the S. Sung Imperial Collection. A version now in the Peking Imperial Palace is widely thought most probably original among more than three dozen now extant, but discussion continues. See Liu Yüan-lin, *Ch'ing-ming shang-ho t'u chih tsung-ho yen-chiu* (Taipei, 1969); Roderick Whitfield, "Chang Tse-tuan's Ch'ing-ming shang-ho t'u, "Diss. Princeton, 1965; Chang An-chih, *Chang Tse-tuan Ch'ing-ming shang-ho t'u yen-chiu* (Peking, 1962); Tung Tso-pin, ed., Chang Tse-tuan, *Ch'ing-ming shang-ho t'u* (Taipei, 1953). The Peking version gives a lively impression of a bustling metropolis, and seems in harmony with the historical evidence. Its handling of details may still be rather free, however, as in the absence of a barbican before the city gate shown (perhaps the New Ch'en gate).

monial way for processions to and from the Imperial Palace, was occupied by the stalls of merchants during the eleventh century.[18]

A combination of practical convenience and permissiveness seems, then, to have won out over scholarly partiality for logical neatness, symmetry, and order in the planning (or nonplanning) for the city walls, the placing of the Imperial Palace, the arrangement of the city boroughs, and the location of the different kinds of city activities during K'ai-feng's earlier years. And if in sheer expanse it was probably triple ancient Rome and twelvefold medieval Paris, it was less remarkable among Chinese dynastic capitals. Its area was certainly not four-fifths that of Ch'ang-an in the T'ang; the circuit of its walls only slightly exceeded that of the Tartar City of Peking and approximated that of the Mongol Cambaluc.*

The densities of population settlement in the different boroughs also tell us much about the city's character. The 1021 list of boroughs with their contingents of officials is particularly valuable for its statistics on the population of the Northern Sung capital; we possess no figures even for the total population within its walls, not to mention borough populations, for any other time in the Sung. The data provided do not, of course, answer all of our questions. They show a population of slightly less than 98,000 households (or around 500,000 people) within the city walls. What of the population of the faubourgs? We may guess that their wards were less crowded than those in the walled city, and the regulations for the appointment of faubourg borough officials distinguish between boroughs with more than 500 households and those with less, of which there were no doubt several. Conceivably the outer boroughs together held between 5,000 and 10,000 households at this time.

In dealing with these figures, we must remember the uncertainties of their exact meaning. Do they refer only to taxable permanent residents, and exclude officials, well-to-do residents formally registered elsewhere, refugees, more or less transient merchants, men in army encampments, students, and the varied floating population of the city?

---

* The "straightened" K'ai-feng walls of 1078, with a perimeter of ca. 27.9 km, must still have encompassed less than 6193.4 ha.; T'ang Ch'ang-an had a perimeter of 37.5 km; Mongol Peking ca. 27 km; the "Tartar City" of Peking 23.55 km. Fourth-century Rome has been estimated as some 1380 ha., perhaps 970 ha. apart from palaces, gardens, public buildings, etc., while Paris in 1292 is credited with 378 ha. See note p. 60; *Hsin T'ang shu*, 37.2; Andrew Boyd, *Chinese Architecture* (University of Chicago Press, 1962), p. 53; Sirén, 25–26; J. C. Russell, *Late Ancient and Medieval Population* (Philadelphia, Amer. Philos. Soc., 1958), 61, 64–65. The area of the old or inner city of K'ai-feng, which may be guessed a little more closely from its probable shape resemblances to the post-Sung city, was perhaps ca. 770 ha. after allowing about 48 ha. for the palace.

If so, we have in these numbers only a part of the actual city population in 1021.*

The year 1021 was also relatively early in the Northern Sung. How much may the population, registered or unregistered, have risen during the following century? On this, one clue might be found in the change of the registered population of the entire K'ai-feng Prefecture during this time. This went from 178,631 households about 975 to 235,599 a century later and 261,117 about 1102. Assuming a somewhat regular growth curve, the prefecture must have had around 200,000 registered households in 1021; if the borough figures rested on a similar basis, more than half the registered prefectural population lived then in the city. It seems a rather safe guess that the city more than held its own with the rural areas, towns, and other cities of the prefecture during the following century, and that by 1102 its registered households might already have reached some 135,000 or more. Poetical references to its million people seem matter-of-fact when we allow for the unregistered.†

We may picture the increasingly crowded conditions of the city during its last hundred years of Sung rule. The greatest conceivable area within the outer wall (assuming it circular, which it clearly was not) would be, in the early eleventh century, about 5,758 hectares. This would mean in 1021, at an absolute minimum, a registered population density of 17 households per hectare. For the old inner city, however, our data suggest a minimum density of over 42 households per hectare. Assuming hypothetically an average of five members per household, one reaches a population density of over 210 persons to a hectare, even excluding those probably unregistered.

One would like to know more about the distribution of population in different boroughs. We are thwarted by the absence of data on borough boundaries. Can the numbers of wards help us? They seem to have a partly spatial connotation. But it becomes clear from the ward and area data that the wards in the new city were much larger, on the average, than those of the old. This suggests, not illogically, that in

---

* While explanations still vary somewhat, it is now rather generally agreed that Sung census figures for individuals are very incomplete. While the true ratio seems to vary by region and place, it appears that on average there were around five persons per household.

† There appear to have been no differences in the actual territory under K'ai-feng prefecture in 976, 1081, and 1100, to account for population growth. One *hsien* was split in 1009; in 1105, however, three *hsien* were removed and added to another prefecture, *reducing* the territory. See *TPHY* 1.3a; *YFCY* (ch. 1), p. 5; Ch'üan Han-sheng, "Pei-Sung Pien-liang ti shu ch'u ju mao-i [Export-import trade of Pien-liang in the Northern Sung]," *Chung-yang Yen-chiu Yüan Li-shih Yü-yen Yen-chiu So chi-k'an* 8, No. 2, pp. 196–200; Robert Hartwell, "A Cycle of Economic Change in Imperial China: Coal and Iron in Northeast China, 750–1350," *Journal of the Economic and Social History of the Orient,* 10 (1967), pp. 125–27.

fact the wards in more thinly peopled parts of the city took in rather larger areas. For the moment, however, we may assume an *equality* of areas for wards in all parts of the city, in order to make our higher population density figures conservative. On this basis, it still seems that the tightest crowding of all was in the northeast corner of the old city, in Borough Left Number Two. If its area was proportional to its number of wards, it might have less than 275 hectares, and with some 80,000 people, it would have around 300 persons per hectare. This would mean a population, for this borough alone, exceeding that of Paris in 1292 but nearly twice as crowded, and indeed there were smaller settlements of that day known to have such population densities.* The Left Number Two Borough, it is interesting to note, is adjacent to the Old Ts'ao Gate (d in plan), center of intense business activity. The data for the Left East Borough suggest that the heavily populated area extended outside of the gate also.†

With such pressure of people even in the early eleventh century, and without counting transients, it is little wonder that beginning at least in 1012 the government was obliged repeatedly to remove the structures put up by citizens and encroaching on public thoroughfares. How could roofs be provided for such a multitude? Did the customary North Chinese single-storied courtyard dwelling prevail even in the places where housing was most in demand? Again evidence is unclear. We do find literary mention of huge inns or taverns of several stories, the largest accommodating over a thousand patrons. Seventy-two inns of the first class and three thousand more humble ones are referred to, but perhaps most were more modest in scale. Chang Tse-tuan's Ch'ing-

---

* For areas, see note p. 65; for populations by borough see Fig. 3.1. The new city, whose area would be ca. 4,950 ha. or less, would have 13 households (65 persons) or more per hectare. Western cities offer few parallels. Estimates of population size and density in ancient Rome and Constantinople vary hugely. Russell, *Ancient and Medieval Population*, pp. 64–66, suggests 200 persons per hectare for the possible 970 ha. within the Aurelian wall actually available for residence; perhaps far more in the time of Augustus. London in the fourteenth century, with 35,200 persons, was one of the greatest cities in later medieval Europe (W. S. and E. S. Woytinsky, *World Population and Production* [New York, 1953], p. 112). Russell, pp. 60–61, however, cites an estimate of 59,200 people for Paris in 1292, and a density of 157 per hectare. He gives still denser populations for some smaller places such as Béziers with 14,476 people (322 per ha.) in 1304. Actual densities, he notes, may have been less, with some of the people really living outside the very cramped walled area. For Paris of 1292 see note p. 65; Béziers was a mere 45 ha. London passed the population of the Northern Sung capital only late in the seventeenth century, and Paris later still (Woytinsky, p. 113). It should be remembered that multi-storied houses were common in Rome as well as in Medieval Europe.

† For the Ts'ao gate district see Ch'üan, "Pei-Sung Pien-liang," p. 204. A full consideration of K'ai-feng's population patterns would require further economic analyses of the Sung that are impossible here. Important studies for this include those by scholars already mentioned, as well as more recent investigations by Shiba Yoshinobu, Umehara Kaoru, and others.

ming Festival scroll adds supporting evidence. In the Peking version
the traveler seems to enter only the southeastern corner of the outer
city, perhaps through the Ch'en-chou Gate (K in plan). Here we do see
several buildings of two stories: one, quite large, seemingly a hostelry.
There is even a two-story place of entertainment in the faubourg near
the Rainbow Bridge. But the perspectives of the scroll do not give us
distant views of the city, in which such taller living places might figure
as a recurrent theme. If single-storied houses remained the more common design, the crowding of people becomes even more dismaying.*

Such were some of the pragmatic aspects of Sung K'ai-feng. How
quickly and how far were these balanced or circumvented by more
appealing elements? Here we must remember that the growth of formalistic attitudes with respect to K'ai-feng was merely one phase of
a similar movement pervading all of Sung intellectual life, and that a
tension between pragmatism and formalism went far back in Chinese
history. It was, in fact, one part of the prolonged political tug between
followers of Confucius and Mencius and those of thinkers somewhat
arbitrarily grouped as Legalists.

Under the term "formalism" we may subsume several broad
aspects of the more traditional Chinese world-view as they are reflected in human actions. In part, formalism is associated with a conviction that the universe, in all of its parts, partakes of a single order that
is both physical and moral. Human, ethical and ritual violations disturb
the total order of nature, which responds with omens or natural
calamities, or ultimately with the overthrow of the reigning dynasty.
The order of nature as represented in objects of a landscape may also
influence the destiny of human beings living there, in ways not physically
explainable and not exactly moral, which one is tempted to call transcendental. Finally, and related to these, there is a deep faith that the
only ultimate and really satisfactory solution of man's problems, whatever their nature, must come from the long and successful cultivation
of a cosmically sanctioned social ethic. These various relations between
man, nature, and the cosmos led men to control the occult forces of
nature beneficially by such devices as placing a family grave or a city,
with geomantic wisdom, auspiciously for the family's or the city's
future fortunes. And since cosmic ethics invested human behavior
patterns (both moral conduct and formalities) with values and consequences apart from those pragmatically justifiable and predictable,

---

* *HCP* 74.14b (1012); 102.9a (1024); 116.7b (1035); Ch'üan, "Pei-Sung Pien-liang,"
p. 215. The order of 1035 refers specifically to the old city.

formulas and rituals assumed great importance both to individuals and to social and political institutions.

In the Sung, the growth of pragmatic habits of thought and behavior, and a more critical intellectual attitude, had (as we have seen) noticeably weakened the commitment to formalism. Sung pragmatism, however, retained very markedly the value-orientation usually characteristic of Confucian thought. It stressed the ethical purpose of the state and its duties to its subjects; references to the cosmic basis and limitations of political power were common in the Imperial Court. Confucian concepts were taught in texts which also stressed ritual behavior. The ever-present elements of formalism were available when the situation grew more favorable for a countertrend to that of pragmatism.

Related to formalism was an instinctive wish for intellectual neatness, for institutions and practices that were consistent and in accord with their labels; the preference for these seemed to go beyond concern with rationalization for the sake of purely practical consequences. And if institutions ought to be set in order, reformers needed suitable models. Since dynasties after the Ch'in were tainted with despotic and disapproved Legalism, and time had obscured the harsher realities of the earlier dynasties and invested them with edifying myths, it was natural that men should find desirable models especially in antiquity. Thus it was that efforts at improvement in all aspects of life easily became exercises in avid antiquarianism. Ancient precedents assumed the force of cosmic truth.

In this period scholars were developing a new view of the past through the systematic study of ancient bronzes and of history. They were increasingly critical of the legendary elements embodied in ancient texts, and gradually more analytical in their attitudes toward nature and the supernatural. This makes it at times all the more difficult to be sure of men's motives in using conventional precedents, rituals, and interpretations of natural omens. In some cases their attitude may have been ambiguous; in some, a cynical playing on widely held beliefs; in some, it was surely sincere. The question of motivation is further complicated by the fact that many constructive deeds of government were formalistic as well as pragmatic: a very practical policy might simultaneously be a gesture to appease an offended Heaven, or to display piety. Some actions, such as the frequent amnesties, became rather conventional formalistic expressions.*

---

* The combination of Confucian ideals with a realistic attitude influenced by Legalism is well exemplified by Li Kou: see Etienne Balazs, *Chinese Civilization and Bureaucracy* (New Haven, Yale Univ. Press, 1964) and S. Y. Hsieh, "Li Kou," Diss. Univ. of Chicago, 1972. A reaction against disorders accompanying contemporary change no doubt added attraction to social norms believed to be ancient.

Measures and programs of reform illustrate this point. Many, more especially during the dynasty's first century, seem almost purely pragmatic in their inspiration. As the eleventh century progressed and administrative problems became more acute, the programs of reform tended to grow broader, more utopian and sweeping. Simultaneously, they tended to have a greater reference to classical precedents. Individualism and commercial activity, which found little praise in the old texts, fell once more into increasing ideological disfavor. And by the early twelfth century, under Hui-tsung, there appeared a growing tendency to introduce titles and institutions with an antiquarian flavor. An element of formalism may be sensed also in the recasting of Sung governmental organization around 1080. It is no doubt true that the earlier complicated structure of offices with ambiguities of responsibility and duplications (at least on paper), had been somewhat conducive to inefficiency. But the protests against these features, which are found earlier in the century, seem to imply, too, a certain moral blemish in lack of order, disparities of titles and functions, and departure from tradition. The reformed structure that emerged had a strong resemblance superficially to that of earlier T'ang officialdom, but in fact many late-T'ang and Sung innovations were preserved under more conventional titles and terminology.*

Even in the weighing of political actions, while historical experience could be used pragmatically, old precedents could also be applied formalistically so as to inhibit a realistic choice between alternatives, as we shall see in the events of 1126−1127, treated in Chapter 6. In philosophy, formalism was advanced with the growing popularity of the *tao-hsüeh* movement, though this had certain pragmatic justifications as well. The final triumph of *tao-hsüeh* over the pragmatic philosophers would not, however, come until the full acceptance of Chu Hsi's interpretations a century after the fall of K'ai-feng.†

---

* Proposals to restore T'ang forms of administrative organization were found as early as 998: see *HCP* 43.15b−17a. The new classification title system (*chieh-kuan*) used after 1080 borrowed titles used in the T'ang prime for other purposes, while in actuality they preserved the function of the titular "pay offices" (*chi-lu kuan*) conceived from late T'ang to early Sung, in neatened form. The 1080 reorganization of the Secretariat-Chancellery involved similar compromises. Antiquarianism appeared in usages in the late Northern Sung, such as Hui-tsung's terms of Pi-yung for the University, *ta ssu-ch'eng* for the head educational official, the new titles for the chief councilors, and so forth.

† Still considered a heretic at his death in 1200, he emerged from disfavor slowly. Only in 1241 did he share sacrifices in the Confucian temple along with other eminent scholars; in 1313 his commentaries became orthodox for the examinations (see J. P. Bruce, *Chu Hsi and his Masters* [London: Probsthain, 1923], p. 91; J. W. Haeger, "The Intellectual Context of Neo-Confucian Syncretism," *Journal of Asian Studies*, 31, 499−513; and Chapter 7).

Formalism made its impact on K'ai-feng in a number of ways, of which many (not all) involved physical aspects of the city. As a capital, it ought not only to meet the geomantic requirements common to all cities: it should also symbolize the empire and the emperor's central place in it. Merging with the transcendental symbolism proper to a capital, there was also a very practical political end: that of expressing the dynasty's greatness through the majesty, beauty, and fitness of the city. A given building or piece of landscaping often served both purposes.* K'ai-feng in its early years as capital fell short, as we have seen, in most respects, lacking grandeur, symmetry, regularity, and comfort. Divination had played no role in its selection as a site for a capital. But it had at least a general southern orientation, with the Palace more or less central, and soon began to acquire other suitable features.

One of the simplest ways of improving the city's symbolism was the use of appropriate nomenclature for its features. At first the Sung did not trouble to alter inherited place names, but before long these began to seem inappropriate for the role their capital was to play. The old names for the city's wards were held to be vulgar, and all but four in 995 were changed for new and more elegant designations, largely auspicious in flavor or describing public virtues. Meanwhile, gates of the inner and outer walls, previously often called after cities or towns to which they led, were renamed, some in 960 and all by 979, to carry associations with the state cult ("Obedient to Heaven") or geomantic appropriateness ("Morning Sun" on the East, "Vermilion Bird" on the inner South). Some were renamed from time to time. (In popular usage, however, the old names continued in favor, and a gate opened in the old city during the previous dynasty, named the "Gate for the Flourishing of Ritual" and renamed the "Gate for the Exaltation of Brilliance" was generally called to the end the "New Gate.")†

Sung rulers also began early a rather modest effort to make their capital more suitable in concrete ways. Considerations both of space and of fiscal stringency limited the size of the Imperial Palace, but it

---

* The process was felt to be within nature, hence not "supernatural." Needham terms it "pseudo-scientific." The formalistic principles of the traditional Chinese city plan are well presented in Paul Wheatley, *The Pivot of the Four Quarters* (Chicago: Aldine, 1971), pp. 411–51. Drawn much from the late *K'ao-kung chi* chapter of the *Chou li*, they included axiality, symmetry, the three gates on each side, cardinal orientation, and geomantic significance for the whole. For these principles as applied to Sui-T'ang Ch'ang-an, see also A. F. Wright, "Viewpoints on a City: Ch'ang-an," *Ventures,* Winter 1965, 15–23; Wright, "Symbolism and Function," *Journal of Asian Studies,* 24,667–73.

† See K'ai-feng plan and notes. The southern gate of the Imperial City in T'ang Ch'ang-an was also named "Gate of the Vermilion Bird" (Chu-ch'iao Men).

was renovated by the first emperor with elegance and symmetry.* In 1012 a third gate was opened in the southern wall of the inner city. This was quite possibly a practical step, but its formal significance was scarcely altogether coincidental. It gave the inner city, at least, the classical twelve gates, symbolizing the twelve months of the year, and equally distributed in the four walls.† More than a century after the dynasty's founding, the outer city walls received an extensive and much-needed renovation, in the course of which they were strengthened, provided with more impressive moats, and also somewhat lengthened and straightened. But all of this evidently fell far short of giving them any real regularity and symmetry.‡

The Sung emperors provided the proper temples and installations for the many rituals of the state cult. They showed far less enthusiasm than their T'ang predecessors for the most impressive and costly rites of all, the sacrifices to Heaven performed atop one or another of the five sacred mountains in the several parts of China. But they were prompt and more consistent than the T'ang in carrying out the next most important, the sacrifice to Heaven on a raised open circular altar outside the capital's southern wall. Altars and accessory buildings were provided for this, and for the complementary sacrifice to Earth outside the northern wall. Care was given also to provide, in the proper locations, buildings for the other national cult ceremonies.§

---

* T'ai-tsung rejected a plan to enlarge his palace, which would have encroached on dwellings of the citizens (*SHY* [vol. 15], 1.11b−12a).

† See note 16 and note p. 71.

‡ The walls seem to have been rather higher and stouter than those of previous capitals, perhaps in response to the use of explosives in warfare. They were 12.29 meters (4 *chang*) high and 17.82 meters (5 *chang* 9 *ch'ih*) thick at the base. This perhaps discouraged more extensive relocation. The moats were enlarged in 1082 to 76.8 meters (50 *pu*) in breadth at the top, 66.4 meters (40 *pu*) at the bottom, and 4.6 meters (1 *chang* 5 *ch'ih*) in depth (*SHY* [vol. 15], *fang-yü* 1.17a). The walls were white, the gates vermilion, and the moats were planted, in the twelfth century at least, with willows on both banks. Except for the processional main gateway on each side, the gates were all furnished with curved barbicans with oblique openings (*MHL* [ch. 1], 17−19).

§ The T'ang ruler T'ai-tsung abandoned projects to carry out the elaborate sacrificial rituals at the base and summit of T'ai-shan, but they were completed by Kao-tsung, Empress Wu, and Hsüan-tsung. Sung Chen-tsung performed them as a part of his fantastic ritual splurges after the peace of Shan-yüan, but he was the last in Chinese history to do so. See Edouard Chavannes, *Le T'ai Chan* (Paris: Leroux, 1910), pp. 169−261. The sacrifices to Heaven at the Southern Suburb, however, were only performed by the T'ang rulers about once in ten years, on the average, while the Sung rulers performed them more than twice as often. The Sung court gave much attention to their relation to the Ming-t'ang ritual, which has been construed as an effort to strengthen the emperor's position in the mid-eleventh century. See *YH*, ch. 93; Liu Tzu-chien, "Feng-Shan wenhua yü Sung tai Ming-t'ang chi T'ien [The *Feng* and *Shan* cult and the Ming-t'ang sacrifices]," *Chung-yang Yen-chiu Yüan min-tsu hsüeh yen-chiu chi-k'an*, 18 (Aut. 1964), 45−49; Werner Eichhorn, "Die Wiedereinrichtung des Staatsreligion im Anfang der Sungzeit," *Monumenta Serica*, 23, 205−63.

Finally, to complete the religious character proper to a national capital, K'ai-feng had an increasing array of Buddhist and Taoist temples and shrines.

The various more religious edifices joined with the more mundane governmental ones (for nothing was strictly secular) to invest the city with a certain splendor. A vast Taoist temple complex was built under Imperial auspices early in the eleventh century. The Hsiang-kuo Buddhist temple compound was expanded, with fine halls and a central gate of several stories. Perhaps the crowding of the city encouraged Sung builders to seek monumentality in the vertical form of lofty temple-gates and pagodas, since horizontal spaciousness was hard to achieve. A number of great pagodas appeared: the most famous was that erected by the noted architect Yü Hao, skillfully constructed of wood and rising to some 110 meters. The still-surviving lofty and slender brick "Iron Pagoda" of 1041 and the gigantic but incomplete "Fan-t'a" have already been mentioned. The Sung code included punishments for any failure of builders to conform with official building regulations as well as for those who failed to keep buildings in good repair. The oldest preserved builder's manual comes from the end of the Northern Sung.*

Formalism probably made its deepest impression on K'ai-feng in the reign of Hui-tsung, from 1100 to 1125. That most paradoxical emperor – at once notable painter and calligrapher, patron of arts, science, and archeology, political and social reformer, devoted son of Shen-tsung and prodigal hedonist, promoter of eunuch power and indulger of administrative corruption – made the city more impressive and attractive than ever before. His promotion of antique terms has been noted above, and more of his political acts will be seen in a later chapter. He initiated charitable institutions, hospitals, and medical schools throughout the empire, and carried the expansion of the state educational system to an unprecedented point. In the southern suburb of the capital he built an elaborate complex to house the lower classes of the enlarged National University, which in name, location, and layout all copied supposedly ancient models. (Its buildings were designed by Li Chieh, scholar and engineer, probably the most learned architect

---

* *Hsing t'ung* (Chia-yeh T'ang ed.), 26.10b, 27.2a; Yang; Pao Ting, "T'ang-Sung t'a chih ch'u-pu fen-hsi [Primary distinctions between T'ang and Sung pagodas]," *Chung-kuo Ying-tsao Hsüeh-she hui-k'an,* 6, No. 4, plate 5 and pp. 10, 11, 23, and passim; Li Chieh, *Ying-tsao fa-shih* [Standards of architecture] (Shanghai: Commercial Press, 1925). The last named, first published in 1103, shows due concern with the precepts of the *Chou li* as well as with the latest structural and decorative techniques. See also Laurence Sickman and Alexander Soper, *The Art and Architecture of China* (Baltimore: Penguin, 1956), pp. 255 – 56.

of the Sung.)* On the advice of a Taoist geomancer and in order, it was said, to ensure himself many sons, he caused a symbolic mountain, some 138 meters high and over five kilometers in circuit, to be raised in the northeast corner of the old city. He turned the artificial mountain into a park stocked with rarities including a magnificent collection of the stones eroded into fantastic shapes that were already fashionable as garden adornments. He expelled the merchants and their booths from the colonnaded Imperial Avenue and redesigned it as a lovely boulevard with flowering trees and reflecting pools. To render more impressive the ceremonies of the state cult he replaced with permanent edifices the temporary "Black City" of tents outside the new city, used in connection with the suburban sacrifices to Heaven.† The annual processions from the Palace to the Altar of Heaven evidently provided a gorgeous show for the populace.

The needs of K'ai-feng's citizens, apart from public order and fire protection, seem to have been supplied for the most part through private initiatives. But where these fell short, the state endeavored to meet the deficiency by supplying food, heating, and even public entertainment.‡

Thus through a combination of state and individual action, the city of 960 had become scarcely recognizable in that of 1125. Symbolically and esthetically it had come to fulfill its national and dynastic role with greater fitness; certainly the pleasures it offered were far greater in variety and more stimulating in quality. It must have been a far less austere and graceless place. Yet despite this, the physical ir-

---

* Inspired by the "hall with its circlet of water" praised in the Book of Odes, the group built in 1102, "round outside and square inside," housed 3,000 students. There were 100 buildings, each of five bays and holding 30 students, in addition to four lecture halls; the entire complex extended 1,872 bays. See T'an Chung-lin, *Hsü Tzu-chih t'ung-chien ch'ang-pien shih-pu* [Restorations to *HCP*] (Chekiang Shu-chü, 1883), 20.18a-b. For Li Chieh, see note p. 73.

† Li Lien, 4.13a; 14.1a—14a; *HFHC* 14.10a—11b; Edward H. Schafer, *Tu Wan's Stone Catalogue* (Berkeley: Univ. of California Press, 1961), p. 8; *MHL* (ch. 2), p. 33; (ch. 10), pp. 194—201. The permanent buildings for the sacrifices were erected between 1111 and 1119.

‡ See Edward H. Schafer, "The Development of Bathing Customs," *Jour. of the Amer. Oriental Soc.,* 76, 57—82, esp. 61. Along with the great spontaneous interest in medicine at this time, there was active promotion by rulers (especially Hui-tsung) through new medical schools, hospitals, etc. For brief reference, see K. Chimin Wong and Wu Lien-teh, *History of Chinese Medicine* (Shanghai, 1936), pp. 86—96; 110—126; 132; 139; Hsü I-t'ang, "Sung-tai p'ing-shih ti she-hui chiu-chi hsing-cheng [Normal social relief policies in the Sung]," *Chung-kuo wen-hua yen-chiu hui-k'an,* 5, 33—47. For public supply of fuel, see Hartwell, "A Cycle of Economic Change...Coal and Iron in Northeast China, 750—1350," *Journal of the Economic and Social History of the Orient,* 10 (1967), pp. 138—41. For amusements, see Sogabe Shizuo, *Kaifū to Kōshū* [K'ai-feng and Hang-chou] (Tokyo: Fuzambo, 1940); *MHL,* passim; and a number of modern studies.

regularities were not altered sufficiently to meet the desires of the formalist. And in the century since 1023, the crowding of the city's central areas can scarcely have improved. The growing population must have widened the areas of denser concentrations, and Hui-tsung's landscaping in the crowded central city must have led to worsened crowding elsewhere.

The bustle, noise, and constrictions of the city no doubt added to the attractions of suburban homes for those who could afford the cost. The cases of fourteen men of K'ai-feng origin, who received doctoral degrees in 1148, are interesting in this connection even though the group is too small to be dependable statistically. These fourteen did not, of course, actually live at K'ai-feng, now in Jürchen hands — three of them are known to have lived in various sub-prefectures of Fu-chou — but they still gave K'ai-feng addresses as their official places of residence. For twelve of these graduates we are told whether or not their three immediate antecedents in the paternal line held offices in the nine grades of the upper civil service. Of the twelve, four gave addresses in the suburban countryside of Ch'ui-t'ai, some three kilometers south of the city. All of these had upper civil service antecedents. Four more claimed homes in other places outside of the city, and three of these also had upper civil service ancestry. Finally, in contrast with these suburban people were four who came from within the K'ai-feng city walls: three of these had *no* trace of such official ancestry or connections. Perhaps a suburban home tended to become an enjoyment associated with official position? Even the embellishments that Hui-tsung added to the city may have failed to make it really a place to live if one were free to choose.*

We return, then, to our initial question: what made the lost K'ai-feng more desirable as a Sung capital after 1127 than the actual seat, Hang-chou? While the latter was scarcely more symmetrical or orthodox in its plan, it was with its greater space, broad river, hills, and West

---

* It is of course possible that some with suburban homes had unofficial city residences as well. The charms of the suburbs are described in *MHL;* for Ch'ui-t'ai, which has early historical associations, see *TPHY* 1.5a; Li Lien, 8.13b. For the 1148 graduates see Hsü Nai-ch'ang, *Sung-yüan k'o-chü san lu* [Three lists from Sung-Yüan examinations], 1923, first list. The cases are: Group I, nos. 4, 7; Group II, nos. 1, 2, 3; Group III, nos. 4, 18; Group IV, nos. 9, 18, 53, 57, 76, 119; Group V, no. 99. Of the men with urban backgrounds, one came from the old city (Borough Left #1), and three from the new (one from Borough Left East and two from Right West). One from Right West was descended from three generations of upper civil service officials, suggesting that suburban homes were not universal for such. Note also that the Peking Ch'ing-ming scroll also shows one or two apparent residences of high officials within the city. Ch'ung-ming ward, favored by many scholars because Sung Min-ch'iu lived there with his famous library (see note 5), does not seem to appear among the wards in the *SHY* lists, and its location is unclear.

Lake, surely far more attractive. An element in K'ai-feng's magnetism might well have been a simple lingering hope to regain it together with the northern lands it represented. The loss of K'ai-feng and the iron industries of its market area was no doubt recognized to be a heavy economic blow. Perhaps there was also a kind of irredentist symbolism involved, a feeling that the retention of K'ai-feng as the capital pro forma might somehow help to make it so in reality. And had the passage of time gilded its memory? Or may there have been also a dim sense of something beyond this, an awareness that K'ai-feng had stood for certain individualities that escaped the grasp of later Sung men? Perhaps the courageous realism of its first century, its times of untroubled prosperity, its vital reformism, and some of the restless innovativeness that survived until its loss? If K'ai-feng had never, admittedly, fulfilled very well the ideological requirements for a symbolic capital, yet it could, after all, symbolize some less traditional qualities that distinguished the early Sung period.

Notes to Chapter 3

1. *MHL;* also note p. 64.
2. Ch'üan Han-sheng, "Pei-Sung Pien-liang," 196 – 217; Robert Hartwell, "Markets, Technology, and the Structure of Enterprise in the...11th century Chinese Iron and Steel Industry," *Journal of Economic History,* 26 (1966), 29 – 58; R. Hartwell, "A Cycle of Economic Change...Coal and Iron in Northeast China, 750 – 1350," *Journal of the Economic and Social History of the Orient,* 10 (1967), 102 – 159; Laurance J. C. Ma, *Commercial Development and Urban Change in Sung China* (Ann Arbor, Univ. of Michigan, Dept. of Geography, 1971), 106 – 146.
3. Hartwell, "Cycle," pp. 149 – 52; Ch'üan, *T'ang Sung ti-kuo yü yün-ho* [The T'ang and Sung empires and the Grand Canal] (Taipei: Academia Sinica Historical-Linguistic Section, 1956), pp. 114 – 27.
4. Wang Chien-ch'iu, *Sung tai T'ai-hsüeh yü T'ai-hsüeh sheng* [The Sung National University and its students] (Taipei: Chung-kuo Hsüeh-shu Chu-tso Chiang-chu Wei-yüan-hui, 1965).
5. Chu Pien, *Ch'ü-wei chiu-wen* [Traditions of Ch'ü-wei], Hsüeh-chin t'ao-yüan ed., 4.9a.
6. *HCP* 17.7b.
7. Li Lien, *Pien-ching i-chi chih* [Record of the vestiges of Pien-ching], 1, 3a.
8. *KFFC* 9.11a.
9. *HFHC* 9.11b.
10. Yang T'ing-pao, "Pien Cheng ku chien-chu yu-lan chi-lu [Notes on a tour of architectural antiquities in Pien and Cheng]," *Chung-kuo Ying-tsao Hsüeh-she hui-k'an,* 6, No. 3, 1 – 16, p. 9.
11. Yang, pp. 8 – 9; Chou Ch'eng, *Sung Tung-ching k'ao* [An enquiry into Tung-ching of the Sung] (Liu-yu T'ang, 1731), 14.1a; A. C. Soper, "Hsiang-kuo Ssu, an Imperial Temple of Northern Sung China," *Journal of the American Oriental Society,* 68, 19 – 45.
12. Fu Shou-t'ung, *Pien-ch'eng ch'ou-fang pei-lan* [Investigatory tour of Pien city] (Kaifeng, 1860) 3, 12b; *HFHC* 1.1a, etc.; also note p. 57.
13. For the grand canal and its related waterways, see Aoyama, "Tō-Sō jidai no kōtsū," especially map IV, and Ch'üan, *Yün-ho.*
14. *KFFC* 9.11a.
15. *HFHC* 9.5a; 11a.
16. *Hsin T'ang shu* (Po-na ed.), 38.4b – 5a; *Yüan-ho chün hsien t'u-chih* (Ts'ung-shu chi-ch'eng ed., vol. 3086), ch. 7, p. 189; Hope Wright, *Geographical Names in Sung China* (Paris, Sung Project, 1956); p. 29; p. 82; *TPHY* and *YFCY* under K'ai-feng Fu.
17. *TPHY* 1.1a; *SHY* [vol. 14] *ping* 3.3a – 4b; 6a; [vol. 15] *fang-yü* 1.12a – 13a; *WHTK* 63.5b; *CKFC* 38.21b; *SS* 166.17a. For origins of the *hsiang* see Sogabe Shizuo, "Shō to shōgun no Kankei" [Relation of borough and borough-army], *Tōa keizai kenkyū,* 26, No. 1. A study by Michael Finegan promises further light on its administrative functions.
18. See Kato Shigeshi, "On the Hang," *Memoirs of the Research Department of the Toyo Bunko,* VII, 45 – 83; Ch'üan, "Pei-Sung Pien-liang"; *MHL* (ch. 3), pp. 59 – 61; A. C. Soper, "Hsiang-kuo Ssu," *Jour. Amer. Oriental Soc.,* 68, 19 – 45; street scenes in Peking Ch'ing-ming scroll.

Fiscal Privileges and the Social Order in Sung China

BRIAN E. McKNIGHT

IN COMPLEX SOCIETIES the costs of running the state have rarely if ever been distributed wholly according to the ability of the citizens to pay. Such maldistribution of costs results from at least two major factors. First, people with political power try with varying degrees of success to convert their influence into fiscal privileges. These frequently take the form of exemptions, disguised or open, juridically "legal" or merely tolerated in practice, which are extended to the ruling group and its supporters. Where political power is widely distributed these privileges are by no means universal or complete, for the state must continue to operate, and if sufficient revenues cannot be squeezed from the powerless, then they must be squeezed from those with less power by those with more. Second, maldistribution of costs may also result from a faulty perception on the part of those making policy about the character of their society — specifically of who can pay how much — or in periods of rapid economic change from a lag between the perception of alterations and the legislating of new rules.

But the rulers cannot forever tolerate excessive inequity, particularly if it is blatant, since it disturbs the social equilibrium not only by ruining certain affected households but also by creating a reservoir of anger among those who feel themselves unjustly burdened. The state seeks to avoid this problem by keeping some privileges hidden, by promoting an ideology that justifies the obvious privileges of those with power, and by seeking to distribute the social burden more or less equitably among the weak.

Since the granting of fiscal privileges may result either from the translation of political influence into economic advantage, or from an attempt on the part of the authorities to avoid ruining certain types of

[79]

powerless but economically disadvantaged households, any major alteration in this distribution of fiscal burdens and exemptions presupposes social changes affecting either the distribution of political power, or the perceptions of the rulers, or the ability of households to bear costs.

One such major restructuring of burdens and privileges occurred in the late T'ang with the reform of land taxation and corvee labor symbolized by the Twice-a-Year tax policy of 780. Broadly speaking, prior to these reforms tax exemption privileges were widely distributed, the ruling elite being only the most noteworthy of the privileged groups. The tax reforms were evidence of a tendency to reduce privileges by extending tax liability to previously untouched groups.

A second transformation, less obvious, and therefore not previously described by scholars, occurred in the distribution of administrative labor services (*chih-i*). (These must be distinguished from mere corvee labor — *yao-i* — which in theory had been commuted into money payments by the 780 reforms.) Although the roots of this redistribution of administrative labor services can be traced back into the late T'ang, the major changes began only with the reforms of Wang Anshih and reached their apogee in the Southern Sung. A study of their history will illuminate not only the transformation of rural society that preceded it, but also the redistribution of village-level political power that accompanied it.

The political side effect followed necessarily from the character of the administrative labor service exactions. In traditional China, where the central government could only secure to itself a small part of the gross national product, it was not possible to pay all of those engaged in administration out of government revenues. The formal civil service in Sung times numbered only about twenty-five thousand civil and military officials at a time when the empire contained sixty million people. These civil servants were aided by a host of irregular officials and clerical personnel who outnumbered them perhaps one hundred to one, but even so these groups together could only function on a day-by-day basis in the cities and towns.[1] In rural areas many key functions — tax collection, maintenance of local order, registration of population, compilation of land records, and so on — were assigned under most dynasties to nonsalaried, nonprofessional personnel. Responsibility for these tasks was usually given to selected households, drafted from among those well-to-do inhabitants who lacked exemption privileges. During the Sung these village officers, the functional ancestors of the gentry of later times, were drawn from the top four of the five household grades, which together comprised about one-sixth of the to-

tal population.* These households provided someone to carry out specific functions for limited periods of time in defined jurisdictions, but
were not paid. The responsibility was thus a tax in the broadest sense,
and in some periods people sought assiduously to evade the draft involved. However, although the households called had to bear a variety
of expenses, the positions were not without some compensations. In
particular the higher level village service officers, who could influence
how much each of the households in their jurisdiction had to pay in land
taxes, who had a major role in the making of the records that legalized
landownership, and who held local police powers, of necessity derived
from their authority a considerable amount of influence and power in the
countryside. For this reason, although the primary focus in the following pages will be on privileges and their reduction—a fiscal phenomenon in nature if not in implication—the changes portrayed will re-
veal a transformation in the very nature of Sung rural society, politically as well as economically.

The dimensions and directions of this transformation become fully apparent only in contrast with the situation which existed during
the early T'ang. The T'ang founders' successful attack against the
Sui had been a coup rather than a revolution, since political power
remained in the hands of a small clique of families from the Kuan-
chung region. This group embodied the virtues and vices of an aristocracy—disdain for their inferiors, devotion to military virtues, an intense
pride in their ancestry, and a spare and austere code of honor. Closely
interconnected by bonds of marriage, they set the social tone for the
early T'ang as they had for the Sui and the preceding northern states.
Dominating the higher levels of the nobility and bureaucracy, these
families secured for themselves not only immediate political power but
also privileges for their persons and the large landed estates which
were the economic underpinning of their positions.

The interests of this class were by no means identical with those
of the emperors. Periodically those imperial advisers who identified
themselves more closely with the monarchy than with the class from
which they had sprung attempted to limit the power of this aristocracy.
Most significantly, during the early part of the post-Han interregnum
they sought to limit the amount of land and the number of retainers a
man could legally hold, and coupled this policy of limitation with a sys-

---

* Lü Tsu-ch'ien, writing during the latter half of the twelfth century, reported that in
Yen prefecture of Che-chiang circuit there were 10,718 adult males in grades one through
four, and 71,479 adult males in grade five. Lü Tsu-ch'ien, *Tung lai chi* [Collected Writings
of Lü Tsu-ch'ien] (Hsü chin hua ts'ung-shu ed.), 3.1a—2b.

tem under which, in theory, the emperor as owner periodically re-
distributed land to the people. The restrictive sections of these policies probably were never effectively enforced and soon disappeared,
but redistribution schemes reappeared periodically. The most famous
of these, the *chün-t'ien* or equalized-fields system, was established
under the Northern Wei dynasty and formed the basis for later regulations, including those of the T'ang.

Under the T'ang rules each male peasant between the ages of
eighteen and sixty was supposed to receive from the state twenty
mou (about 2.7 acres) of land held in perpetuity (*yung-yeh t'ien*)
and eighty *mou* (about 10.5 acres) of personal share land (*k'ou-fen
t'ien*).[2] Land held in perpetuity, which was hereditary in the family
of the grantee, had originally been justified as a means for encouraging
the production of crops requiring long-term investment, such as mulberry trees, fruit trees, and so on. Personal share land reverted to
the state when the grantee died or reached sixty years of age. Since
in any locality in any year some people became newly eligible for grants
or personal share land, while other people became ineligible, there was
a system of annual redistribution.

This system of land allotment was intimately interconnected with
systems of taxation, labor services, and military conscription. Having
established the land law, the state could proceed on the assumption
that each peasant unit had an allotment of given minimum size, and
could therefore levy a tax on the head of each household. It was not
necessary to tax by land area since, in theory at least, the land held
by each household was already predetermined. With these head taxes
to be paid in grain and silk were associated a set of labor services due
to the central government and the local authorities, and a militia conscription system.

Allotments of land were not restricted to the adult and adolescent
male peasants who were the actual farmers. Smaller grants were made
to other members of the peasant population, who were presumably not
engaged in any major way in actively farming the land. Women, the
aged, and the young all received land allotments. Members of the ser-
vile population, Buddhists and Taoist monks and nuns, merchants and
artisans, disabled persons, and the nobility and officials all received
grants. Actual cultivators received larger grants of land than most
of the noncultivating groups; only the nobility and officials received still
more. The size of grants to elite households is a clear index of the dimension of their privileges. Whereas under the T'ang rules an adult
male peasant received only twenty *mou* (2.7 acres) of land held in
perpetuity, an imperial prince (*ch'in-wang*) had a right to one hun-

dred *ch'ing* (about 1,330 acres), serving officials of the upper first grade, sixty *ch'ing* (798 acres), princes of commanderies (*chün-wang*) and serving officials of the lower first grade, fifty *ch'ing* (665 acres), and so on down through the hierarchy of serving officials and the nobility to the Director of the Warrior Cavalry (*wu-ch'i wei*) who had an allotment of sixty *mou* (about 8 acres).[3] This last title was a relatively lowly one, corresponding to the second degree of the seventh grade in the T'ang official hierarchy. It was held by officials who merely had attained one "mention" (*chuan*), that is one "right" to an advancement in office.[4] Even so these men were awarded three times the allotment of an adult male farmer. Mandarins carrying titles that did not involve actual functions (*san-kuan*) were to be treated like serving officials if they were of the fifth rank or higher, and even those holding honorary rank were permitted allotments.[5]

Inequities in distribution were magnified by the extension of tax exemption privileges. Broadly speaking, in the early T'ang taxes and services were demanded only from those farmers between twenty-one and fifty-nine who did not come under one of the categories of physical disability or of special privilege. It has been estimated that, at least in part as the result of the wide distribution of privilege, only about 17 percent of the total population were liable for taxes.[6] Landholders exempt from land taxes, corvee labor, and administrative labor services included not only adult males suffering defined disabilities but also overage and adolescent males, all women, Buddhist and Taoist monks and nuns, merchants and artisans, and even individuals whose exemplary moral conduct had been singled out for official commendation. But by far the most important group of the privileged was the ruling elite. All members of the imperial clan, all holders of noble titles, certain relatives of those with noble titles, all officials, relatives of officials of the third rank and up, and all holders of official rank even if they were not actual bureaucrats were exempt. Even minor functionaries (*tsa-jen*) and clerks were exempted as long as they were in service.*

---

* *TLT* 3.38a; *Sung hsing t'ung* [Sung legal code] (Taipei: Wen Hai Publishing Company) 12.11b; *WHTK* 13.142.a-b. *Ku T'ang-lü shu-i* [Old T'ang code with commentary] (Ssu-pu ts'ung-k'an san-pien ed.), 12.13a; Niida, *Tōryō shūi*, p. 686. Twitchett, in *Financial Administration*, p. 146, translated Niida's reconstruction of material on imperial relatives and officials as follows: "All members of the imperial clan who are registered with the Department of Imperial Genealogy, and all kindred of the fifth degree or closer or the empress, empress dowager, or grand empress dowagers, kindred of consorts of the first rank and above, kindred of all civil and military serving officials of the third rank and above, the kindred of those of great merit living in common, and the kin living in common with dukes of states (*kuo-kung*), shall be exempt from tax and labour service." A considerable part of Niida's reconstruction is acceptable, and in my own reconstruction of the T'ang rules. I have largely followed his version. The changes I have

Unfortunately for the T'ang the systems on which these privileges rested were far from stable. When the dynasty was founded, social practice already diverged from the assumption which underlay the
land redistribution system: that land was not alienable by its holders.
Land was being bought, sold, and mortgaged in an economy fast recovering from the depression of post-Han times. The growing gulf between the reality of private landownership and the theory of govern-
ment-controlled land tenure was particularly critical in an agrarian
state where the military and fiscal systems were so closely tied to the
land system. By the early eighth century the disparity had become
obvious, and some piecemeal attempts were made to reform parts of
the total arrangement, but it was not until the rebellion of An Lu-shan
that the state leaders at last began to grope towards a thorough and
fundamental reorganization.

One of the changes which followed the rebellion is central to our
concerns – the reform of land taxation and corvee finally embodied in
the Twice-a-Year tax system of Yang Yen. Prior to the eighth century
there had been taxes which fell on most T'ang landholders, irrespective
of their land-tax privileges. Now, under the financial burdens of the
war, the state moved to extend and broaden such levies. In 769 cer-

---

made are shown in italics. "All members of the imperial clan registered with the Department of Imperial Genealogy, and all kindred of the fifth degree or closer of the empress, empress dowager, or grand empress dowagers, first degree kindred of consorts of
the first degree or above, *grandfathers, fathers, or brothers of concubines of the fifth
degree or above,* relatives of civil and military serving officials of the third rank and
above, first mourning degree relatives of princes of commanderies [Twitchett deletes
this phrase in his translation], *relatives of the* ta-kung *degree of mourning who are living
in the same household with princes of commanderies,* relatives living in the same household with dukes of states, and *fathers and brothers of barons of districts (hsien-nan)* are
all exempt from taxes and labor services." My emendations of the passage are based on
the *TFSL* 48 (p. 450), the *WHTK* 13.142a (where the words *chün-wang* seem to me to
have been misplaced), and on the *Ku T'ang-lü shu-i* 12.13a.

   In 713 it was stated that: "All officials of the sixth rank and below, both in the capital
and in the provinces, and all those holding official posts of various sorts in the offices at
the capital are entitled to exemption for taxation and corvee." *Tse-fu yüan-kuei* [Un-
failing guidelines for the conduct of government] (Li Ssu-ching ed., 1642), 474.13b. The
translation is taken from Twitchett, *Financial Administration,* p. 146. And, also from the
reign of Hsüan-tsung, "all those who receive office according to the statutes should be
exempted from taxes and labor services." *Ryō-no-shūge* [Collected laws with commen-
taries] (Tokyo: Zotei Kokushi taikei edition, 1953), 13 (p. 407). Translation from
Twitchett, *Financial Administration,* p. 146. This exemption even extended to those who
had been struck off the registers of officials, and had not yet been reinstated (as they were
entitled to be after a lapse of six years, albeit at a low rank). *Ku T'ang-lü shu-i* 3.5a;
Twitchett, *Financial Administration,* p. 146. For this process of reinstatement see *Ku
T'ang-lü shu-i* 3.5a-b. For relatives of officials, and non-bureaucrats see *Ku T'ang-lü
shu-i* 12.13a; Twitchett, *Financial Administration,* p. 146; Niida Noboru, *Tōryō shūi,*
[Collected T'ang laws] (Tokyo: 1933), p. 686. (It seems obvious that the character *jo*
at the end of the phrase in Niida is an error for *ch'in.*) Minor functionaries, on being released from service, were supposed to divide a year's exemption with their replacements
on a pro rata basis. *Ryō-no-shūge* 13 (p. 407); Twitchett, *Financial Administration,*
pp. 144–45, 149–50.

tain new taxes were laid against regular officials as individuals. The households of officials were also tapped, albeit at an extremely low rate.* These precedents and others were drawn on by Yang Yen and his colleagues when, in 780, they introduced their new tax system. Under it corvee was in theory commuted to a money payment, and agricultural taxes (collected twice a year) were levied on land rather than on individuals. Most significantly for our purpose they were levied against many previously privileged groups.

In his memorial suggesting the reform, Yang Yen pointed out that the exemption granted previously to officials and monks had been a source of abuses, which implied his desire that such groups lose their exemptions in the future.[7] Under the reform plan taxes were supposed to be equitably assessed according to the land in use as reflected in the green sprouts (*ch'ing-miao*) registers. According to the taxation statutes "every household from those of princes and dukes downwards should annually draw up a separate 'green sprouts register' in accordance with the total average under crops of lands allocated to them [under the land redistribution system] and borrowed wasteland, etc."[8] The implication would seem to be that all were to pay taxes, an implication strongly supported by a document from 852 preserved in the *T'ang hui-yao* which records official disapproval of an attempt on the part of the emperor to grant tax-free status to two estates that he had given to his maternal uncle. Even the properties of the imperial household were now subject to taxation.†

The Twice-a-Year system, which remained the basis of Chinese land taxation until the Single Whip reforms of the Ming period, was the first major step in the reduction of fiscal privileges. As such

---

* *THY* 83 (pp. 1534–35). See Twitchett, *Financial Administration*, p. 262. Here, as elsewhere in this paper, I am forced to assume that the statutes enacted were enforced in practice. Of course it is clear that such enforcement was never perfect. Illegal ways might be found to evade at least a part of the burdens. Unfortunately at the present state of our knowledge it is simply not possible to assess the degree to which such evasion was practiced.

† *THY* 84 (p. 1544). Possibly this discussion refers specifically to policies characteristic of the reign of Hsüan-tsung, and not to conditions prior to his accession in 846, since the officials refer to a number of recent moves on the part of the emperor having as their aim making the treatment of all more equitable. For the imperial household see Twitchett, *Financial Administration*, p. 20. Hino stresses this equalizing aspect of the reform without, however, dealing clearly with the role of privileged groups. See Hino Kaisaburo, "Yō En no Ryōzeiho no genkyo gensoku to sensu, senno gensoku" [The Principles of Payment at the residential place and of payment in copper coins in the *liang-shui* tax system proposed by Yang Yen], *Shien* (Kyushu), 84 (1961). Other secondary works, such as Chü Ch'ing-yüan, *T'ang-tai ching-chi shih* [T'ang economic history] (Shanghai: 1936) are equally reticent on this point.

it was by no means thorough or uniform. There is a considerable body of evidence that the burden of taxes was shared more equitably by various groups. Certainly this is the direction in which the reform pointed. But there is also evidence that some of the previously privileged groups managed to hang on to some of their privileges. A decree of 819 seems to imply that active incumbent bureaucrats could avoid taxes, and the Act of Grace of 845 indicates that the holding of any office carried with it the right to pay much reduced taxes.*

Early in the Sung dynasty the government began an effort to collect land taxes from officials' estates. In 962 local administrations were ordered to compile tax quota documents annually for active civil and military officials.[9] Their ability to evade taxes prompted the state to inaugurate the Equitable Tax System (chün-shui fa) in the capital area in the early years of the eleventh century. It was soon abandoned as a general state policy but through piecemeal prefecture-by-prefecture adoption it came to be generally enforced (at least in theory) by the beginning of the reign of Jen-tsung in 1022.[10] The liability of officials' estates was reconfirmed under Shen-tsung, with the beginning of the Square Fields Equitable Tax System, and was maintained under the Southern Sung.†

The Twice-a-Year reform would seem to have meant the extension of regular land taxes to the estates of the nobility and the imperial clan during the late T'ang. Although the situation of these groups in the Northern Sung is a little difficult to trace, they probably shared the privileges and liabilities of the official group, since official titles were granted to mourning degree relatives in the patrilineages (tsu) of the Grand Empress Dowagers, the Empress Dowager, and the Empress. Such honors were awarded directly to their male blood relatives, and to the husbands, sons, and grandsons of female blood rela-

---

* *THY* 83 (p. 1539); *Ts'e-fu yüan-kuei* 429.7a-b, 488.7a; Twitchett, *Financial Administration*, p. 268. A decree from 821 suggests that at least prior to that year men subordinate to the various armies, commissioners, or offices had been escaping taxes, and a report from 825 indicates that in some cases a man subordinate to the armies in the capital region could not only evade labor services himself, but could also shelter his father, his sons, and his brothers. *Tse-fu yüan-kuei* 488.8a, 9a. Presumably these statements refer to military officers, and central and local civil officials. The passages imply that these evasions were extra-legal, and therefore they are not of central interest to the purposes of this paper.

† According to Sudō the intent of the Square Fields reform was eventually subverted, though the principle remained unchallenged. Sudō, *Chūgoku tochi shi kenkyū*, pp. 432, 433, 502. For the Southern Sung see *SHY*, shih-huo 61.17a-b. *HNYL* 78 (p. 1277) indicates that for most tax collection purposes *kuan-hu* were treated like *min-hu* from 1134 on. See Sudō, *Chūgoku tochi shi kenkyū*, p. 240.

tives.* In general in the Northern and Southern Sung, imperial relatives seem to have been liable for land taxes, just as other groups classified as official households (*kuan-hu*) were.†

The clergy, specifically attacked by Yang Yen in 780, appears to have retained privileges in practice that they did not hold in theory. We know that during the debates surrounding the great persecution of the 840s the clergy were indicted as parasites because they did not pay taxes. And yet the legal character of their privileges is problematic. It would seem that monasteries were liable for taxes on their estates, although they frequently were able to secure special exemptions. Since the fields the clergy owned as individuals were supposedly held for them by the monastery to which they were attached, it seems probable that these lands were subject to taxation under the 780 rules. Furthermore, during an era when the hold of Buddhism on the minds of the ruling elite was steadily weakening, it seems extremely improbable that a government which was taxing imperial clansmen, the nobility, and the officials would continue to exempt the lands of monks and nuns. By the Southern Sung their land tax liability had been clearly established.‡

In the 780 reforms, it seems that only the disadvantaged households maintained their privileges as before. In the directive of the 2nd/ 780 it was stated that "Widowers, widows, orphans, and childless per-

---

* *SS* 159. 4b-5a. The titles awarded were quite low, from the civil service grade of 8-b down, so the privileges may have been rather limited. Male blood members of the imperial clan were granted nominal offices while still children. Yang Chung-liang, comp., *Hsü tzu-chih t'ung-chien ch'ang-pien chi-shih pen-mo* [The rough draft of the continuation of the comprehensive minor for aid in government rearranged in *chi-shih pen-mo* format] (Taipei: Wen Hai Publishing Co., 1967), 35.4a.

† We do learn of individual instances of imperial relatives avoiding both taxes and labor services, but the privileges involved seem to have been irregularly granted. *HCP* 111.1b (for the year 1032). In the Southern Sung the liability of such people for all levies other than labor service was explicitly stated. *TFSL*, p. 450.

‡ Niida and Twitchett feel the monasteries were liable except where specifically exempted. Twitchett, *Financial Administration*, p. 20. The exemption of individual members of the clergy from head taxes dates from the Three Kingdoms period, and despite the apparent imposition of a levy on the clergy by the Chou, (550−581) the general principle of exemption was maintained. See Jacques Gernet, *Les Aspects Économiques du Bouddhisme* (Saigon: Ecole française d'extrême-orient, 1956), p. 25ff. This was true despite repeated appeals by anti-clerical officials for the extending of fiscal burdens to the members of religious orders. See, for instance, the request of P'eng Yen in 779 (*THY* 47, pp. 837−38). That P'eng Yen's proposals were without issue despite the concurrence of the emperor is made clear in the memorial of Yang Yen in 780 which clearly reveals the privileged position of the clergy, and by the documents from the period of the Hui-ch'ang suppression which indicate that the desire to increase the number of households liable to the Twice-a-Year tax was one consideration in the minds of policymakers. *THY* 47 (pp. 840−41). For the Southern Sung see *TFSL*, p. 447. The properties of the clergy themselves, and the properties of the so-called merit cloisters and other memorial institutions were declared fully liable for all land taxes and surcharges.

sons who are not supported or assisted shall be exempted in accordance with the established system."[11] To this list should be added the impoverished, the aged, and the young.[12] During the Sung, however,
even these disadvantaged groups began to lose their land tax privileges. We know that, at least under the Southern Sung, households
headed by women, households with only a single adult male, and
households where an adult male was caring for overage and infirm
parents were all subject to regular land taxes.* It seems probable
that the same situation held for the other disadvantaged groups, including the elderly, the underage, the ill, and the disabled.†

Thus by the Southern Sung none of the major groups exempt from
land taxes during the early T'ang retained their privileges. The loss
of administrative labor service exemptions began somewhat later, but
by the late Southern Sung the number of groups not liable for requisition had been greatly reduced, and the qualifications for registration
in the remaining privileged categories had been made more strict. In
the early T'ang all of the groups exempt from land taxes were also
exempt from call for village officer duties. The Twice-a-Year reform
seems not to have affected these privileges, which remained for the
most part unchanged until the reforms of Wang An-shih, although some
attacks were staged in the early part of the Northern Sung. We are
told that some types of disadvantaged households, including the old,
the young, the ill, and the disabled were made liable for service requisition in early Sung, but were permitted to hire substitutes to do the
actual work.[13] Officials' privileges were also reduced. At times official households might be called on to fill one of the village officer posts,
that of Elder (ch'i-chang),[14] and in 1022 the state moved to limit the
size of estates officials and clerks could own free from administrative
service obligations. The permitted quotas of obligation-free land varied
with rank, but land owned beyond the quota was subject to taxation
as if it belonged to commoners. This policy was soon abandoned in
practice, but was revived in the late Northern Sung and continued
under the Southern Sung.[15]

---

* *TFSL* 48 (p. 447) says "The various widow household heads living alone whose
households are in the third rank or higher, even if they have sons (who are less than
fifteen years old) should be exempt from one-half of the transportation surtax on their
land taxes. As for all the extra levies they should be treated as households one grade
lower than their actual grade. Households from the fourth grade and down should be
wholly exempt [from these surtaxes]." This passage clearly implies that such households
paid regular land taxes. For *tan-ting hu* see *TFSL* 48 (p. 447). For *shih-ting* see *SHY*,
shih-huo 14.27b. Unfortunately, except for *Sung hsing t'ung* 3.6a, I have no evidence
on the treatment of *shih-ting* in the Northern Sung.

† The other disadvantaged groups were less privileged than were households headed
by women as regards labor services. Therefore it seems probable that they were no more
privileged in terms of land taxes.

In the late 1060s the newly enthroned Emperor Shen-tsung, by choosing Wang An-shih as his chief minister, indicated his deep concern for the state of his empire, and his willingness to support radical attempts at reform. One consequence of the changes introduced by Wang and his followers was a wider distribution of liability for the costs of village service burdens. Under his Hired Service System, inaugurated on a national scale in 1071, government funds were used to hire professional yamen personnel, and for a brief period between 1071 and 1074 village officers were also paid. The needed funds were raised by forcing the previously liable population groups to pay a commutation tax, and by taxing other previously privileged groups. Households headed by Buddhist and Taoist clergy, households headed by a woman (*nü-hu*), households with only a single adult male (*tan-ting-hu*), and official households all had to pay a tax called Aid Money (*chu-i ch'ien*).[16]

Under the Southern Sung the residual privileges of many of these groups were even more sharply reduced, or eliminated altogether. Households headed by Buddhist and Taoist clergy lost all of their privileges, no doubt partly in response to the problems created for the state by the widespread sale of monk certificates (*tu-tieh*). These documents, which certified the clerical status of their holders and carried attendant privileges, were sold by the government to raise revenue. Consequently many "clergy" were merely commoners seeking to evade fiscal obligations, especially the onerous adminstrative labor service requisitions. In 1135 the government moved to close this loophole by making households headed by Buddhist or Taoist monks liable for services on the same terms as commoner households, but permitting them to hire substitutes.* This "privilege" of being allowed

---

* For the sale of monk certificates see Kenneth Ch'en, "The Sale of Monk Certificates," *Harvard Theological Review*, 49, No. 4 (Oct. 1956), pp. 307–27; Yüan Chen, "Liang Sung tu-tieh k'ao" [A study of monk certificates of the two Sung periods], *Chung-kuo she-hui ching-chi shih chi-k'an*, 7, No. 1 (June 1944), pp. 41–70. The Tunhuang documents cite cases of such men heading households. For married Buddhist clergy see Gernet, *Les Aspects*, p. 47, 129, and 248. In some cases these men seem to have been true clergy, albeit married, and not just commoners seeking tax exemptions. The Taoist priesthood had never required strict celibacy. To help in separating real clergy from nominal clergy the Sung also ruled that only monks with shaved heads were to receive any exemptions. *SS* 177.1b. For the Southern Sung rulings see *SHY, shih-huo* 14.24b (for the year 1135), 14.31a (for the year 1149); *SS* 34.12a (for the year 1171); *SHY, shih-huo* 65.101b (for the year 1173); *HNYL* 88 (p. 1472).

Although the problem of the nominal clergy was one factor in the reduction of the privileges of Buddhist and Taoist monks, it was not the only one, for in the middle of the twelfth century a graduated head tax was levied on the regular clergy. The decree involved is dated the first month of 1145. *HNYL* 153 (p. 2463); *SS* 30.8a; Chih P'an, *Fo tsu t'ung chi* [Continuing Memoirs of Buddha and the Patriarchs] (Tokyo tripitaka), 47.452c–453a; *CYTC, chia* 15.13a. See also Sogabe, *Sō-dai zaisei-shi*, p. 421. On the general liability of Buddhist and Taoist properties for land and other taxes see *TFSL* 48 (pp. 447, 454); *SS* 34.12a. Of course many temple properties were exempted by special decrees. See *CYTC* 15.13a.

to hire substitutes became less and less of a privilege as the decades passed, for it was progressively extended to many other groups. By the end of the twelfth century anyone called for labor service could hire a replacement.*

The privileges of certain categories of disadvantaged households also were reduced or eliminated. In 1135 the state began to strip away the remaining privileges of households with only a single adult male. It was ordered that rich *tan-ting-hu* might be asked to provide village officers as long as not more than one such household was called in each superior guard (*tu-pao*) in a year. They were allowed to hire substitutes. There are a number of later suggestions for increasing the liability of such households culminating in a ruling of 1172 under which *tan-ting-hu* were to be treated like commoners in assessing administrative labor services.†

The number of households headed by women who could claim exemption was reduced by defining more closely the qualifications for privilege. In 1135 it was ruled that households headed by women whose adult age sons were Buddhist or Taoist monks were to be liable for requisition, as long as not more than one such household was called in a superior guard in one year. There were other calls for reduction of the privileges of *nü-hu*, and in 1168 rich widows who remarried and rich women who were caring for aged or infirm parents-in-law were made liable on the same terms as widows with adult sons in the clergy. Despite these rulings the bulk of households headed by women (like households headed by minors) remained legally exempt from labor service call.‡

---

* *SHY, shih-huo* 14.24b, 26b−27a, 27a, 29b, 30b, 31a, 66.26a. The labor services for which these households could hire substitutes must not be confused with corvee (*yao-i*). During the Sung corvee was for the most part performed by members of the provincial armies (*hsiang-ping*), although at times fifth grade households were called for such duties. Sun Yü-t'ang, "Kuan-yü Pei Sung fu-i chih-tu te fan ke wen-t'i" [On the question of labor service systems in the Northern Sung], *Li Shih Yen Chiu*, No. 2 (1964); Sogabe Shizuo, *Sōdai zaisei shi* [Sung Dynasty fiscal history] (Tokyo: Chūgoku gaku-jutsu kenkyū-sōsho, 1941), p. 90; *HNYL* 162 (p. 2649); *SHY, shih-huo* 14.44b−45a. Labor services, as the term is used here, correspond rather to *chih-i*, that is, they were administrative labors rather than actual physical labor.

† *SHY, shih-huo* 14.24b; *HNYL* 88 (p. 1472), 109 (p. 1772); *SHY, shih-huo* 14.26a-b, 27a, 29b, 46b. They could hire replacements. A *tu-pao* was an administrative unit theoretically numbering 250 households.

‡ *SHY, shih-huo* 14.26b−27a, 31a, 30b, 43a, 65.101b−102a, 66.22a; *HNYL* 88 (p. 1472), 109 (p. 1772); 160 (p. 2592). Despite their legal claim to exemption *nü-hu* seem to have been called on by local officials rather frequently. In 1149 it was reported that local officials in some cases did not even bother to ascertain whether the sons of female household heads were alive or not. The memorialist also said that women who had no sons or whose sons were minors were being called on to provide services. He asked that all *nü-hu* be fully exempt. *SHY shih-huo* 14.30b; *HNYL* 160 (p. 2592). His request was denied. *SS* 30.14b; *HNYL* 160 (p. 2592). In 1180 it was again reported that *nü-hu* were being drafted, and in response their privilege of exemption was again re-affirmed. *SHY, shih-huo* 66.22a.

In their retention of privileges, households headed by women re-sembled households related to the royal family by blood or marriage. Although such households were legally liable for land taxes in the Sung they seem to have held on to their exemption from service liability. The categories of relatives involved were basically the same as those cited in the T'ang. However, there were certain reductions in the privi-leges of some relatives.*

The rules for granting privileges to the conspicuously filial were also far less generous in the Southern Sung than in the T'ang. Accord-ing to a ruling of 1138, if the son of a rich family remained at home to care for aged or infirm parents his family was to be classified with households of rich widows whose adult age sons were Buddhist or Taoist clergy. Thus the exemption of such men (*shih-ting*) from ser-vice liabilities was not total. Nor were they exempt from land taxes. We do know of individual instances of the granting of full exemption from service liability to paragons of filial piety, but these seem to have been irregular and unusual privileges.†

The data on the privileges given the families of students in Sung times require some interpretation. I have not yet uncovered any clear statements of exemption for the early Sung period.‡ The question then hinges on the background of such students. According to statutes issued early in the dynasty the students at the school for the Sons of the State (*kuo-tzu chien*) were to be sons and grandsons of capital officials of the seventh rank or higher, and students at the Grand Uni-versity (*T'ai-hsüeh*) were in large part relatives of officials of the eighth

---

* The major change concerned concubines of deceased emperors (*huang t'ai-fei*) all of whose mourning degree relatives were exempt, as were certain relatives of the concubines of the heir apparent. *TFSL* 48 (pp. 456–57). Relatives of the *ta-kung* or higher degree of mourning of the concubines (*fei*) of the heir apparent were exempt. For further information on the benefits to be derived from marrying members of the imperial clan in the Sung, see Chu Yü, *P'ing chou k'o-t'an* [Wandering Islands miscellany] (Ts'ung-shu chi-ch'eng edition), 1 (p. 3–4); Chang Pang-chi, *Mo chuang man-lu* [Des-ultory notes from the literary manor] (Ts'ung-shu chi-ch'eng edition), 10 (p. 107); Ch'ao pu-chih, *Chi chu chi* [Collected writings of Chao Pu-chih] (Ssu-pu ts'ung-k'an edition), 62.6a–14b. According to *SHY, shih-huo* 14.27b–28a (date 1138) men married to impe-rial clanswomen, if they did not hold titular court rank, were liable for labor service requisition, but could hire substitutes.

† *SHY, shih-huo* 14.27b. During the T'ang *shih-ting* had been free from services though liable for land taxes. Twitchett, *Financial Administration*, p. 146. This T'ang policy is reiterated in *Sung hsing t'ung* 3.6a. Unfortunately I have found no data beyond this very early Sung date to describe their position in the later Northern Sung. For in-stances of complete exemption see Cheng Yao and Fang Jen-yung, *Ching-ting Yen-chou hsü-chih* [A continuation of the gazetteer of Yen Prefecture from the Ching-ting period] (Ts'ung-shu chi ch'eng edition), 5 (p. 65).

‡ There is one document from 1072 which appears to indicate that certain categories of examination candidates were freed from corvee labor if not necessarily from village services. See Ch'iu Han-p'ing, *Li-tai hsing-fa chih* [The treatises on law and punishments from the various dynasties] (Changsha: Shang-wu yin-shu kuan, 1938), p. 396.

rank or lower.[17] The families of most such students would therefore
have been classified as *kuan-hu* and exempt for that reason, irrespective of their sons' student status. However, with the gradual opening of the schools to commoner students, particularly after the educational reforms under Hui-tsung, a clarification of policy was necessary,
and exemption from service liability was specifically granted to some
categories of government students.[18]

In 1133 labor service exemption was extended to cover some
categories of *chin-shih* candidates, and in 1145 this privilege was extended to students in the imperial academy. But in 1149, as a result
of a dispute over these rules, the circle of the privileged was narrowed.
The households of students in the imperial academy and certified provincial graduates were not to be freed from service liability unless
they had attempted the departmental examinations (*sheng-shih*) and
were the only adult males in their households.*

The Southern Sung also witnessed attempts to reduce further the
service exemption privileges of at least some official households. The
system of 1022, limiting the amount of land that could be held free from
liability, was revived in the Cheng-ho period (1111 – 1118). Under the
rules then set down (which continued in use under the early Southern
Sung) a first grade official could own one hundred *ch'ing* (1,330 acres)
free from service burdens, a second degree official, ninety *ch'ing,* and so
on down to a ninth grade official who could own ten *ch'ing* (133 acres)
free from liabilities.[19] During the twelfth century these limits were
sharply curtailed. In 1180 all quotas were cut by 30 percent, and at
some time between 1180 and 1200 all the Cheng-ho quotas were reduced by 50 percent.† During this same era the state moved to strength-
en the bond between these reduced residual privileges and actual
active and substantive officeholding, by decreasing the benefits
of those who derived their *kuan-hu* status from irregular or inactive
officials, or through inheritance.

In 1159, responding to complaints about the lax enforcement of

---

* Candidates who were certified because they had passed the local examinations
(*te-chieh chü-jen*) and those men who, having failed in the metropolitan examinations,
were being permitted to retake them without having to repeat local tests (*ying mien
chieh-jen*) were exempt from labor services in 1133. *HNYL* 64 (p. 1091); *SHY, shih-huo*
14.27a. See also *HNYL* 160 (p. 2592). For the 1149 restrictions see *SHY, shih-huo*
14.30a – 31a.

† *SHY, shih-huo* 6.7a-b. This 1180 cut did not affect the quotas of descendants of
officials, as long as these men continued to live in the same household. By the close of
the twelfth century a first grade offiicial could own only fifty *ch'ing,* and second grade
officials forty-five *ch'ing,* and so on down to a ninth grade official who could own only
five *ch'ing. TFSL* 48 (p. 454). At least from 1160, mountainous lands, bamboo lands,
woods, dikes, etc. were not counted in the quota. *SHY, shih-huo* 6.4a, 61.79a.

the liability-free land system the authorities ruled that heirs to *kuan-hu* status would have a quota half that of their ancestors. Furthermore, if the quota was based on a living active official his current rank would be used, but if *kuan-hu* status was derived from an official no longer active or was derived from posthumous office, the quota was to be halved.* Two years later an official pointed out that under the 1159 rules if an official had sons who split their dwellings after their father's death, these men could own in total more land than had been in their father's quota. He asked that the descendants be permitted in toto only half their ancestors' quota. Although his advice was not followed immediately, such a ruling was handed down in 1168.[20]

During these same decades the privileges of descendants of men granted nominal or irregular *kuan-hu* status were eliminated. In 1159 descendants of certain men who had been irregularly or provisionally appointed to substantive offices were made liable.[21] In 1166 it was ruled that officials could not pass their status on to their heirs, indeed their own privileges were being progressively reduced.† A few years later, in 1172, it was ruled that no one could claim privileges on the basis of descent from someone with posthumously granted official rank. Finally it would seem that descendants of regular substantive officials of the ninth rank were not privileged during at least part of the twelfth century.‡

---

* If a living father or grandfather of low rank was dwelling with a descendant of higher rank, the descendant's rank determined the quota.

† *TFSL* 48 (p. 455). In the first decades of the Southern Sung it had been possible for the rich, by contributing grain in times of emergency to secure offices that could be used to claim *kuan-hu* status. Li Chao-ch'i, *Yüeh ching chi* [Collected writings of Li Chao-ch'i] (Ssu-k'u ch'üan-shu chen-pen ed.), 29.5b–9a; Feng Shih-hsing, *Chin yüan wen-chi* [Collected writings of Feng Shih-hsing] (Ssu-k'u ch'üan-shu chen-pen ed.), 4.2b–3b; *HNYL* 96 (p. 1584), 78 (p. 1275), 77 (p. 1270). Rich men might also purchase registration in the army, or through favoritism secure registration as supplementary officials and thus evade labor services. *SHY, shih-huo* 6.1b–2b, 61.78b. In the beginning such people could use the *yin* privilege to pass their immunity on for two generations. *HNYL* 77 (p. 1270). In 1134 it was ordered that men who had gained office as irregular military officers of the sixth rank or lower through contribution were to be given exemption from service liability on five *ch'ing* of land. If they owned more than five *ch'ing* they were liable on the excess. *SHY, shih-huo* 14.22a; *HNYL* 78 (p. 1275). In 1149 it was ruled that men who were officials through contribution but were not of titular court rank were liable for services but could hire substitutes. *SHY, shih-huo* 14.31a.

‡ There were some complaints about this policy toward the descendants of men granted posthumous rank. It was contended that officials with posthumous ranks were of two sorts, those who had in life been active substantive officials and were posthumously given a new rank, and those with only posthumous rank. Eventually this problem was dealt with by having descendants of the former group of officials claim their quotas on the basis of the *yin* privilege derived from their ancestor's substantive office, without taking the posthumous rank into account. Since the posthumous rank was presumably higher, this had the effect of reducing the quota in question. Descendants of the latter group lost all privileges. *SHY, shih-huo* 6.5b, 7b, 8b–9a, 61.80b; *WHTK* 13.138c; *TFSL* 48 (pp. 455–56). Privileges were explicitly granted descendants of ninth grade officials by an order dated 1199. *SHY, shih-huo* 6.9a-b.

Certain other categories of irregular or low ranking officials had their privileges reduced or eliminated in these years. In 1138 it was decreed that *pao-chia* officers who had been granted *kuan-hu* status because they had gained merit in military actions or in bandit suppression were liable for services unless they were of court rank. *Pao-chia* officers with *kuan-hu* status, but without such merit, were liable unless they had reached the rank of *tai-fu* or above. In 1186 it was decreed that certain categories of supplementary officials (*fei-fan pu-kuan*) and candidates for positions (*ch'i-se pu-kuan*), even if they were of high rank, were not privileged unless they held substantive posts at court.[22] In addition there are a few scattered pieces of evidence indicating that *kuan-hu* did at times provide men to act as village officers, or to oversee tax collection.*

One final attack on official privileges should be mentioned: Chia Ssu-tao's famous compulsory land purchase policy. In the spring of 1263 some low-ranking officials presented a fiscal reform plan. Among its provisions was a scheme for buying up land owned by officials beyond certain quotas which varied with rank. This system has been succinctly summarized by Herbert Franke:

A certain limit was to be set on the size of landed properties, graduated according to the rank held by the owner. One-third of the land exceeding the limit was to be bought up by the state and converted into public fields, the income from which would meet the requirements of the army. At first this plan applied only to landowning officials, but it was soon extended to cover private landowners as well. The maximum area exempted from obligatory cession was 500 *mou*. The purchase price was paid by the state not only in money but also in rank patents and tax remission certificates. The greater the amount of land offered for sale the more attractive the means of payment was made. A landowner who sold more than 5,000 *mou* was paid for his land in the following way: 50 percent in rank patents, 20 percent in tax remission certificates, 5 percent in silver, and 25 percent in paper bills. The price for sales of land between 300 and 500 *mou* was paid entirely in paper money. A list giving the value of various ranks was drawn up (wives of landowners could also obtain court ranks). The tax remission certificates (*tu-tieh,* originally certificates or ordination for the clergy) also had their fixed prices.†

---

* Chu Hsi cites the case of Chiang Fei who, in the middle of the twelfth century, had to serve as a Superior Guard Leader (*tu-pao cheng*). Li Ching-te, comp., *Chu-tzu yü-lei* [Sayings of Chu Hsi] (woodblock, 1872), 98.24b – 25a. Hu T'ai-ch'u, *Chou lien hsü lun* [Continuing discussions on government administration] (Ts'ung-shu chi-ch'eng ed.), p. 12 indicates that such families sometimes oversaw tax collection. His description would presumable apply to the mid-thirteenth century.

† Herbert Franke, "Chia Ssu-tao (1213 – 1275): A 'Bad Last Minister'?" in Arthur Wright and Denis Twitchett, ed., *Confucian Personalities* (Stanford: Stanford University Press, 1962), pp. 229 – 230. See also Herbert Franke, "Die Agrarreformen des Chia Ssu-tao," *Saeculum,* 9 (1958), pp. 345 – 69. Sudō, *Chūgoku Tochi,* pp. 537 – 602

This policy was bitterly resented by the large landlords, officials and commoners, who moved to abrogate it at the earliest opportunity. In a real sense it marked the furthest advance of the attack on fiscal privileges.*

Perhaps it would be best to summarize the material presented in Table 4.1, with a preliminary caveat for the unavoidable minor inaccuracies introduced by simplification.

The general trend of these changes is clear. In assigning costs and responsibilities the state tended more and more to treat the various categories of rural households as a homogeneous continuum except in terms of wealth, and to reduce or eliminate the special privileges previously accorded to certain of these categories. This transformation had not begun at the mid-eighth century, but was virtually complete by the beginning of the thirteenth. Those affected included officials, clergy, students, the disadvantaged, imperial relatives, and certain other limited groups.

But although the trend itself is quite obvious, the problem of explaining its causes and outlining its implications is much more complicated. The character of the change as a whole can perhaps best be illuminated by focusing on two contemporaneous and related developments: the rise and spread of a money economy, and the progressive replacement of the "aristocracy" in the ruling class by a new literati elite drawn in substantial part from southeastern China.

The spread of a money economy into the countryside was a necessary if not sufficient condition for the withdrawal of labor service exemptions from certain groups. During the early T'ang the means

---

provides the most detailed recent description of this reform. In this article Sudō points out that the policy of buying land from the people for use in paying army expenses already had a precedent in the policies suggested by Yeh Shih during the Chia-ting period (1208 – 1224).

In the light of the evidence just reviewed on the stripping of the clergy of their fiscal privileges it does not seem that *tu-tieh* can have been tax exemption certificates at this time. But if they were not, what were they? I initially conjectured that during the Southern Sung *tu-tieh* were paper monetary instruments. Even if not paper money in the strict sense, they still embodied a number of the functions of money. However, as Professor Franke pointed out, this monetary interpretation is weakened by the degree of control apparently exercised by the state over the sale and repurchase of these certificates. Possibly the certificates were valued because they permitted their holders to commute certain petty crimes.

* In this regard I would like to suggest a modification of the old suggestion that the rise of land tax rates contributed to the fall of dynasties. It was not simply the rise in rates but the redistribution of burdens that weakened the dynasties. In a number of dynasties (T'ang, Sung, and Ming, for example) the fiscal problems that had arisen by the middle of the dynasty provoked the authorities to attack fiscal privileges and thus the interests of the rich. These attacks in turn, by weakening the commitment of these men to the state, weakened the state itself.

TABLE 4.1
Land Tax and Labor Service Requirements.

Group	T'ang Dynasty 618–780		T'ang Dynasty 780–907		Sung Dynasty (ca. 1200)	
	land tax	labor service	land tax	labor service	land tax	labor service
officials	E*	E	L*	E	L	liable on all land in excess of a fixed quota
Buddhist and Taoist clergy	E	E	L(?)	E	L	L
imperial relatives	E	E	L(?)	E	L	E
students at the imperial schools	E	E	E	E	L	limited numbers exempt under certain conditions
filial and virtuous	E	E	E(?)	E	L	limited numbers exempt
widows, widowers, orphans, the childless, the aged, the impoverished, and the young	E	E	E(?)	E	L	mostly liable

* E = exempt; L = liable.

of exchange were relatively scarce, and were confined largely to cities. A rural household called on to bear the burden of administrative labor services could hardly avoid sending a household member to perform the work in person. Had the liability for administrative labor services fallen on all rural families the economic burden on certain types of disadvantaged households – those headed by women, the young, the elderly, the disabled, and those with only a single adult male – would have been crushing. Later, in the eighth and ninth centuries, the Chinese economy began to develop with unprecedented rapidity. From a society within which barter had dominated rural exchange China was transformed by the middle of the Sung into a society within which money circulated into all regions and among all levels of people. It then became possible for those drafted to hire professional substitutes. Thus what had previously been an onerous or demeaning burden of personal service became a more tolerable assessment of money.

It is more difficult to connect monetary developments with these groups' loss of tax exemptions (as opposed to labor service privileges). I would suggest that tax exemptions were reduced as one facet of the change of aim reflected in the Twice-a-Year reform. Since, with the final abandonment of the *chün-t'ien* land redistribution system the state no longer even nominally tried to limit the size of landholdings, it could no longer be presumed that "disadvantaged" households were in fact poor. Therefore the state moved belatedly to reduce the benefits attached to classification in these groups.* Those "disadvantaged" households that were truly poor would presumably pay low taxes because they owned little land, and would escape the labor service burdens through the exemption granted households in the lowest (fifth) grade.[23]

The rise of a money economy also contributed to the decline in the privileges of the clergy. Initially it had made possible the widespread sale of monk certificates. Purchase of a certificate became a loophole through which rich commoners escaped fiscal burdens. The state finally closed the hole by eliminating the privileges.

This encroachment of state power into the preserves of privilege was one aspect of a transformation that reached its highest development during the Southern Sung, when the state was centered more clearly on the economically highly advanced Yangtze delta and the developed south than was to be the case in later times. This also helps explain the median position of the Northern Sung, a period during which the north was still a prime factor in social and political life. Indeed we should keep in mind that it was the *Northern* Sung, a successor to the Five Dynasties of the north (907 — 960), not to the Ten Kingdoms in the south.

And yet economic developments can explain the social changes only in part. A more encompassing explanation is mirrored in, if not caused by, another transformation that occurred during this era — the circulation of elites that ended with the displacement of the older "aristocratic" ruling class by a new group of literati bureaucrats. In the earlier period China's rulers saw society as naturally divided into discrete groups defined by ascribed characteristics, most importantly by birth. Formal governmental institutions were dominated by members of the handful of great families that effectively ruled society, while in the countryside informal leadership was also in the hands of these same families, through their satellites or dependents. The beginning of the decline in the power of this elite was reflected from the mid-T'ang on in a tendency to place more emphasis on achieved characteristics in determining social status: on examination success per se or

---

*This may help explain the ambiguities in the reports on taxation after 780. The Twice-a-Year tax was in a sense the first major step in this trend against fiscal privileges, but the old aristocratic habits and attitudes lived on for some time, having until the end of the T'ang spokesmen high in government councils.

on amassed wealth. Examination success, which entailed potential access to the policy making levels of the administration, became the key determinant for membership in the highest stratum of society. Once a device for guiding the distribution of power among men who were already members of the ruling class by virtue of aristocratic background, the examination system now became a route by which increasing numbers of men from outside the circle of great families could enter the high levels of the imperial government. Eventually these newcomers dominated the state. This circulation of elites led to the ascendancy of a group of men whose ideology was more "Confucian" than that of their predecessors. This meant among other things that they tended to stress the importance of equality of opportunity, and this in turn implied an underlying commitment to freeing the social order to permit equitable competition.*

The opening up of officialdom which resulted from the increased use of the examination system as an avenue into the ruling elite changed the social composition of the bureaucracy so that the distance which separated officials from other social groups was growing smaller at the same time that some of the outside groups were becoming wealthier and more sophisticated. The new bureaucrats were increasingly drawn from the families of those who had benefited most from the commercial revolution of the T'ang and Sung, the rich merchants and the wealthy landowners. Even when substantive offices were unavailable, the nouveau-riche usually found it possible to purchase for themselves the consolation and the status of nominal official titles.

With this opening up of the bureaucracy many officials ceased to be proteges or members of families powerful in their own right. The position of the individual official vis-à-vis the emperor was greatly weakened. I would suggest that extension of liability for taxes and services is a clear indicator of this decrease in power. (Of course officials did try, with some success, to evade their burdens illegally, but the very fact that they had to resort to extra-legal measures is a clear reflection of their inability to set policy.)

---

* It is perhaps worth noting that this circulation of elites, with the contemporaneous shift in the attitudes characteristic of the ruling group from acceptance of a status system within which primary emphasis was placed on ascribed traits to a system more dependent on achieved characteristics, occurred in China at roughly the same period as the birth of "capitalistic" traits in the economy. A somewhat similar shift in attitudes is said to have been one aspect of the constellation of events usually connected with the rise of capitalism in Europe. We might also take note of the fact that the cry of "equal competition" came from men from the Southeast and other economically advanced regions, a cry rejected by the "conservatives" from the north and west.

The restructuring of power revealed by this loss of official privileges also affected, in more direct fashion, the structure of village level power in rural areas. The aristocratic system, under which village level authorities had at least the tacit approval of the locally dominant magnate (if indeed they were not his clients) was gone by the end of the T'ang. The "gentry" system of Ming and Ch'ing China, under which rural functions were divided among a number of groups, while social leadership rested with households whose status depended on having degree holders among their members, was only in the process of coming into being. Village level leadership perforce rested more than it did in any other period of the empire in the hands of the rich. Perhaps aided by the state's tendency to ignore distinctions among them other than degrees of wealth, the rich seem to have functioned, for a brief period at least, as a self-conscious group.*

This development came to an abrupt end with the Mongol conquest. The Yüan armies brought with them into the south a set of social values reminiscent of traditional T'ang China, where society was composed of groups distinguished by ascribed traits. Like its northern models and predecessors the Yüan accorded privileges to many groups, and discriminated against others. The Yüan was in this as in so many other ways a true heir of the Chin, the Liao, and the T'ang. The result of the conquest was not the "barbarization" of the South but rather a "northernization," a reinfusion of T'ang values into the south. This is not to imply that earlier Chinese social ideals necessarily influenced the Mongol leaders, only that these leaders found the earlier Chinese ideals, still current among the Chinese under Chin control, to be in general harmony with their own autochthonous attitudes. When the Yüan heritage was passed to the Ming, much of the remarkable social history of the Southern Sung was interred forever.

---

* This group consciousness is clearly reflected in the creation of the "righteous service" institutions in Southern Sung. See Brian E. McKnight, *Village and Bureaucracy in Southern Sung China* (Chicago: University of Chicago Press, 1972), pp. 157–170.

Notes to Chapter Four

1. For the estimate of the number of officials see E. A. Kracke, Jr., *Civil Service in Early Sung China* (Cambridge: Harvard University Press, 1953), p. 55. For the population figures see Kato Shigeru, *Shina keizai-shi kosho* [Studies in Chinese economic history] (Tokyo: Toyo Bunko, 1952–53), II, p. 318. For numbers of clerks see Sudō Yoshiyuki, *Sō-dai keizai-shi kenkyū* [Researches on Sung economic history] (Tokyo: Tokyo Daigaku Shuppan Kai, 1962), pp. 763–65.
2. This description is drawn from Denis Twitchett, *Financial Administration under the T'ang Dynasty,* 2nd ed. (Cambridge: Cambridge University Press, 1970), chapter one.
3. Niida Noboru, *Tōryō shūi* [Collected T'ang laws] (Tokyo: 1933), p. 617.
4. Robert des Rotours, *Traité des Fonctionnaires et Traité de l'Armée* (Leiden: E. J. Brill, 1948), p. 50ff.
5. Niida, *Tōryō shūi,* p. 617.
6. Twitchett, *Financial Administration,* p. 34.
7. *Ts'e-fu yüan-kuei* 488.2b.
8. *TLT* 3.53a-b; Twitchett, *Financial Administration,* p. 143.
9. *WHTK* 4.54a.
10. Sudō Yoshiyuki, *Chūgoku tochi shi kenkyū* [Studies on the history of Chinese land systems] (Tokyo: Toyo Bunko, 1954), p. 498.
11. Twitchett, *Financial Administration,* p. 30, 162. *THY* 83 (p. 1535).
12. *Ts'e-fu yüan-kuei* 486.20a.
13. *SHY,* shih-huo 66.22a, 14.27a.
14. Sudō Yoshiyuki, *Tōsō shakai keizai shi kenkyū* (Tokyo: Tokyo Daigaku Shuppan Kai, 1965), p. 636.
15. *SHY,* shih-huo 1.19b–20b. Maritami Katsumi, *Chung-kuo she-hui ching-chi-shih* [Chinese social and economic history], trans. Sung Huai-jen (Chung-hua Shu-chü, 1935), p. 206. For its revival under the late Northern Sung see *SHY, shih-huo* 61.78a, 6.1b.
16. *SHY, shih-huo* 66.60a-b, 13.29a; *HCP* 227.2a ff.
17. *SS* 157.1a.
18. *SS* 157.6b–7b.
19. *SHY, shih-huo* 61.78a; 6.1b.
20. *SHY, shih-huo* 6.4b, 5a, 61.78b–79a, 80a.
21. *TFSL* 48 (p. 455).
22. *SHY, shih-huo* 14.27b–28a, 32a, 66.24a; *SS* 35.18a; *TFSL* 48 (p. 456).
23. On the treatment of the different grades see Brian E. McKnight, *Village and Bureaucracy in Southern Sung China* (Chicago: University of Chicago Press, 1972), pp. 126–29.

Regional Control in the Southern Sung Salt Administration

EDMUND H. WORTHY

EVER SINCE PRE-IMPERIAL TIMES when Kuan Chung advised the Duke of Huan to establish a salt monopoly, government control of salt production and sales has been recognized as a potential source of prosperity for the state.* But it was not until the Former Han that the government salt monopoly was instituted to help alleviate the financial deficits Emperor Wu faced because of the rising cost of his military campaigns. The successful lesson of the Han was not lost on succeeding dynasties. When many later financial crises arose, often brought about by heavy military expenditures, rulers and officials instinctively looked to the salt monopoly as one convenient, more or less certain means to extract additional income for the state.

The T'ang and Sung in particular turned to salt monopoly revenue to replenish government coffers during their greatest financial and military crises. With the outbreak of the An Lu-shan rebellion in mid-T'ang, Ti-wu Ch'i (flourished mid-eighth century) and Liu Yen (715 – 780) revived the salt monopoly on a national scale, and during the two decades following 760 the revenue earned from salt became one of the main financial pillars supporting the state.† No less important

* I am indebted to Professor James T. C. Liu for critical stimulation as well as advice on various points in the preparation of this paper. Professor Lien-sheng Yang also kindly answered several technical questions. In addition to the conference participants, many others, including Professors F. W. Mote and Thomas Metzger, generously proffered suggestions on different aspects of a draft version.

† A number of studies in English are available on the T'ang salt administration. Denis Twitchett, "The Salt Commissioners after the Rebellion of An Lu-shan," *Asia Major*, NS 4, No. 1 (1954), pp. 60 – 89; Twitchett, *Financial Administration under the T'ang Dynasty* (Cambridge, England: Cambridge University Press, 1963), pp. 49 – 58; and Hino Kaisaburō, "Government Monopoly on Salt in T'ang in the Period before the Enforcement of the *Liang-shui fa*," *Memoirs of the Research Department of the Tōyō Bunko*, 22 (1963), pp. 1 – 55. Esson M. Gale and Ch'en Sung-ch'iao have translated a large number of documents from various sources pertaining to the salt administration from Han through Ch'ing times; see their "China's Salt Administration, Excerpts from Native Sources," *The Journal of Asiatic Studies* (Seoul: Korea University), 1, No. 1 (March, 1958), pp. 137 – 217; 1, No. 2 (December, 1958), pp. 193 – 216; 2, No. 1 (June, 1959), pp. 137 – 217. These translations should be used with caution as they are at times imprecise.

to the general prosperity and solvency of the Sung and, on occasion, to its very stability, were the proceeds from the salt monopoly. In the precarious early years of the Southern Sung, salt monopoly income underwrote most of the military budget. Some years later one official in a memorial of 1160 neatly summed up the situation: "Salt is a national commodity. It neither causes the people distress, nor harms the resources; rather, it is the basis for a prosperous country and a strong military."[1]

In part because of every man's biochemical needs, salt was an obvious commodity for monopolization by the state. Also, because of the relatively limited and clearly defined areas of production, salt was susceptible to bureaucratic management. The salt monopoly never was to surpass the land tax as the state's most lucrative source of income, but when diligently managed it did, throughout most of the last millennium of imperial history, rank second as a revenue producer.

Key to evaluating a monopoly is assessment of the means and effectiveness of the system of controls. Such will be the focus of the present paper. How did the three functional levels of the salt monopoly — production, distribution, and official administration — operate? What were the restrictions placed on salt workers, merchants, and officials; how effective were these regulations; where and how did they break down? How extensive were illicit salt sales (ssu-yen), and how did they affect the monopoly and Southern Sung state income? Answers to these basic questions will not only provide a descriptive analysis of the salt monopoly and its importance to the state's prosperity, but will also illuminate some of the more general problems confronting a bureaucratic managed economy.

The Chinese salt administration is intricately complex in its evolution, regional differentiations, and varying local customary practices. The three primary production areas in Ssu-ch'uan, Shan-hsi, and the six southeastern coastal circuits (lu), running in the Southern Sung from Huai-nan East to Kuang-tung West, all varied in method of production as well as in administrative and monopoly procedures.* In this paper, one small area has been selected for a case study, the administrative region known as Liang-che which roughly encompasses today's Chekiang province and that part of Kiangsu south of the Yangtze River. Liang-che was chosen for two reasons: the importance of the area to the Sung salt production and the availability of an unusually

---

* For further details consult, among other works, Lin Jui-han, "Sung-tai yen-chüeh" [The Sung dynasty salt monopoly], Ta-lu tsa-chih, 28, No. 6 (March 31, 1964), pp. 15–20.

wide range of complementary source materials for the entire Southern Sung period. In the approximately 150 years of Southern Sung rule, Liang-che ranked second in output behind Huai-nan East.

The comparative wealth of materials extant for study of the Liang-che salt administration enables scholars to probe to a depth not always possible in Sung economic history. In addition to several gazetteers, the Sung dynastic history, and the *Sung hui-yao*, two private sources in particular shed considerable light on both the operation and problems of the monopoly and on production procedures. Huang Chen (1213 – 1280)* is a comparatively obscure figure to us now, but during his day and in later times he was regarded as a noteworthy classicist and thinker and as an able local administrator. During the closing years of Li-tsung's reign (1225 – 1264) and also during the very last years of the Sung's existence, Huang served as a salt official first in the western circuit of Liang-che and then in the eastern circuit. In his collected writings (*Huang-shih jih-ch'ao fen-lei*) he has left a valuable legacy of memorials and other documents pertaining to his administration of the salt monopoly. These provide details where the official records leave off, particularly the *Sung hui-yao* whose coverage of the salt administration terminates at 1215.

By fortunate coincidence the second private source deals with a Liang-che West salt works in the very area under Huang Chen's administrative purview. The *Ao-po t'u* is a compilation of pictures, forty-seven of which remain today, each accompanied by an explanatory passage and poem, depicting the process of salt production and the life cycle of the salt workers.† Although compiled in the Yüan period – the preface is dated the third month of 1334, but the paintings were prepared a number of years earlier – this work can nevertheless serve as a source for late Sung history.

---

* For biographical information see *SS* 438.17a – 20a; also the long biography taken from *Yin-hsien chih* [The Yin county gazetteer] and included in the prefatory material to Huang's *Ku-chin chi-yao i-pien* [Record of important events from old and modern times, compiled in retirement], *Ssu-ming ts'ung-shu*, First series (Taipei: 1964 facsimile reproduction of 1932 edition). Huang's major piece of writing is *Huang-shih jih-ch'ao fen-lei* [Daily copyings of Mr. Huang organized by categories] (1767 woodblock edition).

† *APT*. Since there is no pagination in this work, all references are to the number of the illustration and its accompanying text. In a brief article Yoshida Tora introduces the *APT* and in his first footnote (p. 43) discusses the various extant editions. See "Gōha zu to Sō Gen jitai no seien gijutsu," [The *Ao-po t'u* and salt production in the Sung and Yuan periods], *Reikishi kyōiku*, 11, No. 9 (September, 1963), pp. 38 – 43.

In addition to the numerous pictures in the *APT*, three others dating from the twelfth century can be found in T'ang Shen-wei, *Ch'ung-hsiu cheng-ho ching-shih cheng-lei pei-yung pen-ts'ao* [Cheng-ho reign period herbal in readiness for emergencies, drawn from the classics and histories and verified according to category] (Peking: Jen-min wei-sheng ch'u-pan she, 1957, rpt. of Ming woodblock) 4.10a – 12b.

Modern scholarship on the Sung salt administration was greatly stimulated by the appearance in 1957 of Tai I-hsüan's monograph on salt vouchers (*yen-ch'ao*) which explores most every aspect of the salt monopoly.* Tai, however, has devoted a proportionately small segment of his work to the Southern Sung and has organized his materials more around an institutional framework than a regional approach. It has remained for Japanese scholars in the past decade, most notably Yoshida Tora and Kawakami Kōichi, to launch examinations of the various regional administrations. Chang Chia-chü was the first, thirty-five years ago, to treat the Southern Sung salt monopoly, albeit in a cursory fashion.[2] Since then Yoshida has dwelt on the topic,[3] but no scholar to date has marshalled together and fully utilized all the sources available for a full-scale analytical study.

Historical and Administrative Background

The monopoly procedures set up by Ti-wu Ch'i and Liu Yen in the mid-T'ang required salt producers to sell all their salt exclusively to a government agency which, in turn, resold it to merchants after imposing a stiff tax. This was a system known as *kuan-mai* or official sales. This system and *t'ung-shang* — merchant sales whereby the monopoly was only partial and the rights to sales were purchased by the merchants — were operated exclusively or simultaneously by most of the T'ang successor states although frequent shifts of power complicate any overall description of the salt monopoly in the Five Dynasties and Ten Kingdoms period.† Numerous variations of these two systems also prevailed in the Sung, particularly in the first half of the dynasty.[4] In broad terms, two general trends can be distinguished during the Northern Sung: one toward a nationwide system of *t'ung-shang*, and the other toward concentrating complete control of the salt administration in the hands of the central government.

In the Northern Sung Fan Hsiang (flourished mid-eleventh century) and Ts'ai Ching (1046–1126) stand out for the enduring reforms they initiated. Fan is noted for his development of the salt voucher (*yen-ch'ao*) system, proposed in 1044 and carried out a few years

---

* Tai I-hsüan, *Sung-tai ch'ao-yen chih-tu yen-chiu* [A study of the salt voucher system in the Sung dynasty] (Shanghai: Commercial Press, 1957).

Another work presenting an overview of the entire Sung salt administration has not been available to me in my research, only having come to my attention after submission of this article for publication. Stanislas K. P. Ts'ien, "Production, marché, et régie du sel en Chine sous les Song (960–1279)," Diss. University of Paris 1958.

† Tseng Yang-feng, *Chung-kuo yen-cheng shih* [A history of China's salt administration] (Taipei: Commercial Press, 1966), pp. 98, 152–58. Tseng, a one-time salt official in the Republican period, includes information about all the dynasties and substantial data for the modern era.

later. Before that time merchants were asked to ship grain and fodder to the northern border areas to support the army in its defense against the Hsi Hsia. In return they received vouchers of exchange (*ch'ao-yin*) which could be cashed in at central government offices for cash, tea, spices, ivory, or salt, the last being obtained from the highly productive, government operated salt pools in Shan-hsi.[5] In time the merchants began falsely to jack up the prices (*hsü-ku*) of the supplies they shipped to the border troops or of the goods they turned in to the government for exchange. Furthermore, the people's transportation burden under the total government monopoly in Shan-hsi became excessive. To correct these two problems, Fan Hsiang instituted the *yen-ch'ao* system whereby the Shan-hsi salt would be transported and sold by the merchants who would merely have to pay cash to the central government for the vouchers without having first to ship supplies to the border outposts.[6]

In the first two decades of the twelfth century Ts'ai Ching began to consolidate all of the Sung salt administration under the control of the central government and to extend the *yen-ch'ao* system to the entire country. At the same time he stepped up the practice of issuing new vouchers as a means of extracting additional money from the merchants who had to trade in their old vouchers at a disadvantageous discount.[7] His policies and manipulatory devices paid off handsomely for the national and imperial coffers, and for the most part they were copied throughout the Southern Sung.* In fact, the system worked out at the end of the Northern Sung contained the rudiments of the salt monopoly that functioned for the remainder of the imperial period of Chinese history.†

---

* For a general discussion of the Southern Sung salt monopoly, see Yoshida Tora, "Sōmatsu no sembai seido un-ei, Nansō no en sembai seido o chūsin toshite" [The operation of the monopoly system in late Sung, with focus on the Southern Sung salt monopoly], *Reikishi kyōiku*, 7, No. 6 (June, 1959), pp. 61 – 67.

† For purposes of comparison to later developments see the following: H. Franz Schurmann, *Economic Structure of the Yüan Dynasty* (Cambridge, Mass.: Harvard University Press, 1956), pp. 166 – 192; Ping-ti Ho, "The Salt Merchants of Yang-chou, A Study of Commercial Capitalism in Eighteenth Century China," *Harvard Journal of Asiatic Studies* 17 (1954), pp. 130 – 168; Thomas A. Metzger, "T'ao Chu's Reform of the Huai-pei Salt Monopoly," *Papers on China*, 16 (1962), pp. 1 – 39; Metzger, "The Organizational Capabilities of the Ch'ing State in the Field of Commerce: The Liang-huai Salt Monopoly, 1740 – 1840," in *Economic Organization in Chinese Society*, ed. W. E. Willmott (Stanford: Stanford University Press, 1972), pp. 9 – 45; S. A. M. Adshead, *The Modernization of the Chinese Salt Administration* (Cambridge, Mass.: Harvard University Press, 1970). Numerous articles and monographs on the Ming and Ch'ing salt administration exist in Chinese and especially Japanese, the most noteworthy being Saeki Tomi's *Shindai ensei no kenkyū* [A study of the salt administration in the Ch'ing dynasty] (Kyoto: The Society of Oriental Researches, Kyoto University, 1962).

The topography of the Liang-che circuit is highly varied. The northern sector (or in terms of the Western and Eastern circuits into which Liang-che finally divided in the Southern Sung,[8] the Western circuit) is a deltaic plain between the Yangtze River at the very northernmost boundary of the circuit and the Ch'ien-t'ang River which drains into Hangchow Bay. Interlacing waterways and lakes facilitate transportation by boat. The Eastern circuit runs roughly from the southern shore of Hangchow Bay to the south below Wen-chou. Except for the shoreline and river valleys, this half of Liang-che is quite mountainous—a fact which, as will be seen later, influenced the distribution of salt particularly at Wen-chou and T'ai-chou (present-day Lin-hai *hsien*).

Rainfall in Liang-che also affected salt production, for rain prevented the salt workers from boiling brine. According to present climatic conditions, Wen-chou and T'ai-chou are in a high precipitation belt with rainfall totaling approximately seventy inches per year. Rainfall north of Ming-chou averages some ten or twenty inches less, depending on the particular area.[9] Furthermore, the entire Liang-che coast, particularly the southern segment, is often the victim of destructive typhoons.

Requiring tracts of highly saline soil and the availability of very brackish seawater, salterns were scattered the length of the serpentine Liang-che coastline. The vast majority, however, were concentrated along the shores of Hangchow Bay. Although the figure was periodically changing due to decreases or increases in productivity or due to administrative exigencies, the *ch'ang** in Liang-che West during the Shao-hsing period (1131–1162) were distributed as follows: Hsiu-chou (after 1195 raised to Chia-hsing fu), 10; P'ing-chiang fu (in the Northern Sung known as Su-chou, but not producing then), 4; and Lin-an fu, 10.[10] These *ch'ang* were not all actually producing salt, for calculated into the figures are the *mai-na ch'ang*, or sales-procurement *ch'ang*, which primarily served as collection points where salters turned in their salt. These sales-procurement *ch'ang* also were at times the sites to which merchants came to collect or "buy" their salt; at other times they went to storage depots (*ts'ang*) generally located in

---

* Because of its differing levels of usage, *ch'ang* is troublesome to interpret, much less translate. Sometimes it is used to refer to places where salt is produced—salterns—and in this sense it is merely an abbreviation for the equivalent terms of *yen-ch'ang* or *t'ing-ch'ang*. Whenever used in this sense, the term will be translated simply as "saltern." However, *ch'ang* carries a much broader meaning that includes administrative offices such as *ts'ui-chien ch'ang* translated as production-supervisory *ch'ang*, and *mai-na ch'ang* rendered as sales-procurement *ch'ang*. In these circumstances of extended meaning, no translation for *ch'ang* is given; rather the transliteration is preferred for lack of a suitable English equivalent.

or near prefectural (*chou* or *fu*) cities. Subordinate to a *mai-na ch'ang* were usually several *ts'ui-chien ch'ang*, or production-supervisory *ch'ang*, from which point officials oversaw production at many salterns to check irregular practices and illegal sales.

Lowest in the salt administrative hierarchy were the *tsao*, or furnaces, where the brine was boiled and crystallized into salt. A large but unfixed number of these furnaces would be under the superintendence of each *ts'ui-chien ch'ang*. At one point in the Southern Sung they totalled 2,400 for all of Liang-che.[11] In some probably highly irregular proportion which we cannot know precisely today, the furnaces were grouped together as production units or salterns. The *Ao-po t'u* speaks of two or three furnaces being gathered into a *t'uan*.[12] In another Southern Sung source, ten furnaces formed one "*ch'ang*," *ch'ang* obviously referring to a saltern, as opposed to the administrative *ch'ang*.[13] The furnaces and/or the salters' families, like other sectors of society, were organized into *chia* for purposes of mutual assistance and surveillance. Again it is impossible to know the exact situation for the sources are at variance with each other. In the Northern Sung it was ordered that three to ten furnaces form a *chia*,[14] while Huang Chen wanted ten salters' families to compose a *chia*.*

The administrative organization or hierarchical chain of *ch'ang* differs somewhat in Liang-che East. According to *Yü hai*,[15] the regional breakdown of *ch'ang* in the Shao-hsing period is as follows: Shao-hsing fu (before 1131 known as Yüeh-chou and for most of the Northern Sung not producing salt), 4; Ming-chou (after 1194 raised to Ch'ing-yüan fu), 6;† T'ai-chou, 3; and Wen-chou (after 1265 raised to Jui-an fu), 5. A list from the *Sung hui-yao* for approximately the same period corroborates this number of *ch'ang* but terms most of them as sales-procurement *ch'ang* (*mai-na ch'ang*) and none of them as production-supervisory *ch'ang* (*ts'ui-chien ch'ang*),[16] an administrative distinction which was completely missing from Liang-che East. There were sometimes smaller, branch salterns (*tzu-ch'ang*) as adjuncts of the larger *mai-na ch'ang*, but they do not functionally correspond to the *ts'ui-chien ch'ang* of Liang-che West.‡ The explana-

---

* *HSJC* 80.9a; Kawakami Kōichi discusses a similar problem in regard to Huai-nan; "Hokusō-dai Wainan en so seisan kōzōkō to shūen kikō," [The production and procurement of salt in Huai-nan under the Northern Sung], *Shigaku zasshi*, 73, No. 12 (December, 1964), pp. 39–63.

† The *PCSMC* (6.27a) says another seven *ch'ang* were established after the K'ai-hsi period (1205–1207). Huang Chen records (*HSJC* 77.4a) that there were 20 *ch'ang* in Shao-hsing and Ching-yüan fu.

‡ *PCSMC* 6.27b–28b. The Ming-ho *ch'ang* is omitted from this list but is given in one to be found at 16.11a. There were also a few branch salterns in Liang-che West.

tion for this apparent lack of production-supervisory *ch'ang* in Liang-che East is that the functions of production-supervision (*ts'ui-chien*) and sales-procurement (*mai-na*) were performed out of one office often having two officials.* As true also of Liang-che West, merchants were sometimes required to pick up their salt at the sales-procurement *ch'ang*. Thus, at some periods during both the Northern and Southern Sung, the three activities of salt production supervision, procurement of the salt from the salters, and distribution of it to merchants were combined at the same administrative level. This provided the opportunity for malpractices that would have been less likely to arise had there been a geographic distance, as well as administrative separation, among the three functions.†

During the Northern Sung other difficulties in Liang-che fore-shadowed to some extent Southern Sung headaches with the salt mo-nopoly. For one, illegal sales of salt were quite pervasive. A memorial jointly submitted by Shen Li (d. ca. 1068) and Li Su-chih (d. ca. 1090), who were then Fiscal Intendants (*chuan-yün shih*) for Liang-che, states:

> The salt levy for this circuit [is set] at 790,000 strings of cash per year. In 1058 it reached only 593,000. Moreover, within one year those punished for illegal sales [totalled] 3,999 people. The problem is in government salt being priced high. Thus illegal sales of salt do not cease, and the government levy is increasingly in arrears.[17]

Although remedial steps were taken, the incidence of illegal salt sales did not abate. In fact, the situation became so serious that in 1073 one thousand troops were brought in from two other areas to help cope with the problem,‡ and this even after Lu Ping (flourished latter half of the eleventh century) had already instituted stern measures to attempt to bring the situation under control.

---

* See the list of officials in *PCSMC* 3.22a-b. The *ch'ang* created after the K'ai-hsi period (see note 16) generally had just one official. It is not at all clear whether these new *ch'ang* were all independent sales-procurement *ch'ang*. *PCSMC* 3.21a.

† Kawakami Kōichi, "Hokusō dai Ryōsetsu-ro enhō ni tsuite" [On the salt monopoly of the Liang-che circuit in Northern Sung], *Shakai keizai shigaku*, 29, No. 6 (1964), pp. 26–41. In this article Kawakami makes illuminating comparisons between the dis-tribution systems in Liang-che and those in Huai-nan, the latter region being one on which he has published several other articles.
Professor Miyazaki Ichisada, in commenting on my paper at the conference, intri-guingly proposed that the Kingdom of Wu Yüeh, which comprised in large part what was to become the Liang-che circuit in the Sung, was peacefully annexed by Sung T'ai-tsu with little administrative shakeup. This fact suggests a possible reason for the Sung problem of administrative organization, the inexplicably large number of salterns, and thus the extensive smuggling in the circuit.

‡ *SHY, shih-huo* 24.6 (p. 5197). I am indebted to Kawakami's article for this ref-erence (see above note).

The plight of the salters was the second common predicament that confronted both Northern and Southern Sung salt administrators. In the Northern Sung, Shen Li as well as Lu Ping, who in 1072 was appointed the Judicial Intendant of Liang-che (*t'i-tien hsing-yü*) with special responsibility for managing salt monopoly affairs, addressed themselves to this problem. At its root was the fact that salters were not being paid regularly, if at all, for the salt they turned over to the government. Lu Ping reimbursed one million strings of cash in back payments due salters.[18] Some years prior to this Shen Li submitted to the throne a twenty-volume compendium detailing salt policies and, in particular, measures to alleviate the salters' hardships. Among other problems Shen also devoted attention to the squeeze exacted by officials and the troubles that arose in transporting the salt, two topics that frequently filled the pages of Southern Sung memorials.[19]

Like Han Wu Ti and the T'ang emperors at the time of the An Lu-shan rebellion, the Southern Sung court was faced with vast military expenditures. And in all three dynasties it was revenue from the salt monopoly that became the lifeblood of the national and especially the military budget. While income from salt was not specifically earmarked for military use, there is no doubt that it was considered the first line of military and fiscal defense. Documents record many instances where officials declared the indispensability of salt and, sometimes for no apparent reason, tea revenue: "The court's major expenses rely completely on the profits from salt and tea,"[20] or "Supporting the army is totally dependent on the tax income from salt and tea."[21]

When it is considered that Yüeh Fei's troops in 1138 required 560,000 strings of cash each month and that Han Shih-chung's force was supported by the court to the extent of 210,000 strings per month —and these amounts are exclusive of grain and other supplies—then the enormity of the early Southern Sung's financial burden becomes vividly clear.* Such economic pressures—as well as the fact that in losing the territory north of the Huai River, the imperial treasury was deprived of proceeds from the two very productive salt pools in Shan-hsi

---

* Chuang Chi-yü, *Chi lei pien,* [Miscellaneous jottings as delectable as a chicken rib], *Ts'ung-shu chi-ch'eng* ed., Vol. 2867, pp. 70—71. Tai has used this source and several others in his discussion (pp. 336—39) of Southern Sung military expenditures. Chang Ju-yü quotes a Sung source giving a breakdown of military cash expenses for most of the Sung; *Ch'ün-shu k'ao-so* [Critical encyclopedia of a myriad sources] (Taipei: Hsin-hsing shu-chü, 1969, facsimile reproduction of 1508 woodblock edition), *hsü-chi* 45.62 (p. 4561). According to this, the monthly military cash expenses in 1135, exclusive of grain and other supplies, totalled one million strings of cash.

and salterns in other northern areas — demanded an almost immediate and miraculous recovery from the Huai-nan and Liang-che salterns.

During the turmoil of the flight south, the work of the Huai-nan and Liang-che salterns was so disrupted that, for example, the revenue from Huai-nan salt in the opening years of the Shao-hsing period was reduced from a previous eight million strings of cash to only 350,000 strings.[22] Thus, the salt administrators' first order of business was to reorganize the saltworks and regroup the many salters who had fled. Toward this end, special dispensations and loans were offered the salters in Huai-nan and Liang-che as an inducement to return to work.[23] The results were little short of remarkable, for in a brief span of time the income doubled at the three Monopoly Bureaus (*chüeh-huo wu*) which sold to merchants vouchers and rights to purchase tea, alum, incense, and salt exclusively in Huai-nan and Liang-che. The Bureaus' income of 6.09 million strings in 1130 had by 1136 reached 13 million.[24] Eighty percent of this latter figure (10.4 million) derived from salt, 10 percent from tea, and the remaining 10 percent from spices, alum, and other miscellaneous items.[25] Then a short three years later in 1139, salt revenue for the entire country totalled 13 million, 7.7 million of which originated in Huai-nan.[26]

For the first century of the Northern Sung, salt was not conspicuously more profitable for the state than the other monopolies, but thereafter became the most profitable monopoly. The statistics in Table 5.1 illustrate this development. When these data are placed in the perspective of a profile of the Sung's revenue derived in cash (see Table 5.2), then the mushrooming importance of salt to the state's cash income can be appreciated. These cash revenue figures of course do not take into account the considerable tax payments in kind, and unfortunately, there are no meaningful national income statistics integrating revenue in cash and kind. While cash income is the only available yardstick against which to measure the growth of the salt monopoly, it should be noted that throughout the eleventh century, and most likely for the remainder of the dynasty, cash income increased considerably while tax revenue in the form of various commodities remained constant, or even declined.[27]

Comparing the data in Tables 5.1 and 5.2, we see that the wine monopoly revenues represent 29 percent of the annual cash income in 1017—1021, and salt 6 percent. By 1078 the situation was reversed with salt revenue amounting to 37 percent of the total cash income and wine 20 percent. In 1119 the salt monopoly income of 21 million from Huai-nan and Liang-che alone supplied at least one-third of the

TABLE 5.1.
Sung Monopoly and *Ho-mai* Silk Annual Revenues.

Year/Period	Wine in strings of cash (*kuan*)	Salt in strings of cash (*kuan*)	*Ho-mai* Silk, purchased by agreement; in bolts (*p'i*)	Tea in strings of cash (*kuan*)
995 – 997	3,259,000+†	2,358,000+§	–	1,390,000††
1034 – 1037	4,280,000+	3,550,000+	2,000,000	–
1041 – 1048	17,100,000+	7,150,000+	3,000,000	–
1077 – 1079	12,280,000+‡	22,300,000+**	–	–
1160*	14,000,000+	21,000,000+	3,000,000	2,700,000‡‡

Source: *CYTC* 14.1b (p. 414) unless otherwise noted.

* Figures for this year include only Ssu-ch'uan and the Southeast. The year given is arbitrarily fixed, as the source loosely mentions the end of the Shao-hsing period.

† *HCP*, 97.21b. Although several other sources corroborate this figure, Chang Ju-yü quotes a sum of 1.2 million strings for the same period; see his *Ch'ün-shu k'ao-so* [Critical encyclopedia of a myriad sources] (Taipei: Hsin-hsing shu-chü, 1969, facsimile reproduction of 1508 woodblock edition), *hsü-chi* 45.8a – b (pp. 4565 – 4566).

‡ Takeda Kinsaku has derived this total from the reports of numerous prefectures (*SHY*, shih-huo 19); see his "Sōdai no kakuko ni tsuite" [The Sung wine monopoly], *Shigaku zassi* 45, No. 5/6 (1935).

§ Chang Ju-yü, *Ch'ün-shu k'ao-so, hou-chi* 57.7a (p. 3167).

** Shen Kua, *Meng-hsi p'i-t'an* [Jottings of Shen Kua], *Ts'ung-shu chi-ch'eng* ed. vol. 281, p. 77. No date is given by Shen Kua for these data, but by correlating other relevant sources, Ch'üan Han-sheng (see footnote 27) has pinpointed the date as 1078 – 79.

†† The source for this is Chang Ju-yü (*hou-chi* 56.9b [p. 3148]). The data are for 998.

‡‡ The source for this figure is *CYTC* 14.12a (p. 435).

national cash income,* if we hypothetically use as a base the highest known Northern Sung cash income of 60 million.†

Additional data (see Table 5.3) found in the *Sung hui-yao* facilitate a comparison of the different monopoly incomes in the Southern Sung. In 1162 the salt revenues from Huai-nan and Liang-che still

* Lü I-hao, *Chung-mu chi* [Collected writings of Lü I-hao], *Ssu-k'u shan-pen ts'ung-shu ch'u-pien* (Taipei, 1959 rotographic reproduction), *han* 48, 2.11a. Tai makes use of this source (pp. 339 – 340).

† Stipulating 60 million as the maximum Northern Sung cash income in pure supposition. Nevertheless, this sum does not seem unrealistic in light of the highest known Southern Sung cash revenue of 65.3 million. We can assume with some justification that the cash revenues toward the end of the Northern Sung were high, for this was just the time that Ts'ai Ching and others were squeezing as much money out of the country and populace as possible.

TABLE 5.2.
Northern and Southern Sung Annual Cash Income.
(in millions of strings of cash)

Period	Income
Early N. Sung	16.0+
1019 – 1021*	26.5+
1056 – 1064	36.8+
1068 – 1078	60.0+
1086 – 1090*	48.0+
Early S. Sung	under 10.0
1160 – 1162*	64.0
1185 – 1189*	65.3+†

Source: *CYTC* 14.1a–b (pp. 413 – 14): the same data have been copied into *YH* 186.14b – 15a (pp. 3505 – 3506).

* These dates are arbitrarily fixed, as the sources merely indicate the beginning or the end of a given reign period.

† This figure is derived from Sogabe Shizuo, *Sōdai zaisei shi* [History of the Sung financial administration] (Tokyo: Daian, 1966; rpt. of 1941 ed.), pp. 38 – 39.

did not match those of the late Northern Sung, and it was not until a few years later that they did. Nevertheless, Huai-nan and Liang-che revenues at this time amounted to 28 percent of the national cash income. When the proceeds from Ssu-ch'uan are added in (this accounts for the apparent discrepancy between the two salt figures for 1160 – 62 in Tables 5.1 and 5.3; Li Hsin-ch'uan's total of 21 million includes Ssu-ch'uan), overall salt monopoly proceeds totalled 33 percent of the 64 million cash income for the late Shao-hsing period. In contrast, wine monopoly revenues from the entire country remained in secondary position, representing 22 percent of the annual cash income.

The salt receipts from Huai-nan and Liang-che continued to mount at least over the next twenty years. The only firm statistics that exist to substantiate this are for 1170 when the sales of Huai-nan vouchers totalled 21.963 million, while those in Liang-che reached only 5.012 million,[28] making a sum total of 26.975 million, the last and the highest figure ever quoted in extant sources.* In comparing this Huai-nan/Liang-che breakdown for 1170 with the comparable figures for 1119 (Huai-nan, 14 – 15 million/Liang-che, 7 – 8 million), it becomes apparent that over the fifty-odd years there was a noticeable

---

* It should be pointed out that data quantifying salt in terms of money, especially for the national or a broad regional level, are seldom found, while weights for production quotas and actual output are more commonplace.

TABLE 5.3.
Monopoly Incomes for Three Monopoly Bureaus.

Year	Salt	Tea	Spices/Alum	Miscellaneous	Total
1154	15,665,615/430*	2,694,004/577	1,099,108/685	1,208,762/514	20,667,491/206
1162	17,969,011/609	2,121,477/758	1,195,854/246	279,449/058	21,556,792/671†

Source: *SHY*, *shih-huo* 55.27a–28b (pp. 5761–62). The three bureaus were located at Hsing-tsai, Chien-k'ang, and Chen-chiang.

* Figures before slash are strings of cash (*kuan*), and after the slash, cash (*wen*). The *wen* to *kuan* conversion ratio used in this table is 1,000 to 1, and not the Sung *sheng-pai* of 770 cash per string. For a discussion of this problem see Ku Yen-wu, *Yüan-ch'ao-pen jih-chih lu* (Taipei, 1970), ch. 15, pp. 334–335; also, Lien-sheng Yang, *Money and Credit in China* (Cambridge, Mass.: Harvard University Press, 1952), pp. 36–37.

† A discrepancy exists in the *SHY* either for the grand total reported as 21,566,092/671 or for the figures given for the four monopoly incomes, as an independently calculated sum of these four incomes yields a total of 21,556,792/671.

decline in sales of Liang-che salt vouchers and a very marked increase
in Huai-nan sales. This is not to say that the actual overall production
of Liang-che in 1170 was reduced. To the contrary, according to this
1170 report,[29] there was a flourishing trade of illicit salt in Liang-che.

Irrespective of the existence of illegal salt sales, we may still
attempt to reach some speculative conclusions regarding the quanti-
tative importance of *official* Liang-che salt sales relative to the state's
total cash income. In the Northern Sung up until the time of Ts'ai
Ching's prime ministership, Liang-che's salt revenues were negligible.
The 1058 income of 530,000 strings of cash represented a mere 1.4
percent of the state's cash intake, while if the quota of 790,000 had
been met, only 2.2 percent of the government's cash revenue would
have derived from Liang-che salt.* The quota of 871,800 for 1080,
if actually filled, would have yielded between 1.4 and 1.8 percent,
depending on the state's income.† With the commencement of the
voucher system there was a multifold increase in the relative yield,
but exactly to what degree cannot be determined in the absence of
data for the state's cash income. After the salt administration had
rallied in the Southern Sung to the heights of the late Northern Sung
production rate, Liang-che salt contributed at least 7.7 percent to
the state's cash income, and this is based on a year (1170) when the
quota was not reached.‡ Although the percentage of Liang-che salt
revenues cannot begin to compare to Huai-nan's, they nonetheless
were an indispensable source for the national budget, illicit salt sales
or not. It was therefore paramount for the salt administrators to con-
serve this fiscal resource through every possible means of control.

Production and Controls

From at least as early as the Sung, the first period for which we
possess detailed information about salt technology, and even until
the present century, the process of manufacturing salt along the southeastern coast of China has essentially involved producing a brine of
very high saline content and then decocting it until pure salt crystals
form. Exact production methods, of course, differed somewhat by
region due to climatic conditions and by locality due to established
customs. In Liang-che East and West the technique, generally speak-

---

* *SS, shih-huo* 182.3a. A cash income base of 36.8 million was used for this computation. See Table 5.2.

† *YH* 181.24b (p. 3433). This is calculated on the basis of state cash receipts being
somewhere between 60 and 48 million. See Table 5.2.

‡ The state's cash income here is set at 65 million, midway between the figures for
the late Shao-hsing and Ch'ien-tao periods. See Table 5.2.

ing, varied in two respects. The first difference is that Liang-che West used an iron caldron (*p'an*) while Liang-che East used a caldron made out of bamboo.[30] This bamboo caldron could withstand only two or three days of intense usage.[31] Salt produced in the iron caldron turned out whiter and was considered superior to the yellowish variety boiled in the bamboo pan.*

The second difference lies in the preparation of the substance from which the brine is made. The *Ao-po t'u* mentions that Liang-che West used a method termed *shai-hui*, and Liang-che East practiced what is called *kua t'u*. This latter term is never explained satisfactorily in any source, but the description in a Sung gazetteer from K'uai-chi (Shao-hsing fu),[32] which was in the northern part of Liang-che East and not necessarily representative of the entire circuit, reveals that a field was flooded with sea water and allowed to dry in the sun; in the evening the crystals in the alkaline soil were scraped off the surface (*kua chien* or *kua t'u*). This procedure was repeated five or six days until there were sufficient crystals to fill the percolating vat in which the brine was made. The Liang-che West method, as described in the *Ao-po t'u,* varied in that before the drying beds were flooded with sea water, embers and ashes (the *hui*) from the reeds used to stoke the caldron fires were spread on the field; they were also layered in the percolating vat. These differences in production techniques apparently were not fundamental.†

The salt production quotas are much more clearly known, for abundant Southern Sung data exist on this topic. Table 5.4 lists the quotas established for two periods in the third quarter of the twelfth century. Due entirely to significant reductions for the Ming, T'ai and Wen-chou quotas in the Ch'ien-tao period, the total Liang-che production quota in this period is almost 100,000 *tan* below that for Shao-hsing. In the case of T'ai and Wen-chou the reason for the quota reduction was not an inability to produce sufficient salt but an inability

---

* Fang Shao, *P'o-chai pien* [Writings in a tranquil dwelling], *Pai hai, han* 3, *ts'e* 18, 2.1b. Tai's study, which contains a concise description of the production process on pages 4 – 7, utilizes this source.

† For further discussion of this problem and for references to additional and sometimes confusing sources, readers are referred to Yoshida's article on the *Ao-po t'u* (see note, p. 103) in addition to Tai's monograph. For purposes of comparison, interesting discussions of ancient and medieval Western methods can be found in R. J. Forbes, *Studies in Ancient Technology* (Leiden: Brill, 1955), III, 157 – 174; and A. R. Bridbury, *England and the Salt Trade in the Later Middle Ages* (Oxford: Oxford University Press, 1955), pp. 3 – 21. In his major study of Japanese salt production techniques in modern and premodern times, Kodama Yōichi presents detailed information that can shed light on the Chinese procedures. *Kinsei enden no seiritsu* [The establishment of salt fields in recent times] (Tokyo: Nihon gakujutsu shinkō kai, 1961).

TABLE 5.4.
Southern Sung Salt Production Quotas.

Circuit/Prefecture	Late Shao-hsing Period, 1131–62	Ch'ien-tao Period, 1165–73
Liang-che West	1,137,145*	1,144,177
Hsiu-chou	818,697	818,697
P'ing-chiang fu	75,718	79,627
Lin-an fu	242,729	245,852
Liang-che East	848,283	743,201
Shao-hsing fu	116,920	140,637
Ming-chou	392,670	374,494
T'ai-chou	144,313	90,000†
Wen-chou	194,379	138,069†
Huai-nan East	2,683,711	2,683,711
Kuang-nan East	331,060	331,060
Kuang-nan West	231,689	229,097
Fu-chien	333,389‡	333,389‡
Ssu-ch'uan	1,200,000§	—

Source: With the exception of the Ssu-ch'uan total, the Shao-hsing figures are found in *SHY* (*shih-huo* 23.13 – 17 [pp. 5181 – 5183]). Although no date is given, the *SHY* cites the *Chung-hsing hui-yao* as the source. *CYTC* (14.5b – 6a [pp. 422 – 423]) quotes the same figures and dates them as late Shao-hsing period. The Ch'ien-tao figures are located in *SHY* (*shih-huo* 23.17 – 18 [p. 5183]) which quotes the *Ch'ien-tao hui-yao*.

* Units are *tan*. According to the Huai-nan and Liang-che salt measuring practice (*CYTC* 14.5b – 6a), 50 *chin* constituted one *tan*. In Sung times one *chin* was the equivalent of 596.82 grams (cf., Wu Ch'eng-lo's *Chung-kuo tu-liang-heng shih*, Shanghai, 1937, p. 74). Thus, if one pound equals 453.59 grams, one *chin* roughly weighs 1⅓ pounds and one *tan* of salt approximately 66 pounds.

† *SHY, shih-huo* 28.1 – 2 (p. 5279) records that not until 1174 was a petition submitted to the emperor requesting a reduction in the quota for Wen-chou and T'ai-chou. Therefore, it is likely that some, if not all, of the quota listed for the Ch'ien-tao period really dates from this somewhat later period.

‡ These figures have been converted into *tan* from *chin* at the rate of 50 *chin* per *tan*, the prevailing conversion rate in Huai-nan and Liang-che. According to Li Hsin-ch'uan, though (*CYTC* 14.6a [p. 423]), Fukien did not use this rate; but he provides no other conversion equivalent. Thus, this figure in *tan* is only an estimate. A significant discrepancy exists between the amount of *chin* for Fu-chien quoted in *SHY* and *CYTC*, the former reading 16 odd million and the latter 26. The lower figure seems more reliable since it is cited twice in *SHY*.

§ The source for this is *CYTC* 14.9a (p. 429); again the figure originally in *chin* has been converted to *tan* at 50:1.

to market what was produced.[33] Because of the inaccessibility of the two areas by land or inland water routes, the only way large-scale merchants were able to transport their salt was by sea, and this they obviously were unwilling to undertake, so much so that approximately two-thirds of the salt produced in these two prefectures remained unsold. Rather than have this surplus salt go to waste, or worse still be used for illicit sales, the authorities, uncharacteristically taking into account realistic market conditions, reduced the quota.

With these exceptions the quotas for all other Liang-che districts were increased in the Ch'ien-tao period. It was the output in this period and the immediately succeeding one of Ch'un-hsi (1174–1189) which Huang Chen said served as the basis for quotas (*tsu-e*) when he served as salt administrator in the waning years of the dynasty.[34] Huang's high regard for the achievements of the salt administration in these two periods notwithstanding, there is solid evidence that there were vast discrepancies between the amount of salt collected by officials (not actual production, for this would include illegally sold salt which there is no way to calculate) and the established quota. In 1170 Liang-che fell short of the mark by approximately 700,000 *tan*.[35] In spite of this conflicting evidence, Huang considered the point marking the downward turn in the salt administration and production to come after the Chia-ting period (1208–1224) when corruption became more outrageous, inflation more pronounced and various malpractices more prevalent.[36] Production figures bear witness to this phenomenon. In 1235 it was reported that Huai-nan and Liang-che had for the preceding two or three years accumulated a deficit of some six million *tan*.[37] Although comprehensive figures do not exist for any later periods, Huang Chen often commented that in his day officials were not able to meet their quota.

In spite of this incidence of default, Huang Chen cannot be strictly faulted for considering the Ch'ien-tao and Ch'un-hsi periods as the pinnacle of production. At some point during this time an apparent breakthrough in technology allowed the salters almost to double their production capacity. In the manufacturing process testing and controlling the degree of salinity of the brine to be boiled into salt crystals was a key, timesaving step. If the brine was too diluted, not much salt would be forthcoming for the effort and fuel expended in the boiling. Even prior to the Sung,[38] salters had employed an ingenious method of floating in the brine lotus seeds that had been cured in brine solutions of differing consistencies.[39] Each lotus seed would have a different specific gravity allowing it to float only in brine of equal or greater strength. According to the *Sung hui-yao*, some advance was apparently made in application of the technique at the beginning of the Ch'un-hsi period.* Although this development is reported to have occurred first in Huai-nan, such an important achievement, allowing for an increase in production from a maximum of 1,700 *chin* per day to an average of 2,500 to 3,000 *chin*, surely must have spread to other salt-producing areas, such as in adjacent Liang-che.

Li Hsin-ch'uan also provides information about the quantity of salt a furnace in Huai-nan and Liang-che could produce. "Each furnace in a day and a night decocts six caldrons of salt, one caldron [being equal to] 300 *chin*"[40] In other words, a furnace turned out 1,800 *chin* (or thirty-six *tan*) per twenty-four hour period, slightly more than the production rate in Huai-nan *prior* to the technological advance. With this knowledge of the daily production rate of a furnace combined with data both for the number of furnaces in Liang-che (approximately 2,400 in 1170)[41] and for the annual production quota, we can easily compute the length of time, that is the number of twenty-four hour boiling periods, it took to meet a quota. And for Liang-che we arrive at the astonishing result that each of the 2,400 furnaces had to operate an average of only twenty-one days before meeting the quota for the entire year.†

The bulk of the salt production took place throughout the nine months of the spring, summer, and fall.[42] Of course not every day was suitable for optimal production because of rain or other reasons, and not every furnace turned out 1,800 *chin* in twenty-four hours. The *Ao-po t'u* reveals that in good months, when the saline content of the brine solution was high, the salters could take crystallized salt from the caldrons while simultaneously pouring in fresh brine. In poor months when the solution was weak, presumably because of dilution by rain and other factors, salters could not continuously boil salt but would have to wait until each caldron's brine had completely evaporated into crystals and then start afresh.[43] Moreover, the availability of fuel to stoke the furnace affected the length of time salt could be

---

* *SHY, shih-huo* 28.20 (p. 5288): "In the early Shao-hsing period each furnace— boiling one day and night, and calculated by the amount of salt boiled in one boiling session [*huo-fu*]—[could produce] at the maximum 17 *ch'ou*, one *ch'ou* [being the equivalent] of 100 *chin* of salt. Recently in the early Ch'un-hsi period, the salters have obtained a method for testing the brine solution. They cast ten lotus seeds into the brine, and if five float then the brine has five parts [salt consistency]; if seven float, then the brine has seven parts [salt consistency]. In the event the brine is not seven parts, then [the salters], using an ox, dig and scrape up the salty soil again and percolate this with the weak brine solution. It is necessary to wait for brine to be thick enough to use before boiling it. Every furnace, in one firing, boils 25 to 30 *ch'ou*. . . . "

† The computations were made as follows: 2400 (furnaces in Liang-che) x 36 *tan* (daily production) = 86,400 *tan* (total optimal Liang-che production in one day). 1,887,378 *tan* (annual Ch'ien-tao Liang-che quota) ÷ 86,400 *tan* = 21 days.

produced. By the eighth or ninth month of each season, fuel supplies dwindled so that production was impeded. And in the late Sung and Yüan, when the marshes, where the reeds for fuel grew, were allowed to deteriorate or be switched to other uses, there simply was not enough fuel to keep fires burning continuously.[44] In spite of these extenuating circumstances, the fact remains that only an average of twenty-one production days out of nine months was needed for all Liang-che furnaces functioning at the optimal rate to meet their quota.*

Aside from production delays mentioned above and rainy weather, neither of which could have cut into overall production time too greatly, how can we account for the salt produced during the obviously large number of days when salters were free to, and inevitably did, produce excess quota salt? By law all salt was to be sold to the government; whatever was manufactured over the quota was considered surplus (*fou-yen*) and was purchased by the government supposedly at a higher price than the regular salt. This, then, is one, and legally the only, possibility for disposing of extra-quota salt.

A second and more likely possibility (which will be discussed more fully later in this paper) is that officials through many nefarious practices extracted or extorted extra salt from the salters. Even rainy days, for example, occasioned the opportunity for chicanery. "If there was rain one day, then it was falsely reported as three days. If in one season there were ten days of rain, then one saltern could illegally produce 360,000 *chin* [720 *tan*]."†

Illicit sales to merchants or to ordinary individuals is the third most likely means of disposing of non-quota salt. As a matter of fact, all salt, quota and extra-quota alike, tended at all times—and especially in times of lax administration—to be attracted toward officials' pockets and the salters' own purses. Either deprived the state of its due revenue. Exact figures of salt lost to corruption of one sort or another or to illegal sales can naturally never be computed, but the amount must have been substantial judging simply from the dimensions of the possibility for producing extra-quota salt.

The case of Huai-nan suggests a fundamental cause for the prevalence of illegal salt sales in Liang-che, or in other words for the lack

---

* Only in the case of T'ai and Wen-chou are there sufficiently detailed data (*SHY, shih-huo* 28.1a–2b [p. 5279]) to compute the average production rate of a furnace on the local level. Such a computation corroborates the more general findings for the whole of Liang-che.

† *CYTC*, 14.6b (p. 424). This is calculated in the following way. One saltern has ten furnaces each of which produces 1,800 *chin* or 36 *tan* per day; thus each saltern produces 18,000 *chin* daily. With ten days of rain, an additional 20 are falsely reported as having inclement weather. Therefore 20 x 18,000 = 360,000.

of control over production. Huai-nan's quota was 2,683,711 *tan* per year, but its 411 furnaces were only a small fraction of the number in Liang-che.[45] Operating at the *pre*-technological advance rate of thirty-six *tan* per day, each furnace would on the average require 114 days to meet its quota. Obviously Huai-nan salters had little extra time during a season to manufacture non—quota salt. This comparison suggests that Liang-che furnaces were simply too numerous to be subject to effective control. It would have been far better for Liang-che administrators to have reduced drastically the number of furnaces and demand a greater production from each one, yet there is only one recorded instance of such a measure being taken in Liang-che. In 1174 the eight *ch'ang* of T'ai and Wen-chou eliminated almost 170 furnaces, but even so, 302 remained.[46]

Given so many furnaces it was imperative that production controls be strictly enforced. A hasty recapitulation of the steps in the production process as presented in the *Ao-po t'u* supplemented with information from other sources will show how and to what extent controls were practiced. Evidently they were not imposed until the boiling stage. Prior to this, salters had to undertake extensive preliminary work in the preparation of the brine to be boiled. First and foremost, this involved substantial hydraulic works, for the sea water had to be drawn up to the drying beds (*t'an-ch'ang*) through a series of pumps and ditches. Moreover, as the drying beds were necessarily near the sea, and on high ground if possible, the construction of locks and dikes was mandatory if high tides and storms were not to flood the beds. A flooded bed would be as long as a week in drying out.[47] The labor required for these hydraulic works and their upkeep meant that all members of salters' families in addition to hired laborers had to pool their efforts. The drying beds were surrounded by ditches from which the brackish water was methodically dipped onto each bed. In the summer months it took one day before the bed would dry and form salty particles (also called *hui*) but in the winter, two or three days.[48] These particles would be swept up and placed in the nearby percolating vat to which was connected an underground storage well via a bamboo pipe. Sea water poured into the vat would filter through the layers of crystallized particles and ashes, and finally pass as brine into the storage well. The brine was then transported, by boat or in buckets toted by porters, to the furnaces, two or three of which were grouped into a *t'uan*, at least in Yüan times.[49] These *t'uan* had walls built around them to protect the brine stored there and any salt boiled within the confines. It is at this point that controls were institutionalized. There were regulations concerning the use of the brine, the starting and stopping of the fires, and the size of the boiling caldrons. In the mid-eleventh century Lu Ping, in an effort to restrict illicit sales of salt, fixed the number of boilings and caldrons.[50] However, by 1138 an official complained that for a number of years the rules regarding the starting and stopping of boiling fires had been abolished, so that there was no way to know how much salt salters manufactured nor any way to control the amount produced.[51] A long sealed memorial of 1163 suggesting specific reforms in the salt administration had much to say about the control of fires and caldrons:

[Salt production] heretofore has had established regulations. Caldrons were divided into three classes, each having an order [of use].... For example at one boiling session [one] could boil so much salt. The starting and stopping times of the fires were set. Each time [one] came to start a fire the production-supervisory *ch'ang* applied for the brine solution. As soon as [one] stopped the fire, [the official] immediately collected [the salt] and stored the brine in the *ch'ang*.... Recently the production-supervisory [official] has not even controlled the firings and has allowed the salters to monopolize the caldrons and the furnace. [The officials] do not ask about the order [in which the salters were supposed to boil their salt*] so that the poor [lower ranking] salters who have gathered their fuel in the *ch'ang* cannot boil [their salt].[52]

This memorial further points out that the production quota for a caldron per boiling was formerly 500 *chin*. Gradually this was reduced to 300 *chin*, and by the time of this memorial to 200 *chin*; and many times even 100 *chin* or less per boiling. Needless to say, the salt boiled in each caldron over and above these low quotas did not reach the officials. To circumvent these malpractices, the memorialist proposed that a fixed number of caldrons and boilings be re-established. As an additional control device, a record book should be drawn up so that each time a fire was started or stopped the *chia-t'ou* of the furnace would have to have the fact duly recorded.[53] Finally, the production-supervisory officials (*ts'ui-chien kuan*) were ordered personally to oversee the boiling of the salt, indicating that in the past they had been lax in this duty and had most likely delegated the responsibility to someone else, such as a clerk. By virtue of the fact that a similar proposal was made eight years later in 1171, we know that the earlier reform measures apparently were not successful, if they were implemented at all.[54] There is no reason to believe that the results of

---

* The *APT* (47) mentions that salters took turns using the caldrons according to an order that is not specified.

this second proposal were any more fruitful than the first. Thus, it may be concluded that throughout most of the Southern Sung production control regulations were for all intents and purposes a dead letter.

After the salt was manufactured it would be turned over daily to the officials to be measured and stored temporarily in the *t'uan* which, according to the *Ao-po t'u*, had five or seven storage rooms.[55] They were for the convenience of the salters so that they would not have to be perpetually transporting their salt to the salt distribution storage depots (*chih-yen ts'ang*) which could be some distance away. When this temporary storage space was full, the salt would then be shipped under the seal of each household[56] and measured again upon arrival.

This measuring or weighing, the final production procedure, was a point where precise controls were absolutely necessary if the salters and/or porters were not to be cheated out of their just due. Variation in and official manipulation of measuring units and utensils were not problems novel to the Sung. Huang Chen was particularly conscious of them. He attempted to standardize all the measuring units and equipment at the level of both the saltern and the storage depot. At the saltern the salters were often shortchanged in the weighing process; the porters who transported the salt to the distribution storage depots were the victims of the same malpractice. Standardization of measures at both ends of the transportation route was, Huang believed, the most efficacious means of checking the pilferage of salt in transit. As a realist, though, Huang understood that it would be impossible and even inadvisable to put a complete stop to the "wastage" lost to porters, but he wanted to reduce it to more or less acceptable levels. He also realized that enforcement of strict measurements had to be carried out simultaneously at both the storage depot and the saltern. "Now if we wish to eliminate [the problem of] overmeasuring at the salterns, we must first eliminate it at the salt storage depot. But the storage depot's clerks [depend] on this for their livelihood. [Corruption] is like a rat's nest; if this place is stopped up, another will be bored out."[57] There is of course no way to know how effective Huang's or other officials' control of this problem was, but we can be certain that at no time was it ever completely eradicated.

Because of the necessity of a ready supply of fuel the government placed restrictions on the use and disposal of the marsh lands (*lü-ch'ang* or *ts'ao-ch'ang*) in which grew the reeds and rushes used for fuel and for weaving the bags in which the salt was packaged. There was also a prohibition against any of the salters' property being mortgaged or sold, lest the salters become rootless and change occupations,* but this prohibition was frequently violated.† There can be little doubt that property gradually accumulated in the hands of the richer salters; and even in one case near the fall of the dynasty, an unscrupulous official confiscated a great deal of salters' land with no apparent legal justification.[58]

In the highly labor-intensive production of salt the expenses of the salters were not light. They had to pay for any labor hired, such as for hydraulic works and the cutting of fuel, for any construction supplies needed, and for taxes. Because they were supposed only to manufacture salt, they were allowed to commute their taxes (*che-na*) with salt. "The salters are secluded along the sea coves and just boil salt for an occupation. They have never tilled and cultivated the soil; so they are allowed to commute the *liang-shui* [tax] with salt."[59] The officials would pay cash for them, and they, in turn, would repay the officials with the salt they manufactured. According to an imperially approved memorial of 1163, they were permitted to pay their tax out of extra-quota salt (*e-wai yen*). Every three years the tax was supposed to be computed according to a salter's manpower and rate of output.[60] All salters were completely absolved of corvee conscription so as to let them concentrate on their production.

To meet the salters' production expenses and to provide them with some means of subsistence, the government gave them what was known as "principal" (*pen-ch'ien*). Implied in the use of this term is the fact that salters were not selling something to which they had sole possession or which they had manufactured for retail distribution at a profit. This was, after all, a salt monopoly, and the salters were only servants of the state, not free agents. They did not receive "wages" as such, but "capital" in the sense of "starting money" or funds contributed to an enterprise by the owners. They were to receive their *pen-ch'ien* in two equal installments, the first before they actually started to produce the salt and the second after they had turned in their stipulated quota. The first installment was collected at the pro-

---

* Huang Chen, "Ch'uang-lun fu tsu-e tsai hsü t'ing-ting liu-ts'e" [A memorial proposing six plans for restoring the original quotas to relieve the salters] in Sun Hsing-yen et al., comp., *Sung-chiang fu-chih* [Gazetteer for Sung-chiang prefecture] (Taipei, 1970 facsimile reproduction of 1817 woodblock edition), 29.3b–4b (p. 643). This highly informative memorial is not included in *HSJC*.

† These violations are evidenced by officials seeking to strengthen the prohibition. For example, see *SHY, shih-huo* 27.11–12 (p. 5261); Huang also says in the above mentioned document that several different types of land belonging to the salters had passed into the control of the wealthy.

duction-supervisory *ch'ang* and the second portion at the sales-procurement *ch'ang*.[61]

This is the way the system was supposed to operate in the Southern Sung; however, as should be expected, many irregularities arose and eventually became customary practice. By 1157, for example, salters had to wait until they weighed their salt at the sales-procurement *ch'ang* before they could receive any of their money. This imposed a severe hardship on the poorer salters who could not easily obtain funds to tide them over.[62] In Huang Chen's time it was the practice for the richer salters (the so-called *shang-hu*) to distribute the money to the other salters. This inevitably led to their collusion with the officials for the purpose of pocketing the money themselves.[63] Li Hsin-ch'uan also reveals that late in the Ch'un-hsi period the *chia-t'ou* and the *tsung-hsia*, who were the designated "foremen" of the furnaces, would expropriate the *pen-ch'ien* and then for fear the other salters would report them, would allow them to produce illegal salt.*

As if these malpractices were not enough, the salters frequently went empty-handed for their efforts, because officials simply did not distribute the *pen-ch'ien*. The prevalence of this flagrant corruption can be forcefully demonstrated by the amounts that virtuous officials returned to the salters. Huang Chen distributed more than 600,000 strings of cash,[64] his highly admired predecessor Sun Tzu-hsiu, 500,000 strings,[65] and Yen Shih-lu in the mid-Shao-hsing era repaid even vaster sums owed to the salters.[66] Part of the problem with the officials' management of the *pen-ch'ien* was that they were allowed some flexibility with its use, as long as they eventually paid out what was owed. By long standing practice they borrowed against the *pen-ch'ien* funds for various reasons. One legitimate reason that easily degenerated into corruption was for officials to draw their living and expense allowances from this source of funds. Due to lax accounting procedures, though, the money at times was never returned or was diverted to other purposes.[67] Another particularly malicious practice that Huang Chen railed against was known as "certificate fees" (*wen-p'ing ch'ien*) whereby officials and clerks, on the pretext that salters owed them money, would lay claim to the *pen-ch'ien* and use it to cover their expenses or to curry favor with their superiors.[68]

Judging from the extensiveness and multiplicity of problems surrounding the payment of *pen-ch'ien* to salters, apparently few, if any, effective controls could be instituted. The devious ways of the officials and clerks proliferated in proportion to the restrictions. There were of

---

* *CYTC* 14.6b (p. 424). Huang Chen also discusses this problem (*HSJC* 80.8b–9a).

course penalties for illegal use of these funds, and there was a regulation to the effect that officials needed to prove upon expiration of their term of office that they owed no *pen-ch'ien*.[69] If these rules had been conscientiously carried out, however, few officials would have remained in the salt administration. The only recourse the salters had to collect or recover their money was, first, the right to report cases of injustice and, second, the system of pocket account books in which supposedly were entered the amount of salt they turned in and the amount of *pen-ch'ien* to be received.[70]

In cases when salters did receive their money, they were paid fourteen cash for each *chin* of regular quota salt and seventeen cash for each *chin* above their quota; [71] in 1175 these rates were increased to sixteen and nineteen cash, respectively.[72] The intention of setting a higher price for surplus quota salt was to attract it into the government storage depots and away from illicit trade. But since the distinction between the two prices was not always observed,[73] this incentive often had little appeal. Compared to the price at which officials sold salt to merchants, the *pen-ch'ien* rate seems paltry. Exclusive of extra fees and miscellaneous charges, one bag of salt (the equivalent of 300 *chin*) was sold to merchants in Liang-che at one time in the Southern Sung for eighteen strings of cash, or 18,000 cash,* but the government supposedly paid only 4,200 cash to the salters for the same bag. The ravages of inflation also made the little money received by the salters seem even less. Huang Chen tells how in about 1260 each *chin* of salt was priced at 200 "old" *hui-tzu* (note that at least by this time the easily devalued paper currency rather than specie was used for payment), but in terms of actual purchasing power this was worth only eleven cash.†

Payments to the salters were further reduced by numerous charges so that in the end the salters received next to nothing. Although these fees were common in all periods of the Sung salt monopoly,‡

---

* *SHY, shih-huo* 26.4 (p. 5243). There is no evidence whether the price merchants paid was figured in long or short strings (see the discussion on units, Table 5.3). Here for no other reason than to expect the government to collect as much money as possible, the long strings are used to make the calculation.
  In Kuang-nan the buying price was 18 cash per *chin* and the selling price 50 cash; cf. *SHY, shih-huo* 27.14 (p. 5262).

† *Sung-chiang fu-chih*, 29.3a (p. 643). See also *HSJC* 77.3a–b. On the general problem of inflation in the late Sung see: Ch'üan Han-sheng, "Sung-mo te t'ung-huo p'eng-chang chi ch'i tui-yü wu-chia de ying-shang" [Currency inflation in late Sung and its influence on commodity prices], *Kuo-li chung-yang yen-chiu-yüan li-shih yü-yen yen-chiu-suo chi-k'an*, 10 (1948), pp. 193–222.

‡ For example, see complaints made in 1163; *SHY, SH* 27.12 (p. 5261).

they seemed to be especially onerous in Huang Chen's day. "Since the branch office [*fen-ssu,* see following section] was established, as soon as a salter came to ask for capital money, he had to pay surcharges under the category of routine operating fees [*ch'ang-li ch'ien*]; such charges, I have heard, number twenty-two."[74] In another place Huang catalogs some of these fees,[75] which were not limited to cash payments alone; over and above these there were extra salt charges so extensive that in the late Southern Sung a salter had to turn in an extra *chin* of salt to meet the fees on his one *chin* of regular quota salt.[76]

Such extortionist practices at the expense of the salters left them only two alternatives—the sale of illegal salt or flight from their occupation. The first option, which was the usual first resort, started a vicious cycle from which the only escape was flight. Since the source of the salters' *pen-ch'ien* was the fees paid by the merchants for the salt and other charges, anything that deterred merchants from purchasing government salt would influence the *pen-ch'ien* funds. Illicit sales by the salters brought on this very problem in two ways: first, the merchants did not buy the monopoly salt, and second the amount of such salt conceivably available for sale, per chance any merchants should be interested, was reduced. Thus, whenever the salters ceased receiving *pen-ch'ien* and could no longer pay off excessive "squeeze" from the profits they earned through illicit salt sales, their only viable alternative was to flee.*

Even though the law bound salters to a particular saltern and prohibited them from moving to another or from changing their jobs, the incidence of violations was beyond calculation. Some salters would run away to another saltern where the quota was over-subscribed, change their names, and enter the registered ranks of salters there; others would join the army.[77] If they were caught, the penalty during the early part of the Southern Sung was banishment to a distant province, usually Kuang-nan; however, this had the undesired and unintended effect of congregating all the violators in one area while simultaneously diminishing the number† of salters in Liang-che.[78] Accordingly, it was proposed that as an alternative to this punishment, offenders receive eighty

---

* One memorial dating from 1160 touches on this problem (*SHY, shih-huo* 27.2 [p. 5256]).

† The total number of salter families (*t'ing-hu*) in Liang-che during the Southern Sung is impossible to determine. The *APT* (1) reveals that in Yüan times there were 9,600 *ting-hu.* Li Hsin-ch'uan (*CYTC* 14.6b [p. 424]) claimed that without doubt each furnace had 20 families (*chia*) connected to it. If all these were salter families, then there would be 48,000 families (2,400 furnaces) in Liang-che; this seems highly improbable when compared to the Yüan figure. Therefore, we can presume that these 20 families per furnace included laborers connected with the salterns but not officially classified *t'ing-hu.*

strokes of the bamboo cane, be returned to their original saltern, and be obligated to meet their original quota. Needless to say, all these attempted controls imposed on runaways and on salters selling illicit salt* were of no avail when the situation became so intolerable that little choice remained to them.

Under the most intolerable circumstances, salters turned to banditry and piracy. Accounts of this are scattered throughout the sources, but the most serious disorders occurred near the fall of the dynasty. Huang Chen reports large-scale melees in Liang-che East during which considerable numbers of people and salters were killed.[79] At times when control mechanisms were on the verge of collapse or indeed had collapsed, the best policy was not a harsh crackdown, but a remission of quotas and a pardon for past breaches of the regulations. Thus it is we read of officials making such requests and emperors voiding overdue and uncollectable quotas. In other words, official acknowledgment, although tacit, that controls had failed became most often the means of reimposing new controls and fresh order.

Administrators and Administration

Although the Southern Sung administrative scheme in Liang-che East and West differed somewhat from *ch'ang* to *ch'ang* in the exact duties, titles, and number of officials, the basic personnel components and functions were more or less constant. A Salt and Tea Intendant (*t'i-chü ch'a-yen kung-shih*) headed each circuit's salt administration. He was immediately responsible to the Ministry of Finance.† Directly under him were one or two executive administrators (*kan-pan kung-shih*) whose purview covered the entire circuit and whose responsibilities, as far as can be ascertained, were to oversee and press for salt revenues and to audit the accounts of storage depots and sales-procurement *ch'ang*.[80] After 1235 another subordinate official (*chu-kuan wen-tzu*) was created in each of the circuits with the explicit duties of restoring the revenues to the quota level and of buying any extra-quota salt.[81] At this level in the administration officials and duties begin to divide along the broad functional lines of sales-procurement, production-supervision, and distribution; titles, though, differed in the two circuits and, in Liang-che East especially, changed periodically as the system evolved. Many times one official concurrent-

---

* For details of the regulations concerning salters selling illicit salt, see *SHY, shih-huo* 26.17–20 (pp. 5242–5243).

† For the evolution of the office of the Tea and Salt Intendant, see Tai I-hsüan, pp. 164–167.

ly carried out two functions, and on occasion *hsien* magistrates concurrently bore the title and responsibility of a salt administrator. Usually every salt producing *ch'ang* had one official responsible for production-supervision, while officials in charge of sales-procurement and distribution each numbered one or two and were located at the *hsien* or prefectural seats. Both civil and military officials filled the ranks of these local posts, and if two officials served in one post, the civil and military bureaucracies usually were represented equally.*

Even though all these officials were as a matter of course charged with the prevention of corruption and of illegal salt production and sales, the primary burden of on-the-spot control of illegal sales devolved to the police inspectors (*hsün-chien*) who by law were supposed to be appointed to each *ch'ang*.[82] Yet they were not particularly suited for the responsibility. They were drawn from military stockades, and many were illiterate. As the temptations for personal gain were often irresistible and the difficulties of halting illegal sales were overwhelming, they regularly colluded with salters and officials alike.

To carry out their duties to the letter of the law, the police inspectors needed to maintain an impartial distance from the salters, but quite the contrary was the case, for as one official described the relationship, the inspectors and salters after long contact became like one family. When salters from their jurisdiction sold salt illegally, the inspectors acted as outside coverup agents; if the salters were arrested in another jurisdiction, inspectors would put up many bribes and also request that their own names be listed as co-captors so that they would be protected from blame and at the same time receive partial credit for the arrest.[83] At other times the inspectors would secretly join the large, uncontrollable bands of smugglers, serving as middlemen in transactions.[84] So rare was it for the police inspectors to capture smugglers personally that one inspector who was wounded in an arrest received an immediate promotion of one rank in spite of the fact that he did not recover enough salt according to regulations to warrant such a reward.[85]

Patrolling the transportation routes between the salterns and the storage depots[86] to prevent highjacking by robbers and pilferage by the transport workers (*shao-kung* or *kang-shao*) was one of the main duties of the police inspectors, but the one at which they were least effective. Officials also were unable to stem the tide of pilferage, for

---

* Cf. *SHY, shih-huo* 25.32 (p. 5230), 26.35 (p. 5251), 27.14 (p. 5262). For concise descriptions of the salt administration in Liang-che East and West during the thirteenth century, see *PCSMC* 3.21a−22a and *Sung-chiang fu-chih* 29.4a (p. 643); Chang Chia-chü (*op. cit.*, pp. 225−226) conveniently summarizes the contents of these materials.

the transport workers put foreign matter – dirt, sand, and even feces – into salt bags to compensate for missing weight and thereby conceal their thefts. Often they did not even bother to take this precaution. Huang Chen considered these losses in transit one of the most pernicious problems confronting the salt administration.

Porters' pilferage affected all aspects of the salt monopoly. Salters were paid *pen-ch'ien* only according to the amount of salt received by officials and so were shortchanged by any thefts in transit. Officials had to justify the amount of salt received with the amount dispatched from the saltern and so were subject to disciplinary action. And the central government's income was diminished because officials were caught in the bind of taking new salt or extorting additional contributions from salters to make back quota payments until eventually there was little salt to meet the current quotas.[87] One cause of the problem lay in the fact that the transport workers did not receive their fees (*shui-chiao ch'ien*) on time or at all.[88] The root of the problem, however, stemmed from the fact that upon reaching the storage depots transport workers had to pay various customary fees which totalled as much as 160 strings of cash.[89] Pilferage was the only means they had of obtaining such payoff money. There seemed to be little way to put a stop to the pilferage, aside from the obvious but not always realizable solution of eliminating or reducing the customary fees and of establishing standardized measures as has been discussed above. Therefore, the transport workers were described as being intimidated not by the threat of punishment but only by the fear of losing their jobs and thereby their source of profit.[90]

Difficulties in shipping the salt, such as caused by the transportation workers, underlay in part an official argument whether salt should be distributed from storage depots in prefectural cities or from the level of the sales-procurement *ch'ang* in *hsien* or *chen* towns. The distances involved in the several legs of the shipping route could be short but more often were not.* Pilferage losses must have increased in direct ratio to the length of the routes. Thus, distribution from the sales-procurement *ch'ang,* one leg nearer to the production-super-

---

* To take an example of the area in Liang-che West where Huang Chen served, the P'u-tung production-supervisory *ch'ang* was 70 *li* to the south of the sales-procurement *ch'ang* at Hua-t'ing; the Yüan-pu production-supervisory ch'ang was 106 *li* to the east. And from Hua-t'ing to the storage depot in Hsiu-chou (later known as Chia-hsing fu) was another 120 *li*. Information from the following two sources was used to compute these distances: Wang Hsiang-chih, *Yü-ti chi-sheng* [Geography of the empire] (Taipei: facsimile reproduction of the *Yüeh-ya t'ang* woodblock edition, 1963), 3.3a (p. 39); Yao Kuang-fu et al., comp., *Ch'ung-hsiu Hua-t'ing hsien-chih* [Revised gazetteer for Hua-t'ing county] (1879) 9.3b.

visory *ch'ang* than the storage depots, would have been less costly in terms of transportation losses. But then merchants had to bear the additional transportation expense of collecting their salt from the sales-procurement *ch'ang* rather than from the distribution storage depots in the prefectural cities, and they were natually reluctant. Accordingly, the officials had to offer covert, illegal bonuses, termed *ta-tai*, as inducement to the merchants. Sometimes these bonuses amounted to as much as eighty *chin* of salt per bag, a bag by regulation being limited to 300 *chin*.[91] Because of losses from these "bonuses," officials proposed in the Cheng-ho period (1111–1117) that distribution points be shifted to the prefectural cities. However, by early in the Southern Sung the extra-legal bonuses were given out at the prefectural storage depots as well. Thus officials reasoned that inasmuch as the added costs of government transportation and administration were not achieving the desired results, the old system should be restored.[92] And so through the Southern Sung the system periodically alternated in what were attempts through ineffectual, superficial changes in the administrative superstructure to cope with a problem whose cause lay elsewhere.

The dual pillars of the salt monopoly controls were a legal code of rewards and punishments for officials and private individuals and an efficiency rating system (*pi-chiao fa*) for officials. All officials were subject to this rating system which essentially was based on their sales or production performance measured against quotas. The elaborateness of the system indicates the reliance the government placed on it as a means of control. According to a stipulated amount or percentage an official exceeded or fell short of a quota, he could receive immediate promotion or demotion, or in less extreme cases, advancement or postponement of the date set for his promotion evaluation review (*mo-k'an*). The ratings were usually made every season or year, but in some instances an official's quota record was computed even by days.[93]

The idea for efficiency rating in the salt administration germinated in the mid-Northern Sung before the salt voucher system had been extended to the southeastern circuits. By the time of Ts'ai Ching the system was widely in use and can be partially credited with the rapid increase in salt revenues at the time.* The Northern Sung did not place much emphasis on production quota efficiency ratings, but more on those for sales quotas. The Southern Sung followed its pre-

---

* Tai's description of the efficiency rating system (pp. 169–176) provides the basis for some of the following discussion.

decessor's model but with one consequential modification: only the officials in those individual districts with the greatest increase and the greatest deficiency received reward and punishment respectively. In the Northern Sung all officials were measured by quota ratings. Such pressure on every official to meet his quota brought about adverse side effects, for the salters were continually forced by various means, legal and illegal, to produce salt and the populace was regularly coerced into buying fixed amounts of salt. Although the Southern Sung modification was intended to eliminate these evils which strained the Northern Sung monopoly to the breaking point, cases of forced salt sales were not uncommon in the Southern Sung.[94] Furthermore, officials felt compelled to resort to more and more illegal bonuses to boost their sales and meet their quotas.*

These incidents of forced sales and illegal bonuses demonstrate the power of the efficiency rating system to prod officials into maintaining a certain level of sales and production. Without this system the entire salt monopoly could have easily fallen apart. Indeed, it was reported in 1160 that the meagerness of rewards for efficiency was sufficient to cause some officials to perform their duties perfunctorily with the concomitant result that salters less vigorously produced salt.†

The laws defining the rewards for officials and private individuals recovering illicit salt and stipulating the penalties for those who produced and sold such salt were as detailed as the regulations for the efficiency rating system,‡ yet not nearly so effective. The penalties for salters selling and/or producing illegal salt have been discussed briefly above. Officials were equally subject to such penalties and, moreover, were liable to prosecution jointly with smugglers for allowing illicit salt to slip past them or for not thoroughly investigating smuggling cases.[95] The thriving illicit salt trade in Liang-che during the Southern

---

* In some cases where there was a large backlog of salt, such as at Wen and T'ai-chou, bonuses were legalized to attract merchants; these dispensations (*chia-jao*) were for restricted periods of time. See *SHY, shih-huo* 26.43 – 44 (pp. 5254 – 55), 27.16 (p. 5263); Tai, pp. 344 – 45; *HSJC* 71.14a – 16a; *SHY, shih-huo* 27.1 (p. 5256). This reference does not make clear which officials were not eligible for sufficient rewards, but a memorial dating from just a few years later (*SHY, shih-huo* 27.1a [p. 5261]) reveals that at least the sales-procurement officials were among this group.

† *SHY, shih-huo* 27.1 (p. 5256). This source does not make clear which officials were not eligible for sufficient rewards, but a memorial dating from just a few years later (*SHY, shih-huo* 27.12 [p. 5261]) reveals that at least the sales-procurement officials were among this group.

‡ For further details see Yoshida Tora, "Nansō no shien tōsei ni tsuite – *Keigen jōhō jirui*, kakukinmon o chūsin toshite" [On the control of illicit salt in Southern Sung, with special focus on the monopoly restriction section of *Ch'ing-yüan t'iao-fa shih-lei*], in Yamazaki sensei taikan kai, ed., *Yamazaki sensei taikan kinen Tōyō shigaku ronshū* (Tokyo: 1967), pp. 501 – 513.

Sung emphatically demonstrates that these penalties were not an adequate deterrent.

Rewards for recovering illegal salt were not much more effective, and could in fact cause other problems. An intricate scheme of promotions, graduated according to the amount of salt captured, was worked out for officials, particularly the police inspectors.[96] On the other hand, private individuals, and sometimes officials, received cash rewards that amounted to several times more than the *pen-ch'ien* that was originally paid for the salt. Funds for rewards came from small amounts retained by local administrators from the sales of salt. This money, though, was often not used for its intended purpose, the officials feeling that the captor's privilege of keeping the smuggler's boat was sufficient reward.[97] In Huang Chen's time there were few funds to pay rewards because sales were low; so rewards had to be squeezed out of other sources. This strongly suggests that rewards could have caused more problems than they solved.

Like any other bureaucracy, the salt administration was eventually plagued by its own cancerous growth. Not only did the administrative machinery become cumbersome, but also it drained monopoly revenues since the swelling number of officials and clerks siphoned off a larger proportion of squeeze. Clerks proliferated in proportion to the number of officials. One salt and tea intendant's branch office in Hua-t'ing had some 400 or 500 clerks and runners.[98] Counting the personnel of this branch office, the two sales-procurement *ch'ang,* and the salt distribution office in the Hua-t'ing region, the total came to more than 1,000 people, all of whom, not to mention their families, depended on the salters for their existence.*

Not only did the number of officials and clerks multiply, new offices were also added to the administrative structure, most notoriously the branch offices. Although Huang Chen railed against the evils of this office most vociferously, it existed long before his time and was the subject of similar complaints. Early in the thirteenth century a branch office was created and then later abolished when it was discovered that revenues were diminishing rather than increasing.[99] The branch office must have re-emerged, for Sung Tzu-hsiu, shortly before Huang's term of appointment, successfully petitioned to have the post eliminated again.[100] Then Huang in 1259 had to request to dismantle the very same office.[101] According to him, the branch office had been set up with the convenience of the salters in mind. How-

---

* *HSJC* 71.7a. For the general problem of clerks in the central government bureaucracy see James T. C. Liu, "The Sung Views on the Control of Government Clerks," *Journal of the Economic and Social History of the Orient,* 10, No. 2 (1967), pp. 317–344.

ever, the abuses inflicted upon them by the clerks and officials from this office were, in his opinion, one of the primary reasons for the calamitous state of the local salt monopoly. Rather than have an official from the regular office go twice a month to the production-supervisory *ch'ang*, someone from the branch office went every five days. Each trip meant 800 strings of cash for document transmission (*p'ai-hsia*) fees, whereas the regular office demanded only 100 strings.[102] And this was just the preliminary round of extortion payments.

Merchants and Marketing

The legal commercial activities of the salt merchants were carefully regulated through a system of vouchers and certificates. Although the red tape involved in processing these documents was not inconsiderable, the system was manageable for the Chinese bureaucracy which excelled in such paperwork. Indeed, from the few records that remain about this subject, it appears that this aspect of the salt monopoly controls was the most successful within its established objectives. Tampering with voucher documents, accounts, and registers which were cross-filed at different offices required infinitely more collusion than that between salters and police who joined to produce and market illicit salt or than the machinations of clerks and officials who misappropriated *pen-ch'ien* or extorted extra fees and salt from the salters. The rarity of reference to flagrant malpractices in the Monopoly Bureaus indicates the effectiveness of their control system. When an official took funds from one of these bureaus in 1172 there was no legal precedent for his punishment.[103]

Although records were kept for other procedures in the production and distribution of salt—for example the number of boilings or the *pen-ch'ien*—such records were sometimes neglected or lackadaisically maintained. They did not lend themselves as readily as voucher records to verification through many administrative levels of cross-checking. For instance, there was no way to double check the actual quantity of salt produced without on-site inspection by officials, even though the number of boilings was supposed to be entered into a register. The meticulous attention paid to the elaborately conceived voucher system suggests that the government ultimately was more interested in controlling the receipt of the voucher sales and the use of these vouchers, for it was at this point that the government made its profit. The purchase of illicit salt by merchants of course was a problem that could be effectively contained only through scrupulous police inspection and investigation, not accounting techniques, as this salt was ipso facto out of the monopoly domain.

Merchants wishing to purchase salt produced in Liang-che first had to buy their vouchers at either of the Monopoly Bureau offices at Hsing-tsai or Chen-chiang.[104] Each of these offices sold vouchers for different production areas. While the voucher prices remained fairly standard between the two Monopoly Bureau offices, the method of payment did not. Very exact payment formulas were established from time to time for each bureau outlet; the ratio of paper currency, coins, silver, and gold was carefully stipulated[105] so that the government received maximum value for the various media of exchange as their market values shifted.

The value of the vouchers themselves also varied from time to time since the government arbitrarily regulated their period of circulation. Issuing new vouchers—a profit-making practice vigorously pursued by the Southern Sung in the exact fashion of the late Northern Sung—would automatically devalue any old, outstanding vouchers. Merchants were naturally required to use the new vouchers when obtaining salt at the distribution storage depots. Sometimes they would pay a surcharge in cash (t'ieh-na) if they used the old vouchers, or else they turned in both old and new vouchers at a stipulated proportion (tui-tai) highly favorable to the government. The application of either method, or both simultaneously, was entirely at the discretion of the government.* New series of vouchers were frequently issued. Just in the period from 1129 to 1134 there were five new issues.[106] After the monopoly revenue declined in the thirteenth century, many new series were brought out.[107] Such issuances of new vouchers could spell considerable financial losses, if not ruin, for many merchants.

Merchants would take their vouchers to the appropriate distribution point—the storage depot at either the prefectural or hsien level—to obtain their salt. When the system whereby they went to the hsien level distribution depot was in effect, they were originally supposed to collect pre-determined amounts of salt from all or several of the various ch'ang under the prefecture's jurisdiction. However, the stringency of this regulation eroded over time to the point where merchants began themselves to designate the particular area where they wished to obtain salt. These areas of course were the ones where they received the most favorable treatment; accordingly, the malpractice of illegal bonuses began.[108]

Based on the time of arrival at the distribution center, merchants were placed in order (tzu-tz'u) to collect their salt. This priority was

---

* Since Tai (pp. 320—21, 342—43) and others have examined this subject, there is little need to go into details here.

of some importance when it is considered that while waiting to obtain their salt—and sometimes there could be a wait of many months—a new series of vouchers could be issued. Because there was so much at stake financially in this priority list, we can easily imagine, in the absence of any concrete evidence, that it was prone to manipulation.

Vouchers were numbered and had the name of the purchaser written on them.* The names of merchants were registered at the Monopoly Bureau so that when the vouchers were returned to this office, there could be a check to see if any irregularities had occurred. The vouchers were to be dispatched under seal to the Monopoly Bureau as soon as they were cashed in to prevent their being used a second time; such was not always the case, though.† All vouchers were eventually incinerated.

With the salt, the merchants were given an accompanying permit (*sui-yen wen-yin*) which proved that the salt they were transporting was legally acquired. This apparently was the one means the police inspectorate had for determining which salt was legal and which illegal. Designated on the accompanying permit, which was valid for one year, were the place(s) the salt was to be sold. All salt produced in Liang-che was for exclusive distribution there and in She-chou (in Chiang-nan East circuit) just across the Liang-che border.‡ Huai-nan salt was also allowed to be distributed in certain areas of Liang-che. If a merchant was not able to dispose of all his salt in the designated area, if he wanted in mid-route to change the distribution area, or if he needed to extend the time limit of his accompanying sales permit, he could apply for such permission through a complicated procedure.

Conclusion

Ultimately the only yardstick for measuring the effectiveness of controls in the salt monopoly is the prevalence of illicit salt production and sales. By this standard, Liang-che monopoly controls must be judged a partial failure, for the incidence of illicit sales is patently obvious. One official in 1160 graphically illustrated the scope of the problem when he pointed out that the city of Shao-hsing and its two surrounding *hsien,* being in a salt producing prefecture that was the

---

* Portions of the following discussion are drawn from Kusano's article (see note 104), pp. 140–145. Tai (pp. 112–114) pieces together the physical appearance and the contents of the vouchers. Note that officials and their relatives were forbidden to buy salt.

† See the case discussed in *SHY, shih-huo* 25.33–34 (p. 5231).

‡ *SS, shih-huo* 182.6a-b; Tai (pp. 75–77) also provides information on the sales distribution territories for all salt.

most populous in Liang-che East, bought from official sources only 16,000 *chin* of salt annually. By comparison, the smaller cities of Wu and Ch'ü-chou and their adjacent *hsien*, which were entirely dependent on salt transported from other areas, purchased each year 500,000 and 300,000 *chin,* respectively.*

In the course of this study we have seen the possibility, in terms of production time, Liang-che salters had for manufacturing illicit salt, the pressures driving them to engage in illegal activities, and the approximate extent of illicit salt production. This examination of the institutional controls has also suggested certain inadequacies in the system—lack of efficient production controls, an unmanageably large number of furnaces in Liang-che, an inability to prevent pilferage by the transport workers, and the malpractice of illegal bonuses. But was there some more fundamental defect (or defects) in the system that underlay the illicit salt and other problems?

First of all, the fact that there were no effective means of controlling production can bear repetition here, for illicit salt originated at this stage of the process, whatever market it may have eventually found. No matter how vigorously carried out, the few controls imposed were simply insufficient to cope with the problem. Essentially all that was needed to manufacture sea salt was sea water, some land, a few pieces of equipment, which would be costly only if used for a large-scale operation, and labor, all of which were in ready abundance. Thus "backyard" production was not only possible, it was probable. Li Hsin-ch'uan called such privately boiled salt "pot salt" (*huo-tzu yen*). He explained that each salter family had its own pot which in a night over a small fire could turn out sixty *chin* of salt in two boilings. Two hundred families with ten furnaces, therefore, could manufacture in one year more than one million *chin*.[109]

Since there was no way to put a stop to this privately manufactured salt, the threat of penalties served little purpose. Like many other officials, Chu Hsi noted that in spite of stern regulations, illicit salt sales still flourished.† Salt producing areas seldom consumed gov-

---

* *SHY, shih-huo* 27.2–3 (pp. 5256–57). In discussion at the conference, Professor Miyazaki hypothesized that one cause for the apparent low level of official sales in Liang-che might be due to the fact that soldiers and officials received salt—exactly to what extent we cannot fully determine—as part of their compensation. With the Southern Sung capital located in Liang-che, the salt paid to the many officials there could easily have flowed into the local black market.

† Chu Hsi, "Tsou yen-chiu-k'e chi ch'ai-i li-hai chuang" [A memorial on the salt and wine tax and the advantages and disadvantages of the drafted service system], in his *Chu-tzu ta-ch'üan* [Complete collected works of Chu Hsi], *Ssu-pu pei-yao* ed., 18.13b.

ernment salt which was more expensive and sold mainly in urban areas. Huang Chen also called attention to the fact that one never saw those who lived in the mountains and rural areas entering the city to buy salt.[110]

Even assuming that it were possible to eliminate all illicit salt production and sales, the fundamental question arises whether such action would be advisable. Huang Chen posed the problem in this way:

Every time we see that the prohibitions against illicit salt are stringent, then the quota of official salt is deficient. If the prohibitions against illicit salt are relaxed, then the quota of official salt is increased. How is it that the multiplicity of illicit sales has contrary [to expectation] benefit for the government?[111]

He answered his question by demonstrating that illegal sales by salters allowed them to acquire the principal not always forthcoming from the government but necessary to produce government quota salt. The management control policy that Huang implies here bears striking similarity to a view that has recently become current in modern management theory. An American industrial psychologist has postulated that "by permitting a controlled amount of [employee] theft, management can avoid reorganizing jobs and raising wages. Management still keeps most business decision-making functions in its own hands and retains workers without increasing salaries and benefits."[112]

Thus it may be argued that illicit salt sales served an indispensable function in the Sung monopoly, whether the officials cared to admit it or not. Drying up this reservoir of extra profit for the salters would mean that they would have to be given enough *pen-ch'ien* to pay in full for their many expenses and customary fees. This, in turn, would necessitate tighter restriction on corruption by officials and clerks, which was beyond the realistic means of the administration. And so permitting illicit sales was the least troublesome solution to the problem. The government, after all, was concerned first and foremost with collecting revenues. As long as they continued to pour into the treasury without serious disruption there was no need to change the system or rumple the feathers of contented officials. Certainly there were laws against officials expropriating the *pen-ch'ien* or against their extorting money and salt from the salters, but as long as the quota was met, violations were not earnestly prosecuted. Only when illicit salt sales ran out of control, when large bands of smugglers formed, or when vast numbers of salters fled, as happened toward the end of the Sung, did the government seriously initiate legal action.

While on the one hand the tacitly allowed illicit salt sales were essential to the operation of the monopoly as it was imperfectly constructed, these illegal sales, on the other hand, always posed a threat to the monopoly. By definition, competition in any form is antithetical to a monopoly, and this is just what the illicit salt sales were. Whether the government could do anything about it or not, its salt was continually in competition with illicit salt. The fact that this salt drove higher priced government salt out of the markets near salt producing areas has already been mentioned. Government salt was three times as expensive as its competitor.[113] There is even one reported case when some salters, whose transportation costs for quota salt were excessive, discovered that it was more economical to buy illicit salt near the sales-procurement *ch'ang* and turn this over to the authorities instead.[114] This competition constrained the government from raising its prices and thereby acquiring more funds with which to pay additional *pen-ch'ien*. At one point when an increased surtax (*t'ieh-na*) of three strings of cash was tacked onto the price of each bag, merchants refused to buy salt, forcing a price rollback.[115] Furthermore, the general demand for salt, even though it was indispensable to human diet, was not totally inelastic; so people would simply buy less salt of either type if prices greatly strained their already low incomes.* In other words, raising the prices beyond a certain point would prove counter-productive in terms of revenue.

Another area of competition in the Sung salt monopoly that is not always recognized lies in the system of production and sales quotas placed upon officials. Just as with the case of illicit salt sales, this efficiency rating system had both desirable and undesirable effects, the undesirable effects paradoxically undermining the very control mechanism designed to overcome them. The need to meet quotas forced officials of the different distribution depots into offering illegal bonuses, in effect competing with each other for merchants' trade. The salt for these bonuses was derived in the long run from extra demands made upon the salters, and so the vicious cycle began. One further problem — and virtue also, as we have discussed previously — of the Southern Sung efficiency rating system was that not every official was liable to penalties or rewards, only those with the great deficits or increases. Thus the vast majority of officials could maintain inefficient and corrupt practices within certain limits and not suffer any consequences.

One principle of a monopoly is: the more essential the monopolized item, the less consumer resistance to monopoly taxes and therefore the greater the potential profits, assuming the implementation of effective controls. However, the converse of this theory holds true too: the more an item, such as salt, is considered a necessity of life, the

---

* I-shuan Sun, "Salt Taxation in China," Diss. University of Wisconsin 1953. For a discussion of the demand curve for salt, see pp. 99 – 102. This thesis focuses on an economic analysis of the twentieth century salt monopoly.

more it tends to resist the constraints of a monopoly. Therefore, inherent in the Sung salt monopoly were centripetal and centrifugal forces that subjected the system to constant tension. The controls imposed on production and administration represent some of the centripetal forces, while the competitive elements in the monopoly were the centrifugal forces. Effective monopoly controls had to balance these forces, to counter one against the other. Such a balance was precarious at best, if not heavily weighted in favor of the centrifugal movement. Imbalance in any one aspect of the monopoly, such as illegal bonuses or pilferage by porters, would set off a chain reaction that Sung officials, given the limits of their expertise and of the management tools at their command, found difficult to bring under control.

Notes to Chapter Five

1. *SHY, shih-huo* 27.2 (p. 5256).
2. "Nan Sung Liang-che chih yen-cheng" [The Liang-che salt administration in the Southern Sung], *Shih-huo*, 1, No. 6 (February, 1935), pp. 19 – 25.
3. "Nansō no engyō keiei, seisanmen o chūsin toshite" [Management of the Southern Sung salt monopoly, focusing on production] in *Sōdai shakai keizai shi kenkyū (jo)* [Studies of Sung social and economic history, part 1], Ajiya-shi kenkyū kai, Sōdai kenkyū bu, ed., *Tōyō shigaku ronshū*, No. 5 (Tokyo, 1960), pp. 71 – 137.
4. Tai I-hsüan, *Sung-tai ch'ao-yen chih-tu yen-chiu* [A study of the salt voucher system in the Sung dynasty] (Shanghai: Commercial Press, 1957), pp. 56 – 73.
5. Tai, pp. 231 – 253; Ch'ien Kung-po, "Sung-tai chieh-yen te sheng-chang ho yun-hsiao chih-tu" [The transportation and production system of the Shensi salt monopoly in the Sung], *Ta-lu tsa-chih*, 28, No. 5 (March 15, 1964), pp. 18 – 22.
6. Tai, pp. 254 – 286.
7. Tai, pp. 307 – 335; Liu Ch'üan, "Sung Yüan kuan-chuan-mai yin-fa te ch'uang-li yü wan-ch'eng" [The establishment and achievement of the official monopoly voucher system in the Sung and Yüan], *Chung-kuo she-hui ching-chi shih chi-k'an*, 6, No. 2 (December, 1939), pp. 217 – 266; Yuki Tōru, "Hokusō jidai tōnan en no kanbaihō no sui-i ni tsuite" [A study of the transition of the official sales system in the Southeast salt monopoly during the Northern Sung], *Tōhō gaku*, 34 (June, 1967), pp. 47 – 61.
8. *SS*, 88.1a.
9. Central Intelligence Agency, Precipitation map in *Communist China Map Folio* (Washington, D.C.: Central Intelligence Agency, 1967).
10. *YH* 181.36a (p. 3434).
11. *SHY, shih-huo* 27.33 (p. 5272).
12. *APT* 2.
13. *CYTC* 14.6a (p. 423).
14. *SS, shih-huo* 182.4b.
15. *YH* 181.36a (p. 3434).
16. *SHY, shih-huo* 23.14 – 15 (pp. 5181 – 5182).
17. *SS, shih-huo* 182.3a.
18. *SS, shih-huo* 182.4a.
19. *SS, shih-huo* 182.3a-b.
20. *SHY, shih-huo* 26.3 (p. 5235).
21. *SHY, shih-huo* 26.5 (p. 5236).
22. *CYTC* 14.5b (p. 422).
23. *SHY, shih-huo* 26.9 (p. 5238); 26.10 – 11 (pp. 5238 – 5239).
24. *CYTC* 17.8b (p. 540).
25. *HNYL*, p. 1703.
26. *HNYL*, p. 2077.

27. Ch'üan Han-sheng, "T'ang Sung cheng-fu sui-ju yü huo-pi ching-chi te kuan-hsi" [The economic relationship between public income and money economy in the T'ang and Sung dynasties], *Kuo-li chung-yang yen-chiu-yüan li-shih yü-yen yen-chiu-so chi-k'an*, 20, No. 1 (June, 1949), pp. 189–221.
28. *SHY, shih-huo* 27.34 (p. 5272).
29. Ibid.
30. *APT*, Introduction (*hsü*), n. pag.
31. *APT* 37.
32. Shih Su, comp., *Chia-t'ai K'uai-chi chih* [Gazetteer for K'uai-chi in the Chia-t'ai period 1201–04] (1926 photo reprint of the Ch'ing Chia-ch'ing edition) 17.44a–45a.
33. *SHY, shih-huo* 28.1–2 (p. 5279).
34. *HSJC* 71.10b.
35. *SHY, shih-huo* 27.33 (p. 5272).
36. *HSJC* 71.10b–11b.
37. *SS, shih-huo* 182.26a-b.
38. Tai I-hsüan, p. 5.
39. *APT* 26.
40. *CYTC* 14.6a (p. 423).
41. *SHY, shih-huo* 27.33 (p. 5272).
42. *APT* "Tzu-t'i."
43. *APT* 44,45.
44. *HSJC* 71.8b–9a; *APT* 33.
45. *SHY, shih-huo* 27.33 (p. 5272).
46. *SHY, shih-huo* 28.1–2 (p. 5279).
47. *APT* 12.
48. *APT* 24.
49. *APT* 2.
50. *SS, shih-huo* 182.4b.
51. *SHY, shih-huo* 26.26–27 (pp. 5246–5247).
52. *SHY, shih-huo* 27.11–12 (p. 5261).
53. *SHY, shih-huo* 27.13 (p. 5262).
54. *SHY, shih-huo* 27.34 (p. 5272).
55. *APT* 5.
56. *APT* 48.
57. *HSJC* 80.10a.
58. *HSJC* 80.12a–14a.
59. *SHY, shih-huo* 26.1–2 (p. 5234).
60. *SHY, shih-huo* 27.12 (p. 5261).
61. *SHY, shih-huo* 27.18 (p. 5264).
62. *SHY, shih-huo* 27.18–19 (pp. 5264–5265).
63. *HSJC* 80.2a.
64. *HSJC* 77.1a.
65. *SS* 424.19a.
66. *SS* 389.9b–10a.
67. *SHY, shih-huo* 26.13 (p. 5240).
68. *HSJC* 80.1b.
69. *SHY, shih-huo* 28.57 (p. 5307).
70. *SHY, shih-huo* 28.3 (p. 5280); see also *HSJC* 80.10a.
71. *SHY, shih-huo* 26.11 (p. 5239).
72. *SHY, shih-huo* 28.3 (p. 5280).
73. *SHY, shih-huo* 27.11 (p. 5261).
74. *HSJC* 71.6b.
75. *Sung-chiang fu-chih* 29.3b–4a (p. 643).
76. Ibid.
77. *SHY, shih-huo* 26.13 (p. 5240).
78. *SHY, shih-huo* 27.22 (p. 5266), 26.13 (p. 5240).
79. *HSJC* 77.1a-b.
80. *SHY, chih-kuan* 43.43, 43.45 (pp. 3295–96).
81. *SS, shih-huo* 182.26a-b.
82. *SHY, shih-huo* 27.1 (p. 5256).
83. *SHY, shih-huo* 27.11 (p. 5261).
84. *SHY, shih-huo* 27.1 (p. 5256).

85. *SHY, shih-huo* 27.28 (p. 5269).
86. *APT* 48; see also *SHY, shih-huo* 27.11 (p. 5261).
87. *HSJC* 71.10a-b.
88. *HSJC* 80.9a.
89. *HSJC* 80.9b.
90. *HSJC* 71.12a.
91. *SHY, shih-huo* 26.36 (p. 5251).
92. *SHY, shih-huo* 25.32 (p. 5230).
93. *SHY, shih-huo* 27.36 (p. 5273).
94. See, for example, *SHY, shih-huo* 26.42 (p. 5254); *SS*, Kao-tsung *pen-chi* 31.14a, Li-tsung *pen-chi* 41.8b; *HSJC* 71.18a.
95. *SHY, shih-huo* 26.3 (p. 5235); 26.32 (p. 5249).
96. For an example see *SHY, shih-huo* 26.26–27 (pp. 5251–52).
97. *SHY, shih-huo* 27.20–21 (pp. 5265–66).
98. *HSJC* 71.17a.
99. *SHY, shih-huo* 27.14 (p. 5262).
100. *SHY*, chih-kuan 43.45 (p. 3296).
101. *SS* 424.19a.
102. *HSJC* 71.6b.
103. *SHY, shih-huo* 27.38 (p. 5274).
104. *SHY, shih-huo* 27.9 (p. 5260). Also see Kusano Yasushi, "Nansō jidai no Wai-setsu enshōhō" [The salt voucher system of Huai-nan and Liang-che in the Southern Sung], *Shien*, 86 (December, 1961), pp. 123–54, esp. p. 137.
105. For example, see *SHY, shih-huo* 26.20 (p. 5243), 27.9 (p. 5260), 27.21–22 (p. 5266), 27.41 (p. 5276).
106. *SS* 182.23b–24a.
107. Tai, p. 343.
108. *SHY, shih-huo* 27.11 (p. 5261).
109. *CYTC* 14.6b (p. 424).
110. *HSJC* 71.20a.
111. *HSJC* 71.19b.
112. Lawrence R. Zeitlin, "A Little Larceny Can Do a Lot for Employee Morale," *Psychology Today,* June 1971, p. 26.
113. *SHY, shih-huo* 26.27 (p. 5247).
114. *SHY, shih-huo* 27.40–41 (pp. 5275–5276).
115. *SHY, shih-huo* 26.21 (p. 5244).

1126-27: Political Crisis and the Integrity of Culture

JOHN WINTHROP HAEGER

THE SUNG LEGACY IS BITTERSWEET. Unable or unwilling to build an empire worthy of the Han and T'ang, the dynasts of Chao inverted the ancient rules of tribute, bought from Jürchen and Khitan the peace they could not win, sold their classical wisdom to the Koreans, manufactured pots of subtle green and gray, painted stunning vibrant birds and flowers, and built the largest cities of the medieval world. This uneasy combination of political failure with cultural effervescence has particularly attracted Chinese scholars to the Sung, but tied their attention to the problem of national and imperial humiliation. Scholars seeking explanations for Sung weakness have produced a large corpus of studies on the institutions of government: on the personality of the emperors, the power of the ministers, the size and organization of the armies, and on the structural problems of society and economy which had implications for the mobilization of resources. The dynasty survived for 320 years, however, and survival is not merely the obverse of weakness. Studies which have tried to show that the persistence of Sung rule across three centuries was only the residue of its founding strength and had no independent spring of life have not only been at odds with the preponderance of cultural and social evidence, but also have proved emotionally unsatisfactory as well. The curiosity of scholars about the ways and means of Sung survival is not really based on a mechanistic interest in the palliatives which avoided or postponed impending doom, but shows instead an implicit interest in the positive achievements of the day. Surely revolutionary advances in literature, education, urban culture, and the arts did not merely gild a dying lily. Humanistic scholarship on culture is a fragmentary answer to the question of survival, but does not enter fully into the determination of historical significance. Questions about survival imply a historical

[143]

interest in the problem of value, which demands some resolution of the politico-cultural dilemma. Not really *how* did the Sung survive, but *why*? What moved these generations who compromised their homeland to non-Chinese, yet built a world of letters and a heritage of grace?

The last months of Northern Sung show the inherent tensions in bold relief. These months culminated foreign policies which had begun in the tenth century and had been christened by the Treaty of Shan-yüan in 1004. They were governed by a set of laws and institutions inherited from T'ang, reformed, then restored, and marked by the attendant travail. They bequeathed to Southern Sung a country reduced by half in size and a preference for concession and negotiation over war which proved remarkably unshakable across the years in spite of repeated trials and sharp dissent. This paper is designed to explore the ways in which men and institutions responded to these months of crisis, based primarily on the testimony of one Li Kang (1083 – 1140) in a remarkable memoir called the *Ching-k'ang ch'uan-hsin lu*. Li, an official in the Board of Ceremonies when Emperor Hui-tsung was persuaded to abdicate at the end of 1125, and later prominent as the first chief minister to Emperor Kao-tsung in 1127, is famous for opposition to accommodation in any form, for his determination to fight the invading Chin armies in an offensive posture, and for his insistence on mobilization to maintain the court and capital in the Yellow River valley at K'ai-feng. As this strong, emotional, and litigious personality interacted with his fellows and with the institutions they shared and recorded the unfolding process through eight troubled months, he told unconsciously the story of values and commitment in his time. The configuration of contemporary tensions and the nature of the Sung achievement is illuminated by Li's window on government at mid-season.

The Crisis of the Monarchy

In the early pages of the *Ching-k'ang ch'uan-hsin lu*, Li Kang's attention is focused on the monarchy. In 12th/1125 Hui-tsung published a proclamation in which he took personal responsibility for the dangerous state of affairs resulting from the Chin invasion, summoned an army, appointed the Grand Heir (Chao Huan, the subsequent Ch'in-tsung) as Governor of K'ai-feng, and made his own preparations to leave K'ai-feng for the south.[1] This investiture of the heir-apparent with chief ceremonial responsibility for the seat of government did not formally withdraw the Emperor from his position as chief of state, but it did strain the cosmological connection between the son of heaven and the symbolic center of the world, infinitely complicated the machinery of government, and brought to mind a score of baleful precedents in time. It drew criticism from Li Kang and some of his associates primarily because of its murkiness and potential ambiguity: an emperor in absentia could not be compensated by other royal blood in an unsubstantial administrative post, especially under fire. When Li went to confer with his friend Wu Min (d. 1131, a Reviewing Policy Adviser), he drew an analogy with the departure of T'ang Hsüan-tsung from the besieged capital of Lo-yang in 755, which had in fact ended Hsüan-tsung's reign, but without benefit of a formal writ of abdication.[2] Had Hsüan-tsung's son not assumed the throne, the Li family would certainly have been lost and the T'ang ended, but Hsüan-tsung's failure to abdicate in proper fashion created an ambiguity so troublesome to posterity that historians had been unable to assign the year 756 clearly to either reign, and had in consequence preserved dual designations.* In the midst of a grave military crisis, Li's first concern was apparently to protect the mandate and to ensure that the conventions and ceremonies by which it was maintained would remain untarnished. This formalistic approach to crisis seems to have been almost instinctive. In the Chinese tradition resort to historical precedent has generally preceded and often substituted for empirical analysis, suggesting that the universal tension between emotional commitment to history and intellectual commitment to value traditionally favored the former. Beyond this initial, emotionalized, analogical response, Li Kang demonstrated practical concerns: he was unimpressed by Hui-tsung's ability and inclination to fight a war, and could readily see that advantages might be derived from a change in leadership. He therefore persuaded Wu Min that they call together for Hui-tsung's abdication. Li's decision followed an instruction from Hui-tsung on 21/12th/1125 which invited his ministers to submit "frank words" (*chih-yen*) on the crisis occasioned by the Chin invasion. Li had answered with a sealed memorial enumerating possible solutions — monarchical self-rectification, acceptance of criticism and suggestions, preparation of military supplies, bureaucratic reform and change of the year-designation — but before the day's end he had rejected them all and concluded that only Hui-tsung's abdication would be really "appropriate."[3]

Although we preserve no formal codification of succession procedures for the house of Chao, abdication had no precedent in fact. With a single exception, each emperor since T'ai-tsu had duly designated an heir to the throne, who had succeeded him at death. Ying-tsung had

---

* The year 756 is designated both as Hsüan-tsung T'ien-pao 15 and Su-tsung Chih-te 1.

been an adopted son, and a regency had been provided for Che-tsung, who ascended at the age of ten, but these were standard aberrations, of far less moment than an abdication under fire.* Yet of all Li Kang's suggestions to the court, the abdication of Hui-tsung met with no recorded opposition. The Emperor himself merely "sighed."[4] The ministers were silent. Li's reaction to a crescendo of crisis was certainly a combination of deliberation and subconscience, but he focused in the end on the monarchy, apparently choosing to change the personnel in order to preserve the institution. He, Wu Min, and the other ministers of the court who offered no objection evidently preferred the loss of an emperor to the end of a dynasty. Wu Min told Hui-tsung that abdication would assure his own longevity and the security of the ancestral shrines. This euphemism for dynastic survival (the ancestral shrines are only secure as long as the dynasty survives) demonstrated a significant ability of contemporary men to abstract their loyalty one step beyond the person whom they served. This was not an easy matter, for the abstraction of loyalty could not be blatant. The well-known figure of Meng-ku, onetime minister to the ancient state of Ch'u, who had rejected the king's badge of office claiming to be "no minister to man, but a servant of the gods" was still entirely unacceptable in the Confucian tradition, and Meng-ku appears only in the uncanonical *Chan-kuo ts'e*. Furthermore, when Hui-tsung left K'ai-feng, he was naturally accompanied by a complement of eunuchs, relatives and minor officials, but of his chief ministers, apparently only Yü-wen Ts'ui-chung, Right Executive of the Department of Ministeries, was in his suite.† Li Pang-yen, Po Shih-chung, Wu Min and the others remained to serve Ch'in-tsung. This remarkable development suggests that the capacity to abstract subtly was widely generalized among Li's contemporaries at the Sung court. In 12th/1125 it served to facilitate Hui-tsung's abdication. In the following months it paved the way for other departures from Sung custom, but finally it would reach beyond the dynasty itself to assure subconsciously a policy of peace.

In spite of his mute willingness to transcend the traditional re-

---

* Ying-tsung had been adopted by Jen-tsung before the latter produced any children of his own, and his early designation as Grand Heir was not changed. Ying-tsung's personal name was Chao Shu; he was T'ai-tsung's great grandson and the thirteenth son of Chao Ch'ung-jang, King of P'u. The regency for Che-tsung was conducted by his mother, the Empress Dowager née Kao. See Chia Hu-ch'en, *Chung-kuo li-tai ti-wang p'u-hsi hui-pien* [Chronological Register of Chinese Royalty] (Taipei: 1966).

† *CKCHL* 1.4b. When Ch'in-tsung wanted to appoint Li Kang to ministerial rank and asked about vacancies, the Right Executive was reported vacant because Yü-wen was accompanying Hui-tsung.

quirements of personal loyalty, Li Kang had difficulty with transcendental symbols. The *tsung-she*, altars of the soil and home of the ruling clan, were the logical focus for loyalty which had passed by the emperor himself, but the *tsung-she* themselves had abstract properties at least as important as their concrete manifestation: the permanent shrines of the dynasty in the city of K'ai-feng. But in this matter of symbolism, Li was hopelessly literalist: the concrete altars were the whole reality, and the dynasty would perish without them as surely as a tree without roots. Moreover, when the literalist attitude toward symbols became emotionalized and obsessive, it turned into a kind of psychologism. Li and his associates became increasingly determined to achieve control over crisis by internalized, symbolic, psychological manipulations. In this context the statesmen of mid-Sung were acting in a traditionally Confucian manner: as the mind dominates nature, so the quality of officials decides the fate of the empire, the conduct of war rests with men, and crises are resolved by psychic cultivation.[5] In the 1120s the motive power of this cultivation was focused on the concrete aspects of symbolic order.

The abdication proved more symbolic than effective, however. Although a major monarchical crisis was temporarily avoided, and the clarity of the mandate was reaffirmed, Hui-tsung's "mobile court" at the Southern Capital was by no means reassuring to his son's new government in K'ai-feng. Having avoided one problem, the ministers were immediately faced with another. Hui-tsung had no sooner arrived south of the Huai than his court became a new kind of threat. In K'ai-feng, Hui-tsung endangered the dynasty because he could evolve no satisfactory policy to counter the Chin invaders. Leaving, he threatened the dynasty because he muddied dynastic authority. In Nan-ching he became immediately a rallying point for potential secessionists. In fact there is no solid evidence that any challenge to Ch'in-tsung's authority was ever generated in the south, but the rumors spread like wind, so that before Hui-tsung had been gone two months, K'ai-feng was set in motion to arrange for his return.

When Li Kang traveled south in 3rd/1126 to play a central role in resolving the dilemma which his own previous suggestion had created, he stopped along the way to deal simultaneously with the so-called Tao-chün t'ai-shang Empress, the Empress née Cheng, who had fled from K'ai-feng along with Hui-tsung and now lodged in extreme southern Honan. Empress Cheng presented no danger of secession, but she might have rallied dissidents. Furthermore, although she was not Ch'in-tsung's real mother, she could still call upon the precedent of regency, three times exercised in Northern Sung, to "lower the screen"

and take the powers of government back into her own hands.* Li
Kang carried out long discussions both with her and later with Hui-
tsung over the arrangements which Ch'in-tsung had ordered for their
accommodation in K'ai-feng. These are clearly significant under the
circumstances. If any concession with regard to honorific terminology
or prospective domicile, both discussed in worrisome detail, had been
made to either; if, for example, the Empress Dowager had been permitted to live in the Forbidden Palace as she demanded, the effect of
Hui-tsung's earlier abdication might have been substantially undone.
Not only would their return then have seemed to void the transmission
of the mandate, and therefore call into question the proper designation
of the year, but the political and diplomatic advantage derived from a
new beginning vis-à-vis the Chin might have been dramatically reversed.

It is clear that these efforts to take into consideration both the
realities of power and the potent influence of titles, ceremony and
convention in shaping policy were not vacuous. Li told the Empress
Dowager that the court wished "to correspond with the ceremonies
and proprieties in order to soothe the expectations of the empire."[6]
This ascription to ceremony of the power to soothe popular sentiment
was another way to say that Li himself and his colleagues at the court
would all have felt more assurance in a time of crisis if they could
have relied on complete consistency and the appearance of order
within the institution of the monarchy. Significantly, the T'ang had
not been lost because Hsüan-tsung failed to abdicate according to the
dictates of custom, but this ceremonial aberration had caused confusion and "regret" to "later generations." Li might have chosen some
other parable, where a real disaster had ensued, but he selected the
Ling-wu affair, where the dynasty survived, and the confusion was
merely ceremonial. In the crisis of 1126, the court had necessarily
to consider the realities of power, but as they mobilized to meet the
crisis, they both abstracted their allegiance toward the dynastic
institution, and simultaneously used the symbols of the dynasty,
with meticulous attention to propriety, to assure themselves that their
world was still in order. It was important to remain convinced that the
crisis was minor, and could be overcome, just as the T'ang had in
fact survived.

---

* Northern Sung saw one formal regency, from 1085–1090 by the Empress née
Kao for her son Che-tsung. But the Empress née Ts'ao was "co-regent" for Ying-tsung
throughout his short reign (1063–1067) even though Ying-tsung ascended at the ripe
age of 32; Jen-tsung's mother had been "close to the government" in the early years of
his reign, after 1022, and Empress Hsiang was briefly co-regent with Hui-tsung. See
Chia. The consort née Cheng had been made Empress upon the death of the former
Empress née Wang in 1108; she was made "dowager" (t'ai-hou) on the eve of Hui-
tsung's departure from K'ai-feng. See SS 243.10b–12b.

The Decline of the Eunuchs

The decline of eunuch power in 1126 is congruent with the court's renewed emphasis on symbolic order. All the influence and obvious importance of eunuchs through the ages, the tacit acceptance of eunuchs as an institution, and the inability of Chinese government to invent an adequate substitute for the services they performed could never alter a fundamental fact: eunuchs were always biologically and politically unnatural, and consequently inconsistent with the best principles of symbolic order. It is therefore entirely reasonable that individual and collective attacks should have been made on eunuchs in an effort to curb their power by men determined to preserve the dynasty by refurbishing its symbolic claims to rule.

The unfortunate plight of eunuchs in 1126 appears most dramatically in a public denunciation of the infamous T'ung Kuan (d. 1126) and his associates by one Ch'en Tung, a student of the Grand University, and in the murder of several eunuchs during the so-called *fu-ch'üeh* demonstration early in the second month, when a group of students and other residents of the capital assembled before the palace gate to demand the reinstatement of Li Kang, earlier removed in consequence of a disagreement over military strategy. The consequences of this plight are seen in a somewhat subtler way when Li Kang was sent to the Southern Capital to negotiate with Hui-tsung and the Empress Dowager, accompanied by eunuchs, but personally charged with a task which would certainly have been left to eunuchs alone during Hui-tsung's reign or during certain earlier dynasties.

While T'ung Kuan was unquestionably the most significant eunuch in late Northern Sung, and represents the culmination of eunuch power, Ch'en Tung's censure only scratched the surface of eunuch influence. By the end of Hui-tsung's reign, which especially indulged them despite the implicit violation of tradition, eunuchs were involved with almost every aspect of military operations and administration, and had come to constitute a virtual counter-bureaucracy throughout the government. Studies indicate that eunuchs were involved in military affairs from the 960s, and that the policy which permitted their employment as generals and legates was entirely consistent, although the weight of their responsibilities varied from reign to reign.[7] At the end of the Cheng-ho period (1111–1117), a pen-note records that the submission of memorials had been badly obstructed by recalcitrant eunuchs:

The Imperial Brush contradicted itself, . . .the ministers and officials were greatly frightened. It was necessary to get the eunuchs and apprehend them. Only then could they send in memorials, and make for some leadership in the crisis. Therefore all the ministries and offices competed to submit memorials requesting the apprehension of the eunuchs. But afterwards the power of large and small offices still returned to the eunuchs, and in the provinces, the circuits . . . established 'receiving officials'.[8]

In the following years, during the Hsüan-ho period, virtually every government office of any consequence was staffed by a "receiver" (*ch'eng-shou kuan*) in addition to its normal civil service complement, and these receivers — eunuchs in each case — often monopolized control, forcing the directors and assistants to follow their decisions.[9] In a final abuse of power, the eunuchs proved unsatisfied with the mere exercise of de facto control in the halls of government and usurped the ceremonial symbolism as well: the eunuch Liang Shih-ch'eng, receiver for the *mi-shu sheng,* actually sat above the director and his assistant when this office transacted its public business.[10]

When the infamous T'ung Kuan, occasional military commander and receiver, left K'ai-feng with Hui-tsung after a long career of participation in the eunuch abuses of his day, a wave of censure washed free, from the censorate and from the Grand University. He was demoted, banished, and finally beheaded at Hsiung-chou under the supervision of an inspecting censor.[11] The attacks made against him, and the summary death which befell some of his lesser colleagues, must be understood against a background of eunuch control in the army, obviously responsible in part for the sorry state of military preparedness which Li Kang discovered, and of visible usurpations of official prerogative, by which T'ung became popularly known as the "old woman minister" (*ao-hsiang*) — a contemptuous reference to his unjustified presumption.[12] By removing the eunuchs from positions of power, the Ching-k'ang ministers not only expected to assert their power at the expense of a "rival elite," to strengthen the army, and to facilitate memorials, but they also hoped to engender the kind of order among the symbols of government which would give them a semblance of psychological security. By its request that either Li Kang or Wu Min be sent from K'ai-feng for negotiations, and by its ultimate willingness to surrender T'ung Kuan for punishment, even Hui-tsung's mobile court expressed a kind of agreement that *li* had been damaged by the aberrations of eunuch power.

T'ung Kuan's demise did not mark the end of eunuch power during the Sung, but the government continued to make efforts at repression. On 28/3rd/1126 the censor Yü Ying-ch'iu submitted a memorial asking to have all eunuchs removed from positions of military authority since, "from ancient times, there has been nothing but trouble from eunuchs in military affairs."[13] On 17/10th/1127, less than a year after the end of Ch'in-tsung's short tenure on the throne, Kao-tsung issued an edict which forbade any eunuch from holding office or having any private consultation or association with military commanders.[14] When Li Ch'ün was appointed Commissioner of Personnel a few years later, he discussed the relationship between the flourishing and decline of eunuchs and the rise and fall of the state. Their flourishing, he said, caused men to fear them until it reached the point where some rose to attack them. It happened in Han and T'ang, but the Ching-k'ang disaster might serve as a more recent example.

It is necessary to reduce and control them if the country is to avoid the worry of previous days. The eunuchs may keep their wealth, but they must be prohibited from entering the halls of government, and have nothing to do with outside [i.e., public] affairs. Scholars, soldiers, generals and officials must avoid communication with them.[15]

Li Ch'ün evidently expressed a majority opinion, for eunuchs were strictly curbed in Southern Sung. The temporary coup d'état engineered by Miao Fu and Liu Yü in 1129 was the occasion for another outburst of public violence against eunuchs, accompanied by demands to reduce their number and influence, and in the collective biography of eunuchs in the *Sung-shih,* only ten persons are mentioned for Southern Sung, and not one of these was involved with military administration.[16]

It is remarkable that Li Kang did not take part in the denunciation of eunuchs during the Ching-k'ang period. He is inevitably associated with the attacks which were made by others, but no attack on eunuch power passed his own lips.* On several occasions, before and after his appointment to the Office of Field Headquarters, Li submitted long memorials on military administration and reform, but he never made eunuchs into scapegoats for mismanagement, abuses or defeat, nor cited their influence as a problem. In his first audience with Ch'in-tsung, Li discussed military affairs primarily in terms of negotiation with the Chin; earlier he issued no recriminations over the disrepair of watchtowers and gun-emplacements in K'ai-feng. In later audiences he talked about logistics, salaries, and the advantages of the hereditary military commanderies of the T'ang, the so-called *fan-chen.* In the seventh month, following the release of the Autumn Defense Armies, introducing his remarks on the armies with a broad accusation that "the military system has not been repaired for thirty years" he proceeded to lament shortages of manpower, and a chronic failure to

---

* Li does record that eunuchs defending the walls of K'ai-feng were dismissed early in 2nd/1126. See *CKCHL* 2.3b.

carry out training exercises, but never mentioned eunuchs.[17] This almost willful evasion of an issue which others clearly saw is probably explained in several ways — that insistence on this issue could jeopardize his relationship to the crown, that he generally avoided personal re-criminations, that he was involved more with militia than eunuch-led standing armies — but most of all by the understanding that in Li's view, the defense of the country was not simply a military problem, but involved a kind of popular apotheosis. Li Kang did not join in the chorus of attacks on the eunuchs because he fell increasingly away from the consensus of his colleagues on policy. He tended to regard symbolic order more as a prerequisite than a goal. It was Li, after all, who had insisted on Hui-tsung's formal abdication in the first place. But it soon became apparent that other ministers of the court derived so much psychological peace from symbolic order that they became unwilling to undertake a subsequent effort to resist the Chin for real. Since the crisis had been met by psychological and symbolic manipu-lation, it followed that rectified symbolic order and the conviction of success were the marks of real victory. Furthermore, symbolic order could readily be turned against the expression of dissenting views, as Li discovered when he tried to memorialize out of proper sequence and had to inveigh against precedent to be heard: "What time is this to use precedent?" he had asked.[18] When the major eunuchs left with Hui-tsung, and when it developed that any serious warfare would have to depend on militia forces, the eunuchs became essentially irrelevant to the success of Li's plans or the safety of K'ai-feng. It is a measure of his positive pattern of thought and his increasingly dissident viewpoint that he avoided recriminations against them. With his col-leagues, he desired the symbolic order which the end of eunuch influ-ence implied, but beyond and against them, he saw that symbolic order was insufficient of itself.

Institutional Limitations and Innovations

Although interlocking patterns of promotion frequently assured that chief ministers for military affairs would have prior experience in finance or vice-versa, the chief ministers of the court were usually denied direct authority over the military and financial affairs of the state during Northern Sung, which necessarily affected the dynasty's capacity to innovate, and deliberately separated authorities whose joint commitment was necessary to the prosecution of a war. This division of power is traditionally described as control of the people by the Chancellery (*chung-shu*), control of soldiers by the Bureau of Military Affairs (*shu-mi yüan*), and control of finances by the Three

Offices (*san ssu*: the *hu-pu, yen-t'ieh ssu,* and *tu-chih-shih ssu*).[19] After the Yüan-feng reorganization, the Three Offices was abolished, and the chief ministers included primarily the three senior officials of the *shang-shu sheng,* two of whom assumed concurrent responsibility for the former *shih-chung* and *chung-shu ling.*[20] These officials were nominally in charge of the entire government, and should have been kept fully informed on all issues, but the Bureau of Military Affairs, because it had exclusive charge of the sword, and the Ministry of Finance, because it controlled the purse, frequently concealed their affairs from the chief ministers.[21]

To complicate still further the tripartite division of power, Emperor Ch'in-tsung created the Office of Field Headquarters on 5/1st/1126, placing Li Kang in charge.[22] This office effectively split authority over military administration with the Bureau of Military Affairs and seems to have been designated to maintain an element of civilian control. When distinguished provincial commanders (Ch'ung Shih-tao and Yao P'ing-chung) arrived in K'ai-feng on 20/1st/1126, the need to preserve some vestige of civilian hegemony over military commanders even in a time of war rapidly became an organizational snafu. To meet the problem, the Emperor decided to create still another office – the Office of Pacification – over which one of these provincial commanders would have direct and primary control, but he then linked this Office of Pacification with the Bureau of Military Affairs by making the same commander concurrently a co-signatory in the latter. To compound the confusion, he then cautioned the two offices not to become involved with each other and instituted secret memoranda to permit their separate communication with the court.[23] Interestingly and somewhat ironically, the institution of the Office of Field Headquarters (*hsing-ying ssu*) derived from a Liao precedent: the *hsing-ying ping-ma tu-t'ung.* According to the *Liao-shih,* whenever the Liao emperor raised soldiers, he personally appointed both a commanding general and "loyal, related ministers" (*hsün-ch'i ta-ch'en*) to serve as Presiding Field Commander, Assisting Field Commander and Inspecting Field Commander – an effort to divide the potentially dangerous authority of an unbridled general.[24]

The Office of Field Headquarters lasted less than a month, but the Ching-k'ang crisis proved a remarkable catalyst for institutional changes at the beginning of Southern Sung. In 1127 Emperor Kao-tsung established a successor to the old Office of Field Headquarters called the *yü-ying ssu* – Office of Imperial Headquarters, and placed a chief minister in charge.[25] This innovation caused more problems than it solved, raised the whole issue of divided powers, and occasioned a complete reorganization of authority. A memorial to Kao-tsung suggested that the Sung was following the unhappy example of the Five Dynasties in thus dividing the administration of military affairs. This memorial asked that the Office of Imperial Headquarters be terminated, that military power be restored to the Bureau of Military Affairs, and finally that the chief ministers concurrently hold office in the Bureau, so that they might begin to discuss problems of military operations and administration.[26] In 1130 Kao-tsung issued an edict permitting the chief ministers concurrent control of the Bureau, and in 1166 Hsiao-tsung formally reaffirmed their authority in financial affairs as well.[27]

It is not surprising that the Sung found it hard to prosecute a war with its military command internally disunified and with the whole command separated from the organs which made policy. But the institutions did not create the problem, rather the problem had given rise to the institutional confusion. Throughout the eleventh and even into the twelfth century, the T'ang heritage was omnipotent. Sung scholars and statesmen, following the lead of the neo-Confucian masters, could denigrate T'ang achievements and claim that it, along with Han, produced no intellect of note, but even this critical attention gainsaid their claim: if the Sung could not build an empire worthy of the T'ang, they could still change the rules to play a civilistic, classically Confucian game. Furthermore, the T'ang had finally succumbed to the same sword by which they lived, and the early Sung were keenly conscious that their own dynasty was born from the military rubble of too successful *chieh-tu-shih*, who pulled the T'ang apart, then built their fortunes on fragmentary efforts at imperial rule. In an effort to learn the central lessons of this ambiguous parable the Sung simultaneously de-emphasized the glories of imperial craft, and modified T'ang institutions so that the centrifugal tendencies of the late ninth century could be reversed and military power deprived of its independence by separation from fiscal and executive authority. The disadvantages of this separation of powers were predictable, but when the crisis came, and the Sung found it hard to fight a war, it was not that their bureaucratic organization refused to serve them, rather that they had built into the bureaucracy their ambiguous assessment of the T'ang heritage.

It seems likely that the Sung would have had great practical difficulty in waging offensive war against the Chin, and indeed such battles as were fought in 1126 saw scant success. Li Kang discovered for himself that the defense accouterments of K'ai-feng were in serious disarray; he bemoaned the shortage of army horses caused by maladministration and neglect of the so-called Inspectorates of Horse

Rearing; he was also certainly aware to what small size the standing armies had sunk, and how greatly the government would now have to rely on special summons. But he may also have been right in believing that a war could be fought if the court were really disposed to fight one. He shared enough of his colleagues' psychologism, after all, to believe in the efficacy of cultivated determination. In response to Ch'in-tsung's early query about leadership in time of war, Li had observed that "in times of peace the court has developed and nourished great ministers by the gift of high rank and rich reward. These men should be used in time of need."[28] He was oblivious to the contradiction, however: from the time when Chao K'uang-yin made the gift of bureaucratic rank to his generals in 960, the Sung had most esteemed civilian achievements, or rewarded military prowess with civilistic gifts. The result had not only been a practical unpreparedness for war — material deficiencies could have been overcome — but a psychological unwillingness to wage war. In Sung times the bureaucracy did not "serve" the state, it *was* the state, and served itself. Waging war would have entailed the cultivation of values and virtues alien to the bureaucracy, and the promotion of men who were not bureaucrats. The bureaucrats were unwilling to witness either: for them the end of the bureaucratic state was the whole end. A Confucian state at war was no Confucian state at all. In the end they valued the bureaucracy and the ideals it represented more than they wanted to prosecute a war. After two efforts to find a bureaucratic expedient by which to ride out the storm — the Office of Field Headquarters and the Office of Imperial Headquarters — they turned to a more straightforward solution by restoring the authority of civilian policy-makers in the military and financial realm. They did the former at the end of the Chien-yen period (1127 – 1130) when the court had reached the new capital at Hang-chou, and the latter five years after concluding their final peace with the Chin, when the primary concern of the court was economic, financial, and commercial development in the south.[29]

The Transcendence of Civilism

Martialism and civilism (*wu* and *wen*) are normally represented as polar values in Chinese history. Like *yin* and *yang, wen* and *wu* are complementary, although their relationship may be temporarily disrupted.* The view that the Sung dynasty represents the disproportionate triumph of civilism is expressed in the *Sung-shih* itself,[30]

---

*For a discussion of the complementary properties of polar pairs in Chinese philosophy, see Hellmut Wilhelm, *Change: Eight Lectures on the I-Ching* (New York: Pantheon Books, 1960).

and the story of the cup of wine which destroyed the Sung armies is by now quite familiar. Sung T'ai-tsu (Chao K'uang-yin), because he was sensitive to the disaster brought on the T'ang and its successors by military men and keenly conscious of the military coup which had brought him to the throne, deprived his generals of the chance to build regional bases of power, brought the famous *chieh-tu-shih* to end their lives as jobless officials in Lo-yang, appointed civil servants to administer regional military commands called *fan-chen*, and unified the military power of the country in his own hands.* In the words of one observer, he "overcompensated" for the T'ang disaster, "emphasized *wen* and deemphasized *wu*," until "there developed the custom of 'highly civilized weakness' among the Chinese people."[31]

At mid-season, however, the working out of Chao K'uang-yin's "civilistic" testament was far from easy. The civil bureaucrats to whom he had entrusted the administration of the state were confronted at the end of 1125 with a military crisis which threatened the life of the civilistic state, but which their training and temperament had equipped them ill to meet. When Ch'in-tsung was trying to decide whether a policy of resistance and war would be feasible, he asked his ministers a fearfully pointed question: "Who can lead?"[32] He did not want to know who could ride at the van of his armies—he had generals for that—he wanted to know who among the ministers of the court was prepared to lead the country into war and to guide the state under conditions of war. Li Kang did not volunteer himself, but suggested that Ch'in-tsung employ Po Shih-chung and Li Pang-yen, his chief civilian ministers, because it was proper to rely in crisis on men who had trained, served and earned reward through the years of peace; "Although [they] are scholars, who do not necessarily know about soldiers . . . , it is their duty to superintend the generals."[33] In theory Li was quite right—senior bureaucrats should have been interposed above the generals to assure civilian control—but Po's temperament was so offended by the idea of military adventure that he failed to appreciate Li's distinction between civilian supervisory control and intimate civilian management. Replying then to Po's anger, Li indicated

---

* "*I-pei chiu shih ping-ch'üan*"—"with a cup of wine he [T'ai-tsu] dissolved the power of the military"—told of the banquet at which T'ai-tsu allegedly deprived his generals of their rank and power. Actually, T'ai-tsu's attack on military power was a complex and long-term matter. The elimination of individual commands in the *chin-chün* was symbolized by the cup of wine episode; the regulation of the *chieh-tu-shih* in the corners of the empire was accomplished by their slow regulation and subsequent replacement, a process not complete until the reign of Jen-tsung. See Nieh Ch'ung-ch'i, "Lun Sung T'ai-tsu shou ping-ch'üan" [On Sung T'ai-tsu's obtaining of military power], *Yen-ching hsüeh-pao* (June 1948), pp. 85–106.

that he too would have practical reservations about trying to command an army in the field, and the outcome of this audience was a high civilian appointment for Li, not a military commission. During all of his later "military" commissions, as Field Headquarters Commissioner, Defendant of K'ai-feng, Chief of the Bureau of Military Affairs, and Legate for Proclamation and Pacification, even when, by force of circumstances, he personally commanded troops, Li never abandoned his fundamentally civilistic bias. He wanted the professional generals (Ch'ung Shih-tao and Yao P'ing-chung, for example) placed under his "civilian" command, incidentally to prevent the division of a command, but also to maintain high-level civilian control. He also resisted appointment in 6th/1125 as Legate for Pacification with a rephrased version of his memorial suggestion that Ch'in-tsung appoint Po and Li: he was a scholar, he did not understand soldiers, he could not fulfill the responsibilities of a field general, and he might injure national affairs if he served. Li tended consistently to approach military problems as exercises in the use of human resources and human will, where psychology and ethics were always of paramount importance. This was an expression of the classical Confucian equilibrium of *wen* and *wu*. Po Shih-chung shied away from military adventures; Li, opposing him, still approached them within a framework of civilian supervision and Confucian moral psychology. Each of them demonstrated one aspect of Sung civilism.

The sources of genuine trepidation among bureaucrats are not hard to find. In their emphasis on civilism, the Sung were unkind to their regular soldiers. In the first place they recruited the hungry and the vagrant, for whom they could find no other use, then branded these soldiers on the face and hands, which simultaneously injured the soldiers, ruined their pride, and demonstrated that the country would take no pride in them.[34] Instead, eunuchs were appointed to command this branded riff-raff, who looked genuinely fearsome, and the phrase "good men do not make soldiers, and good iron does not make nails" began to gain currency. Little wonder that civil bureaucrats nourished contempt for the military, and wanted as little as possible to do with them. Even Li Kang, often their champion, remarked that some would decapitate their fellow soldiers if the head could be traded for some monetary reward.[35]

Li Kang reconciled his latent fear of armies, their instincts and their power with his determination to meet a military crisis by relying on and thinking in terms of militia. Militia share some characteristics with genuine and successful rebels: they are motivated by noble ends, and they partake more of *i* (integrity) than of *wu*, for they emphasize the purpose for which they are called more than the style by which they act. Li explicitly advocated militia recruited from the *pao-chia,* which eliminated expenditures for military support in time of peace, and the problem of relocating soldiers in time of crisis. These militia would fight only to defend their way of life, and especially their own land, and would have no need to rely upon the cultivation of martialism to justify their existence.[36]

Further than militia, however, Li Kang found it difficult to go: he never extolled martialism per se. Yet without using the concept of *wen* and *wu,* he sometimes implied their complementary relationship. When he advocated revival of the T'ang regional military commands (*fan-chen*), he readily acknowledged that they had proved detrimental to the T'ang and had been rightfully abolished by "our ancestors" in the Sung, but he argued that the present time was different, and demanded a modest resurrection of the old institution.[37] Crudely paraphrased, Li argued that too much *wu* was bad, but too little might also be detrimental. Again, in the course of an audience, when he cited the hexagram "army" from the *Classic of Changes* in an effort to show Ch'in-tsung the nature of his imperial task, he argued for balance. Precisely because Ch'in-tsung was a modest sort of ruler, he argued, he should use an army to offset the natural effects of modesty.[38] Polar relationships lie firmly at the base of the *Changes,* and Li's preference for the latter in memorial quotations may have been involved with an almost subconscious feeling that *wen* and *wu* had gotten badly out of line. If so, the feeling never reached the level of logical expression. The great debate over war and peace in the Ching-k'ang period was definitely not a battle between *wen* and *wu:* complementary concepts can have no partial advocates.

Li Kang, by training and argument, and by what he failed to say, was in no sense a martial servant of the crown. In due season the dynasty honored him as a "loyal (*chung*) and stable (*ting*) duke,"* avoiding martial epithets to mark a critic as it avoided them to mark its emperors and its years. Sung is the only major dynasty in Chinese history which had no "martial ancestor" and no year-designation of martial implications. That Li opposed the policy of token resistance and a negotiated peace is clear. He stood against his lord and his colleagues of the court on the issue of Ch'in-tsung's departure from K'ai-feng, on the wisdom

---

* The title was granted in 1169, in response to a request from Li's fifth son, Li Shen. See Chao Hsiao-hsüan, *Li Kang nien-p'u ch'ang-pien* [A study on the chronological biography of Li Kang], Monograph Series, No. 2 (Hong Kong: Institute of Advanced Chinese Studies and Research, New Asia College, The Chinese University of Hong Kong, 1968), p. 225.

of negotiations from a position of weakness, on the consequences of tribute payments to the Chin, on the tolerability of alienating territory which had belonged to the Sung ancestors, on the advisability of escorting the Chin retreat from K'ai-feng, and on the employment of Autumn Defense forces to break the siege at T'ai-yüan. He was loud in his opposition to concessions, persistent in his calls for firm decision, and expansive in his treatment of government problems. But throughout 1126, he differed most dramatically from his colleagues in his apprehension of crisis. The court, he said, was sitting on top of a pile of firewood with the fire already started underneath, impervious to impending doom.[39] Only he spoke out. The *Ching-k'ang ch'uan-hsin lu*, his record of dissent, may be most significant for this perception of crisis, for Li's trumpet throws the diffident equanimity of his colleagues into bold relief. When the Chin armies bore down on K'ai-feng, the ministers were, he says, "bewildered,"[40] although they did react quite sensibly and peacefully by sending an envoy to negotiate, and by dispatching their own dependents to the south. They were entirely prepared to leave K'ai-feng if it proved necessary to do so; Li's impassioned query, "How can there be another place like this capital among all the walled cities of the empire?"[41] evidently fell in part on ears and eyes which knew the splendor of Su-chou and Hang-chou. In the autumn of 1126, when the capital was no longer threatened, Li accused his colleagues of "talking and laughing as before."[42] He remarked himself how quickly the suburbs of K'ai-feng seemed to recover after the weeks of Chin siege. The resilience of the country and the unshakable equanimity of his colleagues are both the object and lesson of Li's dissent. Li could agree with his colleagues and they with him on the importance of symbolic order, especially in troubled times. But Li's sense of crisis and vibrant temperament set him at odds thereafter with the court. He was no more filled with martial valor than they, no more fond of armies than his peers, no less a scholar, by his own admission, than Po Shih-chung. But he was seized with a vision of crisis: if it could not field an army, the country would be ruined, psychologism notwithstanding. But others surely thought (as Ch'in Kuei would later say)[43] that fighting a war could ruin civilism equally. Culture in the broadest sense was at stake: whether to use craft (in the literal etymological sense) to fight the "crafty Chin" in order to save the Way of the ancestors in North China, or to stand back, rely on the *li*, and let the ancient Confucian structure of values for once be worked out. When Tzu-kung had asked Confucius about government, he was told that food, soldiers, and the confidence of the people were the three requisites of the state. And if one had to be forgone which should be omitted first? Omit soldiers, the Master had replied.[44] Li Kang disagreed: his realism exceeded his psychologism and clashed with the Confucian ideal. Without soldiers, he argued, the country is humiliated, and then lands, valuable goods, and people are finally taken away. But his colleagues were idealist Confucians who lived in an age of classical rediscoveries, who took satisfaction and comfort from symbolic order, who remembered too vividly the military demise of the T'ang, and who relied on a growing sensation of mobility to move not only themselves up in society and toward the capital, but also their capital, their emperor, and their culture elsewhere if the need developed. "In Sung times," one scholar has written,

a kind of 'peaceful culture' developed to an especially advanced degree, which made the physical strength of the Chinese daily weaker until they were no longer able to face bows, soldiers, and horses from the north. When you add that since the late T'ang, Chinese women had developed an exaggerated preference for small feet . . . , that the custom of sitting on chairs was even more habitual in Sung, and that after the southern retreat officials did not ride horses to court, but rode sedan chairs, [you see that] these things contributed to the weakening of the Chinese, which was shown clearly on the battlefield.[45]

This view is probably exaggerated; advances in Sung technology probably counterbalanced the decline in military bearing of the Chinese elite to some degree. Still, the commitment of the Chinese had perceptibly changed. The transcendent values ascribed to the reformers of the eleventh century, which once justified their dissent, gave way in the twelfth century to those whose outlook favored negotiation and abstracted beyond the dynasty to "civilism" above all. Li Kang shared more of this civilistic heritage than he would usually admit, and his sharing gave him at least the common ground of symbolic order, but the apprehension of crisis brought out a kind of legalistic realism which demanded an army and a war.

The idealists transcended even the crisis, and the Sung lived on for six generations.

Notes to Chapter 6

1. *CKCHL* 1.1a.
2. *CKCHL* 1.1b.
3. *PMHP* 25.10−11. See also Chao Hsiao-hsüan, *Li Kang nien-p'u ch'ang-pien* [A study on the chronological biography of Li Kang], Monograph Series, No. 2 (Hong Kong: Institute of Advanced Chinese Studies and Research, New Asia College, The Chinese University of Hong Kong, 1968), pp. 46−48.
4. *CKCHL* 1.2a.
5. See Robert Jay Lifton, *Revolutionary Immortality* (New York: Random House, 1968), p. 32.

6. *CKCHL* 2.7b.
7. Ch'ai Te-keng, "Sung huan-kuan ts'an-yü chün-shih k'ao" [An examination of the involvement of eunuchs in military affairs during the Sung], *Fu-jen* (December 1941), p. 217.
8. Cited in Ch'ai, p. 216.
9. *Lao-hsüeh-an pi-chi* [Pen-notes from Lao-hsüeh's (Lu Yu's) studio], 3. Cited in Ch'ai, p. 216.
10. Ch'ai, p. 216.
11. *TTSL* 121.5a.
12. Ch'ai, pp. 191 – 92.
13. *PMHP* 44.12b.
14. Ch'ai, p. 217.
15. Ch'ai, p. 220.
16. Ch'ai, p. 217.
17. *CKCHL* 3.10a.
18. *CKCHL* 1.3b.
19. Ch'ien Mu, "Lun Sung-tai hsiang-ch'üan" [On the power of chief ministers in Sung], in Chao T'ieh-han, ed. *Sung-shih yen-chiu chi* [Collected Research on Sung History] (Taipei: Chung-hua ts'ung-shu pien-fan wei-yüan-hui yin-hang, 1958), I, p. 456.
20. *SS* 161; Yang Shu-fan, "Sung-tai tsai-hsiang chih-tu" [The Prime Ministership in Sung], *Cheng-chih ta-hsüeh hsüeh-pao* (December 1964), p. 233.
21. Yang, p. 239.
22. *SS* 5 (*hsin-wei*)/1st/1126; Chao Hsiao-hsüan, pp. 51 – 52.
23. *CKCHL* 1.11a.
24. *LS, Ping-wei chih* section. See *Chung-wen ta tz'u-tien* (Taipei: Chung-kuo wen hua yen-chiu so, 1962 – 1966), p. 13041.
25. See *SS, Chih-kuan chih* section; *Lao-hsüeh-an pi-chi* 1, in Ch'ai *op. cit.*; *Chung-wen ta tz'u-tien*, p. 5135.
26. Ch'ien, p. 457.
27. Ch'ien, p. 457.
28. Yang, p. 240.
29. *CKCHL* 3.4b; Chao Hsiao-hsüan, pp. 67 – 68.
30. *SS* 202.1a.
31. Li Chi, "Liang-Sung ch'i-ho te chiao-hsün" [Instruction on the search for peace under the two Sung], *Tung-fang tsa-chih* (May 1941), p. 35.
32. *CKCHL* 1.4b.
33. *CKCHL* 3.6b; 3.8a.
34. Fang Hao, "Lun Sung-tai te chün-tuei" [On the army in Sung times], *Min-chu p'ing-lun* (January 1954), p. 23.
35. *CKCHL* 1.7b.
36. *CKCHL* 3.3a.
37. *CKCHL* 3.2b.
38. *CKCHL* 1.11b.
39. *CKCHL* 3.11b.
40. *CKCHL* 1.1a.
41. *CKCHL* 1.4a.
42. *CKCHL* 3.11b.
43. *CSPM* 72 (p. 585). Entry for 3rd/1142.
44. Confucius, *Analects,* xii, 7, in James Legge, *The Chinese Classics* (London: Oxford University Press, 1867 – 1876) I, p. 254.
45. Li, p. 35.

Neo-Confucians Under Attack: The Condemnation of Wei-hsüeh

CONRAD SCHIROKAUER

DURING THE SUNG the strands of political and intellectual life were closely intertwined, but never combined to create the harmonious pattern which is the Confucian ideal. On the contrary, they frequently pulled in opposite directions sometimes producing and at other times merely revealing strains and tensions in the fabric of state and society. In the last decade of the twelfth century, political and intellectual history intersected in a particularly dramatic way when the associates of Han T'o-chou (d. 1207) attacked a number of eminent scholars as part of their successful campaign to oust Chao Ju-yü (1140–96) as chief minister and remove other political enemies from positions of power. It is one of the ironies of history that among those charged at the time with *wei-hsüeh*, "false" or "spurious learning," was Chu Hsi (1130–1200) who came to be regarded in later centuries as the very font of Neo-Confucian orthodoxy.* The loser became the ultimate victor. If Chu Hsi's triumph was posthumous, not so Han's defeat, for in 1207 he had to pay with his head for his mistake in launching a war against the Chin. Nor did his death soften his posthumous notoriety.

A substantial portion of the research for this paper was conducted in Kyoto where during 1967–68 I was the recipient of a grant from the American Council of Learned Societies – Social Science Research Council under the program for Grants for Research on Asia. I am most grateful for this support.

* The transformation of Chu Hsi's philosophy into the state orthodoxy is discussed by James T. C. Liu in his essay, "The Road to Neo-Confucian Orthodoxy: An Interpretation" originally presented to the Sung Conference in Feldafing and scheduled for publication in *Philosophy East and West*, 23:4 (1973) pp. 483–505. I am indebted to Professor Liu for sending me a draft of his paper before I wrote my own and for serving as the conference discussant of my paper. I also wish to thank Professors Wing-tsit Chan and John Dardess for their comments. For another stimulating recent discussion of the history of Southern Sung Neo-Confucianism see John W. Haeger, "The Intellectual Context of Neo-Confucian Syncretism," *The Journal of Asian Studies*, 31 (1972), pp. 499–513.

Critical intellectuals and resentful politicians were not creations of the Southern Sung. The attack on *wei-hsüeh* was the last clash of this type during the dynasty, but it was hardly the first time a group of Sung intellectuals found themselves in political difficulty. The roots of the troubles of the 1190's can easily be traced to the beginning of the Southern Sung and even to the political and intellectual controversies of the Northern Sung; participants on both sides had furthermore studied history and were well aware of still earlier factional turmoil during the Later Han and T'ang. Thus even as a boy, Yüan Hsieh (1144 – 1224), later among those accused of "spurious learning," drew inspiration from the example of the Confucian literati who were embroiled in the struggle at the court of the Later Han.[1] Most men, however, looked back to more recent events, especially Ts'ai Ching's (1046 – 1126) proscription of the conservative Yüan-yu party late in the Northern Sung[2] and the struggle between war and peace advocates under the first Southern Sung emperor, Kao-tsung. The first two reigns of the Southern Sung witnessed what turned out to be a prelude to the attack on *wei-hsüeh*, and these were also the years when all but the youngest of the participants reached their maturity and first joined government service.

The Political Status of Neo-Confucianism under Kao-tsung (r. 1127 – 62) and Hsiao-tsung (r. 1162 – 89)

At the very beginning of the Southern Sung the political climate favored the opponents of reform since the loss of the north was blamed on the reformers. It was in keeping with this sentiment that special posthumous honors were conferred on, among others, Ch'eng I (1033 – 1107), the great Neo-Confucian philosopher who in his day had opposed Wang An-shih's (1021 – 86) program of extensive reform. Ch'eng I's enhanced reputation did not go long unchallenged, however.[3] Early in 1136 Ch'en Kung-fu (1076 – 1141) performed a major political service for the peace advocate Ch'in Kuei (1090 – 1155) by indicting Ch'in's political rival Chao Ting (1085 – 1147); later in the year Ch'en began an attack on Ch'eng I and the divisive pretensions of his followers.* His stance was quite typical; opposition to Neo-Confucian philosophers continued to be associated with support for Ch'in Kuei both during his rise to power and in the years from 1138 to 1155, when he was the most influential minister in the government.

---

* *TML*, pp. 24 – 25; *HNYL*, pp. 1747 – 48. For a survey of the attacks on Ch'eng philosophy in this period see Terada Ko, *Sodai kyoiku shi gaisetzu* [A general history of Sung education] (Tokyo: Hakubunsha, 1965), p. 227ff.

The attack continued early in 1137 when the Vice Minister for Personnel Lü Chih (d. 1137) criticized not Ch'eng I himself who, Lü conceded, had attained the Confucian Mean, but his followers, who exploited their association with this tradition for political purposes thus exemplifying the counterfeit "mean" of the petty man who lacks scruples. Lü succeeded in obtaining an order to be posted in all circuit, prefectural, and subprefectural schools advising students to stay with the old teachings and not engage in the practices of modern petty men, i. e., the followers of Ch'eng I.[4] Ch'en Kung-fu then returned to the campaign by denouncing Hu An-kuo (1074–1138). Hu was a leading Neo-Confucian most famous for his commentary on the *Spring and Autumn Annals*, which turned this dry chronicle, rejected by the great reformer Wang An-shih,[*] into a patriotic text capable of inspiring the young Lu Chiu-yüan (1139–92) to understand the difference between Chinese and "barbarians."[†] Hu had requested accessory sacrifices for the men he considered the main Confucian thinkers of the dynasty, Shao Yung (1011–77), Chang Tsai (1020–77), Ch'eng I, and his brother Ch'eng Hao (1032–85). He restated the standard Neo-Confucian claim that after Mencius there was a long interruption in the transmission of the True Way which was revived at last by the Ch'engs, and then came to the heart of the matter:

Today we want to have scholars follow The Mean and take Confucius and Mencius as their teachers but forbid them to follow the teachings of Ch'eng I. This is like wanting to enter a house but not allowing it by the door.[‡]

The intellectual persuasiveness of the scholarly and speculative activities of the Neo-Confucians and, to some extent at least, also the acceptability of their ideas ultimately depended on their success in opening a door to the classics by making the old tradition intelligible,

---

[*] For the role of the *Annals* in the conflict between Wang and his opponents, see James T. C. Liu, *Reform in Sung China* (Cambridge, Massachusetts: Harvard University Press, 1959), pp. 30–33. Hu An-kuo's views are discussed in Kusumoto Masatsugu, *So-Mei jidai jugaku shiso no kenkyu* [A study of Sung and Ming Confucian thought] (Tokyo: 1952), pp. 184–89. See also Morohashi Tetsuji, *Jugaku no mokuteki to So-ju no katsudō* [The goals of Confucianism and the activities of Sung Confucians] (Tokyo: Daishūkan Shoten, 1930), pp. 342–79; Otto Franke, *Studien zur Geschichte des Konfuzianischen Dogmas und der chinesischen Staatsreligion: Das Problem des Tsch'un-ts'iu und Tung Tschung-schu's Tsch'un-ts'iu fan lu* (Hamburg: Friederichsen, de Gruyter and Comp., 1920).

[†] Takase Takejiro, *Riku Sho-san* [Lu Chiu-yüan] (Kyoto: Naigai Shupan Kabushiki Kaisha, 1924), p. 16. At the age of sixteen, Lu, filled with patriotic indignation, decided to become a warrior, cut his nails and studied archery and horsemanship.

[‡] Hu Yin, *Fei-jan chi* [Collected writings of Hu Yin] (Ssu-k'u ch'üan-shu ed.) 25.64a-b. Quoted in abridged form in *TML*, p. 28 and *HNYL*, p. 1755. Another version quotes Hu as stating, "This is entering a house but shutting the door." See *LCTM* 1, p. 265.

convincing, and meaningful to men who lived in an intellectual, political
and social environment very different from that of the founders of
the Confucian tradition.

While Ch'in Kuei held power, advocacy of the doctrines of the
Ch'eng brothers was identified with support for the political opposition.
It was also associated with a pro-war stance. A brief quotation from a
famous memorial may suffice as an indication of the passions raised
by this issue and a reminder that the men of Chu Hsi's generation had
no monopoly on outspoken criticism of the emperor and his policies,
here denounced in no uncertain terms:

Now a three-foot youngster is most ignorant, but if you point to a dog or a pig
and make him bow to it, he will indignantly fly into a rage. Today the cruel
barbarians are the dogs and pigs, yet gravely the men of the celestial court lead
each other to bow to them. Will Your Majesty put up with what shames a
small boy?*

The memorialist who posed this rhetorical question was Hu Ch'üan
(1102—80), a onetime student of Hu An-kuo and himself an author
of commentaries on the *Annals* and the *I-ching*.[5]

In 1143 Ch'in Kuei personally attacked the theories of the Ch'engs
in an imperial audience. From that time until his death in 1155 the
doctrines of the Ch'engs were denounced a number of times under the
rubric "specialists' learning" (*chuan-men hsüeh*), which must have
greatly distressed men who thought of themselves as propagating
universal truths. "Specialists' learning" was the object of attacks in
1149 and 1152 when, in addition, Chao Ting was charged with establishing it, and in 1155.[6] Unlike later attacks when the students at the
state university supported the victims, in this case at least one university
student joined in the denunciations.† In conjunction with the attack on
the Ch'engs, Ch'in Kuei conducted a campaign against private histories.
Although his initial complaint against them in 1143 was unsuccessful
and had to be repeated the following year, his efforts led to the burning
of a large library belonging to his opponent Li Kuang (1077—1155)
in 1146.[7]

An important consideration in most Sung political disputes was
the examination system, and Ch'in Kuei was also active in this area,

---

* *HNYL*, p. 1997. This memorial was included by Hsieh Fang-te (1226—1289) in
his influential anthology, *Wen-chang kuei-fan*.

† For a student supporter of Ch'in Kuei see *TML*, p. 38. Yeh Shih states that Ch'in
Kuei was able to corrupt students and induce them to support him. See Yeh Shih, *Shui-
hsin chi* [Collected writings of Yeh Shih] (Ssu-pu pei-yao ed.) 3.10a. This passage is
quoted in Terada, *Sodai kyoiku shi gaisetzu*, p. 233.

not only attempting to block students of Ch'eng philosophy but also trying to further the careers of those close to him, including members of his immediate family.[8] However, his control was never complete: Chu Hsi himself received a degree in 1148. Eight men who attained their *chin-shih* while Ch'in Kuei was in power later became participants in the *wei-hsüeh* controversy: four on each side.

For over twenty years after Ch'in Kuei's death, years which saw renewed fighting with the Chin (1160 – 64) and a change of throne (1162), there apparently were no attacks on the proponents of Northern Sung philosophy, perhaps because officials did not want to identify themselves with the discredited Ch'in Kuei. There was in 1169 an unsuccessful request that accessory sacrifices for Wang An-shih be abolished and the Ch'eng brothers honored,* but this was not followed by any great controversy. During this period most of the men involved in the *wei-hsüeh* controversy received their *chin-shih*. Among those who received their degree in the five examinations held from 1157 to 1169, sixteen were to be condemned for *wei-hsüeh* in the 1190's while fifteen were to be among the attackers. Thus there was at least a rough parity between the two groups although it should be borne in mind that data for the enemies of *wei-hsüeh* are less accessible than for their opponents. Interestingly, these figures stand in contrast to those of the next decade: in the four examinations held in 1172, 1175, 1178, and 1181 sixteen men, later to be branded as disciples of "spurious learning," were awarded degrees, but only two degrees went to their enemies (Table 7.1). The examination of 1172 is of special interest since degrees were granted to seven of those charged with *wei-hsüeh*, including the prominent Ch'en Fu-liang but to only one critic of *wei-hsüeh* (1137 – 1203). The famous philosopher Lu Chiu-yüan also received his degree that year. The examiners in 1172 were Yu Mou (1127 – 1194) and Lü Tsu-ch'ien (1137 – 81). Yu later became a staunch defender of "false learning." Lü is well known as a historian and friend of Chu Hsi, and his collaborator in the compilation of the *Chin-ssu lu*. Neither Yu nor Lü lived to see Han T'o-chou's attack on *wei-hsüeh* but both were associated with the men attacked.

Because Ch'in Kuei's opponents championed the ideas of the Ch'eng brothers and because the Ch'engs had been hostile to Wang An-shih, Ch'in has been considered pro-Wang although Emperor Kao-

---

* *SYHA* 97, cited in Mark Chung Kwai [Mai Chung-kuei], *Sung Yüan li-hsüeh-chia chu-shu sheng-tsu nien-piao* [Chronological table of bibliographical and biographical data for the Sung and Yüan Neo-Confucian philosophers] Institute of Advanced Chinese Studies and Research, Monograph Series No. 3 (Hong Kong: New Asia College, 1968). This reference work has been useful in preparing the present study.

TABLE 7.1.
**Dates When Men Involved in the Controversy
Received Their *Chin-shih*.**

Date	Attacked	Opponent
1142		Lin Li
1143	Liu Cheng	
1145		Cheng Ping
1148	Chu Hsi	Mi Shih-tan
1151	Chou Pi-ta	
1154	Ho Yi	Yeh Chu
1157		Yao Yü, Ching T'ang
1160	Lin Ta-chung	Kao Wen-hu, Chang Po-kai
1163	Lou Yau, Sun Feng-chi, Huang Tu, Li Hsiang, Chan T'i-jen, Yang Fang	Hsü Chi-chih, Fu Po-shou, Hu Hung (?)
1166	Chao Ju-yü, Cheng Shih, Ts'eng San-p'ing, Wang Hou-chih	Ho Tan, Ni Ssu, Hsieh Shen-fu
1169	P'eng Kuei-nien, Wang Lin, Huang Fu, Liu Kuang-tsu, Yang Chien	Chang Yen, Chang Kuei-mu, Shih K'ang-nien, Shen Chi-tsu
1172	Ch'en Fu-liang, Ts'ai Yu-hsüeh, Hsüeh Shu-ssu, Wang K'uei, T'ien Tan, Hsü I, Chao Kung	Li Mu
1175	Hsiang An-shih, Wu Lieh, Yu Chung-hung	
1178	Yeh Shih, Shen Yu-k'ai, Fan Chung-fu	Chang Fu
1181	Huang Yu, Yüan Hsieh, Wu Jou-sheng	

tsung on at least one occasion expressed his desire to profit by the strong points of both sets of theories.[9] Similarly, in 1178 the Censor Hsieh K'ou-jan (d. 1182) impartially warned against the excesses of both the advocates of Wang An-shih, who force their way contrary to good sense and lead ultimately to destruction, and the champions of Ch'eng I whom Hsieh portrays as engaged in vacuous bragging and entering into the dangerous and weird.[10] Two years later, Chao Yen-chung directed his remarks against the favorite subject of Neo-Confucian speculation when he complained about the prevalence of theories concerning human nature (*hsing*) and principle (*li*) in the examinations and specifically condemned the members of the Ch'eng school for misrepresentation, charging that they falsified a reputation for sincerity and reverence while furthering a vacuous and false reality.[11]

In 1182 the attack on Northern Sung philosophy flared up again and took a new turn involving for the first time men who were to be

condemned in the 1190s. The immediate stimulus came from Chu
Hsi's indictment of the well-connected scholar-official T'ang Chung-
yu (ca. 1131 – ca. 1183) which induced the Censor Ch'en Chia and the
Minister of Personnel Cheng Ping (d. 1194) to respond by attacking
not Chu Hsi himself but what they thought he stood for. In the process
they initiated the attack on *tao-hsüeh*, "The Doctrine of the True Way."
The better known of the two attackers was Cheng Ping* who had a
reputation as a good administrator and a man of some courage, the
latter demonstrated by his objections against the transfer of a censor
in 1178 who had impeached a man with influential friends, a case so
sensitive that the Censor Hsieh K'ou-jan did not dare to participate.
Cheng died before Han T'o-chou came to power, but is usually assigned to the group opposed to *wei-hsüeh*. It is therefore noteworthy
that he had once been recommended by Wang Lin (*chin-shih* 1169)
and that his epitaph was composed by Chou Pi-ta (1126 – 1204), both
later charged with *wei-hsüeh*, while at the same time he was on good
terms with a number of the men on the other side, including his
brother-in-law, the Censor Lin Ts'ai. Predictably Chou Pi-ta's epitaph
passes over Cheng's 1183 memorial in silence. All that is known about
it now is that it charged the followers of *tao-hsüeh* with "deceiving the
world and stealing a name." In contrast, very little biographical information is available about Ch'en Chia but more of his memorial on *tao-
hsüeh* has been preserved.[12]

Ch'en Chia's charges set the tone for many of the attacks which
followed and contained allegations which were often repeated. Although
he did not use the term *wei-hsüeh* itself, the essence of his indictment
was that the followers of *tao-hsüeh* were a group of fakers and hypo-
crites whose deeds did not match their words, and he emphasized their
alleged lack of sincerity. Affirming that the difference between depravity
and rectitude was entirely a matter of sincerity or falsity (*wei*), he went
on to cite Mencius[13] to bring to bear Confucius' hatred of the insin-
cere "honest villager" and the condemnation in the *School Sayings
of Confucius* of "conduct which is persistent in its depravity" and
"speech which is eloquent in its falsehood."[14] Ch'en warned against
these men who conceal their falsity while they are really out to "deceive
the world and steal a name." Approving of their statements emphasizing

---

* Tombstone inscription by Chou Pi-ta, *Chou I-kuo Wen-chung kung chi* [Collected
writings of Chou Pi-ta] (Ying-t'ang pieh shu ed., 1848) 65.9b – 16a. See also *SS* 349.14a-
b; Ch'iao-ch'uan ch'iao-sou (pseudonym), *Ch'ing-yüan tang-chin* [The party prohibition
of the Ch'ing-yüan period] (Ts'ung-shu chi-ch'eng ed.), and other listings given in
Combined Indices to Forty-seven Collections of Sung Dynasty Biographies, Harvard
Yenching Institute Sinological Series, No. 34 (Second edition, Tokyo: Toyo Bunko,
1959). Also *SSCW* 27.8b – 9a, 27.29b; *HTCTC* 146 (for 1178); 147 (for 1179); 150
(for 1185); *TML*, p. 44. *SYHA* 34 argues that Cheng Ping was not involved in the
attack on *tao-hsüeh*.

the importance of respectfulness, following through, and the obligation to "rectify the mind and make the thoughts sincere" and "rectify the self and restore the rites,"* Ch'en argued that these terms were the rightful common property of all scholars, but that the followers of *tao-hsüeh* tried unfairly to monopolize them even as their actual conduct belied their words. What the *tao-hsüeh* scholars really wanted, according to Ch'en Chia, were salary and position. They maintained they cared nothing for personal appearance or for money, but acted to the contrary. They used the words of the hallowed kings of antiquity but acted like men in the marketplace. Appropriating the designation for a scholar in retirement, they actually plotted for position and despised the statutes. The best succeeded in their villainy, those next to the top protected their shortcomings, while the lowest hid their lack of ability. In this way, they dominated the examination lists and otherwise made careers for themselves. Ch'en then went on to appeal to the emperor to remedy this situation and eliminate such men so that words and actions, the external and the internal, would all proceed from rectitude and there would be no dissolute fashioning of strange theories to offend against the government.

The defense, as might be expected, was that this was slander. Some university students quickly responded by exploiting the fact that a Ch'en Chia, written with identical characters, had once criticized the venerated Duke of Chou. They mocked the censor:

The Great Sage, the Duke of Chou, encountered slander; the famous worthies of I-Lo [i.e., the Ch'eng brothers and their followers] also suffer ridicule. Alas, the two Ch'en Chias, past and present — why do they only take hold of the errors of sages and worthies?[15]

A vigorous defense was presented to the throne by Yu Mou, who asserted that *tao-hsüeh* was that whereby Yao and Shun had been emperors, whereby Yu, T'ang, and Wu had been kings, whereby the Duke of Chou, Confucius, and Mencius had established the teaching, and warned against those who misuse the term to slander noble men.[16] This often repeated claim of intellectual descent from the founding culture heroes and sages of Confucianism ultimately goes back to the essay *"Yüan tao"* by the great T'ang dynasty precursor of Neo-Confucianism, Han Yü (768–824), and represents a lineage of intellectual orthodoxy which, despite the uncertain status of Mencius during the Sung, was not really challenged by the opponents of *tao-hsüeh,*

---

* These quotations which sometimes functioned as mottos or even slogans, were taken from *The Great Learning* and *Analects* XII, 1.1, respectively.

whose point of attack was the claim that the Ch'eng brothers and their disciples had a monopoly of intellectual legitimacy.* The possible inclusion of Wang T'ung and Han Yü himself into this lineage, while debated by scholars and tending to soften the claim made on behalf of the Northern Sung Confucians, did not concern the opponents of *tao-hsüeh*.†

As James T. C. Liu has pointed out, the term *tao-hsüeh* was used sarcastically already during the Northern Sung,[17] but this did not preclude its use in a positive sense too as when Chang Tsai deplored the view that *tao-hsüeh* and statescraft are two different things.[18] The reputed founder of the Yung-chia school, Wang K'ai-tsu, a contemporary of the Ch'engs, said, "Since the time of Mencius, *tao-hsüeh* is not clear."[19] There were similar cases during the early Southern Sung.[20] Chu Hsi began the preface to his commentary on the *Doctrine of the Mean* by stating that it was composed by Tzu Ssu because he was worried that the tradition of *tao-hsüeh* would be lost. It is also worth noting that the two characters *tao* and *hsüeh* occur together in the *Great Learning* even though Chu Hsi in his notes on this passage did not interpret them as forming a compound but understood *tao* verbally in the sense of "to say" or "to mean."‡ Yet the term was increasingly used in a pejorative sense,§ and the implication that it made an excessive claim to sole mastery of the truth was not lost on some of the leading Neo-Confucians. Lu Chiu-yüan, for example, was uneasy about the expression, insisting that the *tao* is basically to be identified with everyday conduct and that those scholars who limit it to one activity so that "the name inflates an empty reputation and exceeds reality" are sure to be profoundly rejected and forcefully criticized.[21] Nevertheless, this term had considerable intrinsic appeal: after all, what should a Confucian scholar study if not the *tao*? Ultimately it became an honored designation, and when the official history of the Sung came to be written under the next dynasty, the historians, as a mark of special distinction, included a special biographical section on

---

* As Professor Liu points out in "The Road to Neo-Confucian Orthodoxy," this claim was "more than pretentious."

† Why the "tough minded" wing of Southern Sung Confucians including Ch'en Liang and members of the Yung-chia school were attracted to Wang T'ung still awaits a satisfactory explanation.

‡ *The Great Learning* III, 4. Chu Hsi's preface to the *Chung Yung* and his interpretation of *tao* in *The Great Learning* may be found in any edition of his commentaries to the Four Books.

§ The term *tao-hsüeh* took on pejorative connotations to the extent that the eighteenth-century scholar Wang Shih-han (b. 1707, *chin-shih* 1733) suggested the term was coined in the Southern Sung as a word of abuse. See Wang Shih-han, *Han-men chui hsüeh* [Connected studies of Wang Shih-han] (Ch'ing ed.) 2.36b.

tao-hsüeh. * Emperor Hsiao-tsung too, in deciding the merits of the charges raised by Ch'en Chia and Cheng Ping and considering Yu Mou's refutation, agreed that *tao-hsüeh* was a beautiful term but expressed the fear that it could be abused.

In 1188 the political career of Chu Hsi and the fate of *tao-hsüeh* were once more intertwined when Lin Li, attacking Chu for failing to take up an appointment, charged him with using the empty name, *tao-hsüeh,* to advance himself.† Yeh Shih, the Professor of Imperial Sacrifices, defended Chu Hsi vigorously in a memorial where he warned against the example of Ts'ai Ching's suppression of the Yüan-yu party and took up the *tao-hsüeh* issue, pointing out that it did not concern Chu Hsi alone but was being used to slander good men, creating in effect a reversal of values so that "worthy men are anxious and frightened; average men disperse, still their voices and destroy their shadows, tarnish their virtue and foul their conduct in order to avoid this name almost like Manicheans obliterating their traces."‡ The outcome was a political stalemate, and in a famous memorial submitted later that year Chu Hsi himself complained about the way the term *tao-hsüeh* was being used. Depicting the lot of the worthy man, he wrote: "The crowd criticizes him, the multitude attacks him, points to him as a *tao-hsüeh* man, and heaps on him the crime of making a special effort to be superior."[22] Thus when Hsiao-tsung abdicated in 2nd/1189 the term *tao-hsüeh* was in some disrepute, but the men so labelled had managed to hold their own.

Tao-hsüeh *under Kuang-tsung (r. 1189 — 94)*

For the first two years of Kuang-tsung's reign it was not clear what direction matters would take. Shortly after the emperor's accession Cheng Shih, later to be attacked for "false learning," sounded an optimistic note when he began a memorial by saying that the dynasty had the best family laws of any since antiquity. In support of this evaluation

---

* It was also used in a positive sense in the thirteenth century as, for example, by Li Hsin-ch'uan in *TML.*

† *TML,* pp. 47 — 48. For the political career of Chu Hsi, see Conrad Schirokauer, "Chu Hsi's Political Career: A Study in Ambivalence," in Arthur Wright and Denis Twitchett, eds., *Confucian Personalities* (Stanford: Stanford University Press, 1962), pp. 162 — 188. The Lin Li episode is discussed on page 176.

‡ Yeh Shih, *Shui-hsin chi* 2.6b — 7a. Haeger, "The Intellectual Context of Neo-Confucian Syncretism," *The Journal of Asian Studies* 31 (1972), p. 507 quotes an earlier passage from the same memorial, but following the Ssu-pu pei-yao edition or the recent punctuated edition of Yeh Shih, *Yeh Shih chi* [Collected writings of Yeh Shih] (Peking: Chung-hua shu-chü, 1962), I would replace his " . . . recently men have gathered under the rubric of *tao-hsüeh*" with "As for the recently created rubric of *tao-hsüeh* [as a term of abuse]" and go on, "Cheng Ping took the lead and Ch'en Chia concurred. . . . "

he discussed the serving of parents, citing the long harmony which had prevailed between Hsiao-tsung and the abdicated Kao-tsung, his father by adoption. Then, turning to regulation of the family, Cheng said, among other things, that the dynasty had never experienced an empress lacking in virtue. Perhaps he had a premonition that the emperor's conduct toward his father and the character of the empress were to be the weak points of the reign, but more likely he was genuinely hopeful. Cheng also discussed the education of children. He concluded that in these three particulars the Han and T'ang had failed to come up to the Sung. He urged the emperor to continue in this tradition and did not refrain from expressing a characteristically Confucian concern over reports of excessive merry-making in the palace.[23]

For the men later involved in the *wei-hsüeh* controversy this was a mixed period. Thus when in 3rd/1189 the offices of Completioner and Reparationer, which had been established at the urging of Lin Li, were again abolished, this brought on the transfer of one adherent of each side of the dispute.[24] When the Left Grand Councilor Chou Pi-ta was dismissed, this was a triumph for an eventual opponent of *wei-hsüeh,* Ho Tan (*chin-shih* 1166), but Chou's colleague Liu Cheng remained in office. In 1190 Liu became Left Grand Councilor, and continued in this office for the remainder of Kuang-tsung's reign. In 5th/1189 Yu Mou was dismissed for criticizing the Administrator of the Palace Postern and imperial favorite Chiang T'e-li (d. ca. 1192), but this was followed by Chiang's own dismissal.[25] In 1190 *tao-hsüeh* figured in the palace examination answer of Wang Chieh (1158– 1213), a student of Chu Hsi and Lü Tsu-ch'ien. His paper, which presented a critique of the abuse of the term, was well received.[26] Yeh Shih's disciple Chou Nan (1159–1213) also submitted a strong essay on this issue,[27] and the Censor Liu Kuang-tsu (1142–1222), apparently motivated by the fear that the removal of Chou Pi-ta might bring on a purge, memorialized that *tao-hsüeh* was not just the private, selfish theory of the Ch'engs, complained that it was being slandered, defended its stress on the key role of "royal perfection" (*huang-chi*) in setting things right, and argued that most of its proponents were good men, even though a few were less than perfect.[28] Liu was dismissed two months later after he persisted in criticizing the palace appointment of a magician-doctor favored by Empress Li (d. 1200). Initially Ho Tan and Hu Hung, later fellow opponents of *wei-hsüeh* had joined Liu in the case, but they obeyed an imperial order to desist which Liu ignored.[29] Ho was promoted at first but then was forced to resign in 8th/1191 after an unsuccessful effort to be excused from observing ritual mourning for a stepmother who had married his father after Ho Tan had already left the family to be adopted by an uncle. Ho's conduct at this time caused considerable commotion and made him a target of strong student criticisms.[30] This incident suggests a reason for Ho's resentment of moralizing intellectuals while it also reflects the importance attached to the value of filial piety—and late in 1191 filial piety was becoming a prime object of concern among scholars and officials.

Even before officialdom became worried about Kuang-tsung's treatment of his father, many people had become disillusioned with the emperor. Consequently, when unseasonable weather prompted an imperial request for advice in 2nd/1191, key officials responded with strong critiques. As the Censor Lin Ta-chung (1131–1208), later included in the *wei-hsüeh* list, put it, "For thunder and lightning to be followed by a great snow in the second month of spring is clear evidence that *yin* is dominating over *yang*."[31] The moral is obvious, and a prime target was surely Empress Li, who was increasingly taking power into her own hands. A stinging rebuke was submitted by a commoner, perhaps a university student, who complained of "merry-making without measure and music without end" into the night, the constant presence of palace girls, the power of eunuchs, the construction of pavilions, exotic music and dance, the antics of actors and the prevalence of bribery so that appointments to posts from lieutenant general to commander of the palace footmen each had its high price.[32]

P'eng Kuei-nien (1142–1206), later one of the strongest supporters of Chao Ju-yü and Chu Hsi, submitted a similar memorial on the theme of *yin* encroaching on *yang* in which he substantiated his interpretation of the weather by citing the *Spring and Autumn Annals* together with Hu An-kuo's commentary and then traced the beginnings of this disarray of cosmic forces to the time of Emperor Hsiao-tsung. His wide-ranging memorial included a dissertation on the importance of firmness (*kang*), lectures on excessive drinking and banqueting in the palace and failure to enter night visits to the palace in the proper register for the Secretariat, as well as appeals for the emperor to cultivate his virtue and take care of himself (*hsiu-te ai-shen*), all aimed directly at Kuang-tsung. But P'eng was really concerned with the entire government and included a critique of personnel policies as well as the treatment of military and economic problems. In a discussion of the predominance of petty men, he urged the need to follow custom and precedent lest profit triumph over right and selfishness over concern for the public good. This was an ever present danger since P'eng shared a widespread conviction that in personnel management, if both the virtuous and the villainous are employed, the latter would be sure to triumph. Indeed, according to P'eng, this had already taken place, and he sketched a picture of the country run by clerks, with district and prefectural clerks controlling the people, clerks in middle-sized cities controlling officials, and clerks in the censorate who are in contact with powerful favorites controlling the court, thereby permitting the entire network of clerks to function.[33]

This and other memorials notwithstanding, Kuang-tsung continued to deteriorate and apparently took a turn for the worse after Empress Li did away with one of his favorite concubines in 11th/1191. Among those who criticized the emperor's drinking was Ni Ssu (1147 – 1220), later an opponent of *wei-hsüeh,* but it was P'eng Kuei-nien who in a memorial on "taking care of oneself, reducing the desires, and attending to studies" warned the emperor that wine resembles women and petty men in that once approached it cannot be removed, and went on to present a classic definition of alcoholism:

Your servant has observed that whenever those who are not addicted to wine, drink, they become muddled, but it is when those who are addicted to wine do not drink that *they* become muddled. In the case of those who drink and become muddled, the vital force [*ch'i*] is in command and therefore when there is wine, their vital force becomes confused. In the case of those who do not drink and become muddled, wine is in command, therefore when there is no wine, they are deprived of their vital force. If they do without wine for one day, their blood, veins, and arteries cannot manage. Now wine has triumphed over the vital force and the vital force cannot rule itself.[34]

P'eng went on to assure the emperor that a bit of feasting and drinking in the palace does not lead to this condition, but expressed his worry that matters had gone past the safe point. He went on to state his hope that the emperor would turn to the company of eminent scholars and advised a gradual reduction in wine consumption.

Kuang-tsung's most shocking offense against Confucian morality was his failure to pay his respects to his abdicated father in the Ch'ung-hua Palace.[35] The rift between the two palaces became a great scandal for which blame was laid on Empress Li and some eunuchs and favorites. In 11th/1192, on the day of the southern solstice, Liu Cheng (1129 – 1206) led a hundred officials to the Ch'ung-hua Palace to offer their congratulations while Lo Tien (d. 1194), Yu Mou, Huang Ch'ang, (1146 – 94), Yeh Shih, and P'eng Kuei-nien memorialized requesting the emperor to call on his father. Chao Ju-yü managed to mediate between the two palaces and induced the emperor to pay his respects,[36] but in 9th/1193 the same trouble flared up again. On this occasion Ch'en Fu-liang almost succeeded in getting the emperor to go when the empress detained him and rewarded Ch'en for his trouble with a tongue lashing. The issue continued to preoccupy officialdom until Hsiao-tsung's death in 6th/1194 brought matters to a crisis. In the meantime, the palace was deluged by memorials including those from a good number of men later accused of *wei-hsüeh*. Among the most active were Ch'en Fu-liang, P'eng Kuei-nien, Wu Lieh (1163–1233), Chan T'i-jen (1143–1206), Huang Tu (1138–1213), and Lou Yüeh (1137–1213), but Huang Yu (d. after 1210), Hsiang An-shih (d. 1208), Ts'ai Yu-hsüeh (1154–1217), Shen Yu-k'ai (1134–1212), Yu Chung-hung (1138–1215), and Chu Hsi also played a role. Wang Chieh, Chu Hsi's disciple, was one of the men close to Chu who participated in this criticism of the emperor but was not later listed as a *wei-hsüeh* partisan. Of the opponents of *wei-hsüeh*, Ni Ssu was active in this matter, memorializing and once advising Kuang-tsung that the old emperor wanted to see him just as he himself wanted to see his son, Prince Chia, the heir-apparent.[37]

Many of the memorialists took a moral stance affirming the universal applicability of the foremost Confucian virtue: in serving one's parents "from the emperor to the masses the rites are the same."[38] To give weight to their admonitions they drew on a wealth of historical examples ranging from the legendary Shun, the paragon of filial piety, to the abdicated emperor himself, whose exceptional filiality had earned him the temple name "The Filial Ancestor" (Hsiao-tsung). He had insisted on returning to the ancient practice of performing a full three years' mourning for Kao-tsung and indeed had given this as his reason for abdicating after several officials, including Yu Mou, had rejected the idea of his sharing the imperial duties with the heir-apparent. The contrast between father and son was apparent to all.

Memorialists also dwelt on the harmful effects of the emperor's conduct on the country and indeed the entire world as evidenced by a series of unsettling meteorological phenomena and earthquakes. Thus P'eng Kuei-nien, in a memorial dated 3rd/1194, responded to an edict ordering an official to pray for rain at a Buddhist temple by discoursing on the need for harmony:

If the two palaces are not in harmony, the world will not be harmonious, and if the world is not harmonious, the sky and the earth will not be in harmony. And if the sky and the earth are not harmonious, then though the Buddhists want to force the rain in order to respond to Your Majesty's wish, they will be unable to succeed.[39]

University students, too, made their appeal: over two hundred petitioned and another hundred did obeisance in front of the palace, the Sung equivalent of picketing the White House. Some students even drew up a biting "Exhortation in Encouragement of Pleasure" proclaiming "The Duke of Chou deceived us: we wish 'The Announcement about Drunkenness' burned in public. Confucius spoke empty words: we wish the *Classic of Filial Piety* be put away on a high shelf."[40] But it is appropriate to give the last word to Chu Hsi who sent in a sealed memorial in 5th/1194:

> Thus what your humble servant has read does not go beyond the *Classic of Filial Piety,* the *Analects, Mencius,* and the Six Classics; what I have studied does not go beyond the Way of Yao and Shun, the Duke of Chou and Confucius; what I know does not go beyond the reason for the failures and successes since the Three Dynasties and the Han; what I have explicated does not go beyond distinguishing the Principle of Humanity, Rites and Music, the Principles of Nature and human desires; what I have observed does not go beyond the laws of the country. When I examine their meaning, it is always that the subject be loyal and the son filial and that is all. . . . Your humble servant today does not venture to expand his previous remarks, to prepare rites and memorialize in order to fish for a reputation as one who dares to speak and to place the blame on Your Majesty. All I request is to weep and explain the natural nature of the relationship between father and son.*

Kuang-tsung's inability, on account of sickness, to perform the mourning for his father ushered in a crisis which was finally resolved by the emperor's abdication. Yeh Shih and Liu Cheng played an important role in having the heir-apparent formally designated crown prince, but in effecting the actual change of throne Chao Ju-yü, a member of a junior branch of the imperial family then serving as Administrator of the Bureau of Military Affairs, took the lead, spurred on partly by a letter from Hsü I (d. 1208) criticizing his inactivity and suggesting that he obtain a decree from the Senior Empress Dowager Wu (1115—97), the widow of Kao-tsung. To accomplish this Chao called on the Administrator of the Palace Postern Han T'o-chou whose mother was the younger sister of Empress Wu and whose deceased wife was Empress Wu's niece. Han T'o-chou used his connections in the palace and, working through a eunuch, obtained the necessary decree from the Empress Dowager.[41]

From Tao-hsüeh *to* Wei-hsüeh: *1194—97*

The accession of Ning-tsung (r. 1194—1224) solved the crisis of the throne but led to bitter rivalry between the two main architects of the succession, now no longer united by a common cause. At first Chao Ju-yü had the upper hand and expressed his hopes for the new

---

* Chu Hsi, *Chu Wen-kung wen-chi* 12.7a. This is quoted in Morohashi, *Jugaku no mokuteki to So-ju no Katsudo,* p. 406. Morohashi discusses the Chung-hua Palace case on pp. 401—407.

regime by adopting the year title Ch'ing-yüan, combining the first character of the year title of the Ch'ing-li period (1041 – 1048), when the reformer Fan Chung-yen (989 – 1052) was active, with the first character of Yüan-yu, when the opponents of Wang An-shih's policies were in power.* Disregarding the advice of Hsü I and others to humor Han with a general's insignia,[42] Chao Ju-yü rebuked Han when he asked for a fitting reward for his services and forced him to be content with a relatively minor post. Chao himself first rejected but then in 8th/1194 accepted the post of Right Grand Councilor, only to lose it again in 2nd/1195. Even before he obtained Chao's ouster Han had won some substantial victories by securing the dismissal of eminent associates of Chao like Ch'en Fu-liang and Liu Kuang-tsu and forcing the departure of Chu Hsi, who had been called to court on Chao's recommendation.

Han T'o-chou's greatest asset in his contest with Chao Ju-yü was his connection with the palace through his niece, the new empress. Chao's family background, in contrast, although an asset when it came to persuading the empress dowager to issue her decree, was now a distinct liability, since his acceptance of high office went directly against dynastic tradition and against the rule established by Kao-tsung that members of the imperial family were not to be appointed councilors of state. This had already been brought up in 3rd/1193 by Wang I-tuan when Chao was first appointed Co-administrator of the Bureau of Military Affairs, but at that time Wang's objection was dismissed on the grounds that Kao-tsung had simply used this rule as a device to block the schemes of Ch'in Kuei. Wang's hostility toward Chao stemmed from an occasion when Chao as examination supervisor had overruled Wang, then acting as a revising official. The argument was now resurrected by the Right Policy Monitor Li Mu (*chin-shih* 1172), but when in 11th/1195 Han T'o-chou had Chao exiled to Yung-chou, it was Wang who had the satisfaction of writing the order. He used the opportunity to compare Chao to Liu Ch'ü-li (d. 90 B.C.) of the Han and Li Lin-fu (d.752) of the T'ang suggesting the harm a dynasty could suffer at the hands of a member of the imperial family.[43] As Moroto Tatsuo has pointed out, Chao Ju-yü remained the only exception to the dynastic rule.[44]

The removal of Chao Ju-yü fed the tide of protest which had set in with the earlier dismissals. After Chu Hsi was let go, for example, requests for his retention came from Ch'en Fu-liang and others later

---

*This is pointed out by Li Hsin-ch'uan in *CYTC*, pp. 45 – 46. *CYTC*, pp. 79 – 81 contains a discussion of *tao-hsüeh* and the *wei-hsüeh* list. See also Ch'en Fu-liang, *Chih-chai hsien-sheng wen-chi* [Collected writings of Ch'en Fu-liang] (Ssu-pu ts'ung-k'an ed.), 10.1a.

condemned for *wei-hsüeh*. Yu Chung-hung at this time criticized the use of imperial orders circumventing the secretariat and irregularities in the dismissals of Liu Cheng, Huang Tu, and Chu Hsi, warning the emperor, "since antiquity it has never happened that one could dismiss chief ministers, admonitory and lecturing officials and yet achieve wisdom." Wang Chieh warned that imperial orders had been used during the first decade of the century with disastrous results. P'eng Kuei-nien bitterly attacked Han T'o-chou for usurping power, complained that only Han knew what was happening and asked the emperor to dismiss "this petty man" so that "the world will not say that Your Majesty finds it easy to dismiss noble men but difficult to remove petty men." When P'eng was in turn dismissed by an imperial order, Lin Ta-chung and Lou Yüeh protested punishing a man for speaking out. The need to keep the channels of criticism open is a constant theme in memorials protesting a dismissal.[45]

Access to the emperor gave Han the opportunity to influence imperial orders, and objection against this practice was a frequent theme in the memorials of his opponents, but once he had obtained the appointment of political allies as censors and policy critics, he could afford to follow more standard procedures. Ch'en Fu-liang was impeached by a censor, and when Yang Chien (1140−1226) protested the removal of Chao, it was again Li Mu who indicted him for being a member of Chao's faction.[46]

Once begun, the exchange of charges and counter-charges built up momentum. The pattern was for a man to file a protest and then be banished. This is what happened to Lü Tsu-chien (d. 1200), younger brother of Lü Tsu-ch'ien, in 4th/1195. His protest was followed by a petition from six university students, later to be known as the "six *chün-tzu*," who charged:

Li Mu himself knows that virtue and depravity cannot coexist and therefore wants to overthrow virtue completely. . . . What we request is that Your Majesty think of Ju-yü's faithful service, ascertain the fact that Li Hsiang and Yang Chien did not establish a faction and be clear about Li Mu's villainy.*

Unlike Ch'in Kuei, Han T'o-chou was unable to muster student support.

It was in the middle of 1195 that Liu Te-hsiu introduced the term *wei-hsüeh* into a memorial, arguing that "the distinction between villainy and rectitude is nothing but that between the genuine and the

---

* Li Hsiang was dismissed as director of education for protesting the removal of Chao Ju-yü and was later included in the *wei hsüeh* list as was Yang Chien, a professor at the time. For the student protest, see the biography of Yang Hung-chung, *SS* 455.15a−17b, quoted in *HTCTC* 154, No. 19 (1195).

false." Neither side had a monopoly on the language of moral indignation. It was also Liu who composed a scathing denunciation of Liu
Cheng charging him with bringing to court men of "spurious learning"
including Chao Ju-yü who was now accused of all kinds of seditious
plots.[47] Liu's memorial led to further dismissals, and the attacks
continued in full swing. In 8th/1196, after a complaint that it had been
dominating the examination halls for the past thirty years, *wei-hsüeh*
was proscribed from the examinations, and candidates had to attest in
writing that they were not men of "false learning."* The campaign
finally led to the compilation of a list of fifty-nine men guilty of belonging to the "rebel clique of spurious learning."[48]

The Arguments Against Wei-hsüeh

Many of the attacks on the friends of Chao Ju-yü repeated earlier
charges against the followers of Ch'eng philosophy. Ho Tan, for example, in a memorial of 7th/1195 again denounced "specialist learning."
Innuendo about the scholarship and character of opponents was standard fare. In 3rd/1197 Yeh Chu (*chin-shih* 1154) charged:

They consider the six classics, the philosophers, and histories not worth looking at. . . . They only engage in discourses [*yü-lei*] and perverse theories in order
to hide their lack of content and their illiterate vulgarity. By scattering Ch'an
terms they are able to fool men. At the triennial examinations when school
entry is decided, they recognize each other by using strange words and pho-
neticizations, and immediately place a paper [by one of their own] in the first
ranks, thereby causing truly talented and capable men to be rejected.[49]

Yeh went on to say that he spoke from recent experience as an examiner.
His was but one of the voices objecting that men of "spurious learning"
had been dominating the examinations.

Yeh Chu's reference to Ch'an Buddhism and esoteric terminology
and the charge of heterodoxy raised by him and others suggest an
anti-Buddhist element in the campaign against *wei-hsüeh*,† but if there
was anything the accused scholars agreed on, it was their open opposition to Buddhism, a stance which was not a political asset under Hsiao-
tsung. Hsiao-tsung was the author of an essay which attempted to
refute Han Yü's *"Yüan tao,"* and instead of rejecting Buddhism out-

---

* *HTCTC* 154, No. 34 (1196). It is likely that most candidates made such a statement
but at least one man who had been studying Ch'eng I's commentary on the *Book of
Changes* decided not to take the examinations.

† See Araki Toshikazu, *Sodai kakyo seido kenkyū* [The civil service examination of
the Sung dynasty] (Kyoto: Tōyōshi-kenkyu-kai, 1969), pp. 397–400. On pp. 397–98
Araki quotes the passage by Yeh Chu.

right, he argued for a synthesis of the three major creeds: Buddhism to be used for cultivating the mind, Taoism to nourish life, and Confucianism to govern the world.[50] Yeh Chu's words reflect an anti-Buddhist tone, but there is no evidence that Buddhism was really at issue in the *wei-hsüeh* controversy.

In place of the "perverse theories" of the men of "spurious learning" their opponents could only offer the fundamentalist slogan of going back to Confucius and Mencius. It is not surprising that some men resented the *tao-hsüeh* claims for reinterpretations of the Confucian canon. These claims were sometimes quite abstruse and seemed to exclude ordinary educated men from full access to the truth (and even to office), but the opponents of *tao-hsüeh* did not formulate a philosophy of their own, nor did they open any new doors through which men of the twelfth century could gain access to the teachings of the sages. They did not even devise a coherent theory to explain how their enemies had come to depart from the "true tradition," other than through sheer perversity. Liu San-chieh, for example, traced *wei-hsüeh* back to Chang Shih who in all good faith developed a theory of the nature and principle which his followers then used for their own selfish ends, but he did not explain why Chang's disciples should have turned out less virtuous than their master.[51] It was Yeh Shih, himself attacked for *wei-hsüeh,* who suggested that the Northern Sung scholars in their eagerness to combat Buddhism and Taoism were led, despite themselves, to incorporate elements of these two creeds into their own theories, using for this purpose the appendices to the *Book of Changes.*[52] Indeed when it came to accusations of straying from the Confucian path and accepting elements of Buddhist or Taoist heterodoxy, the men attacked for "spurious learning" were each other's best critics. The attacked men continued to draw strength and comfort from their unshaken conviction that it was they who were being true to the great tradition.

One intellectual issue with political overtones which may have played a minor part in the *wei-hsüeh* controversy involved the interpretation of the phrase *chien yung huang-chi* in "The Great Plan" chapter of the *Classic of History,* translated by Legge, following Chu Hsi, as "The Establishment and Use of Royal Perfection."[53] Here Chu Hsi rejected the old commentaries which explained *huang* as "great" and *chi* as "the center,"* readings apparently accepted by Han T'o-chou who took the passage to mean "establishing the center and using the great."[54] Appeals to the emperor in terms of *huang-chi,* exploiting its

---

* Chu Hsi, *Chu Wen-kung wen-chi* 72.12a – 15b. Chu Hsi states that he adopted this interpretation from Feng Shih-hsing, a *chin-shih* of 1131 – 62.

rich associations* and ancient provenance, were not uncommon.† As Tomoeda has suggested, Chu Hsi's version emphasized that "the sovereign by his own person establishes the Supreme Standard (*chih-chi*) of the world," an interpretation which places a very heavy moral responsibility on the emperor. Disagreement over the meaning of this expression may reflect a difference at least in emphasis concerning the function of the ruler, but as Tomoeda has also pointed out, Chu Hsi's views were by no means accepted by his intellectual peers. Lu Chiu-yüan, for one, like Han T'o-chou, held to the older interpretation of the text which Lu understood in terms of people "becoming conscious of their innate goodness."[55] Yet Lu was second to none in his insistence that the emperor must cultivate himself, and in one memorial told Hsiao-tsung that His Majesty was devoting too much time to government administration and too little to study and meditation.[56] Lu himself did not live to see the *wei-hsüeh* controversy but several of his disciples were caught up in it. Furthermore, the authenticity of the "Great Plan" chapter, including the relevant passage, was a matter in dispute among Sung scholars.‡ Yeh Shih's disciple Chou Nan in his 1190 palace examination answer even described *huang-chi* as one of the three evils in the world, the first two being *tao-hsüeh* and factionalism, with one leading to the next.[57]

Chao Ju-yü's associates were often charged with arrogance. Liu San-chieh, for example, in his attack of 6th/1197 accused them of behaving like Yen Hui, Min Tzu-ch'ien or even like Confucius and Mencius. They claimed, he said, the virtue of the Duke of Chou when they interpreted unseasonable weather as a sign from Heaven.[58] Another related theme is disobedience to the emperor, or as Chang Fu (*chin-shih* 1178) put it in his indictment of Liu Kuang-tsu, "showing contempt for the sovereign."[59] This must have struck a responsive chord in the emperor whose father had been subjected to a particularly heavy dose of moralizing criticism administered by pedagogic Con-

---

* The metaphysical dimensions of the term are suggested by its prominent occurrence in the title of Shao Yung's major work, the *Huang-chi ching-shih shu,* rendered by Wing-tsit Chan as "Supreme Principles Governing the World." See Wing-tsit Chan, *A Source Book in Chinese Philosophy* (Princeton, New Jersey: Princeton University Press, 1963), p. 483.

† See Liu Kuang-tsu's memorial above. For another example, see the biographical account of Wu Lieh in Wei Liao-weng, *Hou-shan hsien-sheng ta-ch'üan* [Collected writings of Wei Liao-weng] (Ssu-pu ts'ung-k'an ed.), 89.6a.

‡ Naitō Torajirō, *Shina shigaku shi* [A history of Chinese historiography] (Tokyo: Kyomizu Kōbundō shobū, 1967), p. 295. Here "Yeh Shih" is apparently a misprint for "Yeh Meng-te" whose *hao* immediately follows the name. Yeh Shih himself accepted the legitimacy of the term *huang-chi.*

fucians. It is not difficult to understand the appeal of Han T'o-chou's show when he had actors in the palace mimic the pompous Confucian,[60] or to imagine an imperial sigh of relief at the departure of a P'eng Kuei-nien.

In attacking what they ultimately labelled "the rebellious faction of spurious learning," the associates of Han T'o-chou repeated the theme that they were not campaigning against a number of isolated individuals but were uncovering the machinations of a clique. Yet, there was little to substantiate this serious charge other than the fact that some of the accused were connected by bonds of friendship and common intellectual concerns or that they had recommended one another for office and, most frequently, asked for reconsideration when such a prominent man as Chao Ju-yü or Chu Hsi was removed from office. The opponents of *wei-hsüeh* particularly resented the tendency of these men to identify themselves with the Northern Sung Yüan-yu scholars; as Yao Yü (*chih-shih* 1157) put it, "and those who are deepest into the worst habits are obdurate and incorrigible, constantly cherishing grievances against their superiors and comparing themselves to the men in the Yüan-yu party list."[61] Yao went on to draw a series of highly unfavorable comparisons between the two groups, and the point was reiterated in the official edict drafted by Kao Wen-hu (1134–1212).[62]

Many of the charges were ad hominem, abusing a man's character as well as his scholarship. Some alleged seditious plots to place Chao Ju-yü himself on the throne; almost all included accusations of "deceiving the world" sometimes in the form of "spreading doubt among the masses."* Almost inevitable was the charge of "stealing fame" since these men were very sensitive about their reputations, showing a typically Confucian concern not only for the opinions of contemporaries but also for the judgment of posterity. Their only defense against attacks on their moral character were protestations of innocence. In memorial after memorial they had urged on the emperor the importance of "rectifying the mind and making the thoughts sincere" and now they were accused of the gravest character defects, but they could bear this, secure in their faith that it was their opponents who were the villains, and most lived to see themselves vindicated. But before discussing the further course of the *wei-hsüeh* affair, it is appropriate to examine the composition of the two groups.

---

* Liu San-chieh charged them with "ridiculing the sayings of the sovereign father to the barbarians and spreading doubt among the masses through 'three women and one fish' tallies (*san-nü i-yü fu*)." I have been unable to identify these tallies.

The Composition of the Two Groups

Even though the *wei-hsüeh* list included some men not known for their contributions to Sung intellectual life, among them three military men and the "six *chün-tzu*," the university students who protested in 1195, it did contain many of the most prominent thinkers of the time, and Chu Hsi headed the Academician-in-Waiting section of the list.* The fact that Chu Hsi was one of the first targets of the forces of Han T'o-chou, his place on the list itself, and his ultimate prominence in the history of Neo-Confucianism all have tended to divert attention from the presence on the list of scholars of very different intellectual persuasion.[63]

Although discussions of late twelfth-century Confucianism often emphasize the two schools of Chu Hsi and Lu Chiu-yüan, this is to neglect a more empirical orientation represented by Yeh Shih and the Yung-chia school.† As the thinkers of this period are more carefully studied, new categories will suggest themselves,‡ but it suffices here to take note of these three tendencies, since they do represent the major Confucian approaches to the dominant intellectual issues of the day. Unfortunately, while the controversies between Chu Hsi and Lu have been analyzed repeatedly, scholars have until recently paid much less attention to the representatives of the third tendency, perhaps because these men are less interesting philosophically, and given to rejecting not only Neo-Confucian metaphysical terminology (which they believed tainted with Buddhism and Taoism) but metaphysics itself.§

There is perhaps no better way to illustrate the gulf which sepa-

---

* As it appears in Table 7.2, the list has been consolidated and alphabetized. Originally, it began with "Four Councillors of State," then "Thirteen Academicians-in-Waiting," "Thirty-one Other Officials," "Three Military Officers," and "Eight Scholars." Chu Hsi was the first listed of the "Thirteen Academicians-in-Waiting."

† *SYHA* 54. This threefold division is generally recognized in surveys of Sung thought although the recent book by Iwama Kazuo, *Chugoku seiji shisō kenkyu* [A study of Chinese political thought] (Tokyo: Mirai sha, 1968) analyzes the relationship between the thought of Chu Hsi and Lu Chiu-yüan at length without referring to the presence of other tendencies.

‡ Wu Kang, "Nan Sung Hsiang-hsüeh yü Che-hsüeh" [The two schools of thought in the Southern Sung period – the Hunan school and the Chekiang school], *Hsüeh-shu chi-k'an*, 4 (1955), pp. 1 – 9 called attention to the Hunan school recently emphasized by Mou Tsung-san, whose *Hsin-t'i yü hsing-t'i* [Mind and human nature] (Taipei: Cheng-chung, 1968 – 69) is the subject of an important review article by Wei-ming Tu, "*Hsin-t'i yü hsing-t'i*: Mind and Human Nature" *Journal of Asian Studies*, 30 (1971), pp. 642 – 47. See also Okada Takehiko, "Ko Go-ho" [Hu Wu-feng], *Toyobunka*, 10, (1965), pp. 23 – 33; 11, (1965), pp. 30 – 47. However, after the death of Hu Hung in 1155 and Chang Shih's change of mind, the Hunan school seems to have drastically declined in influence.

§ The first full-length study of any member of the Yung-chia school or the tendency it represents is the dissertation by Winston Wan Lo, "The Life and Thought of Yeh Shih (1150 – 1223)," Diss. Harvard University, 1970. There is a resume in *Sung Studies Newsletter*, II (1970), but I have not yet been able to read the dissertation itself.

TABLE 7.2.
Men Listed as Belonging to the
"Rebellious Clique of Spurious Learning."
(rearranged in alphabetical order)

Chan T'i-jen	Hsiang An-shih	Po Yen-chen
Chang Chih-yüan	Hsü Fan	Shen Yu-k'ai
Chang Tao	Hsü I	Sun Feng-chi
Chang Ying	Hsüeh Shu-ssu	Sun Yüan-ch'ing
Chao Ju-t'an	Huang Fu	T'ien Tan
Chao Ju-tang	Huang Hao	Ts'ai Yüan-ting
Chao Ju-yü	Huang Tu	Ts'ai Yu-hsüeh
Chao Kung	Huang Yu	Ts'eng San-p'ing
Ch'en Fu-liang	Huang-fu Pin	Wang Hou-chih
Ch'en Hsien	Li Ch'ih	Wang K'uei
Ch'en Wu	Li Hsiang	Wang Lin
Cheng Shih	Lin Chung-lin	Wu Jou-sheng
Chiang Fu	Lin Ta-chang	Wu Lieh
Chou Nan	Liu Cheng	Yang Chien
Chou Pi-ta	Liu Kuang-tsu	Yang Fang
Chou Tuan-chao	Lou Yüeh	Yang Hung-Chung
Chu Hsi	Lü Tsu-chien	Yeh Shih
Fan Chung-fu	Lü Tsu-t'ai	Yu Chung-hung
Fan Chung-jen	Meng Hao	Yüan Hsien
Ho I	P'eng Kuei-nien	

TABLE 7.3.
Opponents of "Spurious Learning."
(rearranged in alphabetical order)

Chang Fu	Fu Po-chou	Ni Ssu
Chang Kuei-mu	Han T'o-chou	Shao Pao
Chang Po-kai	Ho Tan	Shen Chi-tsu
Chang Yen	Hsü Chi-chih	Shih K'ang-nien
Chao Shan-chien	Hu Hung	Ting Feng
Chao Shih-chao	Huang Lun	Wang Huai
Chao Yen-yü	Kao Wen-hu	Wang I-tuan
Ch'en Chia	Li Mu	Wang Yüan
Ch'en Tang	Lin Li	Yang Ta-fa
Cheng Ping	Lin Ts'ai	Yao Yü
Ch'ien Hsiang-tsu	Liu San-chieh	Yeh Chu
Ch'ien Mou	Liu Te-hsiu	Yü Che
Ching T'ang	Mi Shih-tan	

rates these Confucians than briefly to consider their attitudes toward the revered classics, for they argued not only over conflicting interpretations of the meaning of individual passages but also over which works were to be accepted into the canon and how the classics were to be used by living men. While Chu Hsi was composing the commentaries on the classics which were to insure his influence for centuries to come, Yeh Shih was challenging some old traditions. Yeh's critical eye led him to question the place of Tseng Tzu in the Confucian tradition, which led in turn to doubts about Tseng's reputed work, the *Doctrine of the Mean*. Since Yeh also had serious reservations about Mencius, he in effect rejected two of Chu Hsi's "Four Books." Lu Chiu-yüan, at the opposite pole of the Confucian spectrum, was famous for his statement, "the six classics are all footnotes to me,"[64] for he taught men to look for the truth within themselves. Reflected here are differences concerning not only the means to search for the truth but also the kind of insight to be pursued.

To Yeh Shih the debate between Chu Hsi and Lu Chiu-yüan about "the supreme ultimate" (*t'ai-chi*) was misguided and indeed ultimately meaningless, while to Lu the scholarship of his two eminent contemporaries must have appeared simply bookish; it is no accident that he himself wrote much less than the other two men. Yet it is well to keep in mind that all these men and their associates subscribed to a common set of Confucian values which each of them tried to further in his own way in a world where a divided land clearly indicated that something was drastically wrong.

All three of these intellectual tendencies were represented among those condemned for "false learning." Chu Hsi and Yeh Shih were themselves listed but not Lu Chiu-yüan who died in 1192 and thus did not live to see the proscription of *wei-hsüeh*. Similarly the anti-metaphysical and practical minded wing of Confucianism was weakened by the death of Ch'en Liang (1143–94), a most fervent advocate of the recovery of the north and most radical in his professed willingness to use the means of the strong man (*pa*) and not depend on those of the sages. It was consistent with this view that when he at last received the *chin-shih* in 1193, he was willing to accept the estrangement between the emperor and his father, thereby gaining imperial favor at the expense of offending Confucian sensibilities.* These two deaths contributed to

---

* T'ung Cheng-fu, *Ch'en Liang nien-p'u* [Chronological biography of Ch'en Liang] (Shanghai: Commercial Press, 1936), pp. 69–70. T'ung suggests that Ch'en Fu-liang may have been so offended that he failed to write a funeral ode for Ch'en Liang. For a general discussion of Ch'en Liang, see Helmut Wilhelm, "The Heresies of Ch'en Liang," *Asiatische Studien*, 40 (1950), pp. 102–112.

the prominence of Chu Hsi and his school but the intellectual tendencies represented by Lu and Ch'en did not disappear overnight.

Among the disciples of Yeh Shih condemned for *wei-hsüeh* was Chao Ju-tang (*chin-shih* 1208)* who wrote the preface to Yeh's collected writings. He and his brother Chao Ju-t'an, who was closer to Chu Hsi, traced their descent back to the second Sung emperor.† Both had supported Chao Ju-yü vigorously against Han T'o-chou—Ju-t'an had even argued that Han should be decapitated. Ju-t'an is also known as a scholar of a skeptical frame of mind and critical attitude toward the classics, especially the *chin-wen* text of the *Classic of History* and the "Great Plan" chapter. Later, after the *wei-hsüeh* crisis was over, he opposed Han T'o-chou's war policy, foreseeing the Sung defeat. When it came, in fact, Ju-t'an and his brother were apparently involved in Han's final removal from office. Chou Nan, who had studied under five masters before becoming a disciple of Yeh Shih, was listed for *wei-hsüeh* along with Chou's father-in-law Huang Tu, who was closer to Ch'en Fu-liang than to Yeh Shih but had also once received a political recommendation from Yeh. Huang shared the strong interest of the Yung-chia school in the *Chou-li*‡ and had been active in the controversies of the preceding decade.

Ch'en Fu-liang, second only to Yeh Shih as an influential Yung-chia thinker, was included on the *wei-hsüeh* list as was his cousin and disciple Ch'en Wu (d. ca. 1213) who had memorialized in defense of the "six *chün-tzu*," but Ch'en Fu-liang's most distinguished disciple was Ts'ai Yu-hsüeh who had done even better than Ch'en on his *chin-shih* examination and had joined the chorus of protest at Kuang-tsung's treatment of Hsiao-tsung. Ts'ai had earlier studied with Lu Chiu-yüan. Another Yung-chia man listed for "spurious learning" was Hsüeh Shu-ssu, a nephew of the prominent scholar Hsüeh Chi-hsüan (1134—73), who had been a teacher of Ch'en Fu-liang and a political opponent

---

* The data concerning participants in the *wei-hsüeh* controversy are based on *SYHA* and *SS*, other biographical sources as listed in *Combined Indices to Forty-seven Collections of Sung Dynasty Biographies* (Harvard-Yenching Institute Sinological Index Series No. 34) and *Sojin denki sakuhin* [Sung Biographical Index] (Tokyo: Toyo Bunko, 1968), and the pertinent sections of such chronological accounts as *HTCTC, LCTM, SSCW, Sung tsai-fu pien-nien lu, TML*. Eight of the men attacked (Chao Ju-yü, Ch'en Fu-liang, Chou Pi-ta, Chu Hsi, Hsü I, Liu Cheng, Lou Yao, and Ts'ai Yüan-ting) are included in the Sung Biographical Project, as are six of their opponents (Ching T'ang, Han T'o-chou, Ho Tan, Hu Hung, Lin Li and Ni Ssu).

† They were related to Chao Ju-yü but the exact relationship is not clear.

‡ For a discussion of the Yung-chia school's interest in the *Chou Li*, see Morohashi, *Jugaku no mokuteki to So-ju no katsudō*, pp. 547, 559, and passim.

of Wang Huai (1127 – 90), the minister who protected T'ang Chung-yu. His Yung-chia affiliation did not prevent him from admiring Chu Hsi but was manifest in his basically activist bent. Like Yeh Shih, Hsüeh accepted service under Han T'o-chou once the latter had embarked on his war policy. Another listed man associated with the general Yung-chia tendency was Shen Yu-k'ai, whose intellectual affiliations included Hu Ta-shih, Chang Shih, Ch'en Fu-liang, Lü Tsu-ch'ien, and Hsüeh Chi-hsüan. Chou Tuan-chao (1172 – 1234), one of the "six *chün-tzu*" can also be included in this group since he was from Yung-chia and was related to the early Yung-chia scholar Chou Hsing-chi (b. 1067). Another native of Wen-chou, but not of Yung-chia, was Hsü I, who played an active role in the 1194 change of throne and advised Chao Ju-yü to humor Han T'o-chou by giving him a generous reward. Later he memorialized asking that Chao be retained. Although Yeh Shih wrote his epitaph, Hsü's intellectual orientation was closer to Lu Chiu-yüan.

Of the listed men associated with Chu Hsi, none was closer to him than Ts'ai Yüan-ting (1135 – 98), one of the only two nonoffice-holders on the list if the "six *chün-tzu*" are excluded. As much a friend as a disciple of Chu Hsi, Ts'ai was an expert on mathematics, music, and the *I ching*. Chu Hsi once said of him, "men find it hard to read the *I*, but Ch'i-t'ung [i.e., Ts'ai Yüan-ting] finds it easy (*i*) to read hard books." When Ts'ai was sentenced to banishment there was a poignant scene of leave-taking as Chu Hsi intercepted him and his escorts at a temple. Since he did not have a political career, it was probably his close association with Chu Hsi that led to his inclusion on the list, but this does not explain why he was listed rather than someone like Huang Kan (1152 – 1221), Chu Hsi's son-in-law, or Wang Chieh, one of the more politically active of Chu's disciples. On the other hand, it is not difficult to understand why Chu Hsi's disciple and Chang Shih's son-in-law P'eng Kuei-nien should appear on the list. Similarly, Hsiang An-shih, a man influenced by Lu Chiu-yüan as well as by Chu Hsi, had criticized Kuang-tsung and memorialized for Chu Hsi. Another follower of Chu Hsi who had criticized Kuang-tsung and was charged with being sympathetic to Chao Ju-yü was Ts'eng San-p'ing (*chin-shih* 1165). Likewise, Chan T'i-jen had memorialized under Kuang-tsung although he is perhaps best remembered as the man responsible for the temple names of both Kao-tsung and Hsiao-tsung. Wu Jou-sheng (1154 – 1224) was less active politically although he used his position in the university to drill students in Chu Hsi's commentaries, and the followers of Han T'o-chou had no reason to like the university. The roles of Huang Hao and Yang Fang are more obscure.

A number of the men listed were disciples or friends of men with whom Chu Hsi had been on excellent terms in spite of philosophical disagreements. Most prominent of these were Chang Shih* who had been a follower of Hu Hung but had changed many of his ideas under Chu Hsi's influence, and Lü Tsu-ch'ien, who came from one of the most distinguished families of the Sung and was known for his historical scholarship, his co-editorship with Chu Hsi of the *Chin-ssu lu,* and his practical cast of mind. Among the listed men, Fan Chung-fu, a descendant of the historian Fan Tsu-yü (1041 – 98), was a follower of Chang Shih. He, in turn, influenced Wu Lieh, a man who had been outspokenly critical of Kuang-tsung and later played an important part in the campaigns of Han T'o-chou. Another son of a famous father was Li Chih (1161 – 1238), son of Li Tao (1115 – 84), and a historian in his own right. He studied under a disciple of Lü Tsu-ch'ien and a follower of Chu Hsi, and provides a link between the condemnation of *wei-hsüeh* and the elevation of Neo-Confucianism under Li-tsung (r. 1225 – 65) since he petitioned in 1242 that sacrifices be accorded to Chou Tun-i (1017 – 73), the Ch'engs, and Chang Tsai. Liu Kuang-tsu, Lin Ta-chung, Yu Chung-hung (d. 1215), and Lou Yüeh, the biographer of Fan Chung-yen, all had ties with this group and all had submitted critical memorials since the accession of Kuang-tsung.

Chao Ju-yü himself was associated with Wang Ying-ch'en (d. 1176) who was known more as a statesman opposed to Ch'in Kuei than as a scholar though he did study the writings of the Ch'eng brothers as a young man. Chao Ju-yü's anthology of Northern Sung memorials also reveals an anti-Wang An-shih orientation without indicating any marked philosophical inclinations. Wang K'uei, Ying-ch'en's son, opposed the dismissal of other scholars and was himself included on the list along with two of his father's disciples: Chang Ying, who as left policy critic had requested that Chao Ju-yü be retained, and Ch'en Hsien (1145 – 1212), grandson of another anti-Ch'in Kuei official and himself known more as an official than as a scholar.

The most outstanding disciple of Lu Chiu-yüan to be listed for "false learning" was Yang Chien, who has been called Lu's Wang Chi (1498 – 1583) and is known for his philosophy of mind and stress on quiescence and vacuity. (These did not prevent him from holding strong reformist and restorationist views or from advocating restrictions on

---

* As a son of Chang Chün (1096 – 1164), Chang Shih provides a link with the war party of the previous generation as well as with the thought of the Hunan school as represented by Hu Hung.

land ownership as a way to return gradually to the well-field system.*)
Yüan Hsieh, a friend of Yang Chien, also cultivated Lu Chiu-yüan's
idealistic philosophy of mind but at one time studied under Lü Tsu-
ch'ien and was on good terms with Ch'en Fu-liang and others of similar
views. Wang Hou-chih (1131–1204), a descendant of a younger
brother of Wang An-shih, was also a disciple of Lu, although he was
primarily an expert on bronze and stone inscriptions.

The intellectual affiliation of the remaining men is not as clear.
Huang Fu's intellectual as well as physical pedigree may go back to a
disciple of Ssu-ma Kuang (1019–86). Chou Pi-ta can ultimately be
linked with the teachings of the Ch'engs but it was more likely his
political associations, including recommendations for Chu Hsi and
Lü Tsu-ch'ien, as well as his rivalry with Wang Huai that made him
persona non grata to the Han T'o-chou group. Most of the rest were
involved in the defense of the others. This includes Sun Feng-chi
(1135–99) who as minister of rites made arrangements for the burial
of Hsiao-tsung and became involved in a dispute with Chu Hsi in which
Sun was supported by Lou Yüeh, Ch'en Fu-liang, and Chao Ju-yü.† On
other matters, however, Sun said he agreed with Chu. Other men, like
Liu Cheng, are not known for any particular scholarly interests or
affiliations but had at one time or another recommended men on the
list and otherwise incurred the enmity of Han and his supporters.

Clearly this was a diverse group intellectually. They differed, too,
in their order of political priorities, although they generally agreed
on the need for reform, including tax reform and moral reform in order
to effect the common goal: regaining the north and expelling the "barbarians" from the heartland of Chinese civilization. A good number
had family ties to men who had opposed Ch'in Kuei. Another factor
which should not be discounted is this: if their intellectual pedigree is
traced back in terms of the linkage between master and disciple, a
great many of the scholars charged with "spurious learning," including
those who belonged to the Yung-chia school, were the heirs of the
Ch'eng brothers.‡

---

* Yang Chien, Tz'u-hu i-shu [Literary remains of Yang Chien] (Ssu-ming tsung-shu,
4th collection), 16. The well-fields are discussed on 16.7b–8a. For the comparison
with Wang Chi, see the note by the Ssu-k'u ch'üan-shu editors reprinted immediately
preceding the preface, and Takehiko Okada, "Wang Chi and Existentialism," Wm.
Theodore de Bary, ed., Self and Society in Ming Thought (New York: Columbia University Press, 1970).

† For a discussion of this complicated matter see Goto Shunsui, Shushi [Chu Hsi]
(Tokyo: Nihon Hyōron sha, 1943), pp. 168–73. It is one more illustration of disagreement between the men attacked for wei-hsüeh on an issue they considered important.

‡ For a convenient chart of master-disciple relationships going back to the Ch'eng
brothers, see Uno Tetsuto, Shina tetsugaku shi–kinsei Jugaku [A history of Chinese
philosophy–modern Confucianism] (Tokyo: Hobunkan, 1944), p. 154.

Conspicuous by their absence from either side of the struggle are the three famous poets alive at that time, Yang Wan-li (1127 – 1206), Lu Yu (1125 – 1210), and Hsin Ch'i-chi (1140 – 1207), all known for their fervid advocacy of reconquest of the north. Yang Wan-li may have had friends on both sides of the controversy, as is suggested by the presence of four attackers and four accused on the list of men he recommended in 1184,[65] but he was the most hostile of the three poets in his attitude toward Han T'o-chou, refusing office while Han was in power, turning down Han's request to compose a notice for a garden Han had built and, it is said, writing a denunciation of Han's crimes as the last act of his life.[66] Lu Yu, who had once been indicted by Chao Ju-yü, was more kindly disposed both to Han's war plans and to Han personally – he agreed to write the notice refused by Yang and also once sent Han a birthday poem.[67] Hsin, the organizer of a militia known as the Flying Tigers, remained like the others on excellent terms with Chu Hsi and mourned him in writing when Chu died in 1200, while the proscription of *wei-hsüeh* was still in effect. But Hsin played an important part in persuading Han to launch his war against the Chin arguing that the latter had been so weakened by internal and external difficulties that the Sung forces could count on a revolt.[68]

Few of the opponents of *wei-hsüeh* are known as contributors to Sung intellectual life although Lin Li wrote a commentary on the *I ching* and had genuine intellectual disagreements with Chu Hsi. But Lin was not active in the 1190s. Of the men who were associated with Han T'o-chou at this time, Ni Ssu and Kao Wen-hu had historical and literary interests and some of their works are still extant, while Hsü Chi-chih (d. 1209) was known as a poet as well as a politician. Hsü is a strange case, for the political enemy of Wang Huai and severe critic of Hsiao-tsung's personnel policy bears little resemblance to the man who went on his knees to Han T'o-chou for the sake of a promotion and once entered Han's house through a drainage gate in order not to miss a birthday celebration, giving rise to the saying, "through the drain a minister, on bended knees a councilor." The *Ssu-k'u ch'üan-shu* editors found his poetry far superior to the ornate verse of the Chiang-hu school and singled out his admiring poem "On Reading Wang An-shih's Poetry" for special praise.[69]

Some of Han's associates had quite distinguished official careers before they joined his group although they did not rise to the high level of the chief councilors they attacked. Thus Chang Fu during a lengthy period of provincial service, repaired embankments and dikes, submitted requests for tax alleviation, administered relief, decreased tolls, looked after the military preparedness of his area, established communal loan granaries, supervised water works, recommended worthy men, set up post houses in the mountains, and strove to lessen the hardships brought on by the salt system. Ching T'ang (1139 – 1200), who held high offices after Han came to power, had made a name for himself through his courageous behavior while on a mission to the Chin. Some of the men belonged to old, distinguished families: Han T'o-chou himself was a descendant of Han Ch'i (1008 – 75), the eminent Northern Sung statesman; Chao Shan-chien was related to the imperial family; Fu Po-shou (*chin-shih* 1168) also belonged to a prominent family. In the last case, there was disagreement within the family, for Po-shou's younger brother was a disciple of Chu Hsi, to whom he remained loyal in the *wei-hsüeh* controversy. Po-shou himself may also have undergone the ceremony of becoming Chu's disciple, although he cooperated with Han.

Some of the men associated with Han in the controversy did comparatively little for him, and one is left with the impression that the amount of information available on a man is inversely proportional to the strength of his attack on *wei-hsüeh*. This may be a result both of historiographical bias and of a practice of assigning less prominent men to take political risks. In any case, Kao Wen-hu merely drafted an edict, Ni Ssu joined in a memorial on the examination system, Ch'ien Hsiang-tsu's participation in the affair was apparently limited to arresting the "six *chün-tzu.*" Both Ni and Ch'ien later opposed Han's war policy. Teng Yu-lung, a staunch war advocate, did complain in 1200 about "false learning,"[70] but neither he nor other war advocates nor, for that matter, such personal henchmen of Han's as Su Shih-tan (d. 1207) or Chou Ta played a significant role in the attack on *wei-hsüeh.*

Personal ambition and private resentment are frequently given as the reasons for a man's participation in the attacks on Chao Ju-yü, Chu Hsi, and others. Perhaps one had, like Ho Tan, been passed over for promotion or, like Liu Te-hsiu, been denied a coveted post. One may have been stung by a slighting remark or felt offended at not being entertained properly; these are the reasons given, respectively, for Ching T'ang's hostility toward Chao Ju-yü and Hu Hung's antagonism toward Chu Hsi. As Chiba Hiroshi has pointed out, Han himself was motivated largely by a personal grudge.[71] Such feelings, combined with a desire to silence a chorus of past critics and discourage future criticism, found an outlet in the denunciations of alleged proponents of "false learning."

The Ban on Wei-hsüeh *Runs Its Course, 1197 – 1202*

Attacks on *wei-hsüeh* in general or on specific individuals did not cease with the publication of the list although by then most of the accused had been removed from office and some had even been banished. Memorials by Yao Yü in 5th/1198 and Ting Feng in 7th/1198 did not add anything new but kept the issue alive. In 1st/1199 P'eng Kuei-nien and three others were deprived of their offices on the urging of Chang Fu and fellow *wei-hsüeh* hunters. The following month, 2nd/1199, the same Chang Fu submitted his indictment of Liu Kuang-tsu.[72] Yet the success of the continuing campaign was mixed. There were cases of men disowning their former masters and pretending not to have had any connection with them, but there do not appear to have been any mass desertions. The more normal response was for a man to accept his fate and await better times. Chu Hsi himself refrained from submitting a critical memorial after he had consulted the *I ching* at the request of Ts'ai Yüan-ting. Instead, he turned to his studies and his teaching, and left his fortune to fate.

The tide of critical, moralizing memorials was stemmed, but if the denouncers of "spurious learning" really intended to eliminate the teachings of their opponents from the examinations, they were remarkably unsuccessful. Among those who succeeded in the examination of 1199, the only one held during the ban, were Chen Te-hsiu, (1178–1235), often considered the leading exponent of Chu Hsi's philosophy during the first quarter of the thirteenth century, and Wei Liao-weng (1178–1237) who held a middle position between the thought of Chu Hsi and that of Lu Chiu-yüan. Even the man who placed first in the departmental examination, Su Ta-chang, had *tao-hsüeh* leanings.

In the following year, 1200, there were signs of a slackening of the anti-*wei-hsüeh* campaign, but the death of Chu Hsi brought the issue once again to the fore. The Right Policy Monitor Shih K'ang-nien (*chin-shih* 1169), in a denunciation of the dead Chu Hsi, charged that he and his disciples had met at night like "demon worshippers" and engaged in Taoist-like chanting and Buddhist sitting. Shih predicted that Chu's followers would gather at the forthcoming funeral to discuss government officials and tell lies about the administration. As a result, attendance at the interment became an act of political courage. In 9th/1200 Lü Tsu-t'ai submitted a bitter and very courageous protest and was promptly banished.[73]

The ban was finally lifted in 2nd/1202; lest anyone draw any false conclusions, it was almost immediately followed by a proscription of private histories. The dead, like Chu Hsi, were honored, the retired restored to their titles, and those still active reinstated in government service. Five of the latter, Yeh Shih, Hsü I, Hsüeh Shu-ssu, Wu Lieh, and the military man Huang-fu Pin, accepted positions of authority under Han T'o-chou and came to be more closely identified with his attempt to reconquer the north than any of the opponents of *wei-hsüeh.*

The major immediate result of Han's rise to power was the ill-fated war against the Chin, but foreign policy was not at issue in the *wei-hsüeh* episode. Han's decision for war may, in part, have been prompted by a need to win literati support after the death of Empress Han in 11th/1200 weakened his influence in the palace. If so, it succeeded in gaining him the cooperation of men who surmounted their dislike and distrust of the man when given an opportunity to demonstrate that theirs was not "false learning."

Conclusion

It is tempting to speculate that the *wei-hsüeh* episode like some of its predecessors reflected social, economic, or regional divisions in Sung society, but solid evidence for such an interpretation has not been forthcoming to date.* Nor was the episode a replay of the polit-

---

* For a recent suggestive but not entirely successful attempt to explain Southern Sung political and intellectual history in geographical and class terms, see Yamauchi Masahiro, "Nan-So seiken no suii" [Southern Sung shifts in political power], *Sekai rekishi* [World History] (Tokyo: Iwanami shoten, 1970), IX, pp. 233–266. A geographical breakdown of the list of men charged with *wei-hsüeh* and of their opponents provides the following results:

Circuit	Number of Men Charged with *wei-hsüeh*	Number of Opponents of *wei-hsüeh*
Liang-che E.	16	11
Liang-che W.	8	6
Fu-chien	12	5
Chiang-nan W.	7	3
Chiang-nan E.	3	
Huai-nan E.		2
Huai-nan W.	1	
Ch'eng-tu-fu	3	
Tzu-chou	2	
Ching-hu E.	1	1
Ching-hu S.	1	1
Unknown	5	6
TOTAL	59	35

A further breakdown by prefecture for the circuit with the largest representation yields the following results:

Prefecture	Number of Men Charged with *wei-hsüeh*	Number of Opponents of *wei-hsüeh*
Ch'u		4
Ming	3	1
T'ai		1
Wen	8	1
Wu	3	4
Yüeh	2	
TOTAL	16	11

The prominence of Wen-chou reflects the involvement of men from Yung-chia, which belongs to this prefecture. It is possible that when the intellectual geography of the Southern Sung is further studied, these data may be made to yield some results of significance, but at the present stage of our knowledge it does not offer a basis for drawing any worthwhile conclusions about a geographic component in the *wei-hsüeh* controversy.

ical disputes of the early Southern Sung between war advocates and appeasers, for no one on either side now defended the latter; Han T'o-chou eventually went to war, but his political opponents had impeccable revanchist credentials.

The intellectual element in the controversy was also very limited. It was an age of vigorous intellectual disagreement over the Confucian heritage, but the arguments took place among the men accused of "spurious learning," not between them and the political opposition. Yet in a divided world, those who did not participate in the intellectual debates could easily come to regard them as at the very least a waste of precious energy – Chou Mi (1232 – 99) quotes one man as equating them with the "pure talk" (*ch'ing-t'an*) prevalent under the Western Chin (265 – 313).* Complaints by such as Yeh Shih about impractical, abstract speculation must have fallen on ready ears even if Yeh Shih himself was ultimately charged with "false learning." And disagreements over the classical heritage could easily be construed as divisive, raising all the dangers of factionalism.

Since the sources are quite prolific, further research can clarify the personalities and conduct of some of the men charged with *wei-hsüeh,* but it is unlikely that much more will be discovered about their opponents, whose lives, for obvious reasons, are much less well documented. It is noteworthy, however, that when the attackers devised the rubric *wei-hsüeh* they were able to draw on the content and rhetoric of previous attacks against other Sung philosophers. Furthermore, they expected this campaign to strengthen their own political position, perhaps by exploiting the resentment of other educated men who were not privy to Neo-Confucian speculations and who were therefore prone to be offended by the philosophical claims and the political behavior of a man like Chu Hsi. The absence of a strong intellectual commitment among the followers of Han T'o-chou helps to account for the mildness of the suppression of the real content of "spurious learning" and the willingness of Han and his men to recall and employ some of their former opponents to assist in the fight against the real enemy in the north.

Some of the charges of fakery rang true enough to become part of the image of the pretentious scholar who makes a false show of learning and virtue, such as the stereotype depicted by Chou Mi, himself a critic of men who claimed to be followers of *tao-hsüeh*.[74] Yet the main effect was in the opposite direction: the men denounced

---

* Chou Mi, *Kuei-hsin tsa-shih* [Miscellany from Kuei-hsin Lane] (Chin-tai pi-shu, collection 19), *hsü-chi, hsia,* 4b – 6a. This is mistakenly attributed to Chou Pi-ta in T'ao Hsi-sheng, *Chung-kuo cheng-shih ssu-hsiang shih* [A history of Chinese political thought] (Taiwan: Ch'üan-min ch'u-pan she, 1954), IV, pp. 112 – 113.

for "false learning" emerged with a new prestige as the defeat of Han T'o-chou and his ignominious death seemed to show that history itself was on their side. All the men were rehabilitated, and Chu Hsi came to be venerated.*

This episode also ultimately helped the cause of those attacked by revealing the intellectual bankruptcy of the opposition, and it may also have enhanced the awareness of common values and beliefs among theoreticians who disagreed on so much else. Even before the *wei-hsüeh* episode, the thinkers of the twelfth century had been able to combine intellectual controversy with friendship, denounce a man's ideas in the most vigorous language and defend him politically, tell him that his thinking was muddled but invite him for a lecture. Since the next generation did not include a Chu Hsi, a Lu Chiu-yüan, or a Yeh Shih, scholars have largely neglected it, but a common link to the *wei-hsüeh* suppression could only enhance the sense of cohesion among scholars during the remainder of the dynasty.

Perhaps it is not surprising that what had been attacked as false and spurious came to be valued as true and genuine, but it is noteworthy that the emerging orthodoxy was to be considerably narrower than the intellectual spectrum represented by the men condemned for *wei-hsüeh*. Of the listed men, Chu Hsi alone was held worthy by the Yüan editors of the official Sung history of having his biography included in the four chapters reserved for *tao-hsüeh*, now a term of highest approbation. The breadth of the condemnation of *wei-hsüeh* may have served to preserve, by associating them with Chu Hsi, the writings of some of the men whose ideas were later considered unorthodox and kept open some alternative philosophical directions, but it may also have stimulated a longing for a definitive orthodoxy and clearer guidelines of what was intellectually acceptable, along with a general quest for a closer integration of ideas and politics.

---

* The future belonged to Chu Hsi, but the negative image created by his opponents did not die out completely. It reappeared among the French Jesuits who saw in Chu Hsi the materialistic and atheistic villain of Chinese philosophy. See Olaf Graf, *Tao und Jen: Sein und Sollen im sungchinesischen Monismus* (Wiesbaden: Harrassowitz, 1970), p. 36.

Notes to Chapter 7

1. Chen Te-hsiu, *Hsi-shan hsien-sheng Chen Wen-chung kung wen-chi* [Collected writings of Chen Te-hsiu] (Ssu-pu ts'ung-k'an ed.) 47.1b.
2. For Ts'ai Ching see Rolf Trauzettel, *Ts-ai Ching (1046–1126) als Typus des illegitimen Ministers* (Bamberg: K. Urlaub, 1964).
3. *HNYL*, p. 832; *TML*, p. 21.
4. *HNYL*, pp. 1759–60. Reference is to *The Doctrine of the Mean*, II.
5. *SYHA* 34.
6. *TML*, pp. 34–39.
7. *HNYL*, p. 2548; Terada Ko, *Sodai kyoiku shi gaisetzu* [A general history of Sung education] (Tokyo: Hakubunsha, 1965), p. 229.
8. Terada, pp. 230–31.
9. *HNYL*, p. 2431.
10. *HTCTC* 146 (for 1178).
11. *HTCTC* 147 (for 1180).
12. See *Ch'ing-yüan tang-chin; Combined Indices; TML*, pp. 43–44; *SSCW* 27.12a; *HTCTC* 148 (for 1183); *SS* 35.1a.
13. *Mencius* VII, 2.37.
14. *K'ung-tzu chia-yü* [The school sayings of Confucius] (Ssu-pu pei-yao ed.) 1.2b; Robert Paul Kramers, *K'ung-tzu chia-yü – The School Sayings of Confucius*, Sinica Leidensia 7 (Leiden: Brill, 1950), p. 205.
15. *TML*, p. 44.
16. *SS* 388.7a.
17. See James T. C. Liu, "The Road to Neo-Confucian Orthodoxy: An Interpretation," *Philosophy East and West*, 23:4 (1973) pp. 483–505.
18. Chang Tsai, *Chang Tzu ch'üan-shu* [Complete works of Chang Tsai] (SPPY) 13. 1a. Cf. also 15. 2a where *tao-hsüeh* is used by Lü Ta-lin (1044–93) in his chronological account of Chang Tsai's life.
19. *SYHA* 6.
20. For example, see Hu Yin, *Fei-jan chi* 25.65a, or Chang Shih's preface to Hu Hung, *Chih yen* [Understanding Words] (Yüeh-ya-tang ts'ung-shu ed.) 2a.
21. Lu Chiu-yüan, *Hsiang-shan hsien-sheng ch'üan-chi* [Collected writings of Lu Chiu-yüan] (SPTK) 35.7b–8a. Takase, *Riku Sho-san*, pp. 139–40.
22. Chu Hsi, *Hui-an hsien-sheng Chu Wen-kung wen-chi* [Collected writings of Chu Hsi] (Ssu-pu ts'ung-k'an ed.), 11.29b.
23. *HTCTC* 151 (for 1189).
24. *HTCTC* 151 (for 1189).
25. *HTCTC* 151 (for 1189).
26. *SS* 400.13a.
27. Chou Nan, *Shan fang chi* [Collected Writings of Chou Nan] (*Han-fen lou pi chi*, Collection 8 – from *Yung-lo ta-tien*) 7.1a–19b.
28. *TML*, pp. 52–54. For *huang-chi*, see note on p. 182.
29. *HTCTC* 152 (for 1190).
30. *HTCTC* 152 (for 1191); *SS* 394.2b–4a; *CTYY*, p. 184.
31. *HTCTC* 152 (for 1191).
32. *HTCTC* 152 (for 1191).
33. P'eng Kuei-nien, *Chih-t'ang chi* [Collected Writings of Peng Kuei-nien] (Wu-ying tien edition, Kuang-ya Bookshop), 1.6b–19a.
34. P'eng, *Chih-t'ang chi* 2.5b–9a. The quotation is from 7b–8a.
35. Kuang-tsung's conduct and the events leading to his abdication are discussed in Harold L. Kahn, *Monarchy in the Emperor's Eyes* (Cambridge, Massachusetts: Harvard University Press, 1971), pp. 222–25.
36. *HTCTC* 152 (for 1192).
37. *HTCTC* 153 (for 1193) and passim. Also P'eng, *Chih-t'ang chi* 3.18b–22a, 4.1a–5a; Chan T'i-jen, *Chan Yüan-shan hsien-sheng i-chi* [Collected writings of Chan T'i-jen] (*P'u-ch'eng i-shu* 6: P'u-ch'eng Chu shih liu-hsiang shu-wu, 1811–14), 6.4a–6a; Lou Yao, *Kung-k'uei chi* [Collected Writings of Lou Yao] (Ssu-pu ts'ung-k'an ed.) 23.
38. Chan, *Chan Yüan-shan* 6.4a.
39. P'eng, *Chih-t'ang chi* 3.19b.

40. The "Announcement about Drunkenness" is a chapter of the *Classic of History*. The quotation is from Lo Ta-ching, *Ho-lin yü-lu* [Jade dew from Crane Forest] as cited in Wang Chien-ch'iu, *Sung-tai t'ai-hsüeh yü t'ai-hsüeh sheng* [The Sung University and its students] (Taipei: Commercial Press, 1965), p. 367.
41. *SS* 36.17a-b; *HTCTC* 153 (for 1194).
42. *HTCTC* 153.
43. Hsü Tzu-ming, *Sung tsai-fu pien nien lu* [Annals of Sung prime ministers] (Taipei: Wen-hai ch'u-pan she), 19.11a–12a; *Ch'ing-yüan tang-chin; Liang-chao kang-mu pei-yao* [Essentials of an outline of two reigns] 2.19a-b, 2.20b; *HTCTC* 153 (for 1193); 154 (for 1196); 154 (for 1196); 154 (for 1197).
44. Moroto Tatsuo, "Sodai no tai sōshitsu saku ni tsuite" [On the policies for the imperial families in the Sung dynasty], *Bunka*, 22 (1958), pp. 623–40.
45. *HTCTC* 153 (for 1194).
46. *HTCTC* 153–54.
47. *HTCTC* 154 (for 1195); *TML*, pp. 62–65.
48. *HTCTC* 154 (for 1196).
49. *SHY* 109; *hsüan-chü* 5.17b.
50. Chih-p'an, *Fo-tsu t'ung chi* [A general record of the Buddha] (Taisho Tripitaka), 48 (pp. 429–30).
51. *TML*, pp. 76–77; *SSCW* 29.12a; *HTCTC* 154 (for 1197); *LCTM* 5.6a.
52. *SYHA* 54.
53. *Shu ching* V, 14.4. James Legge, *The Chinese Classics* (Hong Kong: Hong Kong University Press, 1960) III, p. 324.
54. *TML*, p. 84.
55. Tomoeda Ryūtaro, *Shu-shi no shisō keisei* [Study of the formation of Chu-tzu's thought] (Tokyo: Shunjū sha, 1969), pp. 494–95.
56. *CSPM*, p. 652.
57. Chou, *Shan fang chi* 7.1a–19b.
58. *TML*, pp. 76–77; *SSCW* 29.12a.
59. *LCTM* 5.25a-b; *HTCTC* 155 (for 1199); *SSCW* 29.15a-b.
60. *CSPM*, p. 682.
61. *TML*, pp. 77–78; *HTCTC* 155 (for 1198).
62. *LCTM* 5.15b–16b; *HTCTC* 155 (for 1198).
63. See Schirokauer, "Chu Hsi's Political Career: A Study in Ambivalence," in Arthur Wright and Denis Twitchett, eds., *Confucian Personalities* (Palo Alto, Calif.: Stanford University Press, 1962), p. 184.
64. Lu Chiu-yüan, *Hsiang-shan hsien-sheng wen-chi* [Collected writings of Lu Chiu-yüan] (Ssu-pu ts'ung-k'an ed.), 34.1a.
65. Yang Wan-li *Ch'un-hsi chien-shih lu* [Record of men recommended during the *Ch'un-hsi* period (1174–90)] (Ts'ung-shu chi-ch'eng ed.).
66. Chou Ju-ch'ang, *Yang Wan-li hsüan-chi* [Selections from Wang Yang-li] (Peking: Chung-hua shu-chü, 1962), p. 36ff.
67. Chu Tung-jun, *Lu Yu yen-chiu* [A study of Lu Yu] (Peking: Chung-hua shu-chü, 1961), pp. 41–55.
68. See Corinna Hana, *Bericht über die Verteidigung der Stadt Te-an*, Münchener Ostasiatische Studien I (Wiesbaden: Franz Steiner Verlag, 1970), p. 27 and passim.
69. Hsü Chi-chih, *She-chai chi* [Collected writings of Hsü Chi-chih] (Ching-hsiang-lou ts'ung-shu). The poem is found in 15.12a.
70. *HTCTC* 155 (for 1200).
71. Chiba Hiroshi, "Kan Taku-chū–Sodai kanshin den" [Han T'o-chou–the biography of a depraved Sung minister], *Yamazaki sensei taikan kinen tōyō shigaku ronshū* (Tokyo: Kinen Kankōkai, 1967), pp. 279–288.
72. *HTCTC* 155 (for 1198); 155 (for 1199).
73. *HTCTC* 155 (for 1198).
74. *CTYY*, pp. 138–39. See also John W. Haeger, "The Intellectual Context of Neo-Confucian Syncretism," *The Journal of Asian Studies*, 31 (1972), p. 509.

Sung Patriotism
as a First Step toward
Chinese Nationalism

ROLF TRAUZETTEL

FROM THE ANTHROPOLOGICAL PERSPECTIVE, Classical Confucianism may be described as an ethic of the extended family: the clan is the designated locus of loyalty and the agent of its celebration from generation to generation.[1] Because kinship organization in China was patriarchally structured, the emphasis of loyalty relations was usually upon the allegiance of clan members to the oldest living male, an obligation which is euphemistically described by the term filial piety (*hsiao*), but which actually involves a considerable element of mutuality and reciprocity. The gradual sophistication of social and political relationships in the earliest periods of Chinese history necessarily involved some ethical reorientation, initially by the simple extension of kinship ethics to a larger, proto-national frame of reference. This development was not peculiarly Chinese, however, and the words of the sixteenth-century Duke of Tavannes that "to govern a kingdom or a home is only a difference in dimension" could have been spoken without incongruity by a Chinese emperor.

The proto-national institutions of the Han and T'ang, however, especially economic and military organizations, very quickly developed their own characteristic dynamic. Both in China and in Europe the inescapable responsibility of the proto-national institutions to restrain the independence of great families and clans precipitated a profusion of small conflicts between them, and a widening gap between familial and political ethos. This gap was a constituent element of classical Greek tragedy which gave rise to a distinctive kind of tragic hero: in the tragedies the conflict of values was often the hero's dilemma, in the course of political history it tended to be resolved in favor of a national ethos bound to rationality and to the state, with only cosmetic attention to the damage which this triumph inflicted upon the "natural" familial ethos.[2] In China, in contrast, the same conflict was resolved in favor of extended familial ethics with only minor concessions to the special problems of the proto-national institutions. The following story from the *Han-shu* may serve to illustrate this development. After his accession to the throne in 179 B.C., Han Wen-ti summoned a certain T'ien Shu to inquire who was the most admirable man in the empire. T'ien Shu replied that the most excellent was Meng Shu, the former governor of Yün-chung. The emperor thereupon explained to T'ien Shu that Meng Shu had been removed from office because of his failure to resist the invading barbarians, as a result of which hundreds of his soldiers had died. But T'ien Shu countered that Meng Shu's soldiers had fought for him of their own free will, "like sons for their father," and that Meng Shu had wanted to spare them when they were finally exhausted as a proper father would always have wanted to spare his own sons. Wen-ti was persuaded, and reappointed Meng Shu to his former office.[3]

The progressive depersonalization of Chinese government during the centuries of Han rule and thereafter reveals more and more serious contradictions in the adaptation of a familial ethos for proto-national ends. The so-called feudalism discussions that went on for centuries are a primary expression of the essential problem, and Liu Tsung-yüan's (773 – 819) "Essay on Feudalism" provides us with a characteristic example. Liu outlines how the development of civilization gradually bred hostility among the people and how the institutions of "Lords and Elders and of penal and government systems" emerged from the struggles among them. The focal point of this and most similar discussions is the gradual destruction of the feudal states of the Chou, considered as "natural" familial units in their own time, and the simultaneous consolidation of the Chinese *oikumene*. Satisfaction and discontent are intermingled in Liu's evaluation of the merits of centralization policy and the new administration of the Ch'in. On the one hand, he recognizes the necessity for this development, but on the other he attributes the failures of their policy and especially their collapse exclusively to the immorality of their emperors: "The reason for [Ch'in] failure is that the people were filled with hatred and not that the system of prefectures and districts proved to be faulty." Or: "The government was at fault, not the system." In these and other arguments it becomes clear that Liu does not recognize the full connection between administrative "systems" and the ethical principles which legitimate them. He blandly praises the government of the Han because it adapted the modern structures of the Ch'in to "humane" rulership.

He apparently believed that the cultivated humanity of the emperors could maintain the preeminence of the kind of morality personified by Meng Shu irrespective of the administrative environment: "Let us suppose," he wrote, "that the Han had dissolved the prefectural and district administrations and had bestowed this territory on the feudal lords, it would then have been a matter of mere regret had these lords incited unrest among the people. The precautions . . . of Meng Shu could not have been employed."[4]

In view of the insistence with which this ethic was portrayed until T'ang times, and particularly considering the strength of the metaphor by which the sovereign was assigned to the position of a father, it is imperative to discover the full context in which the social order was legitimated and managed. The universality of the Chinese *oikumene* is central. The familial ethic was humanitary from the outset, but familial interpretation of humanity (*jen*) was limited to the conduct of individuals in specific small groups. With the analogy between the position of the sovereign and the position of the father, kinship relations were indefinitely expanded and defamilized. The ideal of comprehensive humanity was predestined to become the pacifistic ideology of a territorially expansive civilization, which excluded no one from itself and painted itself in universal terms. Through the endless wars and cultural assimilation by which the *oikumene* expanded, generosity and moderation were maintained as the cardinal virtues. As long as they were apolitical and as long as the organization of society required that loyalty and defense be bound exclusively to the state, these principles redounded to the advantage of the ruling class.

The Sung was a period of great Chinese influence on surrounding peoples and great internal administrative vitality, but it was also a period of incessant warfare during which the problems of loyalty and allegiance were pitted against an unshakable Chinese belief in the universality of their civilization. Internally there were substantial tensions between the bureaucracy, with its extensive power and authority, and the lower classes who tilled the land. Traditional problems stemming from the increasing concentration of landed property in the hands of a few sprang up anew; it also became evident for the first time that the commercial sector of society was being constricted by the insistence of the government on its control and regulation. In foreign policy the difficulties were even more obvious. The so-called barbarians, at first equal and then superior to the Chinese militarily, occupied extensive areas of north Chinese territory. At the same time, these non-Chinese peoples rapidly learned how to establish functional government and how to employ administrative and ethical principles over which the Chinese claimed a cultural monopoly. This barbarian astuteness and its political consequences could not help but shake the self-assurance of the scholar-officials of the Sung; moreover it deepened the division within official ranks over the advisability and feasibility of war. Because it would theoretically have been possible to retain the property and privileges to which they were accustomed under foreign rule, the loss of "national" Sung leadership was not feared as if it meant the simultaneous collapse of the whole social order. The universal conception of culture could consequently be seen to authorize the position of the pacifists within the government.

From one point of view, the essential transformation in the world-view of Sung officials was the slow elaboration of the concept of loyalty (*chung*) and the simultaneous de-emphasis of filial piety. The peasant rebellions and militia forces which were locally organized or spontaneously generated to resist the repeated waves of Chin aggression in North China were the most immediate context for serious conflicts of loyalty during the middle third of the Sung dynasty, and the theoretical elaboration of the concept of loyalty in this context was the immediate ideological environment for the development of Sung patriotism. Rebellions have a place in the development of Chinese patriotism which they do not command in the Occident. It is generally conceded that Western patriotism and later Western nationalism are inseparable from the efforts of the so-called third estate to secure recognition as an autonomous political force and to escape from the domination of the aristocracy and the clergy. There is no analogous occurrence in China; indeed the various classes — a term to be applied with caution in respect to China — had very scant ideological independence. The overarching antithesis in Chinese society was the differentiation between officialdom (*kuan*) and the people (*min*), although some of the clarity and consistency with which this differentiation is described may be more attributable to the preconceptions of Chinese historiography than to the whole reality of the social situation. In any case it is probably fair to say that officialdom as a social stratum tended to focus within itself all ideals of the ideological superstructure and then to project these once more into various levels of the social substructure. For example, at the beginning of the year 1126, a certain Wang Ping (d. 1126) was commander of T'ai-yüan in Shan-hsi. When the Chin laid siege to the city Wang was, according to the records, "determined to remain loyal and righteous." When he learned that the Pacification Commissioner Chang Hsiao-ch'un and the circuit intendant of T'ai-yüan wanted to surrender the city to Chin, he assembled 500 men armed with swords, led them in formation before Chang Hsiao-ch'un and interrogated them as follows: 'You and your like, do you not aspire to office?" They all replied, "Yes, it is so." Wang Ping then said, "Only when our dynasty is consolidated and successful are offices attainable." He inquired further, "You and your like, do you wish to be rewarded?" When the 500 men replied affirmatively once more, Wang Ping declared, "Only when our dynasty resists the enemy can rewards be procured."*

The officials who served the Sung had an obvious vested interest in the perpetuation of the system. The replies which Wang Ping apparently elicited from his assembled *min* are evidence for the dissemination of official values into nonofficial segments of society, presumably because throughout most of the later empire the promise of peasant success in open civil service examinations was not wholly illusory.

This downward diffusion of official values can be repeatedly documented. The specific and special interests of other social groups are more rarely articulated, however. The following petition from Tsung Tse (1059 – 1128) to Kao-tsung dated in the summer of 1127 is exceptional in this regard.[5] Tsung wanted Kao-tsung to defend K'ai-feng against the Chin, but he argued more broadly than most of his contemporaries would probably have been able to do. For the military, he said, K'ai-feng was the most important base; for the merchants it was the trading center of the empire; and for the farmers it was the most excellent land in the country. Although this articulation seems unusual, it must be taken into account that the sources are partial, because Chinese historians did not regard certain aspects of reality as deserving of transmission.

It is obvious that the pervasion of the concept of loyalty with patriotic significance did not occur in one continuous, slowly swelling stream. The traditional concept of loyalty inherited from the Chou and Han endured throughout the Sung, and from the time of the fall of the northern dynasty until the beginning of the decline of Southern Sung, we find little more than traces of the new loyalty-inspired patriotism which represents the earliest form of Chinese nationalism. In 1125 – 26, when the existence of the Northern Sung was endangered by the pressing threat of the Chin, it was inevitable that loyalty would undergo an especially severe test. This test took on the dimensions of a crisis when it became apparent during the winter season of that year that the actual instrument of national defense, the professional

---

* Wang Ming-ch'ing, *Hui-chu san-lu* [Various conversations on the Sung, third collection] (Pai-pu ts'ung-shu ed.), 2.12b. For Wang Ping's biography see *SS* 452. For Chang Hsiao-ch'un's biography see Ch'ien Shih-sheng, ed., *Nan-Sung shu* [The book of Southern Sung] (Nan-sha: 1797) 13.

army, would not be sufficient to repel the Chin. The response to this
deficiency of professional standing forces was the spontaneous local
organization of civil armies recruited on short notice by regional leaders. The court found itself in a dilemma: it needed these militia forces
to preserve the dynasty, but it could not be certain that loyal patriotic
feeling prevailed among them. Tradition had made loyalty a virtue
only for officialdom; control of the moral conduct of the people had
been left to legalist practice. The experience of the T'ang period had
done little to inspire confidence in the loyalty of any military organization, so the court was understandably suspicious of the newly formed
militia. In the summer of 1127, Tsung Tse opposed negotiations for
peace with the Chin and therefore ignored government instructions
to treat their emissaries with consideration. In 1128 an imperial dec-
laration accused Tsung Tse and his followers of having publicly committed the offense of "forming illegal bands" under the pretext of
supporting the emperor.[6]

During these and the following years, the first *chung-i chün* (loyal
and righteous-minded troops) appeared on the political scene. These
organizations emerged intermittently until the end of Southern Sung,
designated by a great number of appellations which appear in the ency-
clopedias under the general heading of *min-ping* (people's army, or
militia). Their origins, organization, and type of leadership were diverse, and the sources provide us with scant and inaccurate information, especially with respect to ideology and presumptive loyalty.
During the initial phase of the Chin wars and especially in the occupied
areas of the circuits of Ho-tung and Ho-hsi, these militia troops often
formed quite spontaneously. There are numerous accounts in the *San-
ch'ao pei-meng hui-pien,* of which the following may serve as a typical
example. Chang Jung, a fisherman from the Liang-shan moor in Shantung province, assembled between 200 and 300 men equipped with
boats, and "attacked the Chin constantly." The Sung administration
bestowed office on Chang, and he later retreated to the south, still
battling unceasingly against the Chin.[7] The gift of office to Chang
Jung is typical of official response to the growth of *min-ping.* A number of local officials attempted to gain control over these movements
either by their own initiative or with the approval of the court. In 1158
a commander from Fu-chou called Shen T'iao wrote the following
memorandum to the throne:

The societies for loyalty and righteousness (*chung-i she*) have existed for
many years in all districts of this prefecture. Membership in these societies
is sometimes great and sometimes small. Those who are regarded as the most
courageous in their assemblage and who support the masses become leaders

of the rest. . . . They manufacture weapons and other implements. Robberies have ceased because of this and the people have given [the societies] their trust. When the authorities have tried to direct these discontented people, they have suffered failure. May it therefore be ordered that [local] commanders watch over the people and that they distribute the necessary orders.[8]

This suggestion was accepted. Despite the defeat of 1126 – 27, the fear of internal unrest apparently outweighed by far the fear of external enemies as far as the court was concerned.

The court and the officials ignored their fundamental distrust of *min-ping* forces only when emergencies made it imperative. In some such situations local officials took initiatives at their own risk. In 1178 in Ssu-ch'uan, for example, local officials set about organizing existing "people's armies" for their own purposes, but because these armies numbered only a little over two thousand men, the central government was requested to initiate further conscription and to prescribe guidelines for the payment of rewards.[9] Information in the sources concerning similar actions drastically increases during the second, third, and fourth decades of the thirteenth century. Between 1210 and 1224 more than 20,000 men were enlisted from the prefecture of Tsao-yang alone. Recruiting efforts by one Chang Shun, the military governor of Ching-chou and O-chou in modern Hupei, were completely autonomous—the sources tell us that he employed his own private means.[10] Sometimes the *pao-wu* system seems to have served as a model for such undertakings. The prefect of Yang-chou in modern Kiangsu province had the enlisted troops perform field work during each spring and summer, and confined his training to the winter months.

Although there is very little information in the sources concerning the social composition of the *min-ping* troops, some inferences can occasionally be made from the accounts of the dismissal of individual enlisted men or the dissolution of privately organized units. As soon as the final phase of the Sung-Chin war was concluded and the new reign period Chia-ting was declared in 1208, a certain Ch'iu Ch'ung, fiscal intendant of Huai-nan, promptly expressed his deep concern over the possibility of widespread rebellion. In this case it was clear that financial considerations of substantial magnitude were mingled with the fear of rebellions. Ho Tan, an official of Ch'iu Ch'ung's board, wrote a memorandum to the court describing the demobilization: 20,586 men were involved; all were ordered to return to their professions; and specific costs of demobilization were paid for each soldier involved.[11] It is clear from other accounts that vagabonds and criminals ("the branded") were sometimes included in *min-ping* armies, and this was probably no accident since they could be employed as spies and informants for the court. A memorandum of 1268 notes, "it was impossible not to unite the [regular] troops and the peasants [soldiers]."[12] On the positive side the sources contain numerous accounts of bravery in the *min-ping*, and numerous statements by officials confirming the superiority of these forces over the regular troops, a judgment which is eventually attested by the installation of *min-ping* forces in the vanguard of the regular army.

While it is hard to generalize from such scant testimony, it is probably fair to say that among the majority of Sung Chinese hatred for the Chin overshadowed all internal social tensions, at least during the periods of extreme crisis occasioned by the Chin invasion of Honan in 1126−27 and again during the war of 1206−8. Ethnic contradictions outweighed class contradictions.[13] Although the Chinese traditionally tended to define their civilization in terms of cultural commitments, some elements of a genuine ethnic revulsion against these foreigners seem to be implied by the manner in which Chin policies for the governance of North China after the fall of K'ai-feng are described:

At that time [1129] the Chin decided to shave the heads of the southern people [*nan-min*]. The people were overcome with anger and sadness and day after day they considered fleeing southwards. Even in the district of Yen, the sons of Han suffered bitter oppression. In their minds they nurtured thoughts of resistance. Some rebelled and withdrew to the uninhabited mountains, while others went southwards and resigned themselves to the inevitable.*

In spite of the Confucian historian's predilection for considering loyalty an issue of concern only to high officials, the downward social diffusion of Confucian values is also well attested. Studies of popular literature and of novels like the *Shui-hu chuan*, for example, demonstrate to what extent the lower classes adopted the moral standards of the upper class. In many accounts, the alleged harmony between loyalty-consciousness among the people and required loyalty among the officials seems highly idealized. In the *San-ch'ao pei-meng hui-pien*, for example, we are told the story of a certain Ma K'uo, who battled the Chin from mountain fortresses in Hopei throughout 1127 until he was finally compelled to flee to the western mountains.

---

* *PMHP* 123.9b−10a. In 1129 the Chin issued the notorious edict in which they forbade the Chinese people to wear Chinese-style clothing and, in the case of contravention, threatened the Chinese with capital punishment. See Hsiung K'o, *Chung-hsing hsiao-chi* [Notes on the period of restoration] (Shanghai: 1937), Vol. I, 7.80. See also O. Franke, *Geschichte des chinesischen Reiches* (Berlin: 1948), IV, p. 225.

At this time the righteous troops [*i-ping*] from the circuits of Ho-tung and Ho-hsi secured themselves in fortified huts and assembled in camps for self-defense. They all wanted to have Ma K'uo as their leader. Ma K'uo said to them: "Soldiers from the mountain fortresses, you are all loyal and righteous heroes. If you now wish that I be elected, [it is necessary to remember] that this is impossible unless you establish correctly the difference between high and low, for only then will I be able to distribute orders and provide appropriate strength for upholding the laws. If this does not occur, lawlessness and disorder will reign, and then how could I accomplish this task?" The assembly responded, "What you command [will prevail]." Thereupon Ma went before them and assumed their leadership. He ordered an altar erected and then bowing southward he worshipped, saying: "Standing here I gaze into the distance to the imperial palace and receive the commands of the lord whom I serve. Great is the honor of our state. With all my strength I will plan for victory and the reconquest of our lost territory." At the end of this devotion, Ma stood facing south. The crowd showed its respect and called, "From this time forth only one command is to be obeyed. Whoever dares to offer opposition shall be subjected to military law."[14]

Yet even this display of common people as loyal to their leader as the court was to its emperor was deeply ambiguous: although Ma proclaims his loyalty by facing south toward the Sung capital, only the emperor himself could truly face south — his vassals faced north wherever they might be.

Furthermore, the loyalty of the people was thrown into question by the peasant rebellions of mid-Sung, and these rebellions were by no means divorced from the foreign policies of the Sung court.[15] One of Fang La's purported speeches to his associates during the uprising of 1120 – 22 complains bitterly about Sung tribute to the barbarian states of Liao and Hsi Hsia: what the court could not dissipate in its own extravagance it doled out as gifts "worth millions in silver and silk," because it lacked the courage to bring this infamous practice to an end.[16] Confucian vocabulary permeates another account of the social aspirations of the Fang La rebellion. In the *Chi-le-pien* by Chuang Chi-yü, one of Fang La's followers remarks in a conversation that the rebellion is dedicated to achieving the state of "relative prosperity" (*hsiao-k'ang*).[17] *Hsiao-k'ang* has an unimpeachable Confucian pedigree, however, since it appears in the "*li-yün*" chapter of the *Rites of Li* as the second best utopia that Confucianism could offer.

The documentation on the Fang La rebellion suggests that the "loyalty" of the rebels, so mistrusted by the court, was no longer interpreted primarily as loyalty to the ruler or to the dynasty, but as loyalty directly to the state. Such a definition of loyalty provided rebels, deserters, and other opportunists with a basis for legitimating their conduct. Political opportunists adorned themselves with the attributes of legitimate power: in 1128 when Liu Yü had defected to the Chin and had taken up arms against troops still loyal to the Sung, he proclaimed an amnesty "to divide the sympathy of the masses."[18] The definition of pure banditry remained flexible: Li Ch'üan, an ex-cattle dealer, and his adopted son Li T'an formed a band called the Redcoat Loyalists (*Hung-ao chung-i chün*) in 1205. He fought against the Chin in the area of Shan-tung, taking substantial territory away from Chin control. After the death of his father, Li T'an assumed the leadership of the band, took over the administration of the reconquered areas, and called himself emperor. In spite of this apparent usurpation of dynastic prerogative, his relationship to the Sung court remained ambivalent and his death did not come until after a risky seesaw policy of accommodation with the Mongols collapsed and his forces were subdued by Kublai Khan's troops in 1262.[19]

Although rebels like Fang La and gang leaders like Li Ch'üan and Li T'an came from the lower levels of society, their proclamations never suggested any serious attempt to advance class oriented interest. The new loyalty of mid-Sung was totally uninvolved with any demand for lower class autonomy. Neither the *min-ping* nor the rebels nor the loyalists developed any distinct ideology of their own, invariably preferring to adopt the norms and values of existing officialdom. But in spite of the overwhelming tendency for ideological values to be diffused downwards in society, the slow development of a new, broadly based concept of patriotic loyalty is itself evidence of the lower classes' ability to have some influence on the configuration of ideology at the top.

Since the loyal feelings of the lower strata of society were more in the nature of a social and emotional undercurrent than a major ideological development, it is necessary to concentrate primarily on the theory and practice of the upper classes in order to verify the dim outlines of a truly patriotic concept of loyalty. As far as the practice of loyalty is concerned, it is clear that political disagreements particularly with respect to the proper posture for Sung response to the Chin invasion never became absolute but always recognized some "national" good, some interest in the preservation of officialdom and the political process over and beyond the merits or demerits of particular arguments. There was a certain strain of traditional magnanimity in this approach to the management of affairs, not dissimilar perhaps to the generosity of Yüeh Fei after he had subdued the uprising of Chung Hsiang and Yang Yao in 1135. In the *Yang Yao shih-chi,* an anonymous work, the famous general is alleged to have pleaded pardon for the agitators in the following words: "his [Yang Yao's] scores of followers have [again] become good children of the empire. . . . To slaughter and behead them now is not in any way conduct befitting a worthy servant of the state."[20] Yüeh joined the traditional magnanimity of victors with the recurrent Chinese tendency to see rebellion as an inevitable alternate means of survival in times of distress, but there is also some hint in this sort of statement that he placed national patriotic interests above smaller and more limited concerns.

On an ideological level, there was also considerable development of issues related to loyalty and patriotism. New responses were sought to the challenges posed by internal and external threats, lest the loyalty of officialdom, a fundamental pillar of the state, be jeopardized. The theoreticians were divided into two main camps: the Neo-Confucianists and the scholars of the utilitarian school, especially Li Kou (1009–1059) and Wang An-shih (1021–1086), and those of the so-called Yung-chia school. Li, Wang and the Yung-chia scholars attempted to reassert an ethos sanctioned by the classics, but gave differing weight to the various original texts. The ambiguity of their interpretations allowed scope for new definitions of ethical norms without destroying traditional ideals or denying the validity of the main Confucian principles. For the Neo-Confucianists, who clung steadfastly to cultural universalism, the greatest problem was the unthinkable shrinking of the Chinese *oikumene*. It was no longer possible for them, even with the best intentions, to maintain that the Chinese *oikumene* comprised the entire civilized world, and if they wished, despite this, to retain claim to universal moral representation of humanity, then the only possible course was an escape from reality: it was necessary to detach theory from fact. In effect they came to skip the link between the family and the nation, and that between the empire and true culture, replacing these with a direct link between the familial imagery of early Confucian times and a metaphysical understanding of the universe. The great eleventh-century Neo-Confucian, Chang Tsai, put it this way: "Heaven is my father; the earth my mother; all people are my blood brothers; the great ruler is the lineal descendant of these my parents."[21] This almost infinite extension of ancient familial relationships strained several superfamilial institutions for social organization. The more serious these developments became and the further kinship bonds departed from reality, the more intensely they were idealized by the Neo-Confucian moralists. Practical attempts to strengthen clan institutions were accompanied by ideological refurbishing. As the construction of clan buildings was financed and schools were established, rituals were also drawn up for the ancestral temples and clan regulations and genealogies were composed.[22] In the course of this ideological redecoration, the concept of loyalty was the first to be substantially redirected. Slowly the entire notion of loyalty was moved from the level of clan ethos to that of state value, primarily through a process of metaphorical extension. Hung Mai (1123 – 1202) quotes the following words by Hsieh Liang-tso: "Lords, teachers, and friends, although they form no natural blood relationship, can be considered as one family."[23] In another context Hung himself wrote: "It is not true that loyalty and righteousness depend on whether or not one holds office or whether one is of high or low social status."[24] It seems that the concept of loyalty was being understood in far more generalized and more abstract terms. At the same time it is clear that the success or failure of loyal conduct no longer served as a criterion for its judgment. Hung Mai criticized the passage from Yang Hsiung's *Fa-yen* which begins: "Someone inquired concerning loyal advice and clever plans,"[25] arguing that loyalty and efficiency were qualities quite independent of one another, and that loyalty especially could be held independent of its consequences in political practice. This distinction is almost reminiscent of the differing tenets of Catholicism and Protestantism — good deeds are essential to the former, while belief alone is significant for the latter.

Loyalty was not merely extended beyond the context of the social relationship it described, it was also internalized in the mind and consciousness of each person and political figure. It is precisely this internalization which led to Confucian eremitism, a pervasive phenomenon at the end of the Sung and throughout most of the Yüan dynasty.[26] Consider, for example, the understanding of loyalty implied in Cheng Ssu-hsiao's autobiography:

The only righteous scholar living in retirement is a man of the Great Sung. He was born under the Sung and will die under the Sung. Today [after the decline of the Sung dynasty], people in the world all believe that it is not the world of the Chao family [the imperial family in the Sung], but how foolish this is! When I review the world from the ancient past until the present in its entirety, I start at the beginning before the existence of heaven and earth, and arrive at a final state when heaven and earth exist — the vast heavens, the entire earth, every blade of grass and every tree I know to be the world of the Sung. Moreover, I do not wish to learn whether in this world there are emperors or kings or usurpers or robbers or criminals, *i* or *ti* barbarians. The absolute oneness of the Great Sung is that of the one entire heaven. [The Great Sung] does not exist merely because it possesses a great territory nor does it disappear for lack of that territory. It experienced times of great cultural creation and times of fatal hardship. It remains even now the mother of all things, never having known its boundaries![27]

Such a rapturous attitude seems to border on insanity when it is judged from the platform of traditional Confucian morality, but Cheng Ssu-hsiao far transcends these norms: he is far more subjective than his traditional Confucian predecessors. His subjectivism, however, is strictly defined — subjective voluntarism as it was expressed, for example, in Wang An-shih's theory of human nature was no more the goal of Neo-Confucian thought than it had been of the classics. Traditionally, Chinese thinkers differentiated clearly between nature (*hsing*) and feelings (*ch'ing*); after the influence of Buddhism they refined the distinction. Han Yü (768 — 824) theorized three gradations of nature — superior, median and inferior — in order to provide a congenial context for moral attributes; Li Ao (772 — 841) argued that nature and feelings were inextricably complementary. Wang An-shih, however, asserted that "nature and feelings are identical with each other, . . .nature is the root of feelings and feelings the actualization of nature."[28] Wang's point is clearly made in his essay "On Yang Hsiung and Meng-tzu," which focuses on the controversy between Meng-tzu's argument that everything in the world has been ordained (*ming*) and Yang Hsiung who holds that good and evil are intermingled in human nature.[29] Wang attempted to resolve this matter as follows: "What Meng-tzu calls nature is [only] the correct nature; what Yang-tzu calls ordination is [only] the correct ordination."[30] Imperfectly hidden behind this allusive discussion is Wang's principal dissent from classical Confucian dogma. He did not believe that all things in the universe had immanent moral qualities of which the moral capacity of men was an outer manifestation. He eschewed the proposition that morality inheres in objective reality, an idea so basic to Confucian thought that it forms the very logic of linguistic rectification (*cheng-ming*) as a means for correcting social disorder; for Wang, it was the human being who *imprints* moral qualities *on* nature. While this position is only dimly described in Wang's essays, the atmosphere of subjective voluntarism is obvious.

The scholars of the Yung-chia school, especially Ch'en Liang (1143 — 94), accomplished this subjective conversion in an emotional rather than philosophically speculative manner. Their emotionality was ignited by their readiness for war — virtually all the scholars of the Yung-chia school together with their predecessors Li Kou and Wang An-shih belonged to the war party. Ch'en Liang violently opposed the court's appeasement policy in respect of the Chin and memorialized Emperor Hsiao-tsung in this regard several times. Yeh Shih (1150 — 1223) participated actively in the 1206 — 8 war against the Chin. Like the Neo-Confucianists, the Yung-chia scholars insisted on the fundamental unity of man and nature, but as sober pragmatists they also insisted upon a holistic relationship between civilism (*wen*) and martialism (*wu*). In the preface to *Cho-ku lun*, Ch'en Liang wrote:

The ways of *wen* and *wu* were originally one. Later generations diverged and created two ways. The scholars employed nothing but pen and ink while warriors served alone with sword and shield, until finally these began deriding one another.[31]

While the ethos of the Neo-Confucian led inevitably to passivity and resignation in the face of crisis, the subjective emotionality of the Yung-chia scholars engendered a militant activism. Ch'en Liang felt that this activism sprang from deep inside each individual man. He asked, "How is it that one always speaks of a Mandate of Heaven?" but answered, "It is far more the plans of men." He was opposed to considering that the success of any task was in the hands of the gods, arguing that the feelings of men and the circumstances under which they acted were normally decisive. "If one underestimates the enemy and then is conquered, it is not that the enemy has brought him defeat, but rather that he conquered himself."[32]

The Neo-Confucianists could maintain universalism under the conditions of the twelfth and thirteenth centuries only by performing two sleights of hand, one which connected individual men directly with the infinite, and another which internalized the determination of personal values. Ch'en Liang and the Yung-chia scholars, on the other hand, renounced universalism. Their patriotism forced them to narrow the boundaries of the Chinese *oikumene*. Their concern was no longer for the *t'ien-hsia* but exclusively for the *kuo*. The barbarians on the frontier who pressed so harshly upon the Sung could no longer be considered as potential members of the inclusive *oikumene*, but only as enemies of the fatherland and as challenges to the wealth and welfare of the *kuo*. The patriotic conception of loyalty which grew out of the vulgarization of traditional Confucian values, the downward diffusion of the Great Tradition, and the philosophical emotionalism of Ch'en Liang was an essential stage in the development of Chinese nationalism.

Notes to Chapter 8

1. Max Weber, *Wirtschaft und Gesellschaft* (Tübingen: 1922), p. 201.
2. See Hegel's interpretation of Sophocles' *Antigone*, F. Bassenge, ed., *Asthetik* (Berlin: 1955), II, pp. 564 – 65.
3. *Han-shu* 37.5b – 8a.
4. "Feng-chien lun" [On feudalism] in *Liu Ho-tung chi* (Peking: 1964), I, pp. 43 – 48.
5. *HNYL* 7 (for the year 1127, 7th month).
6. *HNYL* 12 (for the year 1128, 1st month).
7. *PMHP* 143.5a.
8. *WHTK* 156, ping 8 (p. 1366).
9. *WHTK* 156, ping 8 (p. 1366).
10. *HWHTK* 127, ping 7 (p. 3925).
11. *WHTK* 156, ping 8 (p. 1366).
12. *HWHTK* 127, ping 7 (p. 3925).
13. Chang Cheng-lang, "Sung Chiang k'ao" [An investigation of Sung Chiang], in *Shui-hu yen-chiu lun-wen chi* (Peking: 1957), pp. 207 – 223.
14. *PMHP* 90.12a. See also Ch'ien Shih-sheng, ed., *Nan-Sung shu* [The book of Southern Sung] (Nan-sha: 1797) 27.
15. Kao Yu-kung, "A Study of the Fang La Rebellion," *Harvard Journal of Asiatic Studies,* 24 (1962 – 63), pp. 17 – 63; and *Harvard Journal of Asiatic Studies,* 26 (1966), pp. 211 – 42.
16. Fang Shao, *Ch'ing-hsi k'ou-kuei* [Disturbances by the rebels of Ch'ing-hsi] (Ku-chin shuo-hai ed.), p. 8a. See also Vincent Shih, *The Taiping Ideology* (Seattle: 1967), pp. 353 – 54.
17. Wu Tseng-ch'i, ed., *Chiu hsiao-shuo* [Old stories and records] (Shanghai: 1957), IV, p. 124.
18. Hsiung K'o, *Chung-hsing hsiao-chi* 12, cited in Chang, "Sung Chiang k'ao," p. 219.
19. Shen Ch'i-wei, *Sung Chin chan-cheng shih-lüeh* [Outline history of the wars between the Sung and Chin] (Wu-han: 1958), pp. 166 – 72. Y. Muramatsu, "Some Themes in Chinese Rebel Ideologies," in Arthur Wright, ed., *The Confucian Persuasion* (Stanford: Stanford University Press, 1960), pp. 265 – 66.
20. G. von Sievers, "Das *Yang Yao shih-chi* (Taten und Spuren des Yang Yao): Zur Geschichte der Rebellion des Chung Hsiang und Yang Yao (1130 – 1135)" Diss. University of Munich, 1969, p. 42.
21. Chang Tsai, "Hsi-ming," in W. Eichhorn, *Die Westinschrift des Chang Tsai,* Abhandlungen für die Kunde des Morgenlandes, 22, 7 (1937), p. 36.
22. D. S. Nivison, "Introduction," in Nivison and Wright, ed., *Confucianism in Action* (Stanford: Stanford University Press, 1959), p. 10; H. C. W. Liu, "An Analysis of Chinese Clan Rules: Confucian Theories in Action," *Confucianism in Action,* pp. 63 – 96.
23. Hung Mai, "Jung-chai sui-pi," in *Jung-chai sui-pi wu-chi* (Shanghai: 1935) 2.16 (No. 14).
24. *Ibid.,* 9.84 (No. 10).
25. Yang Hsiung, *Fa-yen* [Model Sayings] 13 (hsiao-chih); Hung Mai, "Jung-chai san-pi" 12.112 (No. 14).
26. F. W. Mote, "Confucian Eremitism in the Yüan Period," *The Confucian Persuasion,* pp. 202 – 40.
27. Cheng Ssu-hsiao, "I-shih chü-shih chuan" [Biography of the only right retired scholar], in *Chiu hsiao-shuo,* pp. 516 – 17.
28. "Hsing ch'ing" [On nature and feelings], Wang An-shih, *Wang Lin-ch'uan ch'üan-chi* (Taipei: Shih-chieh shu-chü, 1966), 67 (p. 425).
29. "Yang Meng" [On Yang Hsiung and Meng-tzu], in Wang, *Wang Lin-ch'uan ch'üan-chi* 64 (pp. 401 – 02).
30. *Ibid.*
31. *Lung-ch'uan wen-chi* (Shanghai: 1937), Vol. I, 5.49.
32. "Cho-ku lun" [Considerations on the Ancients], "Feng Ch'an-ch'ing" in *Lung-ch'uan wen-chi* 8.80.

First Sung Reactions to the Mongol Invasion of the North, 1211-17

CHARLES A. PETERSON

ONE OF THE MOST DRAMATIC AND MOMENTOUS EPISODES in Chinese history began when the Mongols attacked the Chin empire in 1211. A third major power—the Hsi-Hsia to the northwest were a minor one—thus joined the two already on the scene in China, the Chin and the Sung, which had for nearly a century divided the country between them. As we know now, this attack was only the beginning of a long effort which culminated in the conquest of Chin and much later in that of Sung, introducing an epoch which was in many ways peculiar and even traumatic in the Chinese experience. At a distance it appears that nothing could have stopped Mongol military power, which in its own day did not encounter its equal, and that China was destined to be swallowed up like other lands on which the aggressive nomads had set their sights. But nothing of the sort was evident at the time. At the outset in 1211 none of the actors could have predicted even the general course events would take, nor was there anything fixed about the course they did take. Real choices faced the participants more than once along the way, and of the two reigning powers in China, surely the native dynasty in the south—Chin being hard-pressed and on the defensive from the beginning—had the greater options. It would be banal to assert that, had Sung known the Mongols to be even a greater menace than the Jürchen, it would have pursued a different policy. Yet, as it is conceivable that a different policy would have significantly altered the final outcome, it is imperative that we recognize which possibilities appeared available to the Sung and which considerations at least consciously influenced them.

The policy Sung did pursue was a product of several factors— of a specific cultural and intellectual tradition, of an emotional inheritance from the immediate past, of domestic political considerations, and certainly also of a perception of developments in the north at the time. This paper addresses itself primarily to the last of these. In so doing it seeks to open a contemporary window on a fateful sequence of events, focusing attention on the viewer rather than the events. Its overriding objective is to make Sung behavior as fully comprehensible as possible. Secondarily, it attempts to throw light on Sung policy per se. For, even by the most straightforward definition of policy,* it is clear that we have not till now truly identified Sung external policy throughout the early decades of the thirteenth century. The focus here will be specifically on the years 1211 to 1217, or from the first Mongol attacks to the resumption of Sung-Chin hostilities.

That this is the case proceeds in no small measure from the nature of the materials available to us. None of the chronicles of the period are even remotely adequate, certainly not worthy of being mentioned in the same breath as the *Hsü tzu-chih t'ung-chien ch'ang-pien* for the Northern Sung or the *Chien-yen i-lai hsi-nien yao-lu* for early Southern Sung. The *Sung-shih* itself is often enough a mediocre compilation, even if occasionally strong on institutions. And the major documentary collection, the *Sung hui-yao*, has but limited material on external matters, and contains no section at all, in the form in which it has reached us, on Sung relations with the Mongols (nor, in fact, has the *Sung-shih*). The major and obvious reason for this is that most materials on the Sung were compiled under the succeeding Mongol dynasty, a fact affecting both the selection of documents and the quality of compilation. But there is an additional reason, which bears on the treatments we find—or indeed fail to find—on the early decades of the thirteenth century in particular. This period, which featured the lengthy dominance at court of Shih Mi-yüan as Chief Councilor, is held in relative disfavor by traditional Chinese historians. This is in part because of their abhorrence for any long-lived ministry (Has any long-time dominant minister from any period escaped with reputation unscathed?) but mostly because of Shih's installation of Li-tsung on the throne in 1224 against the claims of the legitimate heir. The problem lies not simply or even mainly in the slanted nature of the reporting but rather in the scarcity of the reports in the first place. Thus for virtually every one of the top officials who served during Shih's ministry from 1208 to his death in 1233, including Shih himself, there is very limited biographical information and almost nothing from their own

---

* *Webster's Third New International Dictionary* (Springfield, Massachusetts: G. & C. Merriam, 1971), p. 1754, defines policy as "a definite course or method of action selected. . .from among alternatives and in the light of given conditions to guide and usually determine present and future decisions."

hands.* Hence, on the subject of Sung foreign policy in this period we must acknowledge that we shall find no official spokesman for the powers that ruled at court. What they thought and for what reasons has to be interpreted in large part from their actions. These are also partly to be found, reflected directly or obliquely, in the thoughts and attitudes of some of their contemporaries, and here we do have serviceable sources.

The importance for historians of the collected works (*wen-chi*) of individual scholars and officials has already been amply demonstrated, most recently as sources of economic history and biographical information.[1] In the relative absence of other pertinent material but also because of their own high value as contemporary testimony, they have been utilized here in an effort to determine Sung reactions to the Mongol invasion of the north. I attempt in effect, to recreate the context of Sung opinion in which available foreign policy options presented themselves. My reference is only to explicit assertions, essentially addresses to the throne, bearing on either the external situation for Sung fortunes and policy. To the extent that no attention has been given to implicit evidences, as one might find in belles lettres, for example, the inquiry has not in fact been exhuastive. It will become clear that certain assumptions have been made about the men on whose writings I shall be drawing. I assume, for example, that they were true men of their time and thus that in general outlook, or Weltanschauung, they were representative of the Sung intelligentsia or at least an important segment of it. I also assume that, though for the most part officials of only the middle echelon, what they wrote is a proper index to the kind of information possessed by the government and that it reflects its principal concerns. Certainly the top officials at court had access to a wider range and to special sources of information, but the real difference existed not so much between the various strata of official-

---

* SS 213–214 (*Tsai-fu-piao*) lists ten individuals who, during the period 1208–1233, held top posts at court for three years or more, a necessary qualification for our purposes. These posts are from Chief Councilor (*ch'eng-hsiang*) down through Consignatory Official of the Bureau of Military Affairs (*t'ung-ch'ien-shu shu-mi-yüan shih*), inclusive. The ten, with an indication of an official biography in the SS when available, are: Chang Liang-neng, Cheng Chao-hsien, Cheng Ch'ing-chih (414), Ch'iao Hsing-chien (417), Hsüan Tseng (419), Hsüeh Chi (419), Ke Hung (415), Lou Yüeh (395), Shih Mi-yüan (414), and Tseng Ts'ung-lung (419). Few have privately written biographies and even in the cases of those who do, there is little of value for this reign. Only Lou Yüeh's prose works have survived, but he died in 1213 and there are no relevant pieces from his final years. (One at least has left his collected poetry, Cheng Ch'ing-chih's *An-wan-t'ang shih-chi*.) Contrary to the statement in *Ajia rekishi jiten* 2, p. 405, Ch'iao Hsing-chien's works, *K'ung-shan wen-chi*, have not survived to our day, though they seem to have until the seventeenth century (see the *Ming-shih* bibliographic catalogue).

dom as between officials at court and those out in the provinces. Aside from these broad areas of agreement or similarity, views on specific issues differed sharply, a point to which our documents themselves testify.

Finally, it should be observed that these collections are necessarily spotty sources, apt to yield far more on certain periods and topics than on others. This issues from two of their basic characteristics: that an individual's papers inevitably reflected the whims of his official career and that these are not *complete* but rather *collected* works. Thus a selection has been made, guided by literary and ideological considerations and by a concern to show how conscientious an official and how accurate a judge, of men and situations, the subject was. None of this is peculiar or unnatural, but it is bound to result in some unevenness in a study based on such materials. *

The early years of the thirteenth century introduced into East Asia a new period of international tension following the relative stability which characterized the last half of the twelfth. The rise in strength of the tribes of Mongolia was the principal force shaping these new circumstances whose impact was felt first of all by the Chin empire. Though not united under Cinggis until 1206, Tatar and Mongol attacks along the border from the 1180s placed an increasing strain on Chin finances and the Chin military. Internal problems also plagued the Jürchen state. Wide effects were felt from changes in the Yellow River in the 1190s. Policies which the government subsequently felt obliged to adopt progressively alienated segments of the Chinese and Khitan populations.† Finally, Chin was forced by Sung into an unwanted war in 1206 which, though it won handily, further complicated its affairs.‡ While it has yet to be shown that Chin had entered a stage of active

---

* Though we are very rich in *wen-chi* for the Southern Sung, a number of prominent writers died just prior to our period and another group was still too junior to have left any pertinent writings. This survey has covered the works of the following individuals: Chen Te-hsiu, Chou Nan, Hung Tz'u-k'uei, Liu Tsai, Liu Yüeh (on whose works see note p. 228 below), Lou Yüeh, Ts'ao Yen-yüeh, Tu Cheng, Wei Ching, Wei Liao-weng, Yang Chien, Yeh Shih, Yüan Hsieh and Yüan Yüeh-yu. Some of these were of limited value for this paper (e.g., those of Wei Liao-weng), but offer rich documentation for its projected sequel. It is particularly to be regretted that so perceptive and forthright a writer as Yeh Shih was officially out of circulation from 1208 until his death (1223); only a few of his last pieces will prove of use.

† On Chin's difficulties, external and internal, see Tōyama Gunji, *Kinchōshi kenkyū* [Researches on Chin history] (Kyoto: Tōyōshi Kenkyukai, 1964), pp. 472–504, 545–548 and 565–592.

‡ On this war see Tōyama, *Kinchōshi kenkyū*, pp. 509–564, and the recent and very useful monograph by Corinna Hana, *Bericht über die Verteidigung der Stadt Te-an* (Wiesbaden: Franz Steiner, 1970), especially pp. 21–65.

decline, there is little question that, as a result of these developments, its capacity to determine its own destiny among competing powers had been significantly reduced.

Not unnaturally, the Sung were only marginally aware of these new circumstances. By the end of the first decade of the century the most critical event within recent memory had been the 1206—8 war with Chin. It is easy to dismiss this enterprise as so abject a failure, from start to finish, that it had no serious impact at all. But it is probable that many people had been genuinely encouraged by reports of Chin distress and that there was a good deal more enthusiasm for the war, the first in which Sung took the initiative against Chin (thereby breaking treaty relations), than our sources are prepared to admit. It should in any case not escape notice that, while throughout the twelfth century it was highly virtuous to take a strong, intransigent stand against the Chin, the attempt finally to implement an aggressive policy was quickly and thoroughly repudiated. To be sure, the key figure in the effort, Han T'o-chou, was condemned on the grounds of ill preparation and poor management, not that he was attempting to do the wrong thing. In fact, much of the bitterness exhibited at the time and subsequently toward him was probably due precisely to the danger that, by doing badly what the irredentists had always wanted done, he caused the validity of those very policy aims to be seriously questioned.

The treaty terms to which the Sung were forced to agree were by no means crippling: a twenty-percent increase in the annual subsidy, no loss of territory, but a substantial three million ounces of silver as a war indemnity.* Yet they were humiliating, first, in that they maintained Sung's junior, materially burdensome status in the relationship and, second, in that they required the execution of Han T'o-chou. Since the latter's removal had become widely desired in official circles, the objection here was more to the principle than anything else. Indeed, Han was assassinated long before peace negotiations were completed, and his team of ministers gave way to an entirely new one by the end of 1207. Emperor Ning-tsung, having thrown the rascals out, announced a "renewal" of government (*keng-hua*), changed the reign title (to Chia-ting: "in praise of stability") and, at the beginning of 1208, issued a broad call (*ch'iu-yen*) to officialdom for criticism and discussion.[2] This last step, rather a Sung version of "Let a hundred

---

* Hana, *Bericht,* pp. 57—63; Tōyama, *Kinchōshi kenkyū,* pp. 537—44. On treaty relations in general between Sung and Chin see H. Franke, "Treaties between Sung and Chin," *Études Song,* 1st ser. (1970), pp. 55—84. The Chinese term I render here by annual subsidy, *sui-pi,* is relatively neutral as distinguished from *kung,* "tribute," in use 1141—1164 (see Franke, p. 79). Also, cf. Christian Schwarz-Schilling, *Der Friede von Shan-yüan* (Wiesbaden: Franz Steiner, 1959), p. 57.

flowers bloom," initiated a policy of relatively open discussion, responses to which provide a useful gauge of the mood of the country, or at least that of the elite, at this time.

Common to the three pieces under consideration here are an acceptance of the usual humiliating peace terms as unavoidable, a total and vigorous condemnation (as we would expect) of the recent ministry of Han T'o-chou and its methods, and the conviction that Sung must make full and immediate efforts to recover its strength and assert its ascendancy. Not remarkably, all dwell also on the basic principles of good government, in two cases at very great length. But the tone and points of emphasis differ a good deal from one piece to the next. Lou Yüeh,* who was soon to become one of the leading officials at court and remain so until shortly before his death in 1213, adopts a moderate tone and attempts above all to comfort the emperor, assuring him of his personal blamelessness for the evil conduct of his ministers.† Lou, who had long before urged extensive measures to strengthen the military, both for purposes of defense and for the dreamed of recovery of the north,‡ now reasserts this view; and he goes on to warn against the danger of the country's becoming complacent and neglectful of its military capabilities by putting its trust in the security of the treaty. The same point is taken up by Chen Te-hsiu but even more strongly. In neither case is this surprising since Chu Hsi, who had been dead since 1200 but who cast an enormous shadow over many of the figures I shall discuss, objected to peace agreements in part precisely because they discouraged the nation from making the desired efforts to build up its strength.§

---

* Lou was at this time Han-lin Lecturer (in Waiting) and concurrently Minister of Personnel. In 1209 he became Assistant Executive of the Secretariat-Chancellery. See his biography in SS 395.

† See his "Lun nei-wai chih chih," Kung-k'uei-chi, ch. 25, pp. 362–363 (Ts'ung-shu chi-ch'eng ed.). The piece is not dated, but from internal references (especially to the fact that "successful negotiation of the peace agreement is not yet assured") it must date from early or mid-1208.

‡ See his two pieces, "Lun hui-fu" and "Lun hsün-lien chin-ping," Kung-k'uei-chi, ch. 21, pp. 316–317 and 318–319, respectively, which can both be dated in the early 1190's.

§ See Hsiao Kung-ch'üan, Chung-kuo cheng-chih ssu-hsiang shih [History of Chinese political thought] (Taipei: Chung-hua wen-hua, 1954), p. 505. For a thoroughgoing discussion of Chu's ideas on defense and foreign policy, see Tomoeda Ryutaro, Shushi no shisō keisei [The formation of Chu Hsi's thought] (Tokyo: Shunjūsha, 1969), pp. 419–434. Chu does not, however, always come off well in this realm in the eyes of modern commentators in comparison with contemporaries such as Ch'en Liang and Lu Hsiang-shan. See T'ao Hsi-sheng, Chung-kuo cheng-chih ssu-hsiang shih [History of Chinese political thought] (Shanghai: Hsing-sheng min-shu-chü, 1936), pp. 126–127 and 133, and Hou Wai-lu, Chung-kuo ssu-hsiang t'ung-shih [General history of Chinese thought] (Peking: Jen-min, 1959) vol. 4, p. 596.

In his memorial of the fourth month,* Chen, who will be our mainstay throughout this discussion and who was at the time a Han-lin Academician,† makes a vigorous attempt to convince the Emperor that peace agreements were by their very nature impermanent, potentially harmful and optimally of only tactical use. A state may safely, in his view, only negotiate from strength. If, however, it is obliged momentarily to negotiate from weakness, it must use the opportunity to strengthen itself with the single aim of overcoming its adversary. His paradigm here is the Ch'un-ch'iu prince, Kou Chien of Yüeh, who exploited the chance of survival afforded him by the Duke of Wu to build up his power and eventually annihilate his erstwhile opponent.‡ The road to disaster, when the peace is not so utilized but simply accepted as a blessing, is shown by the six late Chou states, which merely bought time by making treaties with Ch'in only ultimately to be swallowed up by her. Chen goes on bluntly to assert what had become a Neo-Confucian article of faith by then, that real statesmen pay no attention to the condition and actions of the enemy but are concerned only with the rule of their own state. Barbarians across the borders will react accordingly: show respect and submission if that rule is successful; attack if it is not. The immediate and urgent need, therefore, is by the pursuit of the correct principles to strengthen the inner fiber of the country.

The response to the call for criticism made by Ts'ao Yen-yüeh is the most specific and in some ways the best informed.[3] Ts'ao had recently been in the thick of the fighting against the Chin at Han-yang where he distinguished himself by organizing local defense.§ His attack

---

* See *Hsi-shan hsien-sheng Chen Wen-chung kung wen-chi,* 2.1a−4a (SPTK ed.; hereafter referred to as *Hsi-shan wen-chi*). In this paper my years are solar but my months are lunar. The grounds for this procedure are that we can dispense neither with the years according to the Gregorian calendar for convenience nor with the months according to the Chinese calendar for reference to the sources. One may well recall, however, that the lunar year begins a month later on an average than the Gregorian. The years referred to in the course of this paper all fall within the Chia-ting reign period and correspond as follows: 1208, year one; 1209, two; 1210, three; 1211, four; 1212, five; 1213, six; 1214, seven; 1215, eight; 1216, nine; 1217, ten; and 1218, eleven.

† Chen has a biography in *SS* 437, as well as lengthy epitaphs by Wei Liao-weng, in *Hao-shan ch'üan-chi* 69, and by Liu K'e-chuang, in *Hou-Ts'un hsien-sheng ta-ch'üan-chi* 168, the former of which is considerably more useful. (SPTK ed. has been used in both cases.)

‡ See *Shih-chi* 41.1b−6b (Po-na ed.) [E. Chavannes, *Mémoires historiques* (Paris: Leroux, 1895), vol. 4, pp. 420−431]. Kou Chien's final triumph over Wu, taking revenge for the humiliating defeat at Kuei-chi in 494 B. C., occurred in 478.

§ Ts'ao has a biography in *SS* 410 and a far more useful epitaph by Wei Liao-weng in *Hao-shan ch'üan-chi* 87. On this particular exploit see 87.16a-b, in the latter and Ts'ao's own piece in *Ch'ang ku-chi* 9.9a−14a.

on recent policies is even more thoroughgoing than the others, but what is of most interest is his concern for conditions along the border. He describes in some detail the havoc wreaked in the Huai region by the war, not merely destruction but depopulation, unemployment, and inflation. The question of the condition of this area and of what strategic use to make of it is to remain a focus of attention. Ts'ao touches in passing on another vital point in strategic thinking at the time: the reservoir of loyalist sentiment in the north on which Sung hoped it could count. In this case, he points out, "No loyalist rebels came over to us," a fact which would surely make future calculations more conservative. Ts'ao's criticism of the recent war effort runs generally along the same lines as the others, laying the blame on an inadequate buildup beforehand, but he stresses the long-range political harm inflicted on the entire frontier region, both north and south of the border. The people in this region, he observes, bear the brunt of hostilities and, amid the accompanying distress, carry on raids for food and in reprisal against their neighbors across the border. Hence, ill-conceived actions such as this serve, among other things, only to drive apart the Chinese populations living in adjacent Chin and Sung territories. Any effort to recover the north must first adopt a positive policy toward the population and not risk alienating it. Despite these political calculations, a genuine concern for the welfare of the people is perceptible in Ts'ao's discussion.

On the whole, therefore, the recent military debacle had not fundamentally affected sentiment in favor of recovering the north which remained the ultimate aspiration of at least a major segment of the ruling class in the south, a goal which permitted of no question or doubt. But it could not have helped but chasten that sentiment, which even in our writers is not of uniform intensity and which, as they indicate, threatened to give way to complacent acceptance of the status quo. Certainly, as a regulated peace and stability were restored, any practical thinking about again moving north must have been discarded for the foreseeable future. In addition, the Sung could now hardly lend credence to previous reports about Chin decline and weakness — Ts'ao remarks how the Chin were *said* to have become weak — and surely remained puzzled in this respect. Nevertheless, such practical considerations caused not the slightest slackening of the deep and traditional enmity toward the northern alien dynasty, an enmity that offered little hope for conciliation under any circumstances.

Normal diplomatic relations with Chin were resumed immediately after the conclusion of peace negotiations late in the summer of 1208. These involved the exchange of envoys twice a year bearing salutations for the new year and for royal birthdays, the dispatch of envoys on special occasions (a monarch's accession or his death, for example), and, of course, Sung's payment of the annual subsidy.* From all indications these relations were pursued faithfully on both sides until the summer of 1211.† Then the Mongols suddenly intruded.

Though fully aware of Cinggis' hostile intentions since his rejection of vassal status three years earlier, Chin first recognized his real strength when the Mongols began tearing apart its frontier defenses in the spring of that year.‡ Sung gained direct knowledge of these attacks upon dispatch in the sixth month of the regular congratulatory mission for the monarch's birthday. The military crisis forced suspension of ceremonial activities at the Chin court and the Sung mission was actually turned back after having reached Cho-chou in Ho-pei.§ Thus, though word of the attacks might have slipped through earlier, the Sung had clear-cut evidence at an early date of their gravity. This was further confirmed by the failure of Chin's regular birthday mission to arrive at Hang-chou in the fall.[4]

Upon first learning of their attacks on Chin, how much did the Sung know about the Mongols? Here we must largely speculate, but it seems safe to say that any such knowledge was limited and imprecise. Already at the beginning of Northern Sung direct contact had been severed between the tribes in Mongolia and the Sung court; and since its establishment Southern Sung had had virtually no opportunity to maintain intelligence on that part of the world. To be sure, they could find scattered and very general references to those tribes in their own literature, including evidence of Mongol-Chin conflict going back to

---

* On diplomatic intercourse maintained under the force of treaty, see Dagmar Thiele, *Der Abschluss eines Vertrages: Diplomatie zwischen Sung- und Chin-Dynastie, 1117—1123* (Wiesbaden: Franz Steiner, 1971), pp. 142—143, a study which makes a major contribution to Sung-Chin relations in general and to their critical opening phase in particular. It seems not, however, to have been previously noted that the dates for the birthday missions on each side varied with the individual monarch, as *CS* 60—62 (*Chiao-p'in-piao*) makes clear.

† On the exchange of missions, 1208—1211, see *SS* 39.2a—7a, and *CS* 62.25b ff.

‡ For the immediate background of the Mongol invasion of China and the invasion itself up to 1217, see O. Franke, *Geschichte des chinesischen Reiches*, v. 4 (Berlin: de Gruyter, 1948), pp. 263—268; H. Desmond Martin, *The rise of Chingis Khan and his conquest of North China* (Baltimore: John Hopkins University Press, 1950), pp. 113—194; R. Grousset, *L'Empire des steppes* (Paris: Payot, 1939), pp. 286—292; and, particularly as a military analysis, Sun K'o-kuan, *Meng-ku ch'u-chi chih chün-lüeh yü Chin chih p'eng-k'uei* [Early Mongol military strategy and the fall of Chin] (Taipei: Chung-yang wen-wu kung-ying-she, 1955). More recently, a valuable study by Igor de Rachewiltz, "Personnel and Personalities in North China in the Early Mongol Period," *Journal of Economic and Social History of the Orient*, 9 (1966), pp. 88—144, reveals the important role played in the military successes of the Mongols and in their adaptation to Chinese conditions by local elements who rallied to their cause.

§ *SS* 39.8a. Naturally, the possibility cannot be excluded that the Chin simply wanted to deny the Sung envoys the opportunity of gaining further intelligence.

the first half of the twelfth century.* More pertinently, they were well aware of the problems Chin had been having along its northern frontier since late in the century. Some officials at court were thrown into momentary panic in 1196 by reports that disruptions caused by the "Tatars" (ta-tan) might become so serious as to threaten Sung.[5] Such reports eventually encouraged the southern court to undertake its ill-fated war against Chin in 1206,[6] but the results demonstrated that northern frontier problems had not visibly impaired the latter's military capabilities within China proper. News of the Mongol campaign of 1209 – 10 against Hsi-Hsia had certainly reached Hang-chou (though it is worth recalling that Hsi-Hsia yet survived). Perhaps the alert ordered at the Chin capital in the fall of 1210 against rumored Mongol attack did as well.[7]

Something of a reputation, therefore, preceded the Mongols. Yet for Sung, if not for Chin,† this need not have been specific and accurate information. The Sung Chinese knew that there was such an assemblage of peoples "out there" to whom they had somewhat indiscriminately applied a variety of names. Having early in the preceding century made a basic and lasting identification between Mongols and Tatars, they probably still had only limited notion of such tribal distinctions.‡ It was possible on general grounds to distinguish those tribes living nearby who were subject to the influence of (Chinese) civilization from those farther removed who were not. But whether, for example, the distinction had yet been made between "Black" and "White Tatars," which the Chinese would then retain throughout the thirteenth

---

* The materials by Wang Kuo-wei in the following essays in his *Kuan-t'ang chi-lin* (*Hai-ning Wang Chung-ch'üeh kung i-shu*, ed.) collect and discuss virtually all known references to Mongolian tribes in Chinese language sources up through the twelfth century: "Ta-tan k'ao" [A study of the Ta-tan], ch. 14.5a – 26a; "Liao-Chin shih Meng-ku k'ao" [A study of the Mongols in the Liao and Chin periods], ch. 15.1a – 11a; and "Nan-Sung-jen so-chuan Meng-ku shih-liao k'ao" [A study of the historical materials on the Mongols emanating from the Southern Sung], ch. 15.21a – 32a. These studies make absolutely clear how sparse available information on the Mongols and related tribes was to the native dynasty in the south up to our period. As Wang shows in the last of these essays, most of the information that was available (and used by Chinese historians in the twelfth and early thirteenth centuries) issued from two counterfeit and no longer extant works of the early Southern Sung, the *Cheng-Meng chi* (attributed to Li Ta-liang) and the *Hsing-ch'eng-lu* (to Wang Ta-kuan). However, Tōyama makes a convincing case for the historicity of a good deal of this material, even if the works were not authentic accounts by Chin subjects as they pretended. (In dispute, in particular, are reported Mongol attacks on the Chin which, Tōyama argues, induced Chin to come to terms with Sung in 1141.) See Tōyama, *Kinchōshi kenkyū*, [Researches on Chin history] (Kyoto: Tōyōshi Kenkyukai, 1964), pp. 421 – 42.

† De Rachewiltz, "Personnel and Personalities," p. 95, makes the point that the Chin had at least fair intelligence on developments in Mongolia from 1196 surrounding Cinggis Qan. Wang's quotations in the articles cited in note above also make clear how much better opportunity the Chin had than the Sung to become familiar with the Mongols (though they no doubt would happily have foregone this opportunity).

‡ On the variety of designations for the Mongols and for this confusion of the Mongols and Tatars, see Wang, "Liao-Chin shih Meng-ku k'ao," passim, but especially 2b – 3a.

century, is debatable.* It was in any event assumed that they were essentially nomadic peoples whose primitive way of life sustained a warlike nature. Inevitably they were dangerous, though, as history showed, prone to division; hence their current strength, it was probably supposed, resulted from the attainment of some degree of unity. This characterization somewhat anticipates our writers, but, as we shall see, Chinese knowledge of the Mongols expanded only slowly in the course of the following years.

Whereas news of Chin distress would have been received with some satisfaction in the south in any case, it was bound to be seized on with particular fervor by those of more vigorous irredentist persuasion. An address to the throne by Chen Te-hsiu from the end of 1211 predicts the imminent fall of the Chin and warns of the need to prepare for likely contingencies.† But it is important to note that Chen's analysis is made on only general grounds and betrays no especially strong factual knowledge of circumstances in the north. He resorts to the force of history to account for Chin's coming fall:‡ the cycle (of barbarian fortunes) is now complete as once again, like the Jürchen after the Khitan, one barbarian emerges to replace another. Having declined in martial vigor, the Jürchen suffer simultaneously a loss of control over the country, for, having (like ancient Ch'in) ruled by force, they cannot rely on the populace for support. Referring to the attitudes of current leaders, Chen cautions against taking comfort from the coming fall of Chin, for the consequences for Sung, far from happy, may be very serious, both at home and beyond the borders. Citing the *Tso-chuan* and Mencius, he recalls the well-known relationship between external danger and internal alertness and cohesion. The demise of the long-time enemy may lull responsible people into a complacency which would ill serve the country in a time of impending crisis. Externally, a highly dangerous situation could very well materialize upon the collapse of Chin. Sung might be induced to join "the outer barbarians" (*wai-i*) in an attack on Chin but then find itself the recipient of the allegiance of rebels who had risen against their former rulers. This would duplicate the circumstances at the end of Northern Sung when Chang Chüeh created a crisis by switching allegiances from Chin to

---

* See Yanai Wataru's discussion on this distinction in *Mōkōshi kenkyū* (Tokyo: Tōkō shōin, 1966 reprint), pp. 557–564.

† In *Hsi-shan wen-chi* 2. 17b–23b, only the second part of which is directly pertinent. Chen, at this time a secretary in the Royal Library and a division chief in the Ministry of Justice, will remain in positions at court till 1215.

‡ Chen himself, of course, does not grace the northern state with its dynastic name. He and his contemporaries uniformly referred to it in tribal terms (the Jürchen) or as "the enemy" (literally, "the slaves" [*lu*] or "the northern slaves" [*pei-lu*]).

Sung.* Despite these dangers, there is no thought in Chen's view of any rapprochement with Chin; on the contrary, the Emperor must not, in laying his plans, forget Sung's ancient enmity toward its northern neighbor. The proper response is to initiate serious military preparations which will allow the country to meet any contingency. And again: if China itself is well ruled and makes proper use of its resources, it will be in a position to determine events rather than merely to react to them. Chen, then, is anxious rather than optimistic about the crisis in the north, certainly not at this point inclined to see it as an opportunity for the Sung to exploit.

Probably most people at court felt that this prediction of Chin's early fall was premature, especially with the taste of recent defeat still fresh. There are no signs that the government was in the slightest disposed to alter its conciliatory policy. The security precautions it took along the frontier in the fall of 1211, tightening up restrictions on unauthorized movement across the border and putting its border officials on military alert, are indicative of its concern and would have to be considered, under the circumstances, normal.† Since its treaty with Chin obliged it to keep the border sealed, save at authorized points of trade, this can further be interpreted as a conscious effort to avoid any friction with its northern neighbor. For the time being, short of girding itself for an all-out effort as Chen demanded, it could only watch and wait. The withdrawal of the Mongols in early 1212 after their first run of victories necessarily left the question open whether they had come for conquest or merely for plunder. Normal diplomatic exchanges were resumed in 1212, both parties fulfilling the provisions of the treaty in this respect and the Sung no doubt contributing their annual subsidy.‡

Normalcy did not, however, return to Chin in 1212. A serious drought struck the north, compounding the effects of the previous year's troubles.[8] In Shan-tung disorders which may already have been serious took on a new and alarming scale. This was due, not least of all, to the inability of the central government, in the face of external threat, to dispatch adequate military force to deal with the

---

* Chang has biographies in *CS* 133 and *SS* 472. On the events in question, see Franke, *Geschichte* 4, 205 – 207.

† See *SS* 39.8a, for a decree of the ninth month, threatening officials with loss of position for any such action and another of the tenth ordering an alert.

‡ See *SS* 39.8a, and *CS* 62.26b, for the New Year missions; and *SS* 39.8b and 9a, for the congratulatory birthday missions.

disorders.* Meanwhile revolt also broke out among the Khitan in the northeast and intermittent conflicts with Hsi-Hsia, which date from the fall of 1210, continued in the west.† Then in the fall the Mongols reappeared. Their operations were again limited to the northern frontier, where they continued successful, but they were most significant in demonstrating long-range Mongol designs on China. Nevertheless, until well into 1213 no objective observer would have been inclined to dismiss the likelihood of Chin recovery.

Twelve thirteen was, however, the turning point. From autumn on, Chin's military and political position degenerated rapidly and with wide effect. After preparatory steps and a gradual advance into Ho-pei in the summer, the Mongols launched a great offensive which swept across the country and carried them by the end of the year to the Yellow River.‡ Because of their limited numbers and lack of administrative means, this did not give them actual control over the territory they had covered, but it went a long way toward destroying that exerted by the Chin. Moreover, the Mongols were able to, and from the beginning of 1214 did, besiege the Chin capital of Yen-ching itself. Extended now over heavily populated areas and combined with grave problems already present, the war caused severe disruptions and sent thousands of civilians southward in search of safety. Meanwhile, in late summer, the Chin monarch, Wei-shao, was murdered under particularly bloody circumstances, which must have left considerable bitterness and dissension in its wake.§ Chen's prediction in 1211 of Chin's inevitable

---

* *TCKC* (*Sung-Liao-Chin-Yüan ssu-shih* ed.) 23.1b–2a. The first major revolt seems to have been that of Yang An-erh, placed by *CSPM* 87 (p. 759) (also *HTCTC* 159 [p. 4307]) in the eleventh month of this year, but I find no corroboration for this date. Identical accounts of the revolt are found in *CYTC*, *i-chi*, 19.16a, and *TCTC* 24.2a-b, and 25.1b–2a; also see Li Ch'üan's biography (*SS* 476). All sources are vague with respect to time of origin and with a number of secondary revolts in progress at once, probably no one (save the actors) had a very clear idea of when they began. Certainly, Chen's remarks of late 1211 suggest that revolts are already under way. Sun K'o-kuan points out in his *Meng-ku han-chün chi han-wen-hua yen-chiu* [Researches on Chinese military forces and Chinese culture under the Mongols] (Taipei, 1958), p. 21, that Li Ch'üan was sent by Sung authorities to attack a Chin location as early as 1205. See *SS* 38.9a-b. *CS* 12.5a, confirms that such an attack took place, but I am skeptical of the association of Li with it. Sun (pp. 15 ff.) provides a lengthy treatment of these early revolts without, however, throwing much light on their exact chronology.

† On the revolt of Yeh-lü Liu-ko in Manchuria, see Yanai, *Mōkōshi kenkyū*, pp. 33–41, and Franke, *Geschichte* 4, pp. 268ff. See *HTCTC* 159 (p. 4297) for the split between Chin and Hsia and any of the chronicles for the conflicts thereafter.

‡ See references cited in note, p. 223.

§ Substantial accounts of the assassination can be found in *CS* 132 and *TCTC* 23.4a-b; also see Franke, *Geschichte* 4, pp. 261–262.

collapse was becoming more accurate all the time, but this last reversal
of fortunes had been so sudden that it need hardly have established
his reputation as a prophet.

Aside from sources of intelligence within Chin which Sung might
have had, it possessed two clear indicators of the deteriorating situation in the north. One was the inability of its missions of the year 1213
ever to reach the Chin court. These included the regular mission (sent
in the sixth month) which bore birthday salutations; a special mission
(in the tenth month) with congratulations upon accession of the new
monarch; and the regular new year mission (also in the tenth month).[9]
Even the officials responsible for transporting the subsidy ran into
practical difficulties which interfered with its transfer, as we shall see.
The other, and perhaps more graphic, indicator was the appearance on
the borders of large numbers of refugees, which, Liu Yüeh,* in a
memorial of late 1213 tells us, was no blessing. It is noteworthy that a
memorial of the tenth month by Chen Te-hsiu[10] makes no mention of

---

* Liu has a biography in *SS* 401 and a lengthy epitaph of first rate importance by Chen
Te-hsiu in *Hsi-shan wen chi* 41.1a—21a, on which we shall draw heavily. Liu's rather
slender collected words, *Yün-chuang chi,* survive, but available editions raise some peculiar problems. Of the two I have used, both Ming editions, that in the Ssu-k'u ch'üan-shu
chen-pen, series two (reprinted 1971 by the Commercial Press in Taiwan) consists of
twenty *chüan,* while that in the Seikadō collection in Tokyo (of which I used a photocopy
at the Jinkun Kagaku Kenkyūjo in Kyoto), betraying a completely different arrangement,
contains only twelve. There appears, however, to be little difference in actual volume.
Far more striking, both contain (the Chen-pen edition in ch. 17, the Seikadō edition in
ch. 3), as though they were bonafide works of Liu, four memorials in fact written by Chen
Te-hsiu. In the Chen-pen their dates correspond exactly to those found in Chen's works,
but in the Seikadō copy these have been altered in either major or minor fashion. Two
of these documents have been used in this study (see notes, pp. 229 and 239 below), but
the other two (found in *Hsi-shan wen-chi* 2.7b—11a, and 2.16b—17b) have no immediate
relevance. On the basis of other (and substantial) information available there is no question that these pieces are Chen's and not Liu's. I cannot account for this false attribution,
especially involving a figure as well known as Chen; but no doubt the similarity in views
between the two men facilitated it.
The notice on the *Yün-chuang chi* in *Ssu-k'u ch'üan-shu t'i-yao* 160 comments on
the numerous lacunae in existing editions, but betrays no awareness of the presence of
Chen's pieces. According to this notice Liu's works, whose original compilation was
completed in 1222 (see preface by Li Chih), were collected again in separate editions by
two of his tenth generation descendents in the Ming period. It considers that done by Liu
Keng to be superior, primarily on the grounds of completeness, and this is apparently the
one possessed by the Seikadō. It contains, in fact, (in ch. 3) four memorials of unques-
tionable authenticity not found in the Chen-pen edition, two of which are pertinent to
our topic here. This still leaves us with somewhat slim pickings as far as his papers are
concerned; fortunately, however, Chen's epitaph of Liu is so rich in excerpts that it is
a very serviceable source for his stated views and positions. It has yielded significant
portions of nine relevant documents dating from 1213 to early 1215. Indeed, a comparison of the authentic documents with the excerpts included by Chen shows a similarity
so close as almost to suggest that, Liu's memorials having by Ming times largely disappeared, these few were recovered from the latter. Yet differences are present which
indicate an independent source.

this issue, suggesting that it was the Mongol penetration into southern Ho-pei which caused large-scale flight into Honan.

Border officials, unprepared to deal with the refugees coming south, simply turned them away. But this was also no doubt on orders as the Sung court continued to observe its treaty obligations vis-á-vis the Chin. Liu, who held a court appointment at this time, bemoans this state of affairs, but he is not moved by compassion alone.* His primary concern is with the condition of the defenses along the Huai, a matter on which he had some personal knowledge as a result of escorting a Chin envoy to the border early that year.† At that time he submitted proposals arguing the feasibility of pursuing a self-sustaining, self-defense policy (*tsu-shih tsu-ping*) in the Huai region. This featured several measures to restore the productivity of the land, much of which lay neglected and in disuse, and the organization of the populace into militia.‡ Now he relates his contact at that time with a village of battle-hardened peasants near Hsü-i who were feared by the Chin and who wanted only organization and leadership fully to assume their own defense. This probably confirmed ideas on the feasibility of developing a solid soldier-citizenry which he shared with others of his ideological persuasion.[11] He further suggests that refugees can be settled inside the border and incorporated into defense arrangements. As we shall see, he was a strong proponent of maintaining the Huai as the main defense line, as distinguished from those who preferred to concentrate Sung military power along the Yangtze.

Liu, also convinced that Chin must soon fall, projects a chaotic situation in the north in which there will be three competing elements: rebels (*tao-tse*), military adventurers (*hao-chieh*) — effectively successful rebels in command of large forces — and the "outer barbarians." He does not elaborate on the latter at all. He feels, though this may be rhetorical exaggeration, that Sung defenses are not even adequate to

---

* Liu held concurrent posts in the History Office and as Provisional Vice-Minister in the Ministry of Justice at this time. Excerpts from this memorial can be found in *Hsi-shan wen-chi* 41, 10a−11b. By contrast the philosopher Yang Chien was primarily moved by compassion and memorialized, apparently without entering into the practical difficulties, in favor of a more humane policy towards the refugees. See *Tz'u-hu hsien-sheng i-shu, fu*, 18.21b (Ssu-ming ts'ung-shu, 4th series, ed.).

† *Hsi-shan wen-chi* 41.8b; *SS* 401.11a. Though no exact date is indicated, it is most likely that Liu undertook this escort duty early in 1213.

‡ See *Hsi-shan wen-chi* 41.8b−9a, for what I take to be a first memorial on the subject, and *Yün-chuang chi* (Seikadō ed.) 3.16a−17a, as well as *SS* 401.11a-b, for a second one. The date of the *Yün-chuang chi* document is very likely incorrect.

resist defeated armies who come southward in flight; hence, he urges steps be taken to strengthen them.*

One of the envoys sent to Chin in the fall of 1213 was Chen Te-hsiu. Finding it impossible to enter the country, he remained in the border region for several weeks, only returning to court in the second month of the new year.[12] The report he submitted is rich in several respects and has the particular advantage of reflecting information drawn first-hand from sources beyond the confines of the court.[13] This information was not always the most accurate, as Chen himself acknowledges. For example, he mentions having heard that the Hsi-Hsia were attacking Chin positions in the northwest and that rebel forces active in Ho-nan had taken the name "Steel-Spears," both of which were true or partly true,† but also that the Mongols had already taken Yen-ching, which was not true. On the other hand, his analysis of the condition and needs of the Sung defense system must strike one as very well informed.

In the steadily deepening crisis, Chen asserts three immediate objects of concern towards which policy must be directed: the refugees, the rebel groups in Shantung, and the "newly ascendant barbarians." He testifies to the large numbers of refugees seeking to enter, many of whom succeed in doing so despite the efforts of border officials to prevent them. But means are lacking to settle them and, turned away, they can easily become a hostile, rebel force. As far as we can tell, the rebels in Shantung, still fragmented into several groups, first began to launch large-scale operations at the end of 1213. Chen alludes to one who had assumed a royal title‡ and also to hostile actions committed along the border against the Sung. His concern is that, if, as he expects, they attain greater power and come to form an independent political force, they could act as an important swing group, potentially of use

---

* In particular and as the real theme of this memorial, Liu proposes modifications in the selection of officers to serve on the border, putting forth Ou-yang Hsiu's ideas on the subject as the best. He urges more flexibility be permitted officers, including in the selection of subordinates, and that they (i.e., professionals) be placed over his proposed militia. That Liu was highly concerned about getting good military, rather than good literati, leadership over the army is shown by his later memorial complaining that officers in the Yangtze garrisons were being demoted for clerical mistakes. For important excerpts of the memorial as a whole, see *Hsi-shan wen-chi* 41.10a – 11b.

† *HTCTC* 160 (pp. 4328 – 29), mentions Hsi-Hsia attacks, some successful, in the northwest. As for the rebels, it was Li Ch'üan himself who was called "Steel-Spear" because his great strength enabled him to use one. See his biography in *SS*476 and *CSPM* 87 (p. 759). But perhaps the name was applied to his men too.

‡ This could not have been Yang An-erh (cf. above note, p. 225) who did arrogate to himself a royal title but not until the fifth month. It may, however, have been one Hao Pa who is mentioned in *TCKC* 25.2a and *CYTC, i-chi*, 19.16a as having taken such action and who was captured and executed in 1214.

if they can be won over to Sung but highly dangerous if they join the outer barbarians against Chin. Indeed, Sung would be hard pressed to resist a continued movement southward by such combined forces.

In Chen's view the circumstances created by the emergence of the Mongols correspond precisely with those attendant on the rise of the Jürchen against Liao. At that time discerning individuals realized from the outset that the Jürchen would have designs on all of China, for, though these two rivals were both barbarians, "those accustomed to peace were easy to handle but those at the peak of their power could not easily be brought under rein." Now, conquest of the Chin will not satisfy the new barbarian whose appetite is that of the wolf, not that of man.* Moreover, his power promises to swell through the recruitment of former Chin officials, convinced of the defeat of their own leaders and eager to save their own skins. In turn the new power in the north will surely make extortionate demands on the Sung, seeking to place it in the same unfavorable relationship which it occupied vis-à-vis the Jürchen. Compliance with those demands will make it impossible for Sung truly to reestablish an independent status, while refusal will lead to war. Hence, using the earlier, tragic sequence of events as a mirror, the Sung now must obviously prepare to face the same grave dangers.

While Chen was surely eager to put before the Emperor his analysis of the political situation, he was perhaps equally concerned to advance his ideas on military policy.† It would take us too far afield to trace these in any detail, but the objectives of his proposal, his observations on local conditions, and his criticisms provide a good indication of what the Sung conceived their capabilities and options to be. In the main, Chen's idea is to restore the economic health and military potential of the Huai region, pursuing thus the proposal made by Liu Yüeh and sharply attacking the militarily conservative view which held that the best protection lay in taking refuge behind the Yangtze. He resurrects the strategy proposed by Li Kang in the mid-twelfth century calling for the disposition of a thick network of small posts along the frontier which, backed by a large central garrison for the region, can absorb

---

* One of the most deeply held myths about barbarians in China, especially in this period, was that they were fundamentally insatiable – whether by nature or by culture is not clear. The fact that several decades of peaceful coexistence between Chin and Sung belied this notion does not seem to have bothered Chen.

† Chen's exchange with the Emperor, as recorded in *SHY* 186:29, p. 48, reveals that some steps had already been taken along the border, so that one can assume Chen is speaking too with these in mind.

loyalists from the north and solidify the defense line.* Increased regional authority, in the Huai, at Hsiang-yang and at Chiang-ling, is needed, and Chen urges the appointment of high-ranking central officials to manage these key responsibilities.† Since more manpower is required, the 100,000 and more troops stationed along the Yangtze must be moved up. However, the Huai region is, from his own observation, so thoroughly inundated that all markers and boundaries have disappeared and therefore, is in need of vast reclamation efforts. Hence, economic reconstruction goes hand in hand with military measures. Chen is at his most vigorous in condemning those who would maintain the principal line of defense along the Yangtze ("like letting someone put his hands on one's throat") and who, having neglected the region north of the Yangtze, are prepared to abandon it at the drop of a hat. The wise policy, on the contrary, is to rehabilitate it and make it the same kind of strong base of operations that the Wei valley was for Chou and Ch'in. This is, incidentally, merely implying the possibility of territorial gain by historical analogy, as expansive as Chen becomes about future prospects. He goes on to make a final point which needs no elaboration but is of special interest for our general topic. He complains about the state of Sung intelligence on developments in the north and urges that top priority be given to obtaining accurate, up-to-date information ("The true facts must be reported and what *is* reported must be true").

Chen's stated position was, by reference implicitly to that of Shih Mi-yüan's ministry and explicitly to that of the "fortress Yangtze" school, moderately aggressive. Yet it makes no more than oblique reference to recovery of the north and it is distinguished by its relatively limited program of building up the Huai region. In other words, the main impulse was defensive. This most strongly reflects the recent humiliating defeat in the 1206—8 war and to considerable degree the overall experience of Southern Sung. It must also reflect the fragility of Sung's advance position along the Huai. At the other end of the spectrum of opinion stood those who, more sanguine about the possibility of recovering the north (or part of it), stressed the strength of loyalist sentiment among the populace across the border. Probably one such was Li Chih, a member of the abortive new year mission to Chin late in 1213. Li returned to court urging upon the emperor extensive military preparations in view of Chin's imminent collapse and the

---

* The proposal to which Chen evidently refers was submitted by Li Kang in 1135. It is summarized in Li's official biography (*SS* 359.3a—4a) and in *HNYL* 87 (pp. 2832—34).

† A fourth major defense zone was Szechwan to which Chen had directed attention toward the end of 1213. See *Hsi-shan wen-chi* 3.2b—12b.

continued strong loyalism of people in the north.* Of course, this issue could also be used as a tactic by those officials who wanted a more forceful policy. But it was certainly not merely being so used later in 1214 when Liu Yüeh, who had turned again to the refugee problem and whose position was otherwise quite close to Chen's, called for a scrutiny of both Chinese and barbarian refugees. ". . . If in their hearts they have truly come over to us, therein lies hope for recovery!"† At that, Chen himself moved increasingly in that direction.

Though the turmoil in the north multiplied the sources of concern, the focus of Sung policy necessarily remained the Chin and in 1214 the issue which dominated policy considerations was the annual subsidy. Reconstruction of the developments which led up to a crucial policy debate and decision late in the year leaves some shadowy areas, but the main course seems clear. It is necessary to note that the actual transfer of funds (i.e., silver and silk) making up the subsidy was accomplished on the border at Hsü-i late in the spring. Following the precedent set in dealing with Liao, this task was normally undertaken by local financial officials rather than by envoys appointed at court as in cases of formal communications.‡ The disruption which interrupted the movement of envoys to the respective courts seems likewise to have disturbed handling of the subsidy at the border (unless it was a matter of sheer administrative incompetence). Writing in the fall of 1214, Ts'ao Yen-yüeh describes problems which arose on at least two occasions.[14] In one case the Sung officials were permitted to cross the border and deposit the funds, but they were given no formal acknowledgment (*kuo-shu*) for them. In the other the officials reached the border, but did not find the proper Chin authorities to whom to hand over the subsidy and were obliged to wait at great length, during which time the goods involved suffered extensive damage. We do not know

---

* See *SHY* 186:29, p. 49. There was on this occasion an interesting exchange, the emperor checking with Li as to whether he had *personally* heard evidences of loyalism — he claims he had — or whether they were mere rumors. The emperor put off Li's plea for immediate large-scale military efforts on the grounds that funds were not available. Li then urged him to draw upon funds from his personal treasury (*nei-t'ang-ch'ien*), whereupon the emperor returned that those funds were already inadequate. Little biographical information is available on Li, son of the noted historian Li Tao and himself author of the chronicle *Huang-Sung shih-ch'ao kang-yao*. As we have seen, he prefaced Liu Yüeh's works in 1222.

† *Hsi-shan wen-chi* 41.13a: *wen-shen hua-i, min-hsin chi kuei, hui-fu tsai ch'i chung i.*

‡ The original treaty in 1123 is not very explicit on the actual transfer of funds: see Thiele, *Der Abschluss eines Vertrages* (Wiesbaden: Franz Steiner, 1971), pp. 135, 137, 254 – 255. However, Liao precedent was followed, on which see Schwarz-Schilling, *Der Friede von Shan-yüan* (Wiesbaden: Franz Steiner, 1959), pp. 57, 139. For the 1141 treaty, which stipulated Hsü-i as the place of transfer, see Franke, "Treaties between Sung and Chin," *Etudes Song*, 1st ser. (1970) p. 78.

when these incidents occurred, but we can speculate that they came at the beginning of 1212 and 1213, respectively. We must assume that in the second incident reported either the funds were not turned over at all or they were turned over in drastically reduced quantity.

Partly because of these practical difficulties but surely also as a tentative departure from a policy of amity, the Sung government did not send any subsidy for 1214. No information is available on this decision—not altogether surprising in view of contemporary complaints about the lack of open discussion at court*—but we do have a memorial by Liu Yüeh from early in the year which refers to the necessity of finding a proper response to anticipated Chin pressure.† Accordingly, in the third month—well over a month was always calculated for travelling time—a Chin envoy appeared in Hang-chou demanding payment of *two* years' subsidy. He was put off with the remarkably lame excuse that the Sung were having problems with transport because of dried-up canals; he was above all not given a forthright indication of a change in policy.‡ The envoy evidently brought with him instructions for an immediate response should the Sung reaction prove negative. Accordingly, eight days after his first appearance, time spent no doubt awaiting a reply, he announced that Chin was suspending its congratulatory mission for the new year.§ In fact, it did not, but the intent of the move was certainly to threaten a rupture in relations. In considering the Sung position, it is essential to bear in mind that 1213 finished disastrously for the Chin and that throughout the opening months of 1214 their capital itself was under siege. The Sung were, therefore, content to bide their time, awaiting the outcome.

Unable to maintain the siege with adequate rigor, the Mongols, by agreement with the Chin, released it and withdrew in the fourth month. Thereupon the entire Chin court moved in the following month to K'ai-feng, its southern capital, which was regarded (correctly as it turned out) as a strategically and economically more tenable location.**

---

* *Hsi-shan wen-chi* 5.14a—15a. This item is a "discussion of precedents" (*ku-shih*). Time and again Chen returns to the issue of "open discussion," *kung-lun*, and its importance for the health of the state. Also, cf. *Yün-chuang chi* (Seikadō) 3.18a—19a.

† *Hsi-shan wen chi* 41.11b—12b. Chen's prefatory remarks alluding to recent events, strongly suggest an early 1214 date for this memorial.

‡ See Chen's later criticism of this, *Hsi-shan wen-chi* 5.22b.

§ See *SS* 39.10b, and *TCKC* 24.5a, for these appearances of the Chin envoy. *CS* 62 makes no mention of either this or of a subsequent demand for payment.

** The move was undertaken in the fifth month and announced to Sung in the seventh. See *CS* 15.4b—5a; *TCKC* 24.3b—5a; *SS* 39.11a. Also, Martin, *Conquest of North China*, pp. 171—173; Franke, *Geschichte*, 4, 270—271.

Assuming continued severe pressure by the Mongols, this meant that nothing less than a remarkable Chin recovery could save it from losing its northern dominions altogether and becoming a seriously truncated state, confined largely to Honan. When news of the shift reached the Sung court, a controversy soon developed over its significance for Sung policy. Whereas it could hardly be interpreted as other than a demonstration of weakness, questions inevitably arose about whether it was necessarily in Sung's interest to hasten Chin's downfall and, if so, whether it could do so with impunity. For it should not escape notice that the bulk of Chin power lay now virtually at Sung's doorstep, and it was not well known how much of it had survived. The issue of the subsidy served as the pivot of debate. Chen Te-hsiu's memorial of the seventh month has traditionally been held best to represent the true patriotic — we would say the hard-line — position.*

This statement falls into three main sections: Chen begins with an analysis of the current situation and its implications; he moves on to a set of general recommendations whose aim is to achieve "independence" (*tzu-li*); and he undertakes a lengthy consideration of military and strategic matters. He emphasizes that Chin's move southward is a desperate one which cannot bring about any real improvement in its overall situation. One of two consequences is certain to follow: either the "Tatars" will conquer and hold Chin's territories, becoming Sung's immediate neighbor, or North China will collapse into anarchy, divided among rebels. Since neither of these eventualities would be welcome to Sung, the fall of the ancient enemy should not give rise to any false sense of security. At the same time, it is remiss and irresponsible to continue buying peace from the Jürchen and thus with Sung's wealth to strengthen them or the ultimately more powerful successors. Chen returns to his basic view that, if Sung takes the necessary steps, it will achieve such strength that it can handle any situation which arises in the north. He calls this taking an independent course — i.e., free, in the words of Washington, "from all foreign entanglements."

There is no doubt, however, that he is talking about a more, not a less, demanding policy. Though the recommendations he advances to achieve "independence" ring of platitudinous Confucian wisdom, they were intended for genuine application. For example, two of them — the employment of the worthy and (the Emperor's) submitting to the coun-

---

* *Hsi-shan wen-chi* 3.17b—29a. An excerpt has been reproduced in *CSPM* 86 (p. 748), essentially the same as that in *HTCTC* 160 (pp. 4338—39), which Franke has translated in *Geschichte*, 4, pp. 271—272. It has also quoted in *Hsü-Sung pien-nien tzu-chih t'ung-chien* 14 (p. 184) (TSCC ed.), and reproduced entirely in *Liang-ch'ao kang-mu pei-yao* 14.11b—22b (Taipei: Wen-hai, 1967 reprint).

sel of officials — though of lesser special interest to us, were probably criticisms of Shih Mi-yüan and his mode of operation. When it comes to "proper conduct of affairs of government" (*hsiu cheng-shih*), Chen makes clear that he means full mobilization of the resources of the state to achieve superiority over the enemy. As so often, his example is Kou Chien of ancient times. He speaks at greatest length and most pertinently on the importance of gaining popular support (*shou chung-hsin*). He devotes considerable attention to the population of the Huai Valley who have been subjected to hard experiences and, accordingly, for whom a number of steps should be taken, both to improve conditions and to strengthen their resolve. But he is equally concerned, for the first time I believe, about the loyalists in the north. Distressed to find Sung border officials continuing to turn back refugees and those who have revolted against the Chin, he urged humane and generous treatment toward them — though it is not clear precisely what disposition of them he intends. What emerges as his real concern is that Sung, by virtue of its policies along the border, cultivate *a good image* among the population to the north as a whole. In this connection he explicitly mentions, also for the first time, the possibility of recovery.[15] It is, incidentally, no particular surprise that in this elitist society "obtaining popular support" is largely a tactical affair, a policy designed to help the state better to achieve its ends.

Most of the remainder of this memorial is taken up with a thoroughgoing discussion of the military situation, its prospects and needs. Chen, it is fair to say, had no illusions about the consequences of the policies he advocated; in the end things may well be decided on the battlefield, against which eventuality preparations must be made. He is highly critical of the condition of the army, and again, he turns to Li Kang for inspiration. His strategic analysis is impressive both in detail and conception, gainsaying any charge that he was an irresponsible critic. This analysis, by adopting a Chin perspective (still the defensive response), pinpoints the key locations to garrison and fortify, and naturally it still assumes a main line of defense along the Huai. It is worthwhile to note that individuals of Chen's persuasion (there have been many parallels since) felt that Southern Sung's relatively poor performance in defending itself in the past resulted from no basic weakness but rather from its failure to use the right defense. Measures initiated or plans proposed under Kao-tsung and Hsiao-tsung *would* have worked, but the peace treaties led to their being abandoned. Clearly, there was strong need for such a rationale, politically and psychologically.

In conclusion, Chen outlines three policy alternatives in terms of the familiar Chinese best-acceptable-worst formula. The best course of action would be to cut off the subsidy and use that resource in a broad self-strengthening effort. Failing this, one may call first for general discussion of the issues and then decide accordingly. The worst course, tantamount to none at all, would be to continue under present arrangements, that is, to go on honoring the treaty. "We must now take advantage of the enemy's collapse to plan an independent course and, even if his momentary survival limits our options, we must at least provide for our own security."[16]

Thus Chen's position had hardened considerably since the beginning of the year, primarily because of Chin's displacement to K'ai-feng. Earlier he was only tentatively calling for a re-examination of policy toward Chin; now he urges an open and complete break. Implicit in his argument, which unquestionably represented one strong current of opinion in officialdom,[16a] was the view that the Chin court's unilateral decision to relocate further south (and at the Northern Sung capital to boot) released Sung both morally and legally from its treaty commitments. It seems to have gained momentary ascendency at court, for a decision to suspend subsidy payments was made immediately after his memorial was received.* But views on the subject continued to be aired, including some altogether opposed to Chen's. One such was that advanced by Ch'iao Hsing-chien from his post in Huai-hsi. Ch'iao argued that, since the "Tatars" were already strong enough to crush the Chin, they, rather than the latter, were the main source of concern. Hence, Sung should endeavor to maintain Chin as a buffer before this new power. Resorting to ancient phraseology, he warns that "without any lips, the teeth become cold."† Writing shortly afterwards, Ts'ao Yen-yüeh, though accepting with some reservations the pursuit of normal treaty relations with Chin, nevertheless is contemptuous of those who would adopt an antagonistic tone and who talk of recovering the north.[17] At the root of these contrasting views lay differing assessments of Chin's ability to survive under the new circumstances. The hard-liners downgraded these chances; the moderates regarded them as serious. From the point of view of subsequent history, neither side was flatly wrong. But it is worth remarking that there

---

* The decision (following the date of Chen's memorial by two days) is recorded in *SS* 39.11a, and *TCKC* 24.5a.

† *Ssu-ch'ao wen-chien lu, chia,* 26a (Chih-pu-tsu ts'ung-shu ed.). Chiao's biography, *SS* 417.1a-b, quotes a pertinent document from this period put in such abbreviated form that it is impossible to tell whether this is the memorial in question or not.

was a good deal of wishful thinking behind the hard-liners' position and an emotional component which precluded even considering positive action for the sake of Chin's survival.

Shih Mi-yüan and his advisers were not yet prepared to risk an open confrontation and they may even have been persuaded of the validity of the buffer strategy. A second appearance by a Chin envoy to demand payment of the subsidy, in the eighth month, may also have played a role.[18] Amid calls for open discussion and exchanges of views in order to arrive at the best policy, preparations got underway to resume (or continue) diplomatic contact.* Things came to a head in the eleventh month when the appointment of an envoy to go on a new year's mission became publicly known. This was taken simultaneously to mean that subsidy payments were being resumed. The students of the universities in the capital, showing typical disdain for realities in favor of principles, protested vociferously and even demanded the execution of Ch'iao Hsing-chien, who had become regarded as spokesman for the position of compromise.† The memorial of protest by Liu Yüeh, identified as one of the leaders of the opposition, has come down to us, and again we have a long revealing statement by Chen Te-hsiu. But we have no exposition of the official view which must be largely discerned via the criticisms of its opponents.

Liu's and Chen's positions are, of course, very close, but, as their arguments differ, each of them merits examination. Liu assumes that Chin is finished, the only question being who will succeed to its territories, the Mongols now dominant in Ho-pei or the rebels holding Shan-tung.‡ Sung's primary concern, therefore, lies not so much in the immediate consequences of resuming subsidy payments, humiliating in itself though they may be, but in complications to which it will lead in the future. Whoever succeeds Chin will expect to succeed to its subsidy from Sung as well (the Liao-Chin parallel being only too obvious), all the more because the destruction in Ho-pei and the famine in Honan will make the wealth of the south appear that much more attractive. Liu dismisses the view that Chin can act as a buffer as already refuted by its move southward, and by the same token he dismisses

---

* Ts'ao Yen-yüeh's memorial in *Ch'ang-ku chi* 9.8a – 9a, dated the ninth month of this year, was written in response to a directive to authorities at Hsü-i to make preparations for the pursuit of diplomatic relations.

† Several sources record the appointment of envoys and the protests it provoked: *SS* 39.11b; *Ssu-ch'ao chien-wen lu, chia*, 26a; *Sung-shih ch'üan-wen hsü-tzu-chih t'ung-chien* (Taipei: Wen-hai, 1969 reprint) 5, p. 2400; and *Liang-ch'ao kang-mu pei-yao* 14.24b.

‡ See *Yün-chuang chi* (Seikadō ed.) 3.17a – 18a; *Hsi-shan wen-chi* 41.13a – 14a. Significantly, Liu's remarks on the buffer theory are missing from the former text.

the danger of Chin's going to war over the issue of the subsidy. But Sung must arm itself more vigorously. Indeed, he asks, how can we expect to defend ourselves against the "Tatars" or the rebels if we now cannot even do so against a shattered enemy? His recommendation is that a policy be adopted which will make "substance" (i.e., reality) and "appearance" conform, substance being defined as a stout defense and appearance as a rupture of relations with Chin.* (Actually, rather than *not* conforming, it appears that they already did so, but in reverse fashion to that desired by Liu.) Yet for all his zeal in propounding a hard policy, he urges that no open break yet be made and that the court procrastinate until conditions in the north become clear.

Chen's memorial, which constitutes a powerful, if implicit, critique of the regime, was written in response to a new appointment, a situation which normally called for a perfunctory refusal of the appointment (followed by others and all equally ignored).† Though his biography tells us that, like those of others, he eagerly sought a provincial post out of absolute distaste for Shih Mi-yüan, it is likely that he was being exiled for his outspokenness. (Liu Yüeh probably escaped this fate because of his advanced age.) In another year he was shifted to a more distant (though still important) post as the apparent consequence of yet another blunt memorial and was not to return to service at court until the accession of a new emperor a decade later. This memorial of late 1214 is set out in a format of five admonitions to the Emperor, each of which represented in Chen's eyes real or potential weaknesses facing the head of state.

Under the first, on not forgetting the duty of removing the shame of the Emperor's predecessors, Chen exposes the view that Chin-Sung enmity is absolute and eternal. It does not, as in other cases he cites, admit of qualification or compromise. Thus, on purely logical grounds, so to speak, continued relations with Chin are out of the question. He again lays out three alternative courses of action, obviously becoming more bellicose all the time. The first and best would be for Sung to gird its loins and attack the enemy. A reasonable alternative would be to set up a strong defense, break relations, and hold steady awaiting opportunities to exploit. The worst would be to remain conciliatory, thereby bringing aid to the enemy. In point of fact, Chen hedges on the first, confessing that Sung is not yet strong enough to

---

* His formulation here is *pi te sheng-shih chien-ch'üan.*

† *Hsi-shan wen-chi* 4.4a – 10a. Note that *CSPM* 86 (pp. 751 – 752) affixes this memorial (in edited form) to a later one of late 1215 as though it were all a single memorial. Chen was at this time appointed Assistant Accounting and Fiscal Intendent for Chiang-tung.

carry the battle to the enemy and defeat him. Yet support can be drawn away and the populace stirred to action. In effect, then, his three alternatives are reduced to two. Like Liu, he attempts to dispel fears of Chin reprisal, asserting that it is not the fallen enemy whom we should hesitate to provoke but rather the new, powerful one.

A second admonition urges the emperor not to underrate the threat posed by the Mongols and the Shantung rebels. He alludes to current characterizations of the Mongols as "a small, ferocious tribe who have no territorial ambitions" and of the rebels as "small-time bastards whose schemes do not exceed the level of petty thieves." Such complacency, he finds, totally neglects the numerous examples from the past when powerful states emerged out of precisely such beginnings. Surprisingly, he is most anxious over the threat posed by the rebels despite the fact that they were virtually all Chinese. Were the people of North China, who have been left leaderless, to turn *en masse* to the rebels and thus give rise to a new, independent power, this, he warns, would be the worst of all possible calamities. Why was Chen so alarmed over this prospect? Conceivably because a competing Chinese state would render unity against the barbarians all the more difficult and possibly, as a state with native leadership, even compete with Sung in the south.* He goes on to ask that strategies be developed to forestall this eventuality.

Of the remaining admonitions — do not trust to fortune alone, take heed of cajolery,† and do not disregard the importance of open discussion — only the first is of particular interest to us. Chen's remarks here, while exaggerated, give some idea of the temper at court. He claims that in their planning the high ministers were fully counting on Chin's survival, a point which testifies to the strength at court of the buffer view. According to Chen, when news unfavorable to Chin arrived, these ministers refused to lend it any credence; but when the news was good, they accepted it without reserve. Chen is particularly critical of their reliance on the intelligence supplied by border officials, whom he had already once in this memorial attacked as unreliable and too often complaisant. As examples, he cites reports to the effect that the "Tatars" were on the point of making peace with Chin, that the

---

* Chen reports a recent incident in which an emissary with false credentials, who remained unidentified, made a reconnaissance of the Sung coast and then returned northward (7a). He implies that the figure was associated with the rebels, and speculates that he was examining the state of Sung defenses.

† By cajolery here Chen means specifically reliance on portents and signs to reach decisions and make policy. He had earlier, late in 1213 (*Hsi-shan wen-chi* 3.2b – 12b), addressed himself to the same subject, offering a different interpretation of "falling stars" from one then current.

rebels were prepared to put themselves under Sung orders, and that the "Tatars" were willing to return Yen-ching to Sung. On the larger question of Chin's fortunes, Chen's position is that policy must be fixed regardless of what the enemy does or what happens to him. One does not rely on contingencies.

It is impossible to ascertain what impact these protests had in inner court counsels since the full intentions behind the decision to maintain diplomatic contact cannot be known. Chen's removal from court at this time surely suggests that not all of his views were welcome there. Yet the emperor and his advisers had evidently determined on a harder line toward Chin which still, by avoiding a full rupture in relations, would minimize the risk of provoking hostilities. Hence, not only was the congratulatory mission for the new year dispatched,[19] but also one arriving in the third month (1215) for the Chin monarch's birthday.* (These and all subsequent missions, of course, had only to go as far as K'ai-feng.) On the latter occasion, the Sung envoys, inappropriately in the eyes of the Chin ruler, raised the question of the subsidy, indicating that Sung would be prepared to continue payments at the level stipulated in the 1165 treaty (i.e., 250,000 taels of silver and bolts of silk, as against the current 300,000). Since nothing more is heard of such negotiation, it is clear that the Chin refused and that Sung continued, in effect, to disavow this aspect of the treaty. The expectation may well have been that Chin would refuse. Yet, had it accepted, Sung would almost certainly have fulfilled its commitment or else endangered the peace which it still so earnestly desired; hence, this maneuver at least permitted the Sung to stall further while awaiting a clarification of developments in the north — precisely what Liu Yüeh had advocated. In the meantime they continued to observe the formal diplomatic communications, punctiliously sending envoys on every expected occasion until the spring of 1217 when hostilities began.[20]

Chin, too, not yet prepared to face Sung as a belligerent, maintained its obligations in this respect.[21] The reason was simply that its fortunes continued to decline. The fall of Yen-ching in mid-1215 was a major political and psychological setback, and, as the Mongols established a firm base in Ho-pei, they continued to range widely over Chin's dominions north of the Yellow River. The Shantung revolts persisted,

---

* See *CS* 62.28a; cf. *SS* 39.11b. The Sung envoys were Ting Yü and Hou Chung-hsin, neither of whom has an official biography and about whom little seems to be known. Ting subsequently held an important post in Szechwan, negotiating with Hsi-Hsia for an anti-Chin alliance which was never quite realized (see *SS* 40. 5a, 6a).

following a rhythm largely determined by the scale and frequency of government attempts to suppress them.* The Hsia, too, continued their attacks on the west which, if not uniformly successful, at least absorbed additional Chin military strength. Little Chin territory, in short, seemed free from one predator or another. In a final relevant document from this period by Chen Te-hsiu, we find these conditions amply reflected.† Chen, writing from his post in Chiang-tung, alludes to a recent Chin decree which itself exposes their perilous circumstances. But for him the news is bad all over. As he writes at length on internal as well as external affairs, his tone is more strident and his outlook gloomier. No doubt embittered by his removal into the provinces, he mounts a vigorous attack against Shih Mi-yüan's ministry by laying out ten fundamental "faults" (*shih*) which led to the collapse of Northern Sung and which he found were dismayingly reflected in contemporary conditions.²² Of high interest for the historiography of Southern Sung vis-à-vis its predecessor, this diatribe is not least remarkable for its bluntness.

Turning to the external situation, Chen seems convinced that the "new slaves" (*hsin-lu*) will indeed succeed the Chin in the north. In view of this, he warns, Sung's experience with Chin upon its conquest of Liao must be taken as a lesson and great care exercised in dealing with them. Nevertheless, he adjudges Chin still to be the most critical factor in the overall situation; hence, the conduct of diplomatic relations with this old adversary remains paramount. Projecting likely diplomatic moves by Chin, including the promise to return portions of old Sung territory, Chen calls for the court to prepare contingency responses in order to avoid embroilment either in a war with Chin or in the struggle for the north. He goes on to level sharp and specific criticism for the court's handling of these matters so far. First, it has placed itself at long-range diplomatic disadvantage by not breaking clearly with Chin on the subsidy question. By relating its suspension of the subsidy to the Chin court's removal to K'ai-feng, it has implicitly committed itself to resuming these payments should Chin recover Yen-ching. Further, it did not properly justify the suspension of tribute on the grounds that Chin failed to fulfill its original treaty obligations as per the 1123 treaty (Chen here disregarded subsequent treaties and ninety-two years of history). Instead, the pretext given by the court— transport problems—was such as to provoke recriminations from the

---

* By now the main rebel band was known as the "red coats" (*hung-ao*). See *CS* 14.12a, 14a, 17b, 19b.

† *Hsi-shan wen-chi* 5.16b—26b. The date indicated here for this memorial is, however, certainly incorrect. I follow *CSPM* 86 (p. 749), in placing it in the eleventh month of Chia-ting 8 (1215), which is supported by Wei's obituary notice.

Chin and to make Sung a laughing-stock among the northern rebels. Secondly, it has dreadfully mishandled the problem of the northern loyalists, adopting harsh measures along the border which alienate them instead of attempting to win them over. Discouraged, Chen does not even broach the idea of recovery. More generally, he takes the emperor's high ministers to task for their complacency: they are deluded into believing that, if Chin survives, it will act as a shield and, even if it does not and the north falls into chaos, none of the competing powers will threaten Sung. On the contrary, along with rectification of government internally and the adoption of sound external policies, the court must proceed with a military buildup. This was nothing new; but the brief pep talk Chen inserts, demonstrating historically that the south, well-prepared, *can* hold off forces from the north, is noteworthy, a measure perhaps of Sung's less than full confidence in its military capability.[23]

Chen was not being entirely fair to his superiors in Hang-chou, but while discounting his exaggerations, we must acknowledge that he put his finger on the real issues facing Sung policy-makers at the time. In 1214 Sung had seized on the first glaring signs of Chin collapse, the investment of its capital and subsequent relocation of its court, to discontinue the material commitment it had long borne vis-à-vis the northern regime. More than merely eliminating the financial burden, it sought — mindful of the dangers inherent in Northern Sung's original rivalry with the Jürchen over Ho-pei — explicitly to disengage itself from the current struggle over North China. Yet, it did not wish to provoke to war an enemy for whose arms, signs of distress notwithstanding, it maintained a healthy respect. From 1214 to 1217, therefore, the stickiest problems for Sung policy-makers were posed by rebel activity across the border and the obvious need to make military preparations. With regard to the former, we have seen a highly ambiguous reaction thus far: alarm that the rebels may become so strong as to threaten even the south; fascination with the possibility that, won over, they may provide the means for recovery of the north. To the extent that Sung wished to honor its treaty agreement and thus avoid a confrontation with Chin, it was obliged to refuse entry into its own territory to any rebel.* In the interests of internal security and lacking means to make any practical disposition, it may not have wanted to admit these people anyway. Thus we find instances through 1216 of rebels, who were by another definition really loyalists, being turned

---

* All the treaties between the two sides included explicit agreement not to harbor or admit each other's lawbreakers. See Franke, "Treaties between Sung and Chin," *Etudes Song*, 1st ser. (1970) pp. 61 and 63.

back at the border.* But this raised a number of difficulties as a memorial from Ts'ao Yen-yüeh from 1216 indicates.†

Ts'ao was at that time Fiscal Supervisor of the Circuit of Li
(northern Ssu-ch'uan), bordering Chin's western territories. Rebellion
there against the Chin, centering on Ch'in-chou, was of long standing
and, because of more pressing matters in the east, had never been
effectively suppressed. At the same time, the Sung stubbornly refused
to permit any of the rebels to come south. As a result, rebel groups,
indeed in one case a whole population, lived there at length outside the
pale of Chin authority. Ts'ao indicates the presence of 100,000 such
"rebels," of whom 30,000 were fighting men, not far from the Sung
border. He relates having made contact with them and describes the
severe shortage of food from which they were suffering. He himself
sent them grain, ordered border officials to make whatever grain stores
available they could, and gave a tax break to merchants who would
sell out there.

Ts'ao's main preoccupation is to show what problems this situation poses for Sung policy and to suggest an alternative himself. At the
moment, he writes, this rebel population is still somewhat removed
from Sung lines. However, if they should move further south, they will
begin to make contact and Sung officials will have to take some action
one way or the other. Sung forces in his opinion are inadequate to
resist them should they advance in force. Now, by direct allusion Ts'ao
shows that he is fully aware of the government's unwillingness to break
the treaty in giving succor to the rebels, and he also confesses that at
the moment these people are *mere* rebels, no better than the Red Eye-
brows or Yellow Turbans. But he points out that they use the Sung
calendar and count themselves Sung subjects, and he believes that with
organization and discipline they can become a valuable source of
support.‡ Beyond that he fears that, were the Sung to refuse them all
aid, they would become a dangerous adversary. The solution he pro-

---

* Chen's discussion in the memorial we have just considered is itself testimony here
(see *Hsi-shan wen-chi* 5, esp. 23a). Specific cases are recorded of Sung's rejection of
bands seeking to submit in the west, an area which was evidently in a total state of flux;
see *SS* 39.12b and 13b. The case of Ch'eng Yen-hui is particularly regretted by Chen
as a worthy loyalist lost to the cause, while Ts'ao Yen-yüeh (see following) probably
makes reference to that of T'ang Chin and his group. When *CS* 50.2b, records the burning of the state's trade station at Ch'in-chou by "Sung people" in 1213, I assume the
perpetrators were one such group and were not, at least yet, acting under official Sung
sponsorship.

† *Ch'ang-ku chi* 11.12b — 14a. Both the context and Wei's epitaph make it clear that
the document dates from this time.

‡ Ts'ao, endeavoring to win his superiors over to his point of view, takes particular
pains to discredit earlier reports on the rebels, written according to him by mere *k'o-
chü shu-sheng* — "examination candidates."

poses is that a conciliatory policy be adopted which will permit aid to them, induce them to settle down, and keep them favorably disposed toward Sung until the shape of future events becomes clear.

Whether or not the government did adopt Ts'ao's proposal or any part of it we do not know. But it is clear that in some instances it was being drawn into an active role in affairs of the north and that its officials were taking action on their own which Chin could only have interpreted as hostile. In the east there is reason to believe that Sung authorities had long had a clandestine hand in the activities of rebels across the frontier. The key figure here is Li Ch'üan who from 1216 becomes the principal rebel chieftain and also for the next decade and more, the bane of Sung policy.* There is ample information on Li, but for this early stage it is particularly defective as to dates. Officially, he received Sung appointment in return for his formal allegiance at the beginning of 1218.[24] But Sung assistance dates from well before that, certainly from before the beginning of the war in 1217. Initially, it was at a time when Li's and other rebel bands were suffering severely from hunger (1215 or 1216?) that the authorities at Ch'u-chou made contact with them and put provisions at their disposal. This logistic support became a regular operation, probably contributing significantly to subsequent rebel ("loyalist") successes. Reports on it were sent up to Shih Mi-yüan who gave it his blessing but who insisted that it be handled with the greatest of delicacy to avoid a break with Chin.† It was, therefore, not without justification when the Chin monarch complained to Sung envoys at the outset of 1217 that Sung was in collusion with the rebels and thus acting in hostile fashion.[25]

No large-scale military preparations are evident on the Sung side during the years 1214 to 1217; clearly, there was not the slightest intention of entering the fray to the north. Yet defensive preparations must gradually have been undertaken in view of the highly unstable circumstances, even if they did not satisfy the demands of contemporary

---

* Li has a two-part biography in *SS* 476—477; also see Franke, *Geschichte*, 4, pp. 273ff. Two recent accounts in Chinese attempt positive reassessments of Li's career, Shen Ch'i-wei, *Sung-Chin chan-cheng shih-lüeh* [Outline History of Wars between Sung and Chin] (Wuhan: Jen-min, 1958), pp. 166—172, where Li emerges as a hero of the people, and Sun, *Meng-ku han-chün chi han-wen-hua yen-chiu*, pp. 11—43, a lengthy and serious study.

† This reconstruction is based on *SS* 476.2a—3a, and *Sung-shih i* (Taipei: Wen-hai, 1967 reprint), 31.8b. These sources imply that such assistance from Sung authorities came later than I indicate here, but surely Shih would not have been concerned about secrecy had this activity not begun before the outbreak of hostilities. The key figure on the scene, acting as liaison between the rebels and the Sung court, was Ying Ch'un-chih, prefect of Ch'u-chou, about whom additional information is scarce.

critics.* In fact, as time wore on, an increasing need for them was probably felt, for the Chin regime, following its removal to K'ai-feng, not only continued to show signs of life but, by late 1216, even began to recover ground.† Hence, when a debate on defensive strategy was engaged at the Sung court in the fall of that year, it was far from an academic exercise. General fears that the chaos in the north might spill over into the south seem to have given way to specific concern over the possibility of aggression from the Chin who were, of course, no longer under the restraint of a Sung subsidy. The debate pitted the proponents of a strong line along the Huai against those advocating primary reliance on the Yangtze. Reflecting a split which surfaced frequently in the discussions of these critical years, the two sides were essentially divided over the feasibility of defending the Huai region. The "fortress Yangtze" group maintaining that it was indefensible, called for the adoption of policies acknowledging this fact. Their opponents, on the contrary, argued that defense of the Huai region was necessary precisely in order to protect the Yangtze settlements. The debate eventually resolved into one over the proper social and administrative policies to be followed in the regions most exposed to outside attack. Though no new military measures as such are announced, reference is made to preparations which had already been made in the forts along the Huai. If anything more than police measures, these would have represented another breach of the treaty by Sung. Above all, the debate is noteworthy for showing the continuing strength of an extreme defensive mentality which, despite the recent startling changes in the north, still assumed all initiative to lie with the potential outside aggressor. The Huai-line proponents, to be sure, were more sanguine, and of these some at least must have recognized that any Sung gains in the north could only come from having a heavily armed forward line.‡

---

*For an example, see the moderate steps taken in 1213 at Liu-ho, a key point on the route between the Huai and the Yangtze, in *SHY* 174:6, p. 8; but there are few records of any kind of military measures during these years. Chen Te-hsiu finished up his late 1215 memorial (note p. 242), as we have seen, with a plea for military build-up. In Liu Yüeh's final relevant memorials, dating from early 1215, he devotes most of his attention to military matters (see *Hsi-shan wen-chi* 41.14b—15b). Further, a memorial from 1216 by Yüan Hsieh calls for serious military preparations. See *Chieh-chai chi* (Pai-pu ts'ung-shu ed.) 1.3b—7b; also excerpted in *Hsi-shan wen-chi* 47.9b—11a. Ch'iao Hsing-chien, as indicated by *SS* 417.1a-b, also appealed for new military measures.

†See Chin's gains as recorded in *HTCTC* 160 (pp. 4354—58).

‡*SHY* 186:29, pp. 49—50, the only source for this debate, does no more than summarize the positions taken and the arguments advanced. It indicates no advocates by name nor is Chin spelled out as the specific enemy. Yet, as it is clear that a systematic attack is projected, only the Chin were in a position to deliver it.

This defensiveness probably also explains the relatively late date at which Sung entered into contact with the new force in North China, the Mongols. An underlying reason was an intense distaste for attempting positive cooperation of any sort with barbarians, a heritage of the Sung-Jürchen imbroglio nearly a century earlier. The first attested contact on an official level came only in 1221, out of which came the earliest extant work on the Mongols in Chinese, the *Meng-ta pei-lu*.* From this we learn that there had already been contact on at least one occasion, probably shortly before, but complete obscurity surrounds it.† Elsewhere we are told that the Mongols tried twice during the early phase of their invasion of China to reach the Sung court.‡ On one occasion, apparently in 1213, a mission nearly reached the Sung border but was cut off and captured by Chin authorities. On the other, three Mongol representatives appeared in Hao-chou early in 1214, bearing documents, a map on silk, and a request from the "Tatar prince Cinggis" for a military alliance. Border officials were at the time, however, under the strictest injunctions not to admit or give permission for further movement to anyone without first obtaining higher authorization (testimony to Sung's rigorous observance of the treaty provisions at this point). By the time this was procured the representatives had already left. Assuming that these events are not purely apocryphal, an initiative from the Sung vis-à-vis the Mongols might have been anticipated, for the sake of intelligence if nothing else. We cannot, of course, be certain that none was taken at this time.

In the meantime, information on the Mongols, both accurate and otherwise, no doubt continued to filter through to the Sung. Refugees would have been the most frequent source, rebels along the border, too. Such reports also gave rise to written accounts such as the *Nan-ch'ien-lu*.§ Knowledge of some sort must thus have been available on

---

* There has been some question of the precise authorship of this work but not of its authenticity. On this mission and one Chao Hung as probable author, see Wang Kuo-wei's colophons (dated 1925 – 26) to his annotated edition of the *Meng-ta pei-lu* (Meng-ku shih-liao ssu-chung ed.), also summarized by P. Pelliot in *T'oung-pao*, 26 (1929), pp. 165 – 67.

† See *Meng-ta pei-lu*, 1a (Meng-ku shih-liao ssu-chung ed.). One Su-pu-han is said already to have come to treat with Sung prior to 1221 (Cinggis dispatch of a Chu-pu-han being recorded in *The Secret History of the Mongols* but there said to have been blocked by the Chin). Wang in his 1925 colophon (see note above) suggests that Kou Meng-yü's mission to Cinggis (and Chao Meng's to Yen-ching) may have been in response to Su-pu-han's to Sung.

‡ Both of these events are recorded in *CYTC, i,* 19.12a-b, and *Liang-ch'ao kang-mu pei-yao* 14.2a – 3a. That of 1214 is also found in *TCKC* 24.2a-b. These accounts all obviously derive from the same source (cf. note, p. 248).

§ The *Nan-ch'ien-lu,* recounting the Chin court's move to the south, is a Southern Sung fake (see Wang, *Kuan-t'ang chi-lin* 15.30b) but one written not long after the events themselves. Extant, it can be found in the *Hsüeh-hai lei-pien.*

the Mongol army and Mongol occupation policy. Perhaps, too, the fame of their gifted and dynamic leader had spread at an early date. Yet, even if we assume the Sung knew a good deal more about the Mongols in 1217 than they had in 1211, no such growth of knowledge is reflected in our writers. They seem only too prepared to deal in stereotypes, satisfied that the Mongols are simply another wild tribe from the outer fringes — wild because removed from the center of civilization — and like the others warlike and greedy.* Down to the end of 1214, according to Chen Te-hsiu, high officials still questioned their interest in remaining (and possibly their ability to do so), even though the Mongols had already pursued the war against Chin for three years and occupied most of its northern territories. Unfortunately, contemporary documentation fails us for the years 1216 and 1217. But even if the Sung had by this time come to possess a reasonably good knowledge of the Mongols, they would have had a difficult time assessing Mongol military and political potential, almost invariably underrated by contemporaries in any case.† Nor did the drift of events seem unambiguously clear either.‡

---

* The designations applied by our writers to the Mongols are worth noting: the transliterated and apparently neutral "Tatars" (Ta-tan, Ta-jen); the more general "outer barbarians" (*wai-i*); and such typical epithets as "the Tatar (or new) slaves" (*Ta-, hsin-lu*). Interestingly, *Meng* (or *Meng-ku*) does not appear. Later compilations (e.g., the *HTCTC* and even the CSPM) are unreliable in this respect since modifications were made to meet contemporary usage.

† For example, a piece by Yüan Hsieh which probably dates from 1216 still assumes that rebels, not Mongols, will succeed the Chin in control of the north. See *Chieh-chai chi* 2.4b.

‡ Taking the *Meng-ta pei-lu* as the first *relatively* informed repository of information on the Mongols in Chinese, I find it difficult to go beyond these vague speculations on how much the Sung knew in the immediately preceding years. One work which bears an earlier date contains extensive information on the Mongols, the *Chien-yen i-lai ch'ao-yeh tsa-lu, i-chi*, whose preface is dated 1216 (the first half of the work, *chia-chi*, bearing a separate preface dated 1202). Here in chapter 19 of Li Hsin-chuan's work one finds an account of the Mongol invasion down to mid-1215 and rather rich material on early Mongol history and culture (see 11a–17b). It still reflects a strong anti-Chin bias (e.g., Cinggis' break is attributed to Chin treachery) and Cinggis' career is highlighted. Despite its somewhat poor organization, it is a relatively finished piece of writing and remarkably complete in terms of information, especially compared with the *Meng-ta pei-lu*. Indeed, for this general reason but also for specific reasons, these portions of the *CYTC* must be rejected as later additions. One of the specific reasons is mention of Muqali's appointment as Prince of State (*Kuo-wang*), etc. which occurred only in the fall of 1217 (see de Rachewiltz, "Personalities and Personnel," p. 117, note 1, where, however, the author for undisclosed reasons accepts Pelliot and Hambis' suggestion [cited] that Muqali was popularly known by this title before this date). Another is the remark at the end of the section on Chin (19.8b) which explicitly makes reference to a cause of the 1217–24 Sung-Chin conflict. Li Hsin-chuan, who lived until 1243, is known to have compiled two additional parts of the *CYTC*, but they have not survived (see *Ssu-ku ch'üan-shu t'i-yao* 81.10a). It is most likely that he himself made these additions at a later date but, choosing to respect the earlier date of his compilation, did not carry the story past 1215. The close similarity between accounts of the Mongols here and in the *TCKC* and *Liang-ch'ao kang-mu pei-yao* (as well as on other matters) suggests a common source for all of them.

Throughout these years Sung policy remained essentially passive. With one exception it was geared to respond to developments in the north rather than to help shape them. This exception (aid to the rebels being a minor affair) was partial abrogation of its treaty with Chin, at least one of whose motives was further to weaken this old rival. Chin was still alive by the beginning of 1217, but, because of the total depletion of its resources, by no means well. Expansion to the south held out immediate promise of rich stores of food and eventual promise of additional territory. Hence, using Sung's suspension of subsidy payments as the occasion, Chin initiated hostilities that spring which were pursued until 1224 but which realized only the more immediate of Chin's goals.* The long struggle for North China continuing, this war on its southern edge no doubt put a few more nails into Chin's coffin. Would a conciliatory Sung policy have obviated its neighbor's resort to arms and would this have materially altered the fortunes of the latter? Though these considerations anticipate a projected sequel to this paper, the answer to the first question is probably yes, while that to the second could only be wildly speculative. At the least, given the persistence of the Mongol effort, Sung enmity can be said to have sealed the fate of Chin. Hence, compared with events a century earlier, Sung contributed materially to the fall of the Jürchen in a way that it had not to that of Liao.† The contrast is by no means accidental since the subsequent seizure of all of North China by the Jürchen had seemingly exposed the fallacy of ever attempting positive collaboration with barbarian powers. This, odd as it may seem in retrospect, was the lesson drawn from that experience rather than an acknowledgement of the disastrous results of cutting the ground from under an established state which had long since accepted the necessity of peaceful coexistence. But even if the Chin were in the uncertain future to give way to a more potent enemy, Sung policy up to this point hardly ought to be judged short-sighted. Rather, it was defensibly opportunistic, for it reduced Sung's commitment to the northern regime only when the latter could not easily retaliate and it kept Sung's options as open as possible. Whether Sung thereby missed important opportunities for action in the north must await a serious investigation of its financial and military condition

---

* *CS* 15.1a and 2b, and 62.31a. Material need as the real motivation for Chin's attack is generally accepted; see I. Miyazaki, *Ajiashi no kenkyū* [Researches in Asian History], vol. 2 (Kyoto: Toyoshi Kenkyukai, 1959), p. 187; Chin Yü-fu, *Sung-Liao-Chin shih* [History of Sung, Liao and Chin], p. 109; and Tōyama, *Kinchōshi kenkyū* (Kyoto: Tōyōshi Kenkyukai, 1964), p. 54.

† See Thiele's valuable contribution here in *Der Abschluss eines Vertrags*.

at the time.* But our writers, at least, exhibit no particular confidence in the state's military capacity at the time.

Further constraints on Sung policy can be singled out. The defensiveness born of longstanding and confirmed Sung military inferiority vis-à-vis the northern barbarians permitted little initial reaction beyond alarm. The satisfaction at seeing an ancient enemy come under attack did not equal the anxiety felt over whither the chaos might lead. Though the notion of recovering the north had in principle become as fixed as the stars, it was long before the predicted fall of the Chin was even mentioned as an opportunity for realization of this goal. Strikingly, as much fear and distrust were betrayed toward the Chinese rebels in the north as toward either the old or new barbarians.

Opinion on what course to follow was not by any means monolithic but rather was divided into two main streams: the moderate, for most of this time claiming the leaders of government and unquestionably a large segment of officialdom as a whole, and the hard-line, embracing the harsher critics of the current ministry and its policies. The moderates, ill served by the sources, appear cautious and little tempted to take steps which risked the status quo in the south. Having absorbed the lessons of the past, they were reluctant to go to war and, in view of contemporary criticisms of the state of the military, they may also have attempted to keep defense costs pared to a minimum necessary. At the same time they were pragmatists, inclined — to the contempt of their opponents — to frame policy according to conditions rather than principles. The evolution undergone by Sung policy during this period itself demonstrates this.

It would not be accurate to identify the moderates purely and simply with those who espoused a militarily conservative, Yangtze-line strategy. Yet, their acceptance of co-existence with a barbarian northern dynasty necessarily encouraged them to think of Sung as an essentially lower Yangtze valley state. Moreover, to heed their critics they even regarded their northern territory, that is, up to the Huai, as of limited value, of use only as a cushion between the Yangtze heartland and the barbarian to the north. Experience against Chin in the past showed this region to be nearly indefensible; as a result inadequate efforts at reconstruction seem to have been undertaken following the war of 1206 – 8 (or even earlier). It offered by this time, therefore, a fragile base for any recovery attempts to the north. Obviously, viewed

---

* Little research seems to be available on Sung's economic condition at this particular time, but Sogabe Shizuo in *Sōdai zaisei shi* [History of Sung financial administration] (Tokyo: Daian, 1966 reprint), p. 36, indicates a remarkable drop in central revenues from the reign of Hsiao-tsung to that of Ning-tsung.

from the Yangtze and points further south, recovery inevitably appeared less feasible.

For their part, the hard-liners were the heart and soul of irredentism, but there was more to their political position than mere passion for recovery. They nourished a conception of sovereignty which was very nearly metaphysical in character, bearing important external as well as internal implications. Externally, this conception admitted of no relationships of equality between the native dynasty and other states, even when dictated by conditions of power. It admitted of no peace treaties but only of truces. In essence, it rested on a deep belief, a faith, in China's capacity to determine its own fate under any and all conditions. This reached the point of dangerously disregarding external circumstances, by definition of secondary importance. How far the hard-liners would have been prepared to go in undertaking necessary structural reforms and mobilizing the resources of the society in order to achieve their goals, is an intriguing, if unanswerable, question. In any event, it is perhaps in light of the re-emphasis which Neo-Confucianism placed on self-cultivation that this attitude can best be understood, a translation onto the state (and interstate) level of that same preoccupation with self and inner capacity. The hard-liners were not necessarily more anti-foreign than the others, but their uncompromising stand resulted in a shriller tone and had the same effect. By the same token, they were not necessarily more bellicose, but they were inclined to accept a just war with fewer qualifications.

Differences between the two groups naturally went far beyond the realm of external policy, though we cannot attempt to pursue those differences here. In the eyes of the hard-liners, this was only to be expected since the faults of their opponents stemmed from a moral and intellectual position which was at heart weak, deluded and even corrupt. It will not have escaped notice that, sanctioned by the Neo-Confucian tradition, theirs is the only well articulated view of contemporary events to come down to us. Of the others we can perceive but the barest outline. Whether under these circumstances the historian can supply the necessary corrective in recreating these other perspectives is not always a certain proposition.

Notes to Chapter 9

1. See R. Hartwell, *A Guide to Sources of Chinese Economic History, A.D. 618 – 1368* (Chicago: Committee on Far Eastern Civilizations, University of Chicago, 1964) and the Japanese Sung Committee's compilation *Sōjin denki sakuin* [Index to biographies of Sung figures] (Tokyo: Toyo Bunko, 1970).
2. *SS* 39.1a, under the first month of Chia-ting 1.

3. See *Ch'ang-ku chi* (Ssu-ku ch'üan-shu chen-pen, ed.), 5.10a – 24a.
4. *SS* 39.8b.
5. *SHY* 186: 29, 46 – 47.
6. See Tōyama Gunji, *Kinchōshi kenkyū* [Researches on Chin history] (Kyoto: Tōyōshi Kenkyukai, 1964), p. 511ff.
7. *HTCTC* 158 (p. 4297).
8. See *CS* 13.5b.
9. *SS* 39.9b – 10a; *CS* 62.27b – 28b.
10. *Hsi-shan wen-chi* 3.2b – 12b.
11. Cf. Tomoeda, *Shūshi no shisō keisei* [The formation of Chu Hsi's thought] (Tokyo: Shunjūsha, 1969), p. 428ff.
12. *SS* 39.10a; *CS* 62.28a; *Hao-shan ch'üan-chi* 69.14b – 15a.
13. *Hsi-shan wen-chi* 3.12b – 17b; cf. also notice of return in *SHY* 186:29, p. 48.
14. *Ch'ang-ku chi* 9.8a – 9a.
15. See *Hsi-shan wen chi* 3, 24a: *Kuei-hui t'o chih chi shih tsai yü tz'u* ("Laying the foundation for recovery begins here").
16. See *Ibid.*, 28b, for his conclusion and 18a – b for the line quoted.
16a. Cf. *Hsi-shan wen-chi* 41.12b.
17. *Ch'ang-ku chi* 9.8a – 9a.
18. *SS* 39.11a.
19. See *SS* 39.11b; *CS* 14.6a, and 62.28a.
20. See *SS* 39.13a – b and 40.1a; *CS* 14.8a – 15.2a and 62.29b – 30b.
21. See sources in note 20.
22. See *Hsi-shan wen-chi* 5, 18a – 22a.
23. *Ibid*, 25b – 26a.
24. *SHY* 180:17, p. 35; *SS* 40.2a – b.
25. *CS* 15.1a.

Glossary
and
Index

Glossary

ao-hsiang 媼相 150
Ao-po t'u 熬波圖 103, 107, 115, 118, 120, 122
Araki Toshikazu 荒木敏一 n. 180

chai 寨 25
Ch'an 禪 180
Chan T'i-jen 詹體仁 168, 176, 185, 188
ch'ang 場 25, 106, 107, 108, 120, 121, 124, 127–130, 132–134, 138
Chang Chia-chü 張家駒 104, n. 128
Chang Chih-yüan 張致遠 185
Chang Chün 張浚 n. 189
Chang Fu 張金 168, 182, 185, 191, 193
Chang Hsiao-ch'un 張孝純 202, 203
Chang Jung 張榮 204
Chang Ju-yü 章如愚 n. 109, 111
Chang Kuei-mu 張貴謨 168, 185
Chang Liang-neng 章良能 n. 217
Chang Po-kai 張伯垲 168, 185
Chang Shih 張栻 181, n. 184, 188, 189
Chang Shun 張順 205
Chang Tao 張衟 185
Chang Tsai 張載 165, 171, 189, 209
Chang Tse-tuan 張擇端 64, 67
Chang Yen 張嚴 168, 185
Chang Ying 章穎 185, 189
ch'ang-li ch'ien 常例錢 126
Chao 趙 143, 145, 210

Chao Huan 趙桓 144
Chao Hung 趙珙 n. 247
Chao Ju-t'an 趙汝談 185, 187
Chao Ju-tang 趙汝讜 185, 187
Chao Ju-yü 趙汝愚 163, 174, 175, 177, 178, 180, 182, 183, 185, 187–192
Chao K'uang-yin 趙匡胤 3, 8, 155, 156
Chao Kung 趙鞏 168, 185
Chao Shan-chien 趙善堅 185, 192
Chao Shih-chao 趙師召 185
Chao Shu 趙曙 n. 146
Chao Ting 趙鼎 164, 166
Chao Yen-chung 趙彥中 168
Chao Yen-yü 趙彥逾 185
ch'ao-yin 鈔引 105
chen 鎮 25, 26, 28, 43, 129
Ch'en Chia 陳賈 169, 170, 172, 185
Ch'en Fu-liang 陳傅良 167, 175, 176, 178, 179, 185–188, 190
Ch'en Hsien 陳峴 185, 189
Ch'en Kung-fu 陳公輔 164, 165
Ch'en Liang 陳亮 n. 171, 186, 211, 212, n. 220
Ch'en Tang 陳讜 185
Chen Te-hsiu 眞德秀 193, n. 218, 220, 225, n. 228, 230, 235–244, 248
Ch'en Tung 陳東 149
Ch'en Wu 陳武 185, 187
che-na 折納 123
Chen-chiang 鎭江 113, 134
Ch'en-chou (Gate) 陳州 59, n. 61, 68
Cheng Chao-hsien 鄭昭先 n. 217

Index